C000173713

RONNIE WAT

Director of Shotokan of the World Karate Confederation

DR. CLIVE LAYTON

NATIONAL KARATE INSTITUTE (SCOTLAND)

Hadley House, Culter House Road, Milltimber, Aberdeen, AB13 0EN, Scotland

First Published in 2009
by
NATIONAL KARATE INSTITUTE (SCOTLAND)
Hadley House, Culter House Road, Milltimber, Aberdeen, AB13 0EN, Scotland
Tel: +44 (0) 1224 734607
www.nfk-karate.org
email: rwatt@scottishshotokan.freeserve.co.uk

First Edition

British Library Cataloguing-in-Publication Data.
A catalogue record for this book is available from the British Library.

ISBN 978-0-9562602-0-8

RONNIE WATT, 8th DAN

Director of Shotokan of the World Karate Confederation

OTHER BOOKS BY CLIVE LAYTON

DEDICATION

TO

TONY

late of Bedford School and St. Edmund College, University of Oxford
a very dear friend
the consummate lawyer who loved to walk amongst the Scottish mountains
Oss

ACKNOWLEDGEMENTS

The author and publisher are grateful to the following people for their help in the preparation of this book: Rachel Layton; Pandora Layton; Gail Watt; the late Vernon Bell, 10th Dan, Chief Instructor of Tenshin-Shinyo-Ryu Jujitsu (European Jujitsu Union), 3rd Dan Judo, 3rd Dan Karate; William Berry, MBE, 7th Dan, BJA, Chairman of JudoScotland; Harry Cook, 7th Dan, Chief Instructor to the Seijinkai Karate-Do Association; Dr. Fritz Wendland, 5th Dan, Founding President of the World Karate Confederation; Roland Dietrich, 4th Dan, Vice-President, WKC; Compton Ross; William Summers; Gordon McIntosh; Arthur Alsop; Peter Carry; Alistair Grieg; Bill Smith; Leonard Ironside.

Photo Credits: Aberdeen Journals Ltd: front cover, 107, 120; Rachel Layton: 391; (Scotland's) First Minister's Office, ix; Ronnie Watt: front cover, x, xii, xvi, 20, 21, 24, 26, 31-35, 38, 39, 42, 48, 49, 52, 54, 57, 59, 62, 63, 65, 66, 69-71, 73, 74, 77, 78, 80, 82, 84-86, 89, 90, 92, 93, 97, 98, 100-103, 105, 109, 112, 114, 117, 118, 121, 122, 124-126, 131-134, 136, 138-143, 146, 148-150, 152, 155-157, 159, 161-164, 166, 168-176, 180, 181, 184, 186, 191-193, 195-201, 203, 204, 206, 208, 209, 211, 212, 217, 218, 222, 224-228, 230, 232, 235, 238, 239, 242, 244, 245, 247-249, 252, 256-259, 261-264, 268, 269, 271, 273-275, 277-279, 281, 283, 285, 287, 289, 290, 292, 293, 295, 296, 300-302, 304, 306, 308-314, 317, 318, 320, 322, 323, 360-362, 364, 367, 368, 370-381, back cover.

Publisher's Appeal: The publisher of this work has been unable to trace or contact a number of owners (original photographer or other) of photographs used in this book. Such uncredited persons will be duly acknowledged by the publisher in any future edition of this book upon notification of proof of entitlement.

Front cover: Ronnie Watt performing *yoko-tobi-geri* on Paul Allan, who is attacking with a bayonet, at Woolmanhill Barracks (*c.* 1978).

Back cover: Ronnie Watt alongside Masatoshi Nakayama, Chief Instructor of the JKA (Aberdeen, 1981).

CONTENTS

FOREWORD

It is with great pleasure that I write this foreword to Dr. Layton's biography of Ronnie Watt; a man who has worked so hard to develop the art of karate in Scotland.

I have heard how difficult traditional karate training can be and the dedication required to reach black belt level. To gain a masters' grade after more than forty years of training is an exceptional achievement.

I am also aware of the excellent work that Mr. Watt has done in the local community over many years, culminating in him bringing the World Karate Confederation world championships to Aberdeen in 2001, which proved to be a great success.

Mr. Watt has proved himself to be a genuine ambassador for his art, and through his profession, for Aberdeen, and, indeed, his country.

I have great admiration for the manner in which Mr. Watt overcame considerable adversity when starting out on the path of karate and the way that he has positively affected the lives of so many of his students.

Rt. Hon. Alex Salmond, MA, MP, MSP
First Minister for Scotland

FOREWORD

When karate in Europe was still in its infancy, some people, in search of physical and spiritual development, took up this ancient art from the East. Many gave up along the way due to the hard and exhausting training of those days, and only a few stayed and practise still, after nearly fifty years. One of the few is Scotsman, Ronald Watt, from Aberdeen.

In the early sixties there were only a few Japanese masters in Europe to teach the art of karate. They lived mainly in France. Karate-Do training books were also very rare and like most of the beginners in the unknown art of empty-hand fighting, Ronnie had to search and travel a long way to get hold of one of the few books in existence to learn the basics. These hardships and difficulties at the beginning of his life's journey made him so persistent that he never gave up. Many trips to London, the continent, and even to Japan, brought him closer to the real masters and teachers. With daily training sessions, seminars and hardships, Ronnie became a very strong competitor. It was only a matter of time before he was asked to join the British and Scottish national squads and he fought at the top level of world karate.

Renowned world Shotokan masters such as Masatoshi Nakayama, Taiji Kase, Hirokazu Kanazawa, Keniosuke Enoeda, Katsunori Tsuyama, Hiroshi Shirai, Masao Kawasoe, Yoshiharu Osaka and Minoru Kawawada, taught many times at Ronnie's *dojo* in Aberdeen and were guests at his home. After all this time, Ronnie has become known worldwide as a respected master of karate in his own right. In contrast to many other *karateka*, he never changed his style or his approach to the art. He still follows the way of one of the great

Japanese masters, M. Nakayama, whose approach dominates European karate to this day.

Ronnie, a true *karateka* (strong, straight, honest and polite) has actively supported the development of world karate for more than a decade and holds the position of a Director for Shotokan in the World Karate Confederation (WKC). He organised one of the most successful World Championships of the WKC, held in 2001, in Aberdeen, which were attended by teams from all five continents and top instructors from Japan, Okinawa, Africa and Europe. Several *karateka* from the National Karate Federation (NKF {Scotland}) of which he is chief instructor, have won gold medals at world level.

I truly hope that the Scottish samurai, Ronnie Watt, will continue his journey in the Way of karate.

Dr. Fritz Wendland
Founding President
World Karate Confederation

FOREWORD

I was delighted to be asked to write a foreword for this book, on one of the most senior karate instructors to have emerged from Scotland. I have known Ronnie Watt as an active *karateka* at European and World level for many years, indeed, since my own competition days with my national federation, the Serbian Karate Union.

Recently, taking over the Presidency of the WKC, I have been in a position to work more closely with this very humble, honest and hard working *karateka*. I have, on many occasions, invited Ronnie to conduct courses at WKC World and European Championships. With an open-minded policy, Ronnie has helped raise standards, which are now the bench mark of quality for participants, coaches and officials, alike. In this sense, he has been a great asset within our Confederation and to Shotokan in particular, as well as representing the Scottish nation as an ambassador for Karate-Do on the world stage.

Ronnie's NKF organisation, when compared to large WKC national federations in other parts of the world, has achieved remarkable success and provides wonderful, near unequalled opportunities for its members.

I am delighted that Dr. Layton has written a book on someone whom I consider not only a Scottish national treasure, but also a very dear friend.

Marko Nicović
President
World Karate Confederation

PREFACE

The church of All Saints, in Burnham Thorpe, largely obscured by trees, is a little removed from the sleepy Norfolk village it serves. The mellow rays of the late afternoon sun enriched the terracotta coloured roof tiles of the flint, chalk and carrstone walled cottages in the distance, and all around was silent. It was not difficult, given a little imagination, to transport oneself back the two hundred and fifty years to the time Horatio Nelson grew up here, when his father was the incumbent, though the rectory where Nelson was born is long gone. Ronnie Watt, a keen student of military history, requested a visit to All Saints and to walk in the footsteps of England's greatest naval hero.

As we drove from the village along the gently ascending and winding lane, a female Montagu's Harrier, a rare spring visitor freshly arrived from its long flight from the African continent, quartered a field to our left in its typical graceful, buoyant manner, its wings slightly cantered upwards during the glides. Watt had never seen such a bird in Scotland, for only stragglers venture so far north in the British Isles.

Three days of intensive interviewing were over and our journey together ended at Norwich Airport, where, shortly thereafter, Watt and his fellow passengers rose high in their Saab 2000 aeroplane and disappeared far over the North Sea. The material gained from interviewing formed the backbone of this work, and the many hours of telephone conversations and countless emails that subsequently followed allowed for the finishing touches.

The purpose of this book has been to record the extraordinary life, to 2001, of Aberdeen's most celebrated *karateka* and, arguably, Scotland's most famous Shotokan *karateka*. Also included is as much pertinent material on the early Aberdeen Karate Club as has survived through the British Karate Federation archive. Watt began karate training in 1965 and the previous two years of the club's operation is covered in Appendix I.

As in the case of similar works on notable *karateka* by the author – Mitsusuke Harada, Hirokazu Kanazawa, Masao Kawasoe and Michael Randall – the main body of this book is a compilation of recollections largely told in Watt's own words, thus minimising the distance created between the subject and the reader. Whilst Watt's words dominate the text, occasionally it was considered necessary to refer to other sources directly, to provide additional material. Similarly, each chapter contains its own set of superscripted numbers that refer to a substantial collection of references and notes found immediately after the main text. It was felt that this information would be useful to both novice and experienced *karateka* alike, for statements in the text are not only invariably qualified, but, also, further historical facts and figures, and source material, are provided. For a good number of readers, familiar names of *karateka* known to those who have trained for decades will simply be names, so brief and selected biographical material of many of the more significant of these is provided, though some are excluded through lack of sufficient data. Furthermore, by including super-scripts, rather than the material forming part of the main text, continual breaks in Watt's speech, are minimised. The feeling was that if relevant information exists, access should be made available, and it is left up to readers to decide whether they wish to take advantage of it or not. However, continually referring to superscripts whilst reading can get irksome, so readers may care to finish a chapter completely and then refer to the said superscripts whilst the contents of the chapter is still fresh in the mind.

The considerable number of Japanese words, bar two, with the exception of proper nouns, have been italicised for easy reference. The two exceptions to this rule are 'dan' and 'kyu.' 'Dan' (black belt rank) is to be found in most concise English dictionaries, though level of dan is occasionally given in Japanese here, for example, *'Nidan'* (2nd Dan). Numerically, the greater the dan, the greater the proficiency and experience of the individual holding the rank. 'Kyu' (non black belt rank) is not italicised because it contrasts with dan and occurs many times. For those readers unfamiliar with karate gradings, the lower, numerically, the kyu, the greater the proficiency of the individual holding the rank – the kyu system is, therefore, the opposite of the dan system, and if a 1st kyu student is successful in the next grading, then he or she becomes 1st Dan.

Most readers will, of course, be established *karateka*, and thus familiar with most of the Japanese terms used throughout this book, for many are widely referred to in the *dojo* on a daily basis. However, a significant number of readers will, no doubt, have only a limited knowledge of karate terminology, and for these a glossary is provided after the appendices.

Parts of this book are concerned with a period before decimalization took place in Great Britain and in order to keep a sense of the spirit of the time, the author has retained the old monetary system. For readers too young to remember, pre-decimalization employed the rule that there were twelve pennies in a shilling (six pennies in sixpence, of course), and twenty shillings in a pound. If the new values had been placed in brackets after the old values in the text, which would have been a straightforward procedure, the flow of the book, at times, would have been spoilt, and would repeatedly have taken the reader away from the past to the present, and this the author did not wish.

As noted in the prefaces of *Shotokan Dawn* and its associated books, and the author would like to reiterate the point here, if there are errors in the present work relating to BKF material, and, of course, everything possible has been done to minimise such errors, then the author apologises in advance. It has only been possible to work with the material that has survived, or that the author has been privy to, and, once again, any errors are made in good faith. Errors detected to date are almost exclusively related to the late Vernon Bell's handwriting, which can be extremely difficult to read. Also, once again, and with Bell's permission previously given, it was felt that his desire for overly long sentences at times had to be corrected to aid reader comfort; similarly, incorrect grammar has, occasionally, been addressed.

Whilst BKF material is associated with Chapter I, References and Notes, and Appendices, the same provisos regarding material and errors, and so on, may be said for the Watt post-BKF material. Watt read the finished manuscript and his corrections have been included. Having a busy and eventful life, he was understandably unsure of certain dates, and where it hasn't been possible to verify them from other sources, they have been presented as believed correct as given by Watt. So, on occasion, in a work largely constructed chrono-logically, some facts and stories may be presented one or two years out of their exact temporal setting. Whilst both Watt and the author strove for accuracy throughout, certain facts have been impossible to verify.

Watt's life may be said to fall, conveniently, into four distinct episodes that have been largely exploited to form the five chapters in this work (with his Karate Union of Great Britain years being split into two). Today, a World Karate Confederation *hachidan* (8th Dan – awarded 23rd April 2005 after a long and arduous grading), he is Shotokan Director for the WKC, responsible for Britain and Ireland, and is Chief Instructor of the National Karate Federation (Scotland)

Vivienne Milne, wearing her gold medal, standing beside her teacher, Ronnie Watt, at the 6th WKC World Championships (2007).

and the National Karate Institute. His 8th Dan was taken under the auspices of a WKC grading panel, who requested a good number of *kata* be performed and their application explained, in addition to the completion of a thesis on *Sochin*. A highly qualified and experienced coach, Watt has guided his students to numerous trophies in competitions at both European and World level, culminating in Lisa Calder's gold medal in the individual *kumite* at the WKC Children's and Junior World Championships in Hanover, in 2006, when she beat the Russian champion. Similarly, the following year, Vivienne Milne took gold medal at the WKC World Championships in Bergamo, in the Ladies' Senior *Kata*. But there have been other notable results at European level too, including Fiona Ellis's winning of the gold medal in the Ladies' Senior *Kata* in the WKC European Championships in Bratislava in 2006. In total, since becoming a member of the WKC, Watt's students have lifted thirty-three medals at World and European level. Shortly before the manuscript's completion, Watt returned from the WKC Junior and Cadet World Championships held in Novo Mesto, Slovenia (24th-26th October 2008), having raised over twenty thousand pounds in funding to take a squad of fourteen and seven officials, including a physician, taking an astonishing ten medals, two of which were gold (Sara Calder {*shobu-ippon-kumite*} and Morgan Bertram {*kata*}). Watt travels widely in support of the WKC and also teaches abroad, having returned from a *gasshuku* in Haugesund, Norway, where he instructed with Paul Kee, 5th Dan (of Malaysia), in addition to Alf Ronny Fagerland, 4th Dan, and Martin Boag, 5th Dan (both of Norway), in the intervening period between the above WKC Junior and Cadet World Championships and the manuscript's completion.

Today, Watt lives in Milltimber, south-west of Aberdeen, with his wife, Gail, whom he married in 1982. They have two children, Roxanne and Reeve.

There are four significant nouns that come to the author's mind when the name 'Ronnie Watt' is mentioned. The first of these is enthusiasm. This genuine enthusiasm for karate has resulted, for example, in not only his keeping such a fine photographic record, but also in his retaining small items such as tickets to a karate display in 1966 and to a karate club party from 1968. Such attachment brings warmth to the heart of a writer, for he knows that he has chosen his subject well. Watt has managed to retain vigour of interest in Shotokan, despite the passing of more than forty-five years. Make no mistake about it, this is a man who loves his art.

Secondly, he has knowledge, technical and historical, gained from the decades of dedicated training and teaching, in addition to considerable experience of competing, including at international level. One might say that real knowledge of karate is a natural outcome of experience, and most would agree this to be so, but one feels that it is always a question of degree, for, all importantly, Watt has maintained a continued sense of enquiry.

Thirdly, Watt has integrity; a characteristic hardly plentiful these days. Well brought up, he has embraced the five facets of the *Dojo Kun* and the result is a sound, upstanding and rounded individual. He enjoys civic life to the full, was made a Burgess of the City of Aberdeen in 2004, and is an active Freemason, having been initiated in 1989.

Lastly, he has a wonderful sense of humour and one imagines that being able to see the world from this angle has helped him overcome adversity in difficult and worrisome times. Watt relates a good number of humorous stories throughout the book.

Aberdeen has become a centre of excellence for Shotokan not only in Scotland, but throughout the world, with an enviable list of great masters having visited at Watt's invitation since the 1960s. It appears quite clear that Watt's contribution to the City's status in this regard has been without equal.

December, 2008

Clive Layton, M.A., Ph.D (Lond), 7th Dan

I

FROM ODDJOB TO KANAZAWA AND ENOEDA

Ronald Stewart Watt was born at 10.30 a.m. on the 16th April 1947, at 27, Skene Square, Aberdeen, the only child to Leslie Watt (1914-1977)[1], a brickmaker, later labourer/driver for a building contractor, and Marjory Law Cowie Watt (so, unusually, her maiden surname was the same as her married surname {1916-1982}[2]), a farmer's daughter from Milton of Tarrycroys, Keith, Banff. Leslie, the son of a police carter, later farm labourer (from Insch, Aberdeenshire), and his wife to be, who was employed, at the time of her marriage[3], as a fish shop assistant, later as a house keeper, were both living in Aberdeen when they married on the 7th October 1939, just months before Leslie was called up to serve in the Scottish Gunnery Regiment. He saw action in the 8th Army during World War II in North Africa, Italy and France, and a close encounter with a battalion of SS soldiers almost left Marjory a widow, but Leslie survived to fight another day and was demobilised in 1946.

Ronnie Watt recalled: "We lived on the first floor of a block of grey granite tenement flats, four storeys in height. Because the stone contains mica deposits that sparkle, it is known locally as silver granite and Aberdeen is referred to as the Granite City. Immediately above us lived my mother's elder half-sister, Katherine, and her husband, Charlie Gauld. Another uncle, that's my mother's younger brother, James Watt, lived with them and he had the spare room. Jim had been in the Gordon Highlanders and had seen action in France and Germany. He'd received shrapnel wounds in France. He'd been a happy-go-lucky sort of chap before the war by all accounts, but he returned a changed man. I think he'd seen too much. He'd been in Operation Market Garden, the Normandy invasion, and he was a witness to many of his friends being slaughtered. He never really spoke about his exploits, but I know he relived the horrors continuously, through nightmares. My mother told me that he'd been in a bayonet charge, hand-to-hand combat, and had bayoneted a young enemy soldier in the stomach. Jim was haunted by the man's facial contortions during his

Leslie and Marjory Watt (1939)

James Watt

death throes. Today, we know much more about the psychological effects of war and how to treat those so affected, but in those days it was a case of 'You'll just have to get on with it mate.' However, I remember Uncle Jim saying to me that the greatest fear the soldiers had during the war wasn't being killed or maimed, but being blown to pieces, so that there wouldn't be anything to bring home. I was interested in history, especially that of WWI and WWII, and every month, as part of a book club, I'd buy a book, read it, and give it to him. In fact, he was in one of those books, in a photograph, showing him being airlifted out with his wounds. But he didn't really want to talk, he became very quiet, withdrawn actually; I don't think I ever saw him smile. When I was growing up, he was simply Uncle Jim who, like Uncle Charlie, worked as a milkman. They used horses and carts in those days and everything seemed to be at a slower pace. It was simple, methodical work and I doubt if Uncle Jim could have coped with anything more demanding. Jim didn't marry and ended his days a lonely old man who took solace in alcohol. He served his country, worked hard all his life, but died less than a year after he retired. It's a sad story.

"Number 27 Skene Square was a two room flat – a kitchen/through lounge with a recess for a bed, where my parents slept, and a bedroom that was my room. We shared a toilet with another family living on the first floor. To get to the toilet, one had to go out of the flat and walk downstairs to the landing, which wasn't much fun on a Scottish winter's night. It was pretty basic living, but many people existed like this at the time. I was a child and I didn't know any different.

"I had a very happy childhood though; my parents were just wonderful. My father was an honest man, a good person. When he came back from the war he was hooked on full-strength Capston cigarettes. My mother smoked too, most people did at that time, and I remember as a child picking up some cigarettes after opening a sideboard. My mother took them from me and said that they were dirty and, being a sensitive and obedient child, I think that was why I never took up the habit.

"Behind our tenement was a burned out building and two air raid shelters, and I used to play there with my friends. I recall that on one occasion, a playmate, a boy named Brian Rolley, was pretending to be a knight on horseback. He had a soap box on his head for a helmet. We were terrible and I gave him an unintentional reality check. I was on a plank spanning two walls defending my castle and as Brian rode underneath I dropped a brick on his helmet. Well, it was a direct hit and the brick went straight through the cardboard and knocked him senseless. He ended up in hospital.

"I had a cousin on my mother's side, James Stewart, who we all called by his nickname, Toody, and he had a wonderful collection of war memorabilia that he'd often show me. This was a deadly hoard. Live shells, hand grenades, and bits of burned fuselage from a Heinkel shot down over Aberdeen by a Spitfire. Aberdeeen was extensively bombed by the Germans during the war, especially the Hall Russell shipyards. Ships would be built or repaired and then sail up the east coast to join the British fleet at Scapa Flow.

"Toody was in the Merchant Navy and became a head engineer on the Blue Funnel Line, which was a famous name in shipping circles. He'd return home with numerous wonderful things from the Far East, but it was the gifts from Japan that seemed to attract me the most, items such as fans, wind-up racing boats, *zori* and little samurai swords. It was a real delight when he opened up his case because you never knew what was going to be inside. I actually gave a talk on Japan at school based on all the things he had brought back, and that went down very well, so I would say that it was Toody who originally excited my interest in things Japanese.

"I attended Skene Square Primary School and was a member of the Boys' Brigade. I liked stories and always did well in religious education and won a few awards. I also won First Prize for a project I wrote on dinosaurs. Being mildly dyslexic hindered me, but I did a great deal of reading and writing in an attempt to compensate for it.

"I remember Mr. Connicher, who would take us for after school clubs. I recall building a crossbow under his direction and having brilliant competitions firing bolts at old drinking straw boxes. We built things like little cars and Viking ships out of wood and I'd always paint everything I did in black and red, but don't ask me why, because I don't know. Connicher was a young, fit man who had been in the army in World War II, and whilst I was still at Skene School, he suddenly died, and that came as a tremendous shock.

"Then, at eleven, I moved on to Rosemount Secondary Modern School, in Rosemount Place. I tried my best at school and I was considered very good at art, technical drawing and history, good at maths, but not that good at English, though I still enjoyed it. I really developed in subjects that allowed me to dream. My art teacher was Eric Auld, a graduate of the Grays School of Art, a very gifted artist and teacher who is still alive and painting the most wonderful Scottish landscapes, especially in the snow, but also of Aberdeen's architecture. Auld had a profound effect on me and I follow his work to this day,

Ronnie Watt at Skene Square School (1957)

though I regret to say that I haven't yet acquired one of his paintings, and that's something I mean to remedy.

"Art also opened up opportunities of expression and style that gave me freedom from the Presbyterian Scot that I was supposed to be. Surreal painters like Salvidor Dali – his *Christ of Saint John of the Cross* comes to mind – and Paul Delvaux – his *The Village of Mermaids*, and, *The Sleeping Venus*, I liked. I admired the Austrian Expressionist Egon Schiele and the stance he took towards his work.

What a tragedy it was when he died in the flu epidemic of 1918, aged only twenty-eight. In a completely different sense, I found the paintings and woodcuts of the Japanese artist, Katsushika Hokusai, such as his *Great Wave at Kanagawa*, and, the *Hundred Views of Mount Fuji*, strangely appealing.

"Because I love learning, I had a good time at school and I won the award for Best Student in the Fourth Form [Year 10 today]. I didn't like the corporal punishment though and I did get the belt once, because I wrote with the pen backwards as I thought it gave a nice effect. The teacher, a Mr. Murray, hated it and I got the belt. I was so upset. I never did anything wrong and I hadn't even ever been kept back after class, not once. Instead of getting praised for being creative or for showing initiative, I was given the belt for changing my handwriting and I've never forgotten it.

"The school system was really punitive and oppressive. I remember a teacher named Mr. Logie. I thought he was an evil so and so. In his room he had the surnames of pupils on the blackboard and next to each name there were six coloured boxes – white, yellow, orange, green, blue and red. To start out with, at the beginning of the year, in each box there was a number 6 chalked in. Every time Logie thought a pupil had overstepped the mark, the unfortunate student was obliged to go up to the board, rub out the six and insert a five. If a pupil was caught infringing his rules again, he'd have to go up to the blackboard once more, rub out the 5 and insert a 4. If a pupil reached a zero in the white box, he'd receive one lash with the belt. Once he'd reached zero in the white box, the procedure was carried on to the yellow box. If one reached zero in the yellow box, one would receive two lashes with the belt, and so on. Doing something wrong included very minor misdemeanours, such as dropping your pen on the floor, so I was always on edge in his lessons. It was psychological pressure and it kept everyone in their place; well, all except one boy, who was at war with Logie and managed, finally, to get zero in the red box. He received six lashes of the belt and was carted off to the headmaster.

"I love animals – we had a beautiful black and white Persian cat named Louis – and I recall the first lesson I ever had with a strange teacher, Mr. Gerie, who, despite his obvious affection for animals, told the class about a country in the world that blinded eagles and kept them tethered on a perch so that they didn't fly away. I remember that so vividly as it made me feel physically sick to think that people could even consider doing such a wicked thing. I had a vivid imagination and that episode worried me greatly; disturbed me, actually.

Watt, sitting front row, second boy from left, at Rosemount School (1960/61)

"I thought the science teachers were brilliant mind you and we'd go for a week's field trip and walk in the mountains, go skiing and things like that. I really enjoyed it. We were town children and so we had a week away in the country. Having said that though, as we lived close to the sea, we would often go down to the beach.

"I remember another teacher who drove to school in a really ancient Rolls Royce. The teachers were a strange lot then. The problem was that they affected our lives – for better and for worse!

"In the sporting field I enjoyed fencing, swimming, basketball and cricket, which were mostly practised in after-school clubs. I was in the cricket team and I remember we had a match with a tough local school. The Rosemount team were all dressed in white shirts, white flannels and caps, and this other team turned up in all manner of clothes. It was clearly evident that they were envious of our attire. I recall batting and having accrued fourteen runs and someone on the opposing team ambled over to me and said that if I got one more run I'd get beaten up. Well, it so happened that I did get out without scoring any more runs, but I can assure you that chap's threat had nothing to do with it.

"I left school at fifteen and three-quarters with my leavers' certificate and at sixteen I took up a four-year apprenticeship, at one pound ten shillings a week, in a small engineering works that supplied metal parts for ships and the local granite works. I got this job and that's why I left school early, because there was a lot of unemployment in Scotland at that time and I didn't want to lose the position. In the world in which I lived, it was seen as shameful if you were a man and not working. Oddly, the fact that there wasn't much work about didn't seem to enter the equation. In fact, the factory where I was employed was operating short-time work because there weren't enough orders coming in. I think they took apprentices on as cheap labour to be truthful. I used to cycle to work and the handlebars on this racing bike were the cow horn type and it made me feel as though I was riding a Harley-Davidson motorbike.

"Working with metal as I did, and with large, powerful machines all around, was extremely dangerous. I remember when a building weighing hundreds of tons was being lifted and a jack snapped. A metal plate from a door fell on my head. That was a bang I can tell you and I ended up in Accident and Emergency. There wasn't any health and safety in those days and I wasn't even wearing a hat. But that was nothing to what happened shortly afterwards.

"I was working on a large cast plane that planed down metal to one thousandth of an inch. This machine was planing a huge metal box the size of about three double beds and the plane would move back and forth. I was sitting on a plank above the cutting and every time the plane moved back and forth I had to turn down a handle so that the plane cut down another notch. I was quite competent at this job even though I'd just turned sixteen. Anyway, sitting on this plank above the plane was quite uncomfortable and so I decided to adjust my seating. I dropped my left leg to assist my turn and my leg jammed between the plane and the box it was planing and I was pulled into the machine. I heard this sickening crack and my lower left leg was instantly squashed. I screamed in agony and another young apprentice hurriedly switched the machine off, otherwise my leg would have been, quite literally, torn off. Luckily, the machine went into reverse and – I must have had a huge rush of adrenaline – I was able to drag my leg out. I was in a state of shock and as I put the foot of the once trapped leg on the floor it gave way about four inches above the ankle. The lower part of the leg, below the break, bent outwards at a right angle to the rest of the leg, as though made of rubber. You could see the bones sticking out of either end. I was rushed to hospital in an ambulance and a policeman who also attended the accident said, 'It's a terrible thing what's happened to you today.'

"The leg was a total mess, pulped. The colours ranged from black, through blue to purple and green, with two snapped white bones sticking out like broken chopsticks. I lay for a while in indescribable pain until they gave me some morphine, I think. My mother and father rushed up to see me and they were naturally extremely worried. The doctor said that he wanted to see my mother to sign some forms and that was a terrible moment for me because I thought he was seeking permission to take the leg off. I didn't have to have it amputated, but the doctor told me later that if I had been dragged into the machine another inch then I would have lost the leg, because the bones, veins, arteries, muscles and ligaments would have been unrepairable. The surgeon did his best to realign the bones and stitch everything back together. Then they plastered me up, hoping things would knit back, but within three months it became evident that it was wishful thinking and I had to have another operation and the bones pinned in two places. Within three days I was up and walking, tentatively. I was off work a year and a half and I got something like three hundred and fifty pounds compensation, which was a joke, at least by today's standards.

"The consultant said that I was going to have real problems with the leg later in life. For the last forty-five years I have been conscious of what he said and over the last ten years I've had difficulty with the knee, because the ankle is ten degrees off its proper alignment and the knee's compensated. I've had to do a kind of damage limitation job, but it's getting worse.

"At that time, it was the big thing to own a car, and I bought a Ford Cortina 1200 with the money I'd received from the accident. Unfortunately, I took it in for a service and I asked the garage to de-coke it and skim the heads. Now I didn't really know what these meant, they were just words I'd heard that were associated with making a car go faster. Well, I never expected such a bill, but I paid it thinking the improved performance would be worth it. However, I took it out and effectively blew up the engine. When I took it back to the garage and said, 'Look! My car's ruined,' their answer was that it was my fault for asking them to do the work and I should have just had it serviced like any sensible person.

"After I got out of hospital, but when I was still off work, in 1964, I went to the local cinema, the Majestic, to see a black and white film, the name of which I regrettably, despite my best efforts, can't remember, though it starred Patrick Allan. Allan popped up in all sorts of films and made guest appearances on a number of television series. Maybe, I remember it incorrectly, for he appeared in an episode of *Gideon's Way*, entitled, 'A Perfect Crime,' in 1965. Maybe that's what I saw, but I haven't been able to track it down yet, to check. The film involved a series of deaths where the victims had been found with broken necks, and that was the first time I had come across the word, 'karate.' It turned out the lead character had been to Japan and had become an invincible assassin. I came out of the cinema in a whirl and thought to myself, 'If that karate is for real then I've just got to do it.' I had been to judo a few times, a small *dojo* off Union Street, in Aberdeen, but it wasn't really what I was after. The first time I went down to this club, I borrowed a *gi*, and a *judoka*, I think he wore a blue belt, grabbed hold of me and threw me on the mats – bang! He didn't show me what to do, how to break my fall or anything, he just threw me. Well, that landing hurt quite a bit to be truthful; I think I may have been mildly concussed. So although I was very impressed with judo, it just didn't really do anything for me; it just didn't seem to fire my imagination.

"Then, later that year, I saw the James Bond film, *Goldfinger,* at the Palace cinema. Watching Goldfinger's henchman, the seemingly invincible Oddjob, played by Harold Sakata, sealed it for me. I liked Sean Connery's characterization of Bond too – his silver Aston Martin DB5 just added to the suaveness – but Oddjob was something else. There were snippets of karate and karate-like techniques turning up on the television around this time as well, such as in *The Avengers*[4], *The Saint*[5], and, *Danger Man.*[6] Karate just seemed really exciting; it was escapism, enthralling, and I bought a book on the subject, *Mas. Oyama's Karate*, by Bobby Lowe, which was published in 1964. I read it from cover to cover, but I couldn't find anywhere in Aberdeen where karate was being practised.

"I didn't return to work at the same company where my accident had occurred, my apprenticeship was finished anyway, so, instead, I managed to get a job at Richards Ltd, in their Broadford Works, Aberdeen. I really wanted to work, I needed money, so I started out again attending and mending shutters and spindles before being in charge of six looms making canvas. I stayed there for about five years, but the dust, which they said was made from jute, adversely affected me. I was coughing a lot and the noise of the machines was terrible.

"I used to go to St. Katherine's Club, a youth club for boys and girls that had dancing at weekends. The '62 Club was much the same. Aberdeen was much smaller then, before the oil boom, and everyone seemed to know everyone else. I liked the Beatles and the Rolling Stones and quite a few popular bands would come to Aberdeen and I remember one such group, The Herd, the members of which I drove about and took down to Perth in my car. Other bands I recall were Gerry and the Pacemakers, and, The Undertakers, both from Liverpool. Two of my best friends, George Douglas and Brian

Bothwell, were really into the music scene as well. We wore Beatle suits, Beatle boots, and so on. Music and fashion were very much part of our lives and we'd go down to London for a week and stay with people George knew. We'd spend hours wandering up an down Carnaby Street, and spend all our pocket money at shops like Baba's in the Fulham Road. I bought a very expensive pair of pony skin boots and scuffed them badly on a curb. I decided to shave them because it looked as if my boots were going bald! Well, there was I all done up in my Beatle suit and my boots turned pink, the colour of human skin, in front of my very eyes. I looked absolutely ridiculous, but everybody thought it 'cool', to use a word from today, and I became the centre of attention! It's very hard for teenagers today to understand how the 1960s affected young people then. It was like being part of a revolution. Later, I would go to many music festivals all over Britain, including Bath. Today, I have a wide interest in music – from opera to Oasis. I like opera because of the history, the production, and, above all else, the commitment of the singers. I like Wagner – *The Ring Cycle, Rienzi, Lohengrin and Tannhäusser* – and went to see a performance of *Tristan and Isolde* at the Metropolitan in New York. It was an incredible experience lasting five hours. The original star was taken ill and I heard that there were only six people in the world who could have replaced him. I believe Robert Smith took over and he gave an impeccable performance.

"I also like the Canadian band Nickelback and Christina Aguilera. Being a rock and roll fan, the work of the Aberdeen artist Bob Harper, is tremendous, and I have two of his paintings hanging up at home. But let me return to karate.

"In 1965, George and Brian told me that they'd heard that Shotokan karate was being taught in Aberdeen, and so the three of us went along to the Bugeikwai, if memory serves, one Sunday morning to investigate. I was very excited and a little apprehensive as well. The Bugeikwai was a detached granite building and the *dojo* was in the basement, where there were two rooms floored with *tatami;* there were changing facilities too. A chap by the name of John Anderson was instructing and we were invited to train, which we did, for three hours. Whereas Budokan means a hall where Budo is practised, I think Bugeikwai means a group of like-minded people.

"There weren't many students training that night, perhaps ten to twelve, and we were shown how to form a *seiken*, how to get into a *zenkutsu-dachi*, how to do a *gedan-barai*, *oi-zuki*, and so on. After the lesson, George, Brian and I went to a local café, The Sun Café I

The Bugeikwai, Riverside Drive, Aberdeen

believe it was called, off Union Street, and I remember that my body was just pouring with sweat and shaking uncontrollably where I had put so much effort in. I thought the lesson had been absolutely fantastic and everything that I'd dreamed of.

"At that time is was common for people to do fashion sports. By this I mean that teenagers would have a go at fencing for a few months, let's say, then try gliding for few months before moving on to another activity. I went skiing in Aviemore, played a bit of football and dabbled with horse riding, but when I found karate I knew it was for me. It was something that could not be easily discarded like other sports or pastimes. It was captivating, the whole mind body thing, and here was something I could do where my damaged leg would not be a liability. I took to karate like a duck to water; I just loved it. The club trained three times a week at the Bugeikwai and I practised on every occasion; they just couldn't keep me away. We also trained at Torry School and St. Katherine's Hall. The Torry School *dojo* was a typical school gym with a wooden floor, whilst the St. Katherine's *dojo*, which was an assembly hall, was situated upstairs, had a wooden floor and good natural lighting from large windows.

"I think the reason I took to karate so readily was because I saw it

Torry School, now Torry Academy

as an art form, as a means of personal expression. You know how an artist will return to a painting time and time again until it is how he wants it, well, that is how I felt about my karate technique. I saw refined art in the form. I wouldn't be using a paintbrush or a chisel as my tools though, but my arms and legs instead.

"I believe Anderson and his fellow instructor, John Allan, wore yellow belts[7] when I first trained with them, but I could be wrong. Anderson had started training in early 1964[8], I believe, and Allan in late 1965.[9] Because Douglas, Bothwell and I started towards the end of 1965, Anderson didn't register us with the British Karate Federation because we would have had to pay a half-year fee to the BKF, so we just paid training fees. I did actually complete an old-style BKF form, but it was never sent off. I know that because I've still got it.

"Then, not long after I had started, just a few weeks I guess, maybe a month, Anderson informed the class that a famous Japanese *karateka*, a grand champion no less, Master Hirokazu Kanazawa[10], would be visiting our *dojo*. Well, you can imagine how we all felt and what I saw next was to change the direction of my entire life."

At this point it is prudent to intersperse personal recollections from Watt with material that has survived from the BKF archive with regard to the Aberdeen club. Detailed information on the formation of the BKF Aberdeen branch, its early members and training prior to Watt joining, can be found in Appendices I and II. But first, a little

St Katherine's Hall, now the Lemon Tree

background information is necessary.

Vernon Bell[11], the founder of the British karate movement, had founded the BKF on the 1st April in 1957 under the auspices of the Fédération Française de Karaté. He had trained in Paris under Henri Plee[12], Hiroo Mochizuki[13] and Tetsuji Murakami[14], and had arranged for Murakami to come to Britain three or four times a year for the BKF from 1959 to 1964 to tour BKF clubs, run week-long summer schools and grade. Bell was a good organiser and was responsible for carrying through a momentous decision for British Shotokan, when, after the BKF became the official representatives for the JKA in Britain in 1964, he arranged for Kanazawa, 5th Dan, to spend a year in Britain, based in London, but also to teach and grade at BKF branches. As part of a JKA world tour that visited the USA, Germany, Belgium, Holland, France and Great Britain, Taiji Kase[15], Keinosuke Enoeda[16], Hiroshi Shirai[17], and Kanazawa, had arrived in London towards the end of April 1965 and had given demonstrations in the capital, Liverpool and Blackpool, in addition to a televised karate display in Manchester. Kanazawa stayed in Britain and the other three instructors continued on to South Africa.

Between May and November that year, Kanazawa seemingly visited the BKF branches at Blackpool, Liverpool, Nottingham, York and Dundee. So Kanazawa had visited Scotland once before. The

Hemb. No.........

THE BRITISH KARATE'-DO FEDERATION
(affiliated to Japan Karate Fedn.)

Application for Membership/Licence
as
Junior/Full/Service/Foreign/Inactive

I, (Surname).....WATT...............(Christian Names)..RONALD STEWART.
hereby wish to make application for membership of the above organisation and
submit my personal particulars hereunder, for the perusal of the aforesaid
Federation. I confirm that all these particulars are correct and true in every
respect, and I agree, if accepted as a member of this Branch to obey and abide
by its Rules and Regulations, to uphold its Constitution, to conduct myself in
a correct manner, at all times (both in and out of the Branch's premises) and to
further uphold the ideals and principals of the science of Karate as laid down
by the B.K.F. and by the J.K.A. by my personal example and co-operation at all
times.

Signed..R.S.Watt.............
Witnessed......................

1. Surname...WATT...........Christian Names..RONALD STEWART....
2. Permanent address...27 SKENE SQUARE (ABERDEEN).........
3. Telephone No. (if any)............3a. Married/Single.....SINGLE.....
4. Age.....18...........4a. Date of Birth......15/4/47...........
5. If under 18 years of age, have you your parents permission to join.......
6. Hobbies/Interests...SKIN DIVING...CAR RACING.......
7. Occupation......MACHINEMAN......
8.(Condition of Health.....Good......8a. Examiner.......
9.(Date of last medical.11/10/65.......... 9a. Place of Exam......
10.(Have you any Heart/Lung trouble..No......Details...........
11.(Have you High/Low blood pressure.....No.........
12.(Do you suffer from any organic, mental or physical disabilities or weaknesses
...........No...................
13. State names and addresses of present Clubs or Societies which you belong to
....
14. Names/addresses of previous Karate Clubs........
15. Have you had previous Karate instruction....NO.......a. by whom..........
...............place..................
16. Karate Belts held..........a..grade......b. date of grading......
.........c. Examiner.............d. Any further
details of Karate experience..........
17. Where did you hear of this organisation..ASKED...Mr. ROSS...of. A.S.C.
18. How and by whom were you introduced..I and my friends went down to the Club
19. State type of instruction desired - Private lessons.NO.Class Instruction.YES
Complete study of Karate...YES........(Answer Yes or No to above).
20. State precisely why you wish to learn Karate.for Protection......
21. State how you became interested in karate and what decided you that a Course
of training would benefit you. I bought a book by Mr Billy Lowean Karate...
In what way..For the Protection of people myself, family and friends.......
22. Having reached a standard in Karate, to what purpose do you intend using
your knowledge...to advance the Science of Karate in Britain.........
23. How do you think you can further the science of Karate and in what way.....
..I do not think I could further the science of Karate but would like to learn all I can.

35. N.B. Nos. 8 - 12 must be signed by applicant's G.P. himself
on presenting him with this form. P.T.O.

The old-type BKF application form that Watt completed in 1965, but did not
send off.

- 2 -

24. Is your interest in this Branch and Karate as a whole -
 (a) Theoretical (b) Practical (c) Philosophical (d) Cultural
 (e) Scientific (f) Curiosity (g) Knowledge (h) Sport
 .... SCIENTIFIC & PRACTICAL ....
25. For how long do you intend participating in Karate. AS LONG AS POSSIBLE
26. Approx. days and time available for tuition... 1 day. say about 4 hrs ....
27. Do you intend/desire to take Gradings in Karate.....YES...............
28. How far in your studies do you intend to go. AS FAR AS I can ....
29. Do you intend helping the Branch outside instruction hours. YES........
 If so how. IF the instructor ask me to do something out side Club time I will if I can ...
30. State briefly what your conception of Karate is. EMPTY HAND ....
31. Name/Address of your Sponsor in joining this Branch - ....
 ....
32. Name/Address of Seconder in joining... Teccesey ... Nicol ....
 ..8. Hillview Ro Nigg..................................
33. I......................agree to abide by my answers to the above details,
 and if for any reason I desire to resign my Membership I will do so in
 writing, stating my reasons, and giving at least one month's notice to the
 Branch Authorities, and giving one month's Dojo fee to the B.K.F. per pro
 loss of membership vacancy caused by my own personal leaving.
34. I......................pledge myself at all times to keep and honour my
 written Agreements with the B.K.F. and by my integrity to keep all verbal
 and promised arrangements with this Branch forsoever as long as I am a
 Member.
35. I am fully aware and acquainted with the Constitution, Principles and
 Objects of the B.K.F. and with the full knowledge of them I desire to become a member. I declare that at all times during my Membership I will to
 the best of my ability fulfill my obligations as outlined in the
 Constitution.

 Signature.. R.A.Watt..................Date..................................

 Sponsor/Witness...................2nd Witness.........................

 RECEIVED (Date)..........P.O./Cheque/Cash.

 £......s..........d. p.p.........Membership. per pro
 British Karate Fedn.

 M/A/R sent..........J.R.A.Circ./L......... Application...........

 G/C issued...........No........... Refused.......Accepted.........

 LIC. issued...........No.......... Interviewed........Time.........

 Full Membership granted........... Enrolled............

 No.......... A.F.Completed................

 "   "   transferred....... Fee paid.......Amount..........

 Period.......... Resigned.......Cause..........

 Course Paid...........Amount......... Dismissed.......Cause..........

 KARATE-GI. received...............pd.........Delivered................

Urgent N.B. The applicant MUST return and send ALL Documents, Monies, Certificates, Photos, letters and application forms DIRECT by Registered
 MAIL ONLY to office of National Secretary, B.A.F.,
 91, Perryman's Farm Road, Ilford, Essex. (On NO Account Give
 any forms, documents, monies to any other person or hand in at
 any Karate class of B.K.F. EXCEPT where applying DIRECT through
 an affiliated provincial Branch Officer.

N.B. 1. ALL Questions on this form must be fully answered and NOT left.
 Questions 33, 34 & 35 must be signed when enroling.
 2. Leave signatures of all witnesses, sponsors, seconders blank when
 applying for membership. These witness signatures will be made when
 beginning first course lesson in presence of other new members and
 instructors.
 3. DO NOT SEND ANY Registered packets to be delivered on any Saturday.

Dundee *dojo*, or, to give it its full name, the South Angus and Dundee Branch (of the BKF) was run by William McGuire, a thirty-eight year old mill worker by trade when he applied for BKF membership on the 29th February 1964. The club appears to have been based at a number of locations, including the Dundee United Sporting Club, Coupers Alley, Wellgate; the Masonic Halls, Artillery Lane, and, Dudhope Castle. Certainly, for the time, membership was large. As the subject of this book is specifically concerned with the founding and development of Shotokan karate in Aberdeen at this stage, the details on the said Dundee *dojo* will not be gone into here.[18]

However, there is evidence to suggest that Kanazawa's trip to Dundee may have been as early as the last week in June 1965, but correspondence relates to a weekend in July. There are letters between Bell and McGuire to suggest that the latter was having difficulty financing the planned trip by Kanazawa. There was also member dissatisfaction that caused a flurry of correspondence and in an undated letter by John Stables, to Bell, we learn that Kanazawa did visit the club for a weekend and that 'the absolute chaos that attended Mr. Kanazawa's visit was due to the fact that no one knew he was coming,' and in a letter to Bell by journalist, David Danks, dated 21st July 1965, we learn that 'only six of us could attend.' McGuire wrote to Bell on the 5th September 1965 informing him that he had gained direct affiliation to the JKA, and that 'this was granted on a strong recommendation from Mr. Kanazawa.' Bell was none too happy on hearing the news. Bell denied McGuire access to Kanazawa thereafter and McGuire appears to have left the BKF. Whether McGuire became part of the KUGB is unknown, as is whether Kanazawa travelled to Dundee for him again.

Kanazawa's first trip to Aberdeen in November 1965 seems to have been a much happier affair all round. As far as the author is aware, the Aberdeen *dojo* at this time was the only representative of the BKF in Scotland. It is with regard to preparations for this important visit that correspondence between Bell and Anderson (who, along with being the club instructor had taken over the roles of club secretary and BKF area officer), continued after a loss of material between the two men lasting some eighteen months.

In a letter to Anderson, dated the 22nd November 1965, Bell requested Anderson to, 'do everything to get full press coverage, both before and after the [Kanazawa] course, with official photographers and reporters, as well as inviting all the local dignitaries and officials to view the course. If possible, do everything to invite Scottish television to cover the event. I should be glad to hear what arrangements you have made for publicity for this course, especially to invite all the local judo authorities as well as the education experts.'

At 10.15 p.m. on the evening of Friday, 26th November 1965, Master Kanazawa caught the night sleeper train from King's Cross which arrived at Aberdeen just after 9.00 a.m. on the Saturday. The first-class return fare cost £16 10s, and the sleeper berth £2. Kanazawa received £1 10s as a meal allowance for the return trip. On this occasion, he was to teach for six hours – two hours on Saturday afternoon, then two hours on Sunday morning, followed by two hours in the afternoon, concluding with a grading – before catching the 8.30 p.m. train from Aberdeen arriving King's Cross at 7.00 a.m. on the morning of Monday, 29th November.

Bell noted that he would leave it up to Kanazawa to decide if a grading was appropriate, 'if he thinks enough members have progressed on the course.' If a student graded, he was required to pay a registration fee of two shillings to the BKF.

Watt continued: "I didn't know what to expect, none of us did really, though maybe Anderson had trained with Kanazawa since he'd arrived in the country seven months previously, I don't know. Perhaps he'd made a trip down to London, or attended the BKF *gasshuku* [at Grange Farm, Chigwell, Essex, 21st – 28th August]. I recall that he and Allan were having trouble with the *Heian kata* and they wanted to ask Kanazawa about them.

"I attended all the lessons Kanazawa took, including an additional lunch-time session at Torry School, where we trained on the old-type judo mats. The police had heard about this dreaded killer art being taught in Aberdeen and two burly policemen came down to investigate. I got the distinct impression that they were impressed by what they saw and to the best of my knowledge we never heard from them again.

"I was mesmerized as soon as Kanazawa walked into the *dojo*, before he did anything, just his presence. He radiated something. He was the most charismatic man I'd ever met. It was obvious that he was a gentleman too. He tried to make karate personal and he'd walk around the *dojo* carefully correcting individuals, showing aspects of technique and trying to give everyone something they could call their own. He demonstrated a kick on me and I felt so special that I'd been chosen. His *mawashi-geri* just came out of nowhere with mind-boggling speed and accuracy.

"What really impressed me about Kanazawa was watching him

Master Kanazawa performing a fine *yoko-tobi-geri* on an unknown (though non Aberdeen *karateka*) at Torry School (November 1965). Kanazawa brought two English students with him, the other being seated 3rd from the right. Standing: 6th from right, George Douglas; 8th from right, Ronnie Watt; and, Brian Bothwell, 11th from right. Club instructors John Anderson and John Allan are sitting 2nd from right and 4th from right, respectively.

perform *Heian Sandan*. I recall just standing there with eyes as big as saucers. He looked over at me and there was I with this silly, dumbstruck look all over my face. I was in a state of shock – seriously. I was just in total awe of the man. The power that he generated when he did the three *fumikomi* into *kiba-dachi* towards the end of the *kata* was remarkable. The floor shook beneath us when he landed. Nobody had seen anything like it; we just couldn't believe what was happening before us.

"But to top it all, if that was possible, he performed a *yoko-tobi-geri*. That was a genuine jaw-dropping moment. There was just a stunned silence; you could, quite literally, have heard a pin drop. I don't have the words to describe what I thought of Kanazawa and his technique. He had awakened something very deep within me and I knew from that point onwards that I'd give up just about anything and everything to be able to do what he could do.

"Kanazawa was also a very interesting person and I was drawn to him. He had a confidence and a humility that comes from dedicated

Kanazawa performing *yoko-geri-keage* on an English student at Torry School (November 1965). Watt is standing 7th from left. John Allan is sitting 4th from left, Anderson, 6th from left.

training over many years. I found him to be a very friendly man, an intelligent man, someone with depth and bearing."

The course was a great success by all accounts and in a letter to Anderson dated the 13th December 1965, in reply to a now lost letter from Anderson of the 7th December, Bell wrote that he was 'very pleased to hear of the preparations you made for the press coverage and T.V. arrangements for Mr. Kanazawa's course. I am sure the T.V. interview and the film will give the BKF good publicity.' Whether this film still exists is unknown. It may have been broadcast live and no copy made, but this is less likely.

As a letter from Anderson to Bell dated the 18th December reveals, twelve students did indeed grade on the 28th November 1965, as follows: 8th kyu – Derek Butler, Norman Dickinson, John Franklin, John McPhie, Angus Watt; 7th kyu (temporary) – James Brown, Charles MacDonald, John Mitchell; 7th kyu – Angus MacDonald, Kenneth Stopani; 6th kyu – John Allan, John Anderson.

No visitors from Dundee attended Kanazawa's course. Bell learned this fact from Master Kanazawa and Bell wrote to Anderson on the 6th December 1965, to ask for verification of this information. In an undated letter to Bell concerning, amongst other things, the non-appearance of Dundee members, Anderson wrote: 'As you know, I invited Mr. McGuire's BKF members and Mr. Danks's[19] BKF members to attend the course. I heard nothing from Mr. McGuire, but received a letter from Mr. Danks saying that he would not be attending and that his club had severed all connections with the BKF!'

Another feature of Bell's 6th December letter concerned the monies for Kanazawa's course which had apparently not yet been paid to Bell and he wondered why this was. The total due was just over twenty pounds for travelling expenses, a course fee of twenty pounds and an allowance for meals. Anderson replied to Bell on the above noted lost letter of the 7th December and duly sent the money. The reason for the delay in payment is unknown, but whatever it was, Kanazawa accepted it.

Watt continued: "So, Kanazawa had just bowled everyone over, not only by his technical ability, but also by his personality. All we wanted was more of the same. Anderson promised he would get him back as soon as he could, but we had to wait over four months before he taught us again."

To do justice to both Watt and the Aberdeen club, it is necessary to record pertinent information at this time from the BKF archive. In particular, the correspondence between Anderson and Bell provides us with a picture behind the screens, all of which affected Watt either directly or indirectly, and the letters lead up to Kanazawa's next visit.

Bell's letter of the 13th December 1965 is interesting for a number of reasons. Firstly, Anderson had enquired in his earlier letter of 7th December, about the possibility of running both junior and women's karate classes, asking both Kanazawa's and Bell's views on this. An undated letter by Anderson, to Bell, has recently been discovered and this is almost certainly the previously thought lost piece. Anderson wrote: 'I would like your advice and information about junior classes in karate. I teach a class of juniors in judo and most of them are keen to start karate. Would it be possible with strict screening and supervision? Also, since *Sensei* [Kanazawa's] course, I have been approached by several women who desire to learn karate. Could you please advise me about this and other clubs' policies for dealing with it.'

Bell replied: 'I have asked Mr. Kanazawa and he is in agreement that it is OK for you to start such a class [for juniors] since the BKF takes youngsters of fourteen upwards. I suggest you take them from this age only, but first with their parents' written consent and responsibility on all matters affecting their training and commitments.'

Bell continued, 'Regards training for women, Mr. Kanazawa is in favour of this but they should be kept separate from men unless you have no facilities for a separate class. BKF membership has been opened to women for the past year, but in the other BKF *dojo*s most of the area officers include them in the men's classes.' In fact, women had been practising with the BKF since 1957, though the first woman for whom an application form has survived is 1961.[20] This correspondence marks the beginning of women and juniors commencing Shotokan, if not karate, in Aberdeen.

Secondly, Bell makes it clear in his above letter that the BKF annual licence fee of £2-2-0 was payable by all members from January to August and for members starting later in the year, from September to December, £1-1-0. Anderson had apparently made an enquiry as to the annual licence fee for boys, and Bell replied: 'As no rule has been passed regarding boys, to assist you in your junior section I am prepared to accept [a] licence fee of £1-1-0, for those aged fourteen and fifteen, but over sixteen must pay the full fee.'

Thirdly, the BKF had bought a set of six JKA instructional films – almost certainly a unique collection at the time in Britain – three of which were currently with the Liverpool Branch and the other three currently at the York Branch. Anderson was required to write to Andy Sherry[21] and Gordon Thompson[22], respectively, asking for the films to be sent by registered post to Aberdeen. Numbers 4-6 were subsequently received, to be kept for six weeks, and a receipt, dated the 5th January 1966, by Anderson, and sent to Bell to this effect, exists. From later correspondence (letter from Bell to Anderson, 15th February 1966) we learn that the Nottingham BKF *dojo* now had films 1-3, and Enoeda had a JKA Championship film. The six JKA instructional films are now commercially available. In a letter to Bell dated the 28th March 1966, Anderson wrote: 'I have still not yet received the championships film. Since we have been waiting for the film for six months, I think it is about time we had it!'

Watt recalled seeing the set of films: "Anderson showed these one at a time, informally, before lessons. I think one of the members had a projector and screen and watching the films inspired us before training. Although the films were only about five years old, because they were black and white, silent, and a bit jumpy and crackly they seemed to be much older. I remember seeing Kanazawa on film performing the *kata Enpi* and because he had taught at the club it imbued me with confidence. We also got to see many other great JKA masters of the time that were featured showing *kata*, but, of course,

Ronnie Watt (left), wearing a white belt, attacks *jodan oi-zuki* to Jeff Nicol, who blocks *age-uke,* at the Aberdeen Bugeikwai (1965/66).

they were just names to us.[23]

Fourthly, Anderson obviously enquired about a future course with Kanazawa, and Bell suggested late March 1966. Anderson had also asked about the possibility of Enoeda attending too. By this time, Enoeda had returned from teaching for Stan Schmidt in Johannesburg. Bell recommended that Anderson contact Sherry, the Liverpool BKF *dojo* secretary, for, as Bell wrote, 'they employ him [and] permission must be sought from that branch first.' In a recently uncovered, undated letter from Anderson, March, April or May is suggested for a joint Kanazawa and Enoeda course.

Fifthly, the Aberdeen *dojo* wished to have letter-headed paper and Bell advised on this: 'I suggest that new paper be printed for the following items must be deleted from all branch headlines – International Karate Federation, European Karate Federation and any mention of Yoseikan, Shizuoka, for this will only offend Mr. Kanazawa and the JKA. Also refer to Mr. Kanazawa as the National Coach and Technical Director and not as President and refer to myself not as National Coach but National Secretary.'

In a letter to Bell dated the 25th January 1966, Anderson asked about 'hiring [the] film 'Self-Defence' to Grampian T.V. or B.B.C. T.V. to raise funds for a one-week course with Mr. Kanazawa and Mr. Enoeda.' Whether this plan materialised, even though the Aberdeen Branch had the film by this time, is unknown.

As we know, then, Anderson was organising another Aberdeen course with Master Kanazawa and hoping for Master Enoeda, and virtually all the remaining correspondence between Anderson and Bell revolves around this seminal venture. These letters are interesting because they reveal, in detail, not only the amount of work that was put in by Anderson and Bell, but how the Aberdeen club was beginning to forge forwards. So, bearing in mind that Watt was training whilst all this was going on in the background, let us spend time on these letters, for they are of enormous value given their consequence.

In Anderson's letter to Bell dated the 9th February 1966, there are a number of points that are worthy of mention.

Firstly, because the proposed course was for one week's duration, 1st–8th April 1966, Anderson asked Bell whether he had any objection to it being referred to as, 'The BKF (Scottish) Spring Course.'

Secondly, the course fee was £3-3-0 for Aberdeen members and £5-5-0 for non-Aberdeen members. As Anderson wrote: 'The fees for the course are to attract all Aberdeen members and make them think they are getting a really good deal ... the extra £2-2-0 for non-Aberdeen members includes a fee for finding accommodation, etc. We will do our best to help others as much as possible.'

Thirdly, it was proposed that Kanazawa and Enoeda be paid £25 each, for the week. Anderson wondered if the two instructors would object to sharing a flat together during the week, or whether they would be prepared to stay at members' homes.

Fourthly, Anderson noted that the club was 'moving into new premises and is trying to buy our own *dojo*.'

Fifthly, Anderson wrote: 'I hope to be down in London during April for one week (9th–16th), but since I have to hitch-hike down I might not be able to arrive in time for the AGM. What is the possibility of the BKF subsidising my journey, as the only representative from Scotland, so that I arrive in time for the meeting?'

Sixthly, Bell had sent BKF membership forms to Anderson, 'but during the last month over thirty new members have come along to join. Therefore I need at least twenty more sets of forms in order to get them enrolled as soon as possible before they lose interest. We are getting a good response to the junior section and the ladies section, so we want to get them all enrolled while they are enthusiastic.'

Seventhly, Anderson wanted to start karate at Aberdeen University. He had interested the Physical Education Department and they were, apparently, enthusiastic about commencing at the beginning of the next academic year (October). Anderson asked for Kanazawa's views on this proposal. Anderson wrote: 'Therefore Mr. Bell, with a little effort on your part, and my full co-operation here, the BKF could control the Scottish Universities regarding karate; and with a little more work the English universities could all be affiliated. With control of the universities would come eventually control of the whole of Britain. This is not a mad scheme; I have spent some time considering it, and realise that all that is needed is a good deal of clear thinking, straightforwardness and hard work.' Anderson noted that maybe a BUKF (British University Karate Federation) could be formed and asked whether a simpler BKF application form might be appropriate. An interesting quirk of Anderson's, evident in the correspondence of the 9th February 1966, and others, is that he would write the letter 'F' back to front.

Bell replied to Anderson on the 15th February 1966, and Bell's comments to Anderson's question will be dealt with in the same order as presented above.

Kanazawa agreed to attend the course and intended to write to

Enoeda asking him to go too. Bell also wrote to Enoeda and recommended that Anderson did as well. The Japanese were to travel by train, first-class. Bell had no objection to the title 'The BKF Scottish Spring Course.'

On the question of non-Aberdeen members attending the course, Bell provided a list of BKF northern and midland English branch secretaries and their addresses, so: Gordon Thompson (York), Ken Roebuck (Rotherham), Malcolm Gill (Bradford), Andy Sherry (Liverpool), Jack Green (Blackpool) Terry Heaton (Manchester), and Jack Warner (Nottingham).[24]

Twenty-five pounds for each instructor was agreed, plus travel expenses. Bell thought that Kanazawa and Enoeda would have no objection to sharing a flat or residing with Aberdeen members, though he thought the first option was significantly preferable. In fact, as Anderson's letter to Bell dated the 21st March 1966 shows, Kanazawa was booked into the same (unknown) hotel as he stayed in on his first visit to Aberdeen. The author is not sure where Master Enoeda stayed, though it seems highly likely that it was the same hotel.

With regard to Anderson coming to London, Bell suggested that Anderson travel down with Kanazawa and the BKF would subsidise half-fare, which Bell considered fair, since Anderson did not pay for instruction at the London *dojo*. Clearly, then, this suggests that Anderson had trained at either the Horseshoe pub *dojo*, in Clerkenwell, or the Kentish Town Baths *dojo* before Kanazawa's arrival, or at Kentish Town Baths or the Lyndhurst Hall *dojo*, Camden, after Kanazawa's arrival.[25]

Bell duly sent more membership forms to Anderson and noted that smaller and more simple forms would be supplied when available. It was one of these latter forms that Watt completed to apply for BKF membership.

With regard to Aberdeen University, Bell wrote: 'I have discussed with Mr. Kanazawa regarding karate in Aberdeen University and he is entirely in agreement with you and thinks that it is a very good thing, and he wants to establish karate on a national basis, first within the universities, then the police and then the armed services.' Bell continued that when Kanazawa and Enoeda came to Aberdeen for the spring course, Anderson should arrange an interview with the university's PE Department. It was also in this letter that Bell proposed that Anderson, 'adopt the title of BKF Scottish Secretary, which will give you more scope and authority in dealing with these official people. I suggest that you invite all these dignitaries from the university to your course and to your exhibition and then offer them help in the establishment of their club. I hope that you will accept this situation and I think you have discovered an excellent scheme and hope it realises your ambition.' Bell noted that he was not in a position to give an opinion on a BUKF, but noted that this was something to work towards. Anderson did indeed establish a club at Aberdeen University and, as far as the author is aware, it was the first karate club in a British University.

However, in a letter to a Mr. Humphreys of the CCPR (Central Council for Physical Recreation – a forerunner to the Sports Council), dated the 4th March 1966, Bell noted that the BKF were negotiating to establish karate branches at the 'universities at Aberdeen, Hull, Leeds and Liverpool, at this time.' If this is so, then Bell had been quick to seize upon Anderson's initiative. Bell continued: 'It is the ambition and plan of our Japanese Karate Association and its representatives in England … to establish a British Universities Karate Association, affiliated to our own BKF, working through it and with it. We also hope, through our own Federation, to establish authentic Karate-do courses and classes in all leading cities and evening institutes and technical colleges, employing our own Japanese trained and qualified instructors.' Although the BKF did not have any such *dojos*, at least to mid 1966, the Karate Union of Great Britain, the body that resulted after a seismic rift occurred within the BKF, subsequently did.

Anderson had been in correspondence with Tommy Morris, who was based in Shilford, Renfrewshire. Morris was a 1st Dan of the Osaka Karate-Do Renmei and the Association had five clubs when he replied on the 24th February 1966 to a (lost) letter from Anderson, which was, in itself, a reply to a (lost) letter from Morris. Morris studied Shukokai karate, and the Association had Yoshinao Nambu[26], 4th Dan, an 'All Japan' University Champion of 1963, as its honorary president.

Morris[27] was surprised and disappointed by Kanazawa's decision not to encourage BKF members to enter competition at this time, because he felt an international contest, with, potentially, more to follow, could only be good for karate in Scotland and he believed the BKF's attitude was narrow minded.

Morris certainly seems to have been well organised, noting in his letter that his club had one hundred and fifty members and that his Association was affiliated to the Shukokai of Japan, and to the European Union of Karate through the All-British Karate-do Association. It was also planned, in September [1966], to hold the first

Scottish Championships. The author understands that Morris's club initially trained at the Osaka in Albion Street, Glasgow, but was practising at Glasgow's Dixon Halls at the time of the letter.

The BKF, at least at this time, did not have local, regional, or national competitions, though it had sent a team to the first European Karate Championships and competed against France and Belgium in 1963. Details of this exciting event are given in *Shotokan Dawn*.[28]

Anderson wrote to Bell on the 3rd March 1966, suggesting that Kanazawa and Enoeda fly to Aberdeen. Master Kanazawa certainly flew from London (though he seems to have lost his ticket! {Bell's letter to Anderson dated the 4th April}). Anderson had written to the northern BKF branches and had a provisional booking for twelve students from Rotherham. In a letter to Anderson dated the 28th March 1966, Bell wrote: 'The Nottingham Branch is sending you about half-dozen members and the Rotherham Secretary tells me you are receiving about the same from his Branch.'

Anderson wrote to Bell twice on the 4th March 1966. The first letter confirmed Kanazawa's flight times and informing Bell that he would fly down with Kanazawa to attend the AGM. The second letter had an air of panic about it, because Sherry, of Liverpool, had written to Anderson stating that the Aberdeen branch could only have Enoeda for the 6th, 7th and 8th April. As Anderson wrote: 'This course means a great deal to the Aberdeen members and we do not want to be let down. Therefore could you please plead with Mr. Sherry, for me, to release Mr. Enoeda for the period required. Perhaps you could ask Mr. Kanazawa to intervene for our benefit. I have, myself, written to Mr. Sherry asking him to re-consider his decision.'

Bell wrote to Anderson on the 16th March concerning course arrangements. There is little new in this letter, but he noted, having spoken to Enoeda, that the reason why Sherry had allowed only three days for Enoeda to attend the course was because the Liverpool *dojo* had recently started new beginner classes for juniors and women and it was felt that Enoeda should be there for them. Bell asked Enoeda if he could reconsider, with the Liverpool *dojo's* blessing. However, as we learn from a letter to Bell dated the 28th March 1966, Anderson still didn't know when Enoeda was arriving. In his letter of the 16th March, Bell also gave the names and addresses of three BKF southern branch secretaries that Anderson should write to concerning the course: Richard Moffatt (Portsmouth), David Whittaker (Poole) and Richard Kiernan (Plymouth).[29]

Bell actually wrote two letters to Anderson on the 16th March

THE BRITISH KARATE-DO FEDERATION.
Affiliated to Japan Karate Assn., Tokyo.

1508

APPLICATION FOR MEMBERSHIP LICENCE.

SURNAME ...... WATT .... FORENAMES ... Ronald Stewart ....

PERMANENT ADDRESS 27 Skene Square Aberdeen ....

DATE OF BIRTH .... 16/4/47 .... OCCUPATION ... Machineman ....

PREVIOUS KARATE CLUB/EXPERIENCE .... / .... BY WHOM ...... Richards Ltd ....

KARATE GRADE (if any) .... / .... EXAMINER .... DATE ....

State briefly your reason for learning Karate .... For Physical Fitness ....

Are you medically fit? YES/NO .... Yes .... If not, state here nature of ailment .. / ..

I agree to uphold the Constitution, Rules, Regulations, of the Federation and its affiliated Branches at all times. I agree to abide by all laws, constitutions, agreements and committments with the B.K.F., and my affiliated Branch/Club at all times during my membership and after.

I agree at all times to conduct myself in a fit and proper manner as a member of the Federation and its affiliated clubs.

Should I wish to resign from the Branch and B.K.F., I will do so in writing giving 14 days notice of such and paying one month Dojo fees to the Branch in question for loss of my permanent vacancy to that Branch.

I accept and agree to abide by all decisions of B.K.F. and the Branch in all matters affecting my membership/training.

I agree to undertake training in Karate entirely at my own risk, and indemnify the B.K.F. and its branches/clubs completely in respect of any injury, damage to my person or property, at all times.

I will not instruct or teach at any time without the permission of the B.K.F., and I promise to keep all knowledge I gain entirely for the benefit of my own advancement, for my Club and for Karate as a world sport. With full knowledge of Constitution and being fully aware of all my obligations, I wish to become a member of B.K.F., and hereby apply for a Licence which I know at all times remains the property of B.K.F., and I realise I must return this Licence on my resignation to the Federation.

Signed ...... Ronald S. Watt .... (Full Name)

Address ...... 27 Skene Square Aberdeen .... Date .. 16.3.66

Witness .... Address 51 Heathryfield Place Aberdeen

Area Officer Signature ... J. Anderson .... Address ....

1st Committee Member ...... V. Watt .... Address .. 11. Clanywidant Strand ....

2nd Committee Member ...... K. Stephen .... Address 83 .. Gartside Drive ....

Licence Issued ... 16/3/66 .. No. 977 1067 Licence Fee Paid 17/3/66 .. Amount £3.3s. 7/M-

Membership Granted .. 7/3/66 .. No. 1508 Receipt Issued ....

Branch Membership Issued .... No, ... Branch Fee Paid .... Amount ....

Karate .... Paid .... Amount ....

Novice Course commenced .... to .... Paid .... Amount ....

Grading Promotions Kyu .... Date .... Examiner ....

Kyu .... Date .... Examiner ....

C/e 972 Kyu .... Date .... Examiner ....

Kyu .... Date .... Examiner ....

Summer Courses attended .... From .... To .... Fee Paid ....

Place ....

National Secretary's Clearance .... Date ....

The new-type BKF application form that Watt submitted (March 1966)

1966, the second concerned the fact that Kanazawa was to be paid £25 for two hours a day, for five days, therefore at his usual hourly rate of £2-10-0. Because Anderson needed Kanazawa for seven days, overtime was due at the same hourly rate. The Liverpool branch were in-charge of Enoeda's fees. Bell also noted that 'any displays given by

The photograph that Watt submitted with his BKF application form (1966)

Mr. Kanazawa and Enoeda as far as the contract[s] are concerned are included in the price of their weekly salary under the terms of Mr. Kanazawa's contract.'

With all this going on in the background, Ronnie Watt signed his BKF application form on the 16th March 1966, noting his occupation as 'machine man.' His application was supported by Anderson, as BKF Area Officer, and by both Angus Watt and Kenneth Stopani, committee members of the Aberdeen Karate Club. Watt's licence (Nō. 1067), at a cost of £2-2-0, was issued and his BKF membership (Nō. 1508) granted on the 26th March. George Douglas signed his application form on the 20th March, giving his age as eighteen years and occupation as store manager. No BKF application form has survived for Brian Bothwell, though his signature appears as the witness to Douglas's application, so unless something unusual was happening, he must have been a BKF member.

Watt recalled: "Although I had joined the BKF, Anderson never mentioned that organisation, all he ever spoke about was the JKA."

In a letter to Bell dated the 28th March 1966, Anderson requested a copy of the JKA grading syllabus, so that he could, no doubt, teach his members accordingly.

During the first three months of 1966, the following Aberdeen students (excluding Watt and Douglas) whose BKF application forms have survived, arranged in order of signing (dates in brackets) and providing ages and occupations, became members of the BKF: William Smith, 22, scaffolder (6.2.66); William Milne, 18, grocer (10.2.66); Alexander Buchan, 19, mechanic (13.2.66); Bruce Chambers, 18, labourer (13.2.66); James Donaldson, 19, apprentice (13.2.66); Donald McLarty, 19, coach painter (17.2.66); Alexander Johnston, 23, student (20.2.66); Robert Davies, 38, joiner (25.2.66); Harold Flett, 25, gunsmith (25.2.66); John Bremner, 15, schoolboy (5.3.66); George Rennie, 27, draughtsman (18.3.66); Archibald Sim, 27 steel erector (18.3.66); Thomas Brown, 39, foreman (20.3.66). In a letter to Bell dated the 24th March 1966, Anderson also notes a T. A. Sprott and J. Clark as new members, though a T.M. Sprott joined in 1965, and a J. Clark signed his membership form that same year. It is unknown if these individuals are different from the aforementioned, though no membership forms have survived if this is so. It seems almost certain that they refer to the same people. In addition to BKF membership fees, students were obliged to pay two pounds a year to be members of the Aberdeen club. The amount payable for karate lessons is unknown.

In the minutes of the First Annual General Meeting of the Shotokan Club of Aberdeen, held in Torry School, on the 26th April 1966, we learn that 'there were over sixty members on paper; thirty-seven were new members since Mr. Kanazawa's first course; fourteen juniors, of which six were from the judo section; six ladies of whom five were judo; approximately forty active members.'

The minutes also provide us with details of club positions and who held them, so: President – J. Anderson; Vice-President – J. Allan; Active Secretary – A. Watt; Hon. Secretary – D. Anderson (see shortly); Treasurer – C. MacDonald; Committee Members – C. MacPherson, K. Stopani, A. Williamson.

Anderson wrote to Bell on the 21st March 1966 with the proposed course's training times (that we learn from a letter that Bell sent to Anderson on the 28th March 1966, as being acceptable to Kanazawa), from the 1st to the 8th April: Friday – 7.30 p.m. to 9.30 p.m.; Saturday – 9.00 a.m. to 11.00 a.m., 3.00 p.m. to 5.00 p.m.; Sunday – 11.00 a.m. to 1.00 p.m., 5.00 p.m. to 7.00 p.m.; Monday, Tuesday and Wednesday – 9.00 a.m. to 11.00 a.m., 7.30 p.m. to 9.30 p.m.; Thursday – 9.00 a.m. to 11 a.m., 2.00 p.m. to 4.00 p.m.; Friday – 9.00 a.m. to 11.00 a.m. A grading would follow that Friday evening from 7.30 p.m. to 9.30 p.m.

So, Aberdeen students (and visiting *karateka*) were offered twenty-two hours of karate training under top Japanese instructors for only £3-3-0, which was tremendous value, even in 1966! As Anderson noted in his letter to Bell of the 21st March: 'I tried to make these times as similar as possible to the course times at Chigwell, and as suitable to all our members as possible.' Whether Anderson attended the Chigwell, Essex, course, held at the Grange Farm Centre, 21st–28th August 1965, is unknown. However, he did not attend the week-long Lilleshall Hall course, Shropshire, that followed on immediately afterwards.

In addition to the above training/grading, Anderson had arranged a display of karate on the Thursday, 7th April 1966, between 7.30 p.m. and 9.30 p.m. In a letter to Bell on the 21st March 1966, Anderson noted: 'We have hired a large school hall in the centre of Aberdeen for the show ... Most of the tickets for this show have been sold already. The show has been split into four parts: two each of karate and judo. They are arranged alternately, starting with thirty minutes of judo, thirty minutes of karate, thirty minutes of judo and thirty minutes of karate. There will be a 1 vs. 10 judo contest and (we hope) a spectacular final item such as [*tame*]*shiwari* by Mr. Kanazawa and Mr. Enoeda.' Anderson continued, 'All the most important local dignitaries, educationalists and TV personalities have been invited. The local ITA station will be covering the 'Karate Week' and we have arranged for a window display in the Publicity Office in Aberdeen's main street (Union Street). The local press gives me a regular column in their weekly 'Club News' page and should cover events well.'

Watt attended this important spring course, witnessed the demonstrations, and recalled: "We'd seen Kanazawa and he was just mind-blowing, and then we had two JKA champions in our midst with the arrival of Enoeda. Since Kanazawa's first visit, both he and Enoeda had appeared on a popular, up-beat evening television programme at the time, *The Braden Beat*. When I saw Kanazawa on the box, rather like when I'd seen him on film, I felt warm inside because here was someone I knew, personally, on television. If fact, they appeared more than once, over a couple of weeks, and some of the London students joined them. The things I remember were Enoeda breaking four inches of wood with a punch and Kanazawa breaking unbreakable blinds with a *shuto*. That was really inspiring and it showed people up and down the country what real Shotokan karate could do.[30]

"Enoeda was known as the Shotokan Tiger and this name had been given to him in Japan by his peers. In fact, on one of Enoeda early trips

Masters Enoeda and Kanazawa (1966)

up to Aberdeen, I gave him a plate I'd painted with a Shotokan Tiger on it. I was pleased with it and I think he was too, but it was certainly no Michael Parkes[31] – now that man can really paint big cats and somehow captures their power and beauty. Actually, that reminds me

52

of another little artistic endeavour. I carved cufflinks from wood with the Japanese calligraphy for 'karate.' The local hobby shop had the cufflinks ready so that all a student needed to do was stick on the carvings and you could have a set in either light wood to ebony. I showed Kanazawa my handy work and he was impressed, but the finish was not all that good to be truthful.

"Enoeda was a powerhouse of a man, dynamic, aggressive, unpredictable and charged with energy. He was actually daunting; his whole being was just overpowering. The training was fantastic, as you can imagine, and I was like a sponge just soaking up everything I could. Kanazawa would explain everything in detail and Enoeda would drive you on and you'd reach heights you'd never attain by yourself. That was Enoeda's forté, his teaching skill, in my opinion. He was a real motivator, a hard mentor. A smile of approval from Enoeda really meant something. On the last day of the course there was a grading and I was promoted to *hachi-kyu*, 8th kyu, under Kanazawa.[32] I had to perform *kihon*, *Heian Shodan* and *gohon-kumite*. Although I passed my grading, the belt colour didn't change and I still wore white."

A document entitled, *Curriculum For Grading Examination*, and dated 25th September 1964, survives in the BKF archive, and gives details of the JKA requirements for the first four grades. Although Watt may not have been required to demonstrate the contents for the 8th kyu exactly as stated, for there seems to have been some individual grading examiner variation and small changes may have occurred over the eighteen months that had elapsed, the basics for the said grade, and the other three grades to follow, will be given as appropriate:

a) *Zenkutsu-dachi, gedan-gamae* . . . M.F [moving forwards] . . . *oi-zuki*
b) *Zenkutsu-dachi* at *hanmi* . . . M.F . . . *age-uke*
c) *Zenkutsu-dachi* at *hanmi* . . . M..F . . . *shuto-uke*
d) *Kokutsu-dachi, shuto-uke* . . . M.F . . . *shuto-uke*
e) *Zenkutsu-dachi, gedan-game* . . . M.F . . . *mae-geri* with rear leg
f) *Kiba-dachi* . . . crossing legs . . . *yoko-geri-keage*
g) *Kiba-dachi* . . . crossing legs . . . *yoko-geri-kekomi*

Watt continued: "Anderson had arranged a demonstration one evening in the gym of Aberdeen Girls' High School, Albyn Place. It was a bit of a martial arts extravaganza for the time, with karate, judo and kendo displays. I can't remember the sequence of events exactly for the karate, but the Bugeikwai members, of whom I was one, showed the various forms of training that we did and then this was

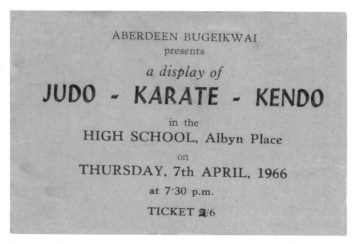

ABERDEEN BUGEIKWAI
presents
a display of
JUDO - KARATE - KENDO
in the
HIGH SCHOOL, Albyn Place
on
THURSDAY, 7th APRIL, 1966
at 7·30 p.m.
TICKET 2/6

The ticket to the demonstration given by the Aberdeen Karate Club and Masters Kanazawa and Enoeda (April, 1966).

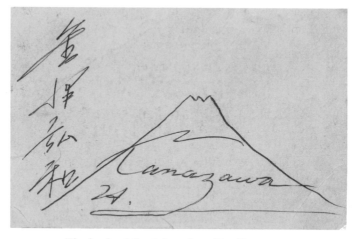

The back of the ticket signed by Kanazawa

interspersed by the two Japanese performing their demonstrations. I remember when Kanazawa and Enoeda paired-up for unrehearsed freestyle. It was just out of this world and the two of them were really going for it. Enoeda charged in with a blistering *mae-geri* and was getting a bit carried away and Kanazawa, who wasn't perturbed, I want to make that quite clear, had to stop him, to say, 'Calm down, this is only a display.' I think that was the time that Kanazawa and Enoeda were at the peak of their ability, and there was no one who could compete with them; they were in a league of their own. There was Kanazawa, the master technician, and Enoeda, the powerhouse. As I've said before, I think I'd have given just about anything to have been one of them. I'm sure a lot of us felt that way. They were superhuman. They also did a *kata* demonstration that evening, *Bassai-dai* maybe, something solid and a form that I'd seen before. The purpose of the demonstrations was to attract new members to the Aberdeen club and the pupils were there to show the type of training any prospective student could expect if they joined. I've still got the orange ticket to that event and Kanazawa was kind enough to sign the back of it."

After the course, Kanazawa did not fly back to London with Anderson as originally planned, but caught the 7.30 a.m. train from Aberdeen, arriving at Newcastle at 1.02 p.m., then continued to Sunderland, catching the 1.12 p.m. train arriving at 1.34 p.m. – the ticket costing £5.1.1d. Kanazawa conducted a week-end course and grading at the *dojo* of Henry and Alan Marr before returning to London and travelling straight on to Poole, Dorset.

The Aberdeen *dojo's* spring course appears to have been a great success, though the names of the students who attended (and which *dojos* they came from), and who graded, other than Watt, is unknown, though Watt's BKF licence shows that he did achieve 8th kyu, even though the entry date is recorded by Bell and not the actual grading date. However, in the minutes of the club's first AGM, we learn that thirty-nine students trained, and that the results of gradings had not come through (from Kanazawa/Bell). A receipt exists, bearing Kanazawa's signature, for £78 for a thirty-two hour course. However, thirty-two multiplied by Kanazawa's hourly rate is £80.

Young men, high on adrenaline and needing a release after hard physical training over a long-awaited week, are apt to act foolishly, and this appears to have been the case for some of the BKF Aberdeen members, as a letter to Bell, by a W. Ross, president of the Bugeikwai Judo Club, indicates. Ross wrote:

'It is with much regret that I hereby inform you of an incident which happened in the *dojo* of the Aberdeen Bugeikwai on Friday, at the end of the BKF spring course. Some of the BKF members had a final night out at a local pub, after which they returned to the *dojo* at about 12.30 a.m. at the invitation of ——— [name removed]. ——— had installed a seventy pint cask of beer in the *dojo* all of which was consumed. The disorder and noise which followed caused the tenants of the flats above the *dojo* to complain about the noise and mess that was being made. The tenants were given a great deal of abuse and the party refused to break up until about 4.00 a.m. after being threatened with police action. I shudder to think what might have happened if the police had been called in.

'The mess left after this party is difficult to describe, no attempt in some cases had been made to go to the toilet, the vomit was all over the pavement, the stairs, the *dojo* floor and [judo] mat, which had also been used for dancing on, broken glass and spilled beer was everywhere, the smell and stench of the beer permeated through the whole building. The mess had to be cleaned up next morning by myself, Mr. MacDonald of the karate section and, unfortunately, young members of the girls' judo section, who practise in the *dojo* on a Saturday morning.

'The owner of the building, who is a very prominent and influential businessman, personally contacted our secretary on Saturday morning after being informed by the tenants. The outcome of this meeting was that we have to be out of the premises by the end of the month.

'The Aberdeen Bugeikwai has built up over the past fourteen years a name which was respected throughout the town, a place where parents could safely bring their children in the sound knowledge that they would be endowed with qualities which would make them good citizens, of good moral character, and now, because of this most distressing business, we shall have lost all the goodwill and respect in one evening.

'The Aberdeen Bugeikwai committee have decided that should we be fortunate enough to find new premises, there will be no place in it for a karate section. I am sure that you will wish to take some disciplinary action which will ensure that the good name of karate in Aberdeen is never again associated with drinking.

'I also wish to inform you that the Aberdeen Bugeikwai will in no way be responsible for any debts incurred by the BKF Area Office in running the BKF spring course.'

As far as the author is aware, this is the only letter of complaint about members of a BKF branch within the surviving BKF archive, at least from 1957–1966. How Bell dealt with the episode is unknown.

Watt went back to the *dojo* with his comrades that evening and recalled: 'Everyone was happy as we walked back to the club after we left the pub. Then, some of the members started drinking again. I left early because I didn't drink and, quite frankly, was worn out, but the next day I heard that things had got a bit out of hand. Evidently, some of the boys couldn't hold their liquor and, amongst other things, had spilt a barrel of beer over the judo mats making them sticky and soggy. The upshot of it was that we were obliged to look for new premises to train in. The club met at Torry school two nights a week and at St. Katherine's Club on Sundays. However, at this time, we could not

John Allan performing *tameshiwari* with *mae-geri* on wood held by Brian Bothwell, with Jeff Nicol supporting, at the Hazelhead Highland Games, Aberdeen, 1966. Watt is to be seen in the background between Bothwell and Nicol.

afford Torry School and were about to look for another school hall nearer the centre of Aberdeen.

"The club did a number of demonstrations at that time. I recall one display in particular that I was involved in at the Hazelhead Highland Games, Aberdeen, in 1966, when a white-belt, and Allan was a green-belt. Allan was good at *tameshiwari* and this always went down well. On one demonstration we did, Allan had, very impressively, punched and kicked through wooden boards and was about to *shuto* through a breezeblock, as a grand finale. Well, at the time, that was just out of this world and would have made people gasp with amazement. It was all set up and the spectators looked on, eagerly. Unfortunately, at the precise moment he was about to perform an *otoshi-shuto-uchi*, a strong wind suddenly got up and somehow the breezeblock toppled over and broke. You could easy smash all the bones in your hand trying to break through a breezeblock, and yet when it fell over it just snapped in two. That really gave the wrong impression, because it made it look as if the block was either easy to break or that it had been treated in some way to make it brittle – which it hadn't. I felt sorry for Allan because that was just really bad luck; he didn't deserve that happening to him. It was like a bricklayer breaking a brick with a trowel, but you try breaking one with your hand and that's a different matter. Well, don't try it. Unless you really know what you're doing and are able to concentrate the force, you'll break your hand. Somehow, when that block fell, the force must have been concentrated on a particular part."

Anderson did attend the BKF AGM and what went on in this meeting changed the face of British Shotokan karate forever, for it resulted in the aforementioned split in the Federation with the majority of clubs leaving to form the KUGB. Essentially, there were two bones of contention. Firstly, there was strong opposition to Kanazawa being obliged to leave Britain when his contract with Bell ran out, and, secondly, the notion of one man, Bell, running the BKF was no longer seen, at least in certain quarters, as desirable. This led to Anderson writing to Bell on the 16th May 1966. Anderson wrote: 'Following your report of the BKF AGM circularised to all Area Officers, in which you declared the meeting null and void, we have decided to withhold BKF fees until this matter is settled. As far as I can gather, you had no right to do what you did and therefore all decisions made at the meeting are valid. I am therefore going ahead with the plans decided on for the formation of the Scottish Area of the BKF. The immediate issues here are the opening of a bank account in the name of the BKF (Scottish Area) and the registration of gradings in Scotland from this office. The next step will be, I assume, the issuing of licences from this office ...' Anderson then discussed the subject of licences and noted that he would appreciate Bell's comments.

In the above letter, Anderson noted that his office had become quite efficient, due to the appointment of his sister, Doris, as Honorary Secretary of the Shotokan Karate Club of Aberdeen, and he intended that she should handle the work for the Scottish Area of the BKF. Matters were in a state of limbo however, for this was before the formation of the KUGB, and Anderson recommended that Bell make Doris an Honorary Member of the BKF. He also asked Bell's view on a design for the headed paper for the Scottish Area and noted a new badge for the Aberdeen club 'consisting of a St. Andrew's Cross with a *seiken* in the middle and two gold crescents bearing the words 'Shotokan Karate'' (a copy of which he enclosed in his letter of the 17th May 1966 {the last known letter between the two men}).

Watt's BKF licence (1966)

Anderson requested more BKF application forms (he had forty prospective members for a beginners' course) and details of the BKF summer course.

Anderson had been fully aware of the situation with regard to Kanazawa's imminent departure, for Bell, in his letter to Anderson dated the 4th April 1966, during the Scottish spring course, had given

Anderson the task of informing Kanazawa that he would be required to leave British shores. Bell wrote: 'I would like you to make a point of seeing Mr. Kanazawa personally and inform him that I have been in touch with the Ministry of Labour headquarters regarding his permit, and the Foreign ... [Labour] division has informed me that his work permit terminates officially on the 18th April.' Bell noted that Kanazawa could not work in this country after that date unless an extension to his permit was granted. Bell was prepared to try to get an extension, for a month, if Kanazawa wanted to stay on and work for the BKF only. Kanazawa subsequently left Britain for a short while and then returned to stay for another two years. In his absence, Enoeda remained, overseeing the formation of the KUGB.

Bell's reflections on Anderson and the Aberdeen club were happy ones. 'His [Anderson] enthusiasm was out of this world,' Bell recalled. 'He would come all the way from Aberdeen to Upminster[33] to train – that must be more than five hundred miles. That sort of dedication is very rare. I liked the fellow. I really liked him. He was down to earth. The Aberdeen *dojo* was nice – compact. He had regular students, terrific students – a most friendly lot. He left [the BKF] and joined the KUGB and I think became a 3rd Dan. I knew he'd reach the top.'

Watt continued: "By the middle of 1966, the club had resigned from the BKF and was then to become part of the newly founded KUGB. I don't know whether Anderson went to the inaugural meeting at Holdsworth Hall, in Manchester, but he may well of done; I imagine it was the sort of thing he would have wanted to attend. It was about this time that we started training at Skene Square School – this was another typical school gym with wooden floor, but in a separate building from the main school building – and I remember we had a meeting in the changing room about leaving one organisation and joining another, how much licences were going to cost, and so on. It didn't mean much to me at the time; I was only a very low grade and didn't know about the politics. I didn't want to know either, because it was only the karate I was interested in. Anderson was the senior at the club and he had brought Kanazawa and Enoeda to our *dojo*. He was highly competent and so I had complete faith in him and in his judgement."

II

BECOMING A PROFESSIONAL KARATE INSTRUCTOR

Watt continued: "Once we'd left the BKF, apart from having KUGB licences, members of the Shotokan Karate Club of Aberdeen were issued with little, wallet size, blue membership books, but these were given up after a couple of years [in 1968].

"Anderson arranged for Kanazawa or Enoeda to come up to Aberdeen quite regularly for courses and I attended every one of these. [On the 14th August 1966] I graded to *shichi-kyu*, 7th kyu, yellow belt, under Kanazawa. I was required to perform the *kata Heian Nidan* and partake in *gohon-kumite* once more. The basics were much the same as for 8th kyu, but techniques performed moving backwards were included." The *kihon* given as in late 1964 for the 7th grade were:

a) *Zenkutsu-dachi, gedan-gamae* ... M.F ... *oi-zuki*
b) *Oi-zuki* ... M.B [moving backwards] ... *age-uke*
c) *Age-uke* ... M..F ... *chudan- (soto) ude-uke*
d) *Ude—uke* ... M.B ... *kokutsu-dachi, shuto-uke*
e) *Zenkutsu-dachi, gedan-game* ... M.F ... *mae-geri*
f) *Kiba-dachi* ... crossing legs ... *yoko-geri-keage*
g) *Kiba-dachi* ... crossing legs ... *yoko-geri-kekomi*

Watt continued: "[On 28th December] I took *roku-kyu*, 6th kyu, green belt, under Kanazawa, and passed, though my later licence stamps show Enoeda for both 7th and 6th kyu gradings. I had to perform the *kata Heian Sandan*, and two *jodan* and two *chudan kihon-ippon-kumite*, both sides." The *kihon* given as in late 1964 for the 6th grade were:

a) *Zenkutsu-dachi, gedan-gamae* ... M.F ... *oi-zuki [and] sanbon-renzuki*
b) *Zenkutsu-dachi, gedan-gamae* ... M.B ... *age-uke,gyaku-zuki*
c) *Gyaku-zuki* ... M..F ... *chudan- (soto) ude-uke, gyaku-zuki*
d) *Gyaku-zuk i* ... M.B ... *kokutsu-dachi, shuto-uke*

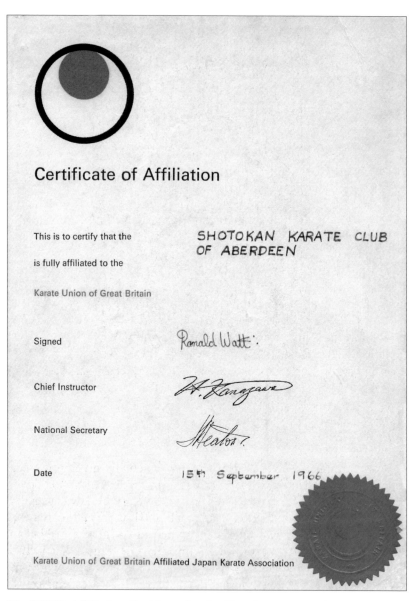

Certificate of Affiliation

This is to certify that the **SHOTOKAN KARATE CLUB OF ABERDEEN**

is fully affiliated to the

Karate Union of Great Britain

Signed — *Ronald Watt:*

Chief Instructor — *H. Kanazawa*

National Secretary — *Heaton*

Date — 15th September 1966

Karate Union of Great Britain Affiliated Japan Karate Association

The KUGB Affiliation Certificate for the Shotokan Karate Club of Aberdeen (1966). Kanazawa is the Chief Instructor and Terry Heaton, of Manchester, the KUGB General Secretary.

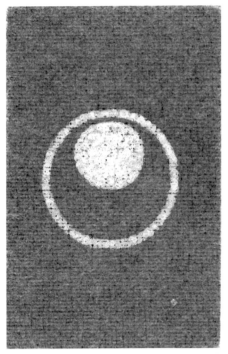

Shotokan Karate Club of Aberdeen membership card (actual size {1967-68})

e) *Zenkutsu-dachi, gedan-game* ... M.F ... *mae-geri*
f) *Kiba-dachi* .... crossing legs ... *yoko-geri-keage*
g) *Kiba-dachi* ... crossing legs ... *yoko-geri-kekomi*

Watt continued: "I remember how I was actually given my green belt. I heard that Kanazawa was going to give a demonstration down in Glasgow and so I informed him that I would travel down specially to watch. I don't think the BKF had a club in Glasgow and so, maybe, after the split, Kanazawa had been invited up to give a display to encourage people to join a fledgling KUGB club.[1] Kanazawa performed a tremendous *mawashi-geri* on Tommy Morris, who was well established in the city, during the display. Afterwards, Kanazawa saw me in the crowd, singled me out, and presented me with my green belt, which he took out of his *gi* bag. Here was a world-class 5th Dan and he remembered *my* green belt. That incident made me feel so proud. It was really wonderful.

"I don't remember now, it may have been at this time, because I was wearing a yellow belt – Kanazawa gave me my green belt at the end of the day – that I entered my first karate competition. Although I recall Kanazawa saying that he didn't practise freestyle until he was a black-belt in Japan, we actually practised at quite an early stage at Aberdeen, though not under Kanazawa's direction. I paired up with John Anderson a good number of times and he would really spar. Of course he was senior to me and much better. Allan was good too, strong.

"My grandfather, on my mother's side, James Watt, had been in the trenches in the First World War and blew out an eye after a gun badly misfired. He bred fine horses and bulls in his youth. He would regularly attend the Great Show, in Keith, which was an annual event. As an impressionable young boy I recall seeing this large silver urn with a wonderful Clydedale horse and Aberdeen Angus bull on it which he'd won in 1908. That urn was just so impressively made, solid, the work of a highly skilled Edwardian silversmith, and I think that trophy was always at the back of my mind and why I later entered so many karate competitions. I wanted to win something splendid like that too.

"I got through a few rounds in that Glasgow tournament and I think I was placed third, but I hurt my foot quite badly. On that occasion Plee and Nambu, both of whom had come over from Paris for the event, were in attendance. I recall Plee quite vividly because he looked like a film star and wore dark glasses throughout the proceedings, though I later heard that he had very sensitive eyes. His beautiful wife accompanied him. I remember Nambu complimenting me on my placing and asking which style I practised.

"As a green-belt I was involved in a demonstration at a school to raise funds for children. As part of the display, Bothwell and I did some *ippon-kumite*. I charged in *chudan oi-zuki*, he blocked me and then performed a *shuto-uchi* to my face. Unfortunately, he got his distancing wrong, so he said, and broke my nose. It was quite bad, there was blood everywhere, and I had to go to the hospital. Well, to be truthful, I wasn't too happy about that incident. I was just standing there letting him counter and he broke my nose, and although he said he was sorry, that it was an accident, I haven't forgiven him and never will. That was the first of thirteen times I had my nose broken over the next forty years. The problem with being quite small – I'm five feet six and a half inches in height – is that I'm always fighting monsters and their arms are about as long as my legs! You see me jumping up in a photograph and the other guy's upper body is four feet out of the photograph. There's a saying: 'a good big one will always take a good

James Watt at Balmedie Farm (*c.* 1916)

little one,' and I'm afraid I've invariably found that to be true.

"But there is a funny ending to the story. I was laying on a hospital table having to breathe in and out through my mouth because my nose

Watt blocking *gyaku-gedan-barai* to Brian Bothwell's *oi-zuki* in Angusfield Avenue, when both 6th kyus (1st half of 1967).

Bothwell delivers a kick upon Watt from the floor (1st half 1967)

was all distorted and blooded up, and the staff were really worried because they thought that I, a 6th kyu, was a karate expert! I remember the doctor being very wary of me in case I reacted suddenly. They were really on edge. Maybe they thought I might explode and jump through the ceiling or something. Actually, I fell asleep!

"Then [on the 7th June 1967], I graded to *go-kyu*, 5th kyu, purple belt, under Yoshikazu Sumi[2], a 3rd Dan, who acted as Kanazawa's assistant. I had to perform the *kata Heian Yondan* and *kihon-ippon-kumite* once more, including *mae-geri*, I think." The *kihon* given as in late 1964 for the 5th grade were:

a) *Zenkutsu-dachi, gedan-gamae ... M.F ... oi-zuki [and, after turning]sanbon-renzuki*
b) *Oi-zuk i ... M.B ... age-uke ... gyaku-zuki*
c) *Gyaku-zuki ... M.F ... chudan- (soto) ude-uke/gyaku-zuki*
d) *Gyaku-zuki ... M.B ... kokutsu-dachi, shuto-uke/zenkutsu-dachi,nukite*
e) *Zenkutsu-dachi, gedan-game ... M.F ... mae-geri (ren-geri* at *chudan* and *jodan)*
f) *Kiba-dachi ... crossing legs ... yoko-geri-keage/yoko-geri-kekomi*
g) *Zenkutsu-dachi ... M.F ... mawashi-geri*

Watt continued: "I took my *shi-kyu*, 4th kyu, purple belt with a white stripe – you had to sow it on in those days – [on the 24th September 1967] again under Sumi. I had to perform the *kata Heian Godan* and *kihon-ippon-kumite*, but this time to kicks – *mae-geri, kekomi*, and, maybe, *mawashi-geri* – as well as punches. Enoeda subsequently stamped my 5th and 4th kyu grades in a later KUGB licence.

"On the 22nd July 1967, I attended the first KUGB championships, which were held at Alexandra Palace, London. There was just a championships that year and no associated *gasshuku*, a feature that was to become an essential part of my calendar in the years to follow. On that first occasion, members of the Aberdeen *dojo* went down by train to King's Cross, and we did so for the next couple of years, though we wised-up to the length of the journey and caught a sleeper. I shared a room with Bothwell and we went through a tunnel. Now we had prepared for the championships and had been training really hard and our reactions and responses were extremely fast, not to say tuned; we were edgy. Well, Bothwell was asleep and he must have heard a change in sound as the train entered the tunnel and he woke up suddenly and put his elbow through the internal wooden wall. I woke up with a start because of the noise, my heart racing, and I was punching and kicking everywhere in the darkness. I put the light on and saw that Bothwell's elbow was leaking blood. Then there was a knock on the door and the guard walked in. I had to think quickly, make something up, and told him that my friend was an epileptic and that he'd had a fit. We cleaned up the blood and were both glad to get off, because the incident had been quite stressful.

"For the large majority of my subsequent annual tips to the KUGB Championships, I drove down. It took fourteen hours in those days, which was a real haul. We flew a few times too.

"At those first championships I saw Shirai, who had come over from Milan to join Kanazawa and Enoeda. He was another top-notch JKA Grand Champion. He looked super-fit; you could sense it. My goodness me, we were spoilt at that time.

"Andy Sherry, from Liverpool, took the *kata* title with *Enpi*, and Jack Green, from Blackpool, took the *kumite*. Green got a nice *jodan uraken* on Andy to win. The team trophy went to Liverpool.

"The normal training in basics at the *dojo* under Anderson and Allan was simple repetition up and down the hall, but it was really top-notch because that's what we all needed. Looking back now, it was hard, tough, traditional karate. The two instructors had good discipline. I don't think any of us really knew what we were doing in the full sense of the word, but we all copied Kanazawa, Enoeda and Sumi, and when they weren't there we copied Anderson and Allan. Kanazawa's English at this time was quite good, and Enoeda's was okay, but they could not get the concept of *hara* across for example, and I don't think we would have understood it at that time even if they could have done so. Well, I know that to be the case, because Kanazawa would say, 'Punch with your stomach,' by which he actually meant from the abdomen, but we would say, pointing to our hands, 'But *Sensei*, this is called a fist!'

"Anderson was a very nice chap, educated, polite, well-mannered. I liked him a lot and still do, though I haven't seen him for years. I had great respect for his karate ability and his dedication. He was a leader you could follow. He was similar to me in that he was a normal guy who tried really hard. He liked the discipline of Budo. He had a wonderful *mawashi-geri*, fast and crisp, and a good punch as well with a sharp snap. He was a real Shotokan man. He studied at Aberdeen University for four years and then moved down to London. In those days, people who went to university were academically extremely bright. I believe I'm correct in saying that he worked at a university, maybe London, in what I took to be social anthropology,

Left to right, standing: John Anderson, Ronnie Watt, Jeff Nicol, unknown, John Burnett, Albert Murray; sitting, Brian Bothwell, unknown, Michael Turnbull, Duncan Beattie, John Allan's son, John Allan – Torry School, (September to December, 1967).

epidemiology, or something similar to do with diseases and death rates. He had lots of books on his shelves in his office on this kind of thing. I went to see him annually when I went down to the KUGB *gasshukus* held at Crystal Palace, Norwood, London, S.E.19. One year I stayed with him throughout the duration of the *gasshuku*, two weeks. He trained at the Budokwai in the Fulham Road and he lived just off that road. He was one of the few people I've come across who you could describe as a really decent man. He later got married in Aberdeen.

"Allan was a good instructor too, and he did push the students on, there's no doubting that. He was a tough mentor who had trained in boxing I believe and had served in the Royal Navy.[3] I found him to be

Watt and Nicol at the Bugeikwai (September to December, 1967)

a very different kind of person to John Anderson and if I have to be honest, I'd have to say that I felt that I got on better, had a greater affinity, with Anderson. Allan was a powerful puncher and kicker.

"Then, in quite a step in those days, I graded to 3rd kyu, brown belt [on the 30th December 1967], under Kanazawa, for which I had to perform the *kata Tekki Shodan*. Once I had a brown belt around my waist I knew I was getting somewhere, for I now had a black belt firmly in my sights.

"After that grading I recall there was a dinner and dance in the Star Ballroom, and Kanazawa attended.

"I remember during one of these early gradings pairing up with a particular student, a large, strong man, for *gohon-kumite*. He said to me prior to the *kumite* that we should be careful, not go in too hard, get carried away. I said that was fine with me because we were beginners

70

Shotokan Karate Club of Aberdeen dinner and dance ticket (actual size {1967}).

and we didn't want any accidents. Then we started. Well, this chap flew in at me with a *jodan oi-zuki* as though there was no tomorrow and caught me with a beauty to the eye. I just wasn't expecting it; I had taken him at his word. Kanazawa didn't like that at all, it was lack of control, and I recall that whereas I passed my grading completely, my partner had to make do with a temporary grade. I had a real shiner of a black eye and that experience taught me not to be so trusting and not to be complacent before *kumite*.

"On that December 1967 occasion, Kanazawa performed the *kata Chinte* and that really had an effect on me, because I found the form so unusual – you know, the opening *tettsuis* performed so slowly, the *fudo-dachi* we'd never seen before, the *tate-ken-gyaku-zuki*, the *haito-barai*, the *otoshi-nakadaka-ken*, and to top it all off, the strange hops at the end. My first reaction to the hops was, 'He's messed the *kata* up and he's hopped back to where he started,' but of course, he hadn't messed it up. I found that *kata* really mysterious and it just fired my imagination. Here we were practising *kihon, gohon-kumite, ippon-kumite*, the *Heian, Tekki* and *Bassai-dai*, and there was this master just so far ahead showing us all these wonderful, stunning movements and techniques.

"Kanazawa had to leave early and Sumi, who had accompanied him, stayed with us over the New Year period. I don't think Sumi, who was staying at a hotel, thought that he was being looked after properly. Basically, one of the Aberdeen students would entertain the Japanese instructor during the daytime, take them about, show them the sights, but Sumi had been left high and dry with nothing to do. I phoned Sumi up about 11.30 p.m. on New Year's Eve, as I'd heard that the chap responsible for him that day hadn't picked him up. The problem was that I don't think this chap had any money and so he couldn't take Sumi about and buy him food and drinks. In many ways it was the fault of the organisers to neglect their guest instructor, to take him for granted really. After all, Scotland is like Japan in that courtesy is very important. So I picked Sumi up and brought him down to my parents' house to celebrate seeing the New Year in. He had a nice time I think, but he wasn't at all happy about being left alone by this other chap. Sumi was in a bad mood and after that, as I recall, he hit the person concerned in the nose during *kumite*. This chap had previously broken his nose and had a plate in there and when Sumi struck him the plate fell out. The blood gushed everywhere.

"But the same sort of thing happened to Kanazawa as well. The fact that the club had a karate superstar in their midst didn't always register with people. I remember that Kanazawa was stuck in his hotel with nothing to eat one evening after training. I suppose everyone thought that someone else would look after him. I went out and bought him fish, a jumbo haddock, some chips, and a few bananas. He was so hungry, famished. He didn't bother about using a knife and fork and just ate it out of the paper as soon as I gave it to him. I didn't like the way some people treated our guest. It struck me that they didn't mean Kanazawa any harm, they just didn't think. I suppose they thought that he was quite capable of looking after himself, which I suppose he was.

"I also took him to my girlfriend's – that's Ethel Trotter – house to

Joan Johnston, Kanazawa, Marjory Watt, Leslie Watt, Ethel Trotter (1967/68)

meet her mother and father to have dinner one evening and he enjoyed that. It's a small world you know, for only last week a member of my *dojo*, a young lady, took out a licence. To my surprise I noticed that she lived at Ethel's old address. I told her that one of the world's great karate masters had had a meal in her house in the 1960s and she was really chuffed by that.

"Because I was living with my parents in a small flat, there was never any room for Kanazawa to stay. However, he would come to my house and sit in the lounge. I remember taking him into my bedroom once and my mother prepared some sandwiches for us. He was very interested in a shrine I had in my room dedicated to karate. In the evenings we would go out tenpin bowling after training and get something to eat. I remember I told Kanazawa that I'd just built a large model boat, the Yamato battleship, and he launched it for me in the bath at home.

"I also recall spending a lunch hour with Kanazawa at the Garth Dee Motel. Anderson and Allan were busy and I took on the responsibility of entertaining Kanazawa, chat to him, because he didn't have anything to do until the evening when the lesson was held. I was so enamoured by Kanazawa and it was a real privilege to be able to speak to him, to have him to myself and to ask all the questions I wanted to. At that time, if you went back late or skipped work, that was

Master Kanazawa relaxing whilst tenpin bowling. From left to right: Kanazawa, Nicol, Bothwell, Watt (1967/68).

From left to right: Bothwell, unknown, Patrice (first name), Murray, Sumi, Watt, Ethel Trotter, Mrs. Allan, Allan, at a party at the Garthdee Motel, where Sumi was staying (1968).

it, they'd fire you, and I think that lunch hour, the really not wanting to go back, had a profound effect on me. I think it made me realise that here was a man who had escaped humdrum existence, and I still regret, more than forty years on, not having the courage not to go back to work that afternoon.

"Kanazawa and I both liked fast cars and we shared an interest in the Ford GT40. You could buy a GT40 in those days for the price of about five Ford Granadas. Today, a GT40 would be worth a million pounds. I drove about in a lime green Escort at the time and Kanazawa had a light blue Volkswagon Beetle, so we shared the same dream![4] Though in Kanazawa's case, I always took his VW as a classy understatement. I remember that he and I went to a showroom in Aberdeen that sold E-Type Jaguars. The great man loved that.

"I also took Kanazawa, Sumi and some other students to a racetrack. One of the members said something, I don't know what it was, but Sumi took real exception to this and slapped this fellow hard across the face. Sumi got his come-uppance though, for I remember, later, when he and Kanazawa were performing a demonstration at Crystal Palace, Kanazawa actually hurt Sumi. I think he was putting Sumi in his place in front of everyone. Well, that was my impression[5] and that was the last time I ever saw Sumi.

"Sumi was a small man. He didn't have the physique of Kanazawa, and I thought that Sumi was a good example of a man who was excellent at karate, a first-rate technician, a very fast puncher, but not with obvious physical attributes. Maybe, being small, he felt that he had to prove himself. Sumi was outclassed by Kanazawa and Enoeda, but they were senior, older, and so that was to be expected.

"Like many students at this time, I hero worshipped Kanazawa. I copied certain little things he did. For example, he seemed to wear his *gi* top short, and when he trained this top would often work its way out from being confined by his belt. I really liked this, so I wore my *gi* jacket short too. Then he had a beautiful blue leather coat that came from the USA and I wanted one just like it. I later had a replica made in Turkey, which I still wear. I also remember that Kanazawa had a new watch and I said to him that it was really nice. He told me how he had problems with the Customs at the airport because of it. I didn't just listen and think, 'That's a shame,' no, I felt really sorry him, because the general impression was that he'd been set-up.

"I took my 2nd kyu under JKA Chief Instructor, Masatoshi Nakayama[6], at the first KUGB *gasshuku* at Crystal Palace [on 17th May 1968]. That was the first of two times Nakayama came to Britain to teach. At that time, 2nd kyu was still brown belt, you didn't change colour or add a white stripe, but for 1st kyu you added a white stripe.

"Training at the 1968 *gasshuku* was in the morning from 10.00 a.m.

to noon and then from 3.00 p.m. to 6.00 p.m., so that was five hours a day. That was a lot and we'd often relax in the swimming pool afterwards. I was young and very keen, but it was tiring." A broad account of this course appeared in an early edition of *Karate* magazine, where it was noted that, 'very few members failed to have a good nights sleep, which is not surprising when one considers the amount of energy expended during the training periods which surely sapped the strength from even the strongest *karateka*. To some of the more exhausted members, the delightful female voice [over the tannoy system] announcing the beginning of another bright day, did not, I suspect, activate the still aching muscles as readily as the previous day's announcement.'[7]

Watt continued: "That was an amazing course if, for nothing else, the number of senior Japanese in attendance. There were an incredible eleven JKA instructors present. I've mentioned Nakayama, Kanazawa, Enoeda, Shirai, and Sumi before, and they were all there, but at the course I was also introduced to Satoshi Miyazaki[8], 4th Dan, Shiro Asano[9], 4th Dan, Akio Nagai[10], 3rd Dan, Koichi Sugimura[11], 3rd Dan, Katsuo Takahashi, 3rd Dan [see shortly], and, Sadashige Kato[12], 2nd Dan. I also recall a Mr. Iwai, 4th Dan.[13]

"I remember Shirai taking us and his instruction was tremendous, and he pulled this big guy, a black-belt, out to demonstrate on. We called Shirai, 'Geronimo', after the Apache Indian. He just emanated fighting spirit and his *katas* were brilliant.

"Miyazaki was living and teaching for the JKA in Belgium, and he was really nice to me. I think he had a problem with one of his eyes. My goodness me, he could certainly knock back the booze though![14]

"Asano had just arrived in Britain. He was quite tall, powerful, solid, yet fluid, with impressive *mae-geris* and *mawashi-geris*. There was no messing about this man.

"I remember that Nakayama was teaching us *Heian Godan* and students were performing the movement that leads up to the first *kiai* point differently. Kanazawa and Shirai went over to Nakayama to question him on this and he showed them. I recall this very vividly. In those days many people opened the left hand, *tate-uke* style, before punching *oi-zuki* with the right fist, but Nakayama said that the left hand should remain as a fist and that one should actually punch with it, and I've practised the move like that ever since. Different masters often perform the same movement differently, and students become confused watching DVDs and practise different variations. I don't think this is a good idea. My view is that it is best to stick to what one

Kanazawa performs a masterly *yoko-tobi-geri* on Enoeda at an early KUGB summer school at Crystal Palace (*c.* 1968).

master you respect does and concentrate on that. However, one mustn't be close-minded and sometimes you may find a variation you prefer. For example, the movement prior to the first *kiai* in *Bassai-dai* is such a technique for me. You know when you are in *kokutsu-dachi* and step across, anti-clockwise, with the right, back leg into a shortened *zenkutsu-dachi*, whilst at the same time blocking with the right hand and with the middle finger of the left hand placed on the base of the right hand, on the wrist, in line with the thumb. Well, I practised like this for twenty years and then I saw Kase perform it without the hands touching. That made more sense to me, I liked the *bunkai,* and so I perform that movement the way he taught it.

"A really funny incident happened on that course, just after one session had ended. Here was Master Nakayama, the highest graded Shotokan *karateka* in the world, and a Wado-ryu guy, a yellow-belt, sauntered up to him and asked how he performed a side-kick. Nakayama, whose English was good, spent considerable time explaining to this chap how to do it. The yellow-belt then went away. We were all surprised that such a low grade should have had the

Watt's competitors' card for the 2nd KUGB National Championships (1968). The signature is that of Terry Heaton, KUGB General Secretary.

audacity to go up to Nakayama, but there are some strange people about. Then, this moron ran over to Kanazawa and asked him how he did a side-kick, and Kanazawa spent time, a long time actually, about twenty minutes, explaining. Still not satisfied, this yellow-belt ran over to Enoeda and asked him. Enoeda didn't explain anything; he just looked at him and growled, 'Train harder.' I believe this episode shows the classic difference between the Nakayama/Kanazawa and Enoeda approaches to teaching karate. Which method is truly best, I cannot say.

"Anyway, this chap came back shortly afterwards and asked Nakayama how he performed a move in *Heian Sandan*, though you could sense that some of the Japanese instructors had had enough of this guy. However, Nakayama took time, once again, to show him how he performed the move, and do you know what this chap said on seeing Nakayama's technique: 'Oh! I do it this way, *Pinan*, because Wado-ryu is better!' I didn't know where to look. It was just so embarrassing. I think this chap must have been one brick short of a load and Enoeda and Miyazaki pulled him away. But this chap was persistent. Finally, I just happened to be in the lift with Nakayama and this yellow-belt tried to get in to tell him how to do karate and Shirai and a few Japanese, laughing, just blocked his entrance.

"I spoke to this chap later and he was really disappointed because he said that the Japanese would not listen to him. He had knowledge and he wanted to share it. I asked him where he had acquired such knowledge and he said that he trained once a week at his Wado-ryu club, read a lot and watched films and TV. I couldn't believe this guy, but I did feel a bit sorry for him as he seemed genuinely hurt.

"I really liked Nakayama. He was actually quite a bit smaller than me and I've seen a photograph of Nakayama and Funakoshi and the difference between Nakayama and Funakoshi was the same as the difference between myself and Nakayama, so Funakoshi must have been tiny, under five foot, and about the size of the average eleven year old today.

"I thought Nakayama was a very cultured man, a very clever man. He was quiet and never pushed himself forward. Everyone had so much respect for him and no one would light up a cigarette in his presence because he didn't smoke. He was also strong. He taught fundamental basics on that course if I remember correctly. I recall doing simple, effective *kihon*, like *gedan-barai/gyaku-zuki*, repeatedly, hips *hanmi*, hips *shomen*. We'd practise going forward, backwards, to the left and to the right, cross-shaped. Then *age-uke/gyaku-zuki*, *soto-ude-uke/gyaku-zuki*, *uchi-ude-uke/gyaku-zuki*, *shuto-uke/nukite*. We then took what we'd learnt and paired-up with a partner, so the *kihon* became *kumite*. I practised this type of *kihon* in Aberdeen of course, but it was the fact that I was being taught by the best in the world that made it so special. I watched Nakayama intensely, to see how he moved. I was so keen to learn.

"I actually had an opportunity to speak to Nakayama when a group of us wandered back the couple of hundred yards to the rooms at the Crystal Palace Centre, where we were all staying. Shirai was there, Andy Sherry and Terry O'Neill[15] were there. I remember asking Nakayama how he was enjoying his visit and how I was looking forward to coming to Japan in the future to train with him. I also mentioned that he would always be very welcome to come to Aberdeen, but I never dreamed for a minute that thirteen years down the line he'd accept my invitation and actually come to my *dojo*. I later asked Nakayama to sign my copy of his famous book, *Dynamic Karate*, and he obliged.

"Enoeda invited me to a meal at a Chinese restaurant with Nakayama, Kase, Kanazawa and Shirai. That was the beginning of a long friendship with Enoeda. I brought quite a lot of students down from Aberdeen and I think Enoeda appreciated that."

Whilst Watt and some of his fellow Aberdeen *karateka* took part in the KUGB championships that year without being placed, the *dojo's* women students did not go unnoticed, for as a report of the time

From left to right: Watt, Allan, Takahashi, Nicol, and three students from Jim Hardie's Fraserburgh *dojo,* outside Aberdeen High School for Girls (*c.* 1968).

shows, 'Four very pretty young ladies from Aberdeen and Liverpool were busy selling hundreds of attractively designed souvenir programmes!'[16]

Watt continued: "I took my 1st kyu[17] under Shiro Asano [on 21st July 1968], in Aberdeen. He was a tremendous fighter and a member of the Takushoku team which included Katsuya Kisaka[18], Hideo Ochi[19] and Miyazaki, that took the JKA university championships, twice. Really top-notch, I thought.

"Katsutaro Takahashi was another of Kanazawa's assistants and he was a genuinely affable person and a happy man, always smiling. I remember a course he gave at the *dojo* we had at the Aberdeen High School for Girls. He taught us the *kata Hangetsu* that night and I thought that was fantastic and so different from the other *katas* I had learned up to that date. Before that lesson I'd looked after him during the day, which was sunny, and took him out for a spin in my green MGB GT sports car. We drove along the River Dee and he was smiling; he loved it. Suddenly he shouted, 'Look! A salmon leaping.'

"'Where? Where?' I replied, and he pointed. Now the river was some considerable distance away and I thought to myself, 'What remarkable eyesight.' So, I decided to get my own back on him and when we were driving through Aberdeen I called out, unexpectedly, 'Cor! Look at that beautiful girl,' and he said, 'Where? Where?' But none was to be seen, for none was around and he gave me a knowing smile.

"Another night I took him dancing after training, by which time he was really hungry because his hotel had stopped serving hours before. We went back to my parents' house and my mother made us a bacon sandwich each in the early hours. I wasn't sure whether he'd eat a bacon sandwich, but he tucked into it as though there was no tomorrow.

"Takahashi was extremely fast and a first-rate technician. His *kata* was of the first order. After he left Britain he went back to Japan and taught at Nakayama's Hoitsugan *dojo* and then, I believe, went to Italy under Shirai. Takahashi is dead now, like his more famous namesake, Yoshimasa Takahashi[20], who I never met.

"I was training four times a week by this time: Tuesday and Thursday evenings and Saturday and Sunday mornings. The venues were Torry School, St. Katherine's Hall and Central School, but I don't remember where and on which day. We also trained in the Star Ballroom, a lounge of the Beach Ballroom. When the facilities were unavailable, we used to go down to the beach, especially in the summer, on a Sunday, to train. We'd often continue on the beach after training at the Star Ballroom for an extra hour and a half. I remember practising on the beach in winter, in the snow. People would walk along the beach wearing snug fur coats and woollen hats taking their dogs for a walk and there were these crazy people leaping about in white pyjamas. We got some strange looks I can tell you. We'd wade out in the near freezing North Sea up to our hips and punch. You couldn't train like that for any length of time of course, just a few seconds really, because it was so cold. I think the life expectancy in that water would have been a couple of minutes at most. Then we'd run back to our cars, put our tracksuits on and drive home as fast as we could to get dried and changed. The car seats would get soaked though and dried with salt marks. The next time we had training after such a session, many of the students would be ill in bed, so it was decided to discontinue this type of practise.

"I recall one winter training session on the beach that Anderson took when it was high tide and the wind was up. He shouted out above the crashing waves that we should bow across the sea to Japan. We all groaned and told him that the direction we were bowing in was towards Norway. He insisted we bow, so we picked him up and threw him into the sea.

"I remember, later, if we ever practised the *kata Unsu* on the beach, when it came time to do the three hundred and sixty degree jump, as we landed the sand that we'd kicked up from making the jump would land plonk, on our heads."

From left to right: unknown, unknown, Watt, Allan, Nicol, Albert Murray, Bothwell (late 1960s).

John Anderson had got the Aberdeen University Karate Club up and running as a report in *Karate* magazine reveals. Dated 19th August 1968, Anderson wrote: 'Despite the university summer vacation, there has been a lot of activity in the club. Most of the team members are to be found training in the gym three or four times during the week.'[21] It had been planned for Enoeda to come and give training at the club from the 24th–28th September and all *karateka* were welcome irrespective of grade or style and training fees were only three pounds for the week. Anderson was a 1st Dan at this stage, but, interestingly, recorded the club's vice-captain as 'Rod Anderson, 4th Dan.' The author can only think that an error has occurred and that 4th kyu was intended.

The University Championships were held at Liverpool University Sports Centre in 1969 and attracted collegiate teams from Liverpool (C. F. Mott Teacher Training College), Bradford, Cardiff, Warwick and Woolwich. Anderson's Aberdeen team had been hotly fancied to take the title, but arrived a week late for the event!Anderson reported at the time: 'The team set out in a blizzard to drive all the way to Liverpool for the British Universities Championships, and on arrival at the Liverpool University Sports Centre at 10.00 a.m. on Saturday

February 8th, found they had arrived a week late. The first reaction was psychopathic inclination towards the host club, until it was pointed out that all five officials of the AUKC [Aberdeen University Karate Club] had indeed mis-read the circulars. So twelve disgruntled *karateka* had a sad return to Scotland.'[22] Steve Cattle's team from C. F. Mott College took all three titles (team *kumite*, individual *kumite*, individual *kata*).[23]

In Anderson's report, we get the names not only of some of some of Watt's fellow KUGB students at the Shotokan Karate Club of Aberdeen (all 4th kyu and below), namely: Cameron, Clarke, Geddie, Murchie and Turnbull, but also some of the members from Aberdeen University (all 4th kyu and below), namely: Ewert, Manson, Stephen, McWhirr and Weyman.

The Aberdeen University team once again travelled down to Liverpool for the 1970 University Championships and Anderson's legacy, for he had left university by this time, was plain to see, as Aberdeen took the team *kumite* title. Other teams came from C. F. Mott Teacher Training College (Liverpool), Bradford, Lancaster, Nottingham, Sheffield and Woolwich. The Aberdeen team members are known: Ewert, Stephen, Reid, Frazer and Hazelwood.[24]

Watt continued: "I did train at the Aberdeen University *dojo* a few times, in the Aberdeen Buchart University Hall. The main hall was large and had an old nylon tiled floor, green I think it was. However, the karate *dojo* I trained in was located in a side gym and had a wooden floor.

"Anderson graded to JKA *Shodan* under Kanazawa, but I'm not sure where he took it, maybe it was in London. He was the first Aberdeen member to be so graded, so that was quite an achievement. John Allan graded to black belt not long afterwards.

"Anderson then left Aberdeen and Allan went down to Dundee for a while, if memory serves. I think he trained at Dempsey's *dojo*, to help them. Pat Dempsey, who was a building contractor by occupation, had two sons, Patrick and Paul, who were later to become prominent. Enoeda used to go up and stay with them and teach at their *dojo*.

"I trained all the time, had no time off, and became the highest grade at the club. I started taking the class and I kept the *dojo* going. Then Allan returned and the word on the street was that he intended opening another *dojo*, or maybe he had opened one, I can't be sure after all these years. I didn't see any point in having two Shotokan clubs in Aberdeen, in being pointless competitors and splitting resources, so I telephoned him and we agreed that we'd have just one

Nicol, Watt, Bothwell and Anderson (who is wearing a black belt {1968})

club.

"We trained at a number of *dojos* at this time, including the aforementioned Torry School and the Central High School, in the centre of Aberdeen, which is now a shopping mall, but we also practised at Woolmanhill Barracks and Powis Academy. The Woolmanhill Barracks was quite a large Victorian building opposite the hospital I had attended when I received my horrendous leg injury. The main hall of the *dojo* was very cold in winter and the whole place smelled of damp. We sometimes used an upstairs room for smaller classes. However, when the building was knocked down, like everything old, we really missed it. Woolmanhill was shared with a judo club and the Spartan Bodybuilding Club.

"In complete contrast, the Powis Academy *dojo* was a school gym in the old style, but, later, we used the Academy's assembly hall and that was modern and very clean.

"Then, not long after Allan's return, he went away again, and when he came back he formed the Aberdeen Shotokan Karate Club. When he did this, I changed my club name to the Scottish Shotokan Karate Centres and this name incorporated my associated *dojos*.

"I waited exactly eight months between passing my 1st kyu and taking my black belt grading. I trained every day in the build up to the big event and I concentrated on getting *Bassai-dai* and the *Heian kata*

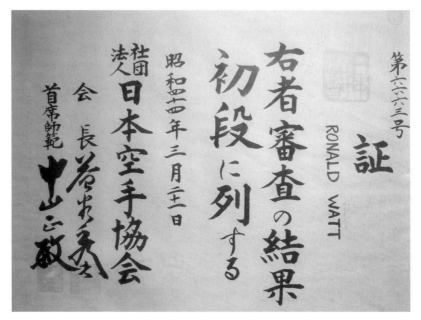

Watt's JKA *Shodan* diploma (1969)

as perfect as I could. I took my *Shodan* with a friend, Jeff Nicol, on the 21st March 1969, under Enoeda, at Torry School. It was a standard JKA black belt grading – *kihon, kumite* and *kata*. The *kihon* was straightforward enough: *sanbon-zuki, age-uke/gyaku-zuki/gedan-barai, soto-ude-uke/empi/uraken/gyaku-zuki/gedan-barai, uchi-ude-uke/kizami-zuki/gyaku-zuki/gedan-barai, shuto-uke/mae-geri* off the front leg/*nukite, mawashi-geri, uraken, gyaku-zuki,* that type of thing. Enoeda could see all that he wanted to see through these basics. There was nothing fancy, no stringing together endless techniques, just good, sound Shotokan. We then did some *ippon-kumite* and *jiyu-ippon-kumite*: two *jodan,* two *chudan,* two *mae-geris,* two *kekomis* and two *mawashi-geris.* The hardest part was the *jiyu-kumite.* Jeff was a powerful man and it was a bit of a ding-dong as I recall, for we both desperately wanted the *Shodan* grade. In the *kata,* we both had to perform *Bassai-dai* and *Heian Godan.*

"Although we had to wait, we were told the results of the grading on the day. When '*Shodan*' was announced we were both overcome with joy. I went home and told my parents. My father was shocked as he thought it was just a hobby.

"Jeff is a nice guy and he later went into the oil business. He

Watt and Nicol not long after achieving their black belts (Woolmanhill Barracks, 1969).

worked as a sprayer of lorries at the time. I remember a demonstration we did together at Woolmanhill Barracks just after we got our *Shodans*. We just went in, on a high, and started sparring. The first technique he did was a *mae-geri*, I didn't block properly and he broke my finger. Next, I kicked him with a *mae-geri* and broke his rib and we both ended up down at the hospital. I recall us standing there, me with my hand all plastered up and Jeff with his chest strapped up. Was it any wonder we had trouble keeping members!

"Black-belts in karate were quite rare at the time and the local press did a write-up on Jeff and I.[25]" The article reveals that the Aberdeen Shotokan Karate Club, with 'around one hundred and twenty members' trained at Torry School on Tuesday and Thursday evenings and on Sunday afternoons.

Watt continued: "The KUGB *gasshuku* was as good as ever in 1969. The usual Japanese were there, and I remember another instructor I hadn't seen before, or since, and that was [K.] Kobayashi, from Denmark.[26]

"It was in 1969 that the Karate Union of Scotland was formed as an offshoot, if that's the right word, of the KUGB, under the chairmanship of Al Doran, and I became a member." In fact, Doran wrote a letter to the editor of *Karate* magazine, presumably just before the re-arrangement (as he is noted as being the KUGB Area Officer and British Karate Control Commission representative), stating the current set up of karate in Scotland, as he saw it. Noting there were three main organisations, he wrote: 'the oldest being the Shotokan clubs who first stared over seven years ago and are all members of the KUGB ...'[27] Doran then mentions the Scottish Karate-Do Association, with Tommy Morris, and Karate-Do Shotokai, with Mitsusuke Harada.

Doran's comment about Shotokan training commencing 'over seven years ago' is interesting, for the article was published in 1969, so presumably Doran was thinking before 1962. In fact, as far as the author is aware, karate, which was indeed Shotokan, was first taught in Scotland near the west coast town of Saltcoats, Ayrshire, by Edward Ainsworth, in 1961, under the auspices of the British Karate Federation. Ainsworth had both trained and graded under Murakami. A short book by the author about this *dojo*, entitled, *Scotland's First Karate Club?* is currently in preparation. Whether Doran knew about this isolated club is unknown.

Mitsusuke Harada first arrived in Britain in November 1963, from Belgium. Born in 1928, he began his study of karate at the famous Shotokan *dojo* a year or so before the building was destroyed in an American bombing raid in 1945. He knew the Shotokan greats of the time – Yoshitaka Funakoshi, Motonobu Hironishi[28], Wado Uemura and Yoshiaki Hayashi. Harada then trained as a private *deshi* of the founder of Shotokan and the man responsible for bringing karate to Japan from Okinawa, Gichin Funakoshi, before attending Waseda University, where, amongst others, he came under the influence of Tadao Okuyama and Toshio Kamata. However, it was in the year of his master's degree that the greatest influence in his life was to be found in the shape of Shigeru Egami.[29] Harada went on to introduce karate to Brazil before coming to Europe, where he continued his association with Shotokai. Harada's lineage is truly exceptional and his story is told in detail in two books by the author.[30] It is understood that Harada did indeed travel up to Scotland quite early on, maybe before the arrival of official JKA instructors in 1965. Tetsuji Murakami never travelled that far north during this period, with Middlesborough being the furthest point. Watt had not heard of Harada teaching in the Dundee, Aberdeen, Inverness triangle at this time, otherwise, as he said, 'I would have sought him out.' However, Watt did recall Harada teaching further south in Stirling, though is unsure about Glasgow and Edinburgh.[31, 32]

Watt continued: "As I've said, I was working as a loom operator and the job necessitated working down by the sides of the machines.

Well, when I needed to do this, I'd have a stretch, practise my karate warming up exercises. One day, I was lying on the floor, stretching, and the company's managing director walked past. He thought I was having some kind of fit. When I got back up, ambulance men with stretchers were waiting at the door, so that took some explaining. I'd also chop up the wooden pins, which were quite valuable and an essential part of the loom, with *shuto*. I shouldn't have done that. Perhaps I just wasn't suited to this kind of work. However, the question of whether I should stay or whether I should leave was taken out of my hands, because doctors thought I might be seriously damaging my lungs breathing in all the tiny particles of dust. I used to come home after work, get the metal bath out of the wash house, next to the coal shed, and bathe in the kitchen. When I took my clothes off, the dust from work went everywhere and the water was discoloured after I'd washed my hair.

"I had some time off from my employment and went to karate courses in London and elsewhere. My lungs cleared and my karate got better.

"But I had to get another job and I worked for another engineering firm, an American Company, as a capstan lathe operator. We used to make power guns for heavy industry which operated on compressed air. I used to work nights for two weeks and then days for two weeks and it just killed me – by the time my body adjusted to the change, I'd have to switch shifts again. I'm quite a creative person, a free spirit, and the repetitive nature of the work was soul destroying. I hated every minute of it and I had to break free. Kanazawa had sent me a card saying that he hoped that I would work hard to become an instructor. He was guiding me and I took his card to mean that he wanted me to have my own *dojo*. In 1970 I said to my mother and father that I really couldn't take that kind of work any more, that I wanted to get a *Nidan* [2nd Dan], and I thought that I could make a go at karate. I told them that people were really interested in the art and I proposed that I should leave my job and start teaching professionally. I wanted to know if they would be prepared to support me in this venture, as it was likely to take time to establish myself, assuming I could make it work at all. They couldn't believe it, they thought I was crazy and said that I ought to have a proper job, but they agreed to back me.

"I put a couple of adverts in the local newspaper and kept my fingers tightly crossed. Quite a few people responded by coming along to my *dojo* and so that is how I got started as a professional karate instructor. This was a few years before the Bruce Lee movies and

The KUGB Affiliation Certificate for the Shotokan Karate Club of Aberdeen (1970).

Kung-fu television series appeared on our screens, and people were still being drawn to *dojos* because of the Bond films. Just to give you an idea of how popular the notion of self-defence was back then in Aberdeen, I could have sixty to seventy people training each night. I remember having well over one hundred on occasion. But I don't want

Kanazawa and Watt in Aberdeen (1970/71)

to give the wrong impression, because people were only paying twenty pence or thirty-five pence to train and halls had to be hired, so no one was making a fortune."

A newspaper article from 1986 reports Watt as saying: 'A lot of people thought I was mad to give up a good job, and I did lose money on it. My parents had to bail me out for over two years until I got on my feet.'[33]

Watt continued: "Those times were different though, because people didn't have the variety they have today. There were no personal computers to spend your life behind and goodness knows how many television channels to choose from. I believe that individuals were more interested in going out and doing things, and personal fitness, personal enquiry, was part of that.

"I found that starting out as a professional karate instructor was quite daunting and I had to get my head around the fact that this was a job, how I earned enough money to eat and keep warm, and yet at the same time I was teaching an art that I loved. I'd never planned to become a karate instructor, never trained with that in mind, it just happened as a consequence of events really. I didn't want to compromise my karate, but on the other hand I had to accept that other people would not be as dedicated as I was and that they might train for different reasons. I was not a big shot in the karate world, but I like to think that I am sincere, and I suppose I hoped that might see me through. I also like to think that I gave good instruction, cheaply, and I'd do my best to get the top Japanese to the *dojo*. I was always a little bit embarrassed when, socially, people I met asked me what I did for a living. I'd say that I was a physical education instructor and leave it like that and hope that they wouldn't enquire further. I was proud of what I did, very proud actually, but I knew they wouldn't understand, as there was no common frame of reference. My idea was then, as it is now, to make high quality karate both amenable and affordable.

"I did not discourage women and children from training because I thought they could achieve something through karate. I remember Norma Amos, who was the first woman to get anywhere in Aberdeen Shotokan as far as I'm aware. She reached black belt level. She started under Anderson and lives in Canada today. She married a Japanese and then an American, I believe. She later changed to Wado-ryu."

There are a good number of newspaper clippings from the 1970s to show that Watt was prepared to teach women both karate and self-defence.[34]

Watt continued: "We had a few child protégés too, who were outstanding at kicking. They were so supple.

"The Aberdeen Shotokan Karate Centre had the following rules that had to be strictly adhered to and each beginner was given a typed copy upon joining:

'1. As you enter or leave the *dojo* you must bow as a sign of respect.
2. The instructor in-charge must be accorded every respect, and must always be called '*Sensei.*'
3. At the beginning of a session the highest pupil at the end of the line, as the class bows at the instructor, [will] say, *Sensei ne rei.*
4. No smoking, spitting or swearing [is permitted] in the *dojo*.
5. If you are late in coming, wait at the end of the *dojo* in the clear view of the instructor and he will tell you when you can come in. Never enter into a class without permission from an instructor.
6. *Dojo* fees must be paid, also club fees must be paid promptly when due.
7. Remember, courtesy, effort and self-discipline are the true ways of a good karate man.'[35]

"Later, I typed a more sophisticated, seventeen-point, *Japanese Martial Arts Etiquette*. I also hand-wrote a list of terms that beginners

Watt performing a *jodan mawashi-geri* (1970/71)

needed to know and this included basic blocks, punches, kicks, stances, types of *kumite*, counting from 1–10, grades and belts worn from novice to 3rd Dan, a short note on *Heian kata* and some general commands such as, *rei, yoi, yame* and *hajime*. I also printed the *Dojo Kun* out on a separate page to show the importance I attached to it.[36]

"I was involved in a fair number of demonstrations at this time as I was trying to encourage students to train with me. One display I remember giving, as a *Shodan*, was at Mike Bissett's Stirling *dojo*, and involved breaking two pieces of two inch thick wood, so that's four

Watt about to break boards, and very nearly his hand, at the Stirling *dojo* (early 1970s).

inches altogether. I made it look as impressive as I could, you know, give the breathing ceremony first. The wood was placed so that it spanned, bridge fashion, two tabletops and students supported the tables either side. I came down with a mighty *shuto*, but the table tops had a lot of play in them and the floor was sprung and the energy bounced back at me. However, the second board broke. I felt a wave of nausea come over me. My hand felt badly injured. Luckily, I didn't break any bones, but in the changing room afterwards, as I tried to dress myself one-handed, I thought to myself, 'Why am I doing stupid things like this?'

"I recall an amusing incident – well, not that amusing for the poor devils involved – that took place in Stirling about this time. We'd hired a hall for a competition and when we got there we found to our dismay that the floor was really slippery, like ice. Everything was set up, people had travelled a good distance, so we decided to proceed with the event. The first two fighters got up and faced each other and began sliding all over the place. It was ridiculous. We asked if anyone had any talcum powder handy that we could sprinkle over the floor, but no one had. What else could we use? The hall had a kitchen attached to it and someone went in to see what they could find and came out clutching a box of scouring powder, which was duly shaken over the contest area. The two fighters faced each other once more and we were in business, or so we thought. One of the combatants launched a fast *mae-geri* that missed, though the upward action of the kick flicked some of the scouring powder into his opponent's eyes. The man couldn't see; his eyes quickly became red, swollen and tearful. The chap who'd kicked, instead of kneeling until some kind of decision had been made by the referee and judges, had, somehow, cut his foot whilst kicking and he had some of the powder in his wound, and he was hopping about because his foot stung. It was then a case of liberal amounts of water being applied to the affected areas. It was a real carry on!

"I enjoyed Japanese films and I thought it would be a good idea to generate some interest in the martial arts by showing a few. It was very difficult to see foreign films then, for you had to find a cinema that specialised in them; they weren't available on DVD as they are today, and that's why I thought it was such a good idea. I managed to get hold of Akira Kurasawa's, *Yojimbo*, and the follow on, *Sanjuro*, both starring Toshiro Mifune, from a firm somewhere in London, who rented them to me. I booked a hall, informed the martial arts' clubs in the local area, and, astonishingly, about three hundred people turned up. Unfortunately, the venture turned out to be a disaster.

"We were all set to go, the lights faded and the projector was on, the film began to roll and everything on the screen was blurred. It turned out that the long lens was fitted. Miraculously, a technically minded fellow fixed that problem eventually, and then, when *Yojimbo* was showing, the film snapped, and some of the frames overheated and caught fire. You could smell burning celluloid and smoke was all around. The audience was becoming very uneasy and it was an absolute nightmare. Whilst the film was being re-spliced I went on stage and performed an impromptu karate demonstration to keep the spectators amused, and accidentally kicked one of my students in the groin. He had to go to hospital. The whole thing was a farce and an experience definitely not to be repeated.[37]

"It was about this time, 1970, when down in London attending the KUGB summer course, that I had a near escape, for I was close to having to use my karate for real. But first of all let me tell you what led up to it.

"I was in Soho and John Anderson was asleep in my car. I was wondering around just taking in the sites of London one night after training with two friends – I'd better not mention their names – from

Glasgow, both of whom were really good competition fighters. Anyway, we went to this local strip club just to see what it was like. I was so naïve. After we left this seedy establishment, we passed one of the strippers on the street and casually said hello. There was nothing in it; we were just being polite. Well, before we could say another word, she was threatening us with a cosh that she whipped out of her handbag. I was really taken aback by her language and ferocity. We decided to move away, out of any trouble, immediately, but, unfortunately, we walked into a lot worse.

"Still in Soho Square, we were standing there trying to come to terms with what had just happened, when we suddenly found ourselves surrounded by a large group of drunken football thugs. They were in a really nasty mood, I suppose their team had lost, and things were building up nicely. The atmosphere was one of extreme danger, but we couldn't get away because they were all around, jostling and jeering, and I expected an attack at any moment. I was on full alert. Then, one of these thugs advanced towards us and one of my friends, in an instant, smashed a Coke bottle over this guy's head. It was a brilliant piece of timing and it gave us that vital split second advantage, when the gang members were in shock, before they retaliated because of what had happened to one of their mates. The three of us burst out of our encirclement and made a hasty run for it.

"My two friends, who, I have to be honest, were not saints, got away in a taxi, but one of the gang, close on their heels, grabbed one of my friend's shoes as he got in. That's how close it was. I went my own way and darted into a restaurant and stayed there for a while, in the shadows. When the coast was clear, I walked back nervously to the car, where Anderson was still fast asleep.

"When I woke up the next morning, I was still a bit shaky from the events of the night before. However, I went training and I was up against an enormous bodybuilder in *jiyu-kumite*, in a bout that Asano was refereeing. Anyway, this man lifted me up and virtually shook me out of my *gi*. As I fell back down, topless as it were, I punched him in the chest and got an *ippon*!

"I bought myself a *makiwara* which I kept in my bedroom. It was built into a wooden platform that you stood on and the body's weight secured the *makiwara* from moving forward as you hit it.[38, 39] Kanazawa told me where I could acquire one and that was somewhere in London. I was dreaming about karate one night and I jumped out of bed and hit this *makiwara*, which was about a foot from the wall. I struck it with a *seiken* at great force and it bent back, smacked against the wall, and the shock toppled over not only my mother's porcelain cabinet but her wardrobe as well. What a mess! There was broken glass and bits of porcelain figurines all over the place and coats and jackets had fallen out of the wardrobe. My mother rushed through to see what had happened. That was an interesting experience, because I was half asleep when I did that, but I probably could never have achieved the same effect when fully awake and concentrating. I think it says something about unconscious power.

"Later, in another house, I had a *makiwara* in the garden and I vowed that every time I came home I'd punch or strike it one hundred times. Sometimes I would come home really exhausted, but I made myself face it. It wasn't easy and when the phone was ringing I didn't answer it because I had to finish my one hundred blows. I suppose that would now be classed as obsessional behaviour.

"I tried all sorts of supplementary training methods that I'd read about. For example, I filled a bucket full of sand and drove my fingers into it, but I gave that up after a while because I wanted to write and needed to be able to hold a pen!

"I also had some iron *geta* made. I knew a chap who cut out metal and he made me a pair of metal flip-flops. They were heavy, but I'd practise kicks in my bedroom. One day, I lifted my knee-up for *mae-geri*, straightened my lower leg, but didn't grip the leather strap so well with my toes, and the *geta* shot off my foot and embedded itself in the wall! I decided not to re-decorate my room until I had mastered the technique.

"Another form of training I did was to wear weights on my lower legs for four months. I didn't bathe in them or sleep in them of course, but I wore them most other times. When you take weights off, your legs feel so light. One day, I was looking at the carpeted floor in my bedroom and I thought to myself, this carpet's in a real mess; I've never noticed all these coffee stains before. I bent down to investigate and found that these weights had suddenly decided to leak iron fillings all over the room. So I had to vacuum it all up before my mother found out. You should have heard the noise as the iron fillings clattered their way up the nozzle and extension pipe.

"In 1972, the KUGB *gasshuku* was held, as usual, in the first two weeks in May. That year, Kase, Enoeda, Shirai, Asano, Ochi, Miyazaki and Kato were there, along with Matsuo Kon[40], who was a 6th Dan in both karate and judo, and editor of the *Tokyo Shimbun* [newspaper].[41] I remember Ochi on this occasion because he performed side-splits standing against the *dojo* wall. He was just superb.

Hideo Ochi performing *yoko-geri-keage* at Crystal Palace (1970s)

"Kon wanted to see Scotland and Enoeda asked me if I could take care of him. I was only too pleased and said as much. So Kon came up and during his visit we had the most wonderful sunshine. I even took him putting at St. Andrews, as he was a keen golfer. Although I really tried, I couldn't get him a round on the famous course. Kon taught at

Watt with Matsuo Kon in Aberdeen (1970s)

my *dojo*. He was good and specialised in judo/karate combinations. I think he was a bit of a one-off, because how many people get 6th Dans in both arts? Anyway, in terms of the weather he had a wonderful time, and when he got back down to London he told Enoeda that Scotland was like Hawaii. Enoeda said to him, 'Are you mad!' Funnily enough, shortly after Kon boarded the plane, it started to rain, and we were back to our usual weather. Enoeda was pleased with the way I'd looked after his friend and asked if there was anything I wanted. I told him that it had been a privilege, but he sent me a lovely blue Tokaido tracksuit with his name embroidered on it. I really appreciated that. Kon gave me one too, before he left, to say thank you, so I was well kitted out. Actually, Enoeda later confided in me that Kon had helped him get on to the JKA Instructors' Course, and I think that he felt indebted to him.

"In fact, later, when I was a 4th Dan, Enoeda gave me a brand new Tokaido *gi* with a gold and black badge embroidered on it. Yukichi Tabata[42], who was Enoeda's *kohai* and a very good friend of his – they used to play golf together – had given it to him. When I was in Dundee on one of Enoeda's courses, he gave me his black belt. I wore that for many, many years, until the silk outer layer wore away so all you could see was the white belt underneath. I stopped wearing it when I got my 8th Dan, because it would have fallen to bits on me.

"The 1973 gasshuku[43] was much the same as 1972, except Kon wasn't there but Tomita[44] and Shimohara[45] were.

"In the early to mid 1970s, Kanazawa and Kato visited the dojo regularly. I remember having a copy of Kanazawa's book, Basic Karate Katas, and requesting a private lesson from Kato on the sai kata that's included. It was funny because Kato asked me whether I had the book, and when I said that I had, he went through it with me using the book for reference. I don't think he knew it either, and I was paying him to do what I could have done by myself!

"Kato was a 4th Dan JKA when he came up to Aberdeen. His dojo was based in the Conservative Club in Crewe, the town in which he lived. He had his North England Karate Centre which was affiliated to the JKA, KUGB and BKCC. When he came up to Aberdeen, we had the courses at the Cowdrey Hall, in Fonthill Road, the YMCA Halls in Union Street and the Woolmanhill Sports Centre, but he would also teach at the clubs in Stirling [Toll Booth, Broad Street], Fraserburgh [Dalrymple Hall, Seaforth Street], and at Elgin [West End School and Museum Hall][46], and Perth.

"I attended what I believe to have been the last course that Kanazawa and Enoeda took together. Although Kanazawa and Enoeda were both top-class JKA karateka, sometimes they would perform movements in kata differently from one another. I wanted to be like them both, but this caused me a few embarrassing moments. I remember attending a course and practising the kata Jion. On the last 'active' movement, you are in kiba-dachi and you keep one foot in place and move the other foot to it. I noticed that Kanazawa and Enoeda moved different feet. What was I to do? I was attempting my 2nd Dan and I was asked to perform Jion, so I faced a quandary as to which leg to bring up. I didn't want to offend either of them, so I brought both legs up at the same time to meet in the middle! I tried to have a foot in both camps you might say. I felt that, politically, Kanazawa and Enoeda became like trying to force two similar poles on two magnets together. Even Nakayama couldn't succeed, and I tried in my own small way to do it in Jion. Kanazawa came up to me and asked why I had done the move in such a way and when I told him, he just nodded. Enoeda just looked at me and pushed me aside as much as to say, 'What a twerp.' That episode shows you their different personalities too. A few months later [on the 23rd August 1973], I took my Nidan again and passed under Enoeda.[47]

cΑberdeen Shotokan Centre

KARATE AS TAUGHT BY THE JAPAN KARATE ASSOC.

Secretary:
Miss N Amos   22 Polmuir Road Aberdeen

Instructors:
R. Watt   27 Skene Square Aberdeen
B. Bothwell   68 Beechwood Avenue Aberdeen

Aberdeen Shotokan Centre card showing Watt and Bothwell as instructors (1973).

"When I was 2nd Dan, I met up with Anderson and he introduced me to a club in Slough, Berkshire. The members enjoyed my karate and there was talk about the possibility of me leaving Aberdeen and moving down south to be an instructor with accommodation provided, but it never happened.

"The year 1973 was when Bruce Lee hit the big screen with *Enter the Dragon*, and, *The Way of the Dragon*. Actually, he made *The Big Boss* [1971], and, *Fist of Fury* [1972] before, but it was *Enter the Dragon* that really sealed it and mainstream audiences went to see him. The fact that Lee died in 1973 just seemed to add to the whole martial arts magic. Much at the same time, *Kung-fu* appeared on television with David Carradine as Kwai Chang Caine. The numbers of students training in the *dojos* soared. Brian Bothwell had gone to England, London I think, to work, and when he came back he asked if he could train with me and I agreed. He then started his own *dojo* at Skene Square School and we had another in Hanover Street." A newspaper report quotes Watt: 'The centre has only been going about five months and already the membership has grown beyond our beliefs.'[48]

"I'll never forget one incident that happened at Skene Square School around this time. We had a brown-belt in the club whose nickname was Kung Ginge [ginge pronounced as in 'fringe'], because he liked kung-fu and his hair was ginger. We were doing some squad training and a white-belt turned up who had recently joined and who was, quite honestly, the weakest-looking student I have ever seen in a *dojo*. The white-belt asked if he could take part and he paired up with Kung Ginge. It looked such an effort for this white-belt to simply raise

Skene Square School

his arms; it was painful to watch. Suddenly, Kung Ginge let out an almighty shriek and jumped high in the air with a view to performing a *yoko-tobi-geri* on his hapless opponent. The white-belt moved about a foot to the side and Kung Ginge flew past him and instead of landing on the floor in a stance, he quite literally landed in the *yoko-tobi-geri* position. Kung Ginge had forgotten to put his legs down and ended up in hospital courtesy of a wide stretcher and an ambulance.

"That reminds me of a foolish thing I did around this time too. I recall going to a *dojo* early to get some practise in before my students arrived. There was no one around so I decided to practise *mae-geri* against the wall. I'd done this before at various locations in the *dojo*, but when I kicked the wall this time, my foot went straight through it, as the part of the wall was made of plywood. The trouble was, my foot went through, but wouldn't came back out! I was stuck, and I had to stand one legged until my students came in. Someone went off to get the caretaker and he had to take a saw to the plywood. I had to apologise to the authorities and assure them that I was not some kind of hooligan. I told them that I'd slipped. Nevertheless, I had to pay three hundred pounds compensation, and that was a lot of money in those days.

"I also recall an exhibition of *kata* that I was supposed to do at the

Watt fighting in an All-Styles British Championships at Crystal Palace, London.

Girls' High School, in Aberdeen. I was dressed not in a *gi*, but in a *hakama*. I stood in *heisoku-dachi*, left hand over right. '*Tekki Shodan'*, I announced, and off I went. First *kosa-dachi*, then right leg up and arms crossed, then down into *fumikomi*. There are twenty-five moves in that *kata*, and that was as far as I got, because my foot went straight through a floor board when I brought the stamping-kick down. My leg was sunk through half way up the calf muscle. Once again, I couldn't retrieve my foot, but this time I'd cut myself. It wasn't bad though and the caretaker had to come and saw me out again.

"I'd been involved in local competitions, inter-club matches, for some years, and I'd also entered the KUGB National Championships, both individually and in the team events, but the standard was so high then. Nevertheless, taking part inspired me, and I passed on to my students all that I had learned.

"I entered an All-Styles competition down in Crystal Palace. I think I fought Billy Higgins[49], now a 7th Dan with the KUGB, but he started in Wado-ryu. Billy was a tremendous freestyle man, and, of course, later went on to captain the British All-Styles World Championship winning team in 1976. Roy Stanhope, another world-class Wado-ryu fighter was also there. In Aberdeen, we did traditional Shotokan training, lots of basics, and I had very little experience in fighting *karateka* from other styles. For me, that competition was really a case

Watt performing *yoko-tobi-geri* on student (*c.* 1974)

of survival. I can't remember now how I got on, I vaguely recall getting through a few rounds, but I couldn't have done too badly because I managed to walk home!

"I also captained a Scottish Shotokan team, but I suppose my biggest success came in 1975, when I won the individual *kata* and individual *kumite* at the Scottish Shotokan National Championships, which were held in Aberdeen. I won a cup for each and was presented with a shield for being Grand Champion. It was quite a big affair and

Kato brought some teams up from England to compete too, and so it was an Open competition as well.

"In the first round of the *kata* in those championships, which was on flag decision, I made a grievous mistake on *Heian Shodan*. It's was just nerves. I missed the *tettsui* out, which is easily done, especially if you practise *Kihon Kata*, or *Taikyoku Shodan* as it is also known, and I'd been teaching that form to beginners the night before. Luckily, my opponent messed the *kata* up too, and did three *oi-zukis* instead of three *age-ukes*.

"Then we were asked to do *Bassai-dai*, and in the final I performed *Nijushiho*.

"In the *kumite* final, as luck would have it, I was up against Bothwell. I watched him loosen up beforehand – he was a really powerful man and a good *karateka* – and I thought to myself, 'I'm going to have my hands full here. This is going to be a good fight.' I felt that there was quite a lot of rivalry between the Aberdeen clubs and you could sense the tension building up.

"Brian and I circled each other first of all and then I lunged in with an *oi-zuki* and followed this immediately with a *gyaku-zuki* and scored a *wazari*. The fight resumed and I went in for an *oi-zuki* again and we clashed. Kato, who was the referee, jumped in with *Yame*. As Kato did this, Brian punched me in the face and broke my nose. That made me see stars, I can tell you. It looks as though I've got a moustache in the photos, but that's actually dried blood. Anyway, Brian had strong fighting spirit, but so did I, there was a lot of adrenalin being pumped around veins, and although my nose was smashed up and I felt a bit sorry for myself, when I saw Bothwell looking at me as much as to say 'There, that's got you out of the game mate,' I was determined to continue and I wasn't going to be dominated by him or his style of fighting. The match resumed and to me Brian's face said, 'I've wounded this guy, but he's still here.' If he'd had a plan, it hadn't worked. The notion of rules didn't seem to apply, otherwise, in my opinion, he should have been disqualified for excessive contact rather than just receiving a caution. I wasn't messing about now, this was as real as it gets. So, we faced each other again and I caught him with a *mae-geri* and that took the match. Brian and I shook hands afterwards and there was no ill-feeling.

"About six months later, Brian and I were sparring on the beach and I broke his nose with a *mawashi-geri*, and that was an accident too.

"Bothwell really made me work hard, spurred me on to train harder.

Watt scores with a *mae-geri* on Brian Bothwell to take the 1975 Scottish Shotokan Open Championships.

Watt being presented with his trophies by Jim Hardie at the 1975 Scottish Shotokan Open Championships.

I found him to be an excellent opponent because it's easy to become complacent, but with Brian about that was never an option.

"I had been a member of the KUS North for about three years and the British Karate Control Commission had registered my Dan grade number, KUS 12.[50] Between 1973 and 1975 we had the beginnings of SKI [Shotokan Karate International] North of Scotland Karate Association, with Kato and Jim Hardie. Hardie ran the Peterhead club and had trained some years with Tommy Morris.

"In 1975 I had my first trip to Japan. The press got wind of it and because it was an unusual thing to do, they did me a little write-up.[51] I think it was Kato who set the trip up and I was invited to go. Students in those days were very loyal and I left the club in capable, secure hands. The idea was to go and attempt my *Sandan* [3rd Dan] with Kanazawa, who was living and training in Tokyo.

"Four British *karateka* went, and if I recall correctly, there was one Englishman, Brian Woods, from East Halton, South Humberside; one Scotsman, yours truly; and two Irishmen, George Reilly from Dublin and Jerry Kelly. We flew Aeroflot into Haneda Airport. I remember sitting on the plane and thinking that I was about to do what just about every *karateka* in Great Britain dreamed about, but then it struck me what I was really letting myself in for, and it wasn't a nice feeling.

"At Moscow, when the plane refuelled, a Russian team boarded. There were twenty of them and they were enormous. When members got up from their seats and walked along the aisle to the toilet, they each had to crouch right down so as not to whack their shoulders, yes, their shoulders, on the ceiling. When I saw these monsters, genuine horror shot through my body, because I thought this was the Russian karate team heading for Tokyo to take part in the JKA championships. I breathed an enormous sigh of relief when they disembarked at Seoul. They turned out to be the Russian basketball team! It shows you what sort of shape I was in.

"Now, Takushoku had a reputation throughout Japan, indeed the world, as being a famous *dojo*, though perhaps infamous would be a better word. The list of world-class Shotokan *karateka* who attended the university is long, including, Nakayama, Kanazawa, Enoeda, Ochi, Miyazaki, Kisaka, Asano and Tabata, all of whom I've already mentioned, and Minoru Miyata[52], Hidetaka Nishiyama[53], Teruyuki Okazaki[54], Hiroshi Shoji[55], Tetsuhiko Asai[56], Katsunori Tsuyama[57], Masao Kawasoe[58], Yoshiharu Osaka[59], and so on.

"We stayed at a university dormitory and the accommodation was free. We slept on the floor and we had to keep the place tidy, but the

Watt waves goodbye to family and friends as he sets off to Japan (1975)

university was very kind. I remember trying to unwind after the journey with a shower and this really tough looking Japanese with a crew-cut walked in. He asked me where I was from, and I said, 'Scotland.' He then asked me who my instructor was, and I answered, 'Enoeda.'

"'If you no training, you down,' he said, gruffly. I took this to mean that if this chap saw any signs of me not practising hard when he was in the *dojo*, I'd pay for it, big time. So, that was a nice welcome.

"The whole Takushoku experience was set up by Tsuyama, who was a lecturer in the Department of Physical Education, teaching karate. The day after we arrived, Kato took the party to a block of offices and, in a room at the end of one corridor, we saw a chair set with its back to us as we entered the room. The chair spun around and there, sitting before us, was Nakayama. It was like something out of a Bond film, you know, when Bond first encounters the head of SPECTRE.

"That first morning, and every morning thereafter, we had to get up and be in the *dojo* by 6.00 a.m. for an hour's training. Then we ate a breakfast of raw fish, raw eggs and rice. In the afternoon, and every subsequent afternoon, we trained for two hours followed by a further two hours in the evening. Assuming you could still stand up, I heard that you could train in the middle of the night too!

"That first day we went to the *dojo* and Tsuyama was teaching and we practised *sanbon-kumite*. I'd practised this before of course, but at Takushoku you really had to have your wits about you. It was three *jodan* attacks and it was clear that these guys didn't mess about. The students were in two lines facing one another, and, after a sequence, one person at the end of the line would run down to the other end and all the class would move up one opponent. I moved up the line of course, and as I moved on my opponents were becoming more senior and they were becoming tougher. Finally I got to Fujikiyo Omura[60] who, in a few years time [1979] would become JKA *kumite* champion by beating Toshihiro Mori.[61] Omura, when the light caught his face in a particular way, looked, at least to my eyes, the spitting image of Shirai. Omura was the senior student there and had warmed up the class beforehand. I attacked and he blocked, then, when he countered, he hit me in the mouth and put one of me teeth through my lip. I was just standing there letting him counter me, as was the practice in Britain, and whack! I didn't realise, and no one had told me, that sometimes, in Japanese *dojos*, one is expected to block and counter again. It's hardly *sanbom-kumite* though, is it? So, that punch came as a complete and painful surprise. I can't read minds, but at the time I took that counter very much in the spirit of, 'You're a visitor, a

From left to right: O'Kelly, unknown, Reilly, Woods and Watt (1975)

foreigner, and that's what you can expect around here mate.' However, in truth, he wasn't 'training me down' at all. It was nobody's fault, because Omura didn't know how we trained in Britain and he did me the honour, if I can put it like that, of treating me in exactly the same manner as he treated his Japanese classmates. I was there with the top boys, the real thing, so I should have been more on guard.

"I ran back down to the end of the line, blood pouring out of my mouth, and worked my way up the line again until I came to Omura once more. The technique had changed and Omura swept me as much as to say, 'I'm the boss.' Now, unfortunately, he swept the leg that had been crushed. My leg ballooned over the next few days to about twice its normal size and bled where Omura's *ashi-barai* had hit the silver pins in my tibia. He wasn't to know about my leg and so I attach no blame. My leg was cut from the inside out. In all seriousness, by today's standards, I would have been in intensive care. The leg looked deformed, but luckily the inflammation went down during the following week.

"My biggest problem throughout my karate training has been my leg. I used to kick with both legs, I love kicking, but now I kick more with my damaged leg and support with the right, for it is the supporting leg that tends to take the strain. I tried to avoid bad habits and I did my best not to condition myself into, 'I'll have to be careful if I do this' mentality, or, 'This is why I can't do this properly,' frame of mind. I did my best to overcome my condition. I am reminded of a student that I taught when I was invited to another *dojo*. I was instructing the class in basics and, as is customary, after every fifth technique I asked the students to *kiai*. Well, I noticed this guy, a black-belt, 2nd Dan I think he was, perform four techniques perfectly normally but when he finished the fifth one, with a *kiai*, he shook his head from side to side whilst at the same time putting his head back. I'd never seen anything like that in my life and wondered if the chap had something wrong with him.

"'What's up with this boy?' I asked his instructor.

"'He's wearing contact lenses,'" came the reply.

"Well my face must have shown that I was none the wiser for the instructor's answer, so he continued.

"'He wore glasses for years and when he did a *kiai* they'd fall down his nose and that's why he shakes his head and tilts it back. That's how he used to keep his glasses on. He still does the movements despite not needing too anymore. He knows he does it, I've told him, but he just does it as a matter of course now.'"

"That is the best example I've come across of how you can get into a bad habit, and that reminds me of another strange story, though I doubt it has anything to do with bad habits.

"I was invited to another *dojo* and the students had been for a run, barefooted, around a lake. One guy, a black-belt, had a hand as red as a pillar box and set out at a right angle. I couldn't take my eyes of this chap's hand that contrasted so strongly with the white of his *gi* that it stood out like a beacon.

"'What's wrong with that student's hand,' I asked the instructor innocently. Well, he started to tell me all that was wrong with this poor chap, how he'd had this operation and that operation – I was amazed this chap was still alive, let alone doing karate – and then it was time to start the lesson and I never actually had my question answered. Anyway, back to Takushoku!

"I had about fifteen freestyle fights with these Japanese everyday. I remember one chap, Kaniko, an Okinawan, who had a good number of teeth broken by a punch. He put his hand to his mouth, collected the broken teeth up, threw them outside and came straight back in and continued. Kaniko was a really nice man outside the *dojo*, but inside, things were different. That's what they were like out there. If you didn't go for it, if they sniffed a weakness, they'd go for it, and your life would have been hell. If you had any sort of ego, they'd knock you off your perch abruptly.

"Tsuyama said that I should pair-up with Omura. I caught him on the chin with *oi-zuki*. I can't say that it was a bonny step forward, but I got him. Omura was not amused. We continued, we clashed and Omura grabbed me between the legs and threw me hard on the floor. It was brutal. I crawled away; my back was really sore. Tsuyama was not happy and he made Omura do bunny-hops around the *dojo*. Then Omura came over to me and asked if I was okay.

"The following day I was fighting again and was pitted against one of my party, but I can't remember which one. I caught him on the chin with a punch and then he caught me on the same lip as Omura had bloodied before. The Japanese looked at each other as if to say, 'They don't just hate us, they hate each other too!'

"I found that I became more aggressive. I recall one bout I had with a Japanese and the senior said, '*Hajime*,' and before my opponent had a chance to move I whacked him in the chin. It really surprised him, and, to tell you the truth, it really surprised me as well. He was okay about it though, and said, 'No. That's good, that's good.'

"The training was intense with few breaks. It was an experience, but I can't say I warmed to it and the atmosphere was always pressured. People who were injured practised *kata*. I don't speak Japanese, but more than once I felt like asking, 'Where do I catch the nearest bus to go home.'

"Fighting like that, day in, day out, meant that I was on a hair trigger. One night, in the Takushoku dormitory, there were a number of very senior grades, Old Boys, Nakayama included, who stayed over and slept there after being taken out for a meal by a Malaysian guy who'd just been awarded his 5th Dan. My leg was still bad from my encounter with Omura and I put my pillow under it to raise it. I slowly drifted off to sleep and then woke up suddenly with a *kiai*. The light went on and there were all these famous people, bleary eyed, looking at me. I apologised and Osaka, half asleep, came over to me and said, 'Ronnie, can't you dream about something other than karate!'

"Before we went to sleep, we told jokes. One of the Japanese told a joke and we understood, so we laughed. Then it was my turn. I told an Englishman, Scotsman and an Irishman type joke which was a bit risqué – I don't feel that I can repeat it here – and it went down well.

Takushoku University

The Japanese had a good giggle. I remember, later, talking about jokes with Kawasoe, and he said you had to be careful in Japan in case people took the joke the wrong way.

"Tsuyama was a fantastic technician and he seemed to exude spirit, though some might call it menace. He was a real innovator and I fully understand why he is held in such high regard in Japan. I thought his style was simple but extremely effective, and I liked that. His stances, especially his back-stance, seemed to be reminiscent of the old Shotokan. His *shuto-uke* was pure."

Watt is quoted in a newspaper eleven years later on this trip to Japan: 'I can only describe it as six weeks of living hell ... On the first day I got my nose broken, my left eye split and my mouth burst ... An American professional who ran his own karate school in the States arrived after us. He left half-way through the first session.'[62]

Watt continued: "I remember, after finishing the third day of this type of training, hobbling down the corridor, feeling every one of my bumps, cuts and bruises, meeting a young *rikishi*. He filled the corridor with his bulk and he stopped to talk to me after I'd said '*Oss*' to him. He explained that he was going to visit two more sumo *dojos* that day because he'd only trained for five hours and he wanted me to train too. He was being friendly and I thanked him, but I explained that I couldn't, which wasn't far from the truth!

"I recall that Osaka gave me some marzipan and I didn't know what to do with it. I was so proud that the great Osaka had given me this sweet. I didn't know if I was supposed to bite a bit off, or break a bit off, or what. Osaka obviously wanted it back. So I thought to myself, 'He won't want me to give it back to him with teeth marks in it,' so I broke a bit off and handed to him. He looked at me with slight disgust and said, 'You keep it.' I still don't know what I was supposed to do with it. Anyway, I was in bare feet and I went to the toilet. Osaka was in there and he told me to put on *zori* when I went to the toilet. He must have thought I was a complete barbarian.

"I found Osaka to be a very charismatic character. He was a tremendous fighter and I sparred with him and he kicked me with a beautiful *mae-geri*. I really felt that kick and he was genuinely worried that he'd hurt me. He was a nice man.

"Our party were taken out a few times in the evening to practise at private *dojos*. There is this false belief that all Japanese are good at karate, but nothing could be further from the truth. Some are good and some are not so good, just like in any other country. The Kanazawas and Enoedas of this world are amongst the very best that Japan has to

Members of the Takushoku Karate Club, 1975. Watt is standing second right.

offer, and that's why they were sent abroad – to promote Japan and karate. Anyway, on one of these outings we visited the private *dojo* of a Takushoku Old Boy, Hamanaka[63], a JKA 5th Dan I believe, who, as you can imagine, was outstanding. We'd been training at Takushoku University where the *karateka* were very dedicated – I won't use the word 'fanatical' – so when you visit a normal *dojo* you have to be very careful, especially in freestyle, for the students work during the day and train in the evening, as a hobby. We were quite aggressive in the *dojo* because that's what we'd been training like each day for weeks, and I got the impression that Mr. Hamanaka was less than happy with Kato for bringing 'head cases' to his *dojo*. Hamanaka was top-rate, he'd been a Takushoku karate club captain and he did a demonstration with Kato. Well, he wasn't too happy with Kato and punched him in the nose as much as to say, 'I'm boss mate.' Afterwards, Hamanaka took us all out to a pub and bought us a bottle of Santori whisky each. We were all required to do our party piece, which is a breaking down of barriers type of exercise. Although it is part of Japanese custom, so they grow up with it, for me, at least, standing up in front of people and singing held considerable fear. I got up and accompanied the karaoke machine to *Road to Dundee*, and, *Flower of Scotland*. I got an enthusiastic response when I'd finished, despite the fact that some members had put their hands over their ears after I'd overcome my initial nerves.

"One of the problems I faced out there was drinking alcohol. I don't drink, as I've said, but those Japanese certainly knew how to knock back the booze. I think they use it more as a come-down after training, but it tended to build up bonding too, with a losing of inhibitions. We went out one evening with members of the Takushoku Sumo Club and had a fine time singing songs and drinking beer. We learned how to sing a sumo victory song. We were guests of these people and after three or four beers you had to be careful to watch your manners – first to refuse a beer and then accept, that kind of thing. I've never found Japanese beer very strong, but because of the heat, you tend to drink a lot of it. In Japan, in that summer, one hour of good karate training a day will keep you slimmed down to muscle." A newspaper report announcing Watt's arrival in Japan noted his dilemma: '[Watt] was forced to down *saki* and whisky, because in Japan it is considered to be an insult if someone refuses a drink.'[64]

Watt continued: "After two weeks of hard training we asked Tsuyama if we could go into Tokyo and have a look around. He said that we could and we relaxed a bit. I went shopping to bring a few things back home as presents. I lost many of those presents on the flight back when they went astray at Moscow Airport.

"We stayed at Takushoku for the three weeks leading up to the university championships, which we attended. I thought Omura was really outstanding. He'd walk out and there was a kind of glow around him, an aura, it was weird. There were a number of styles represented from the various universities and I was told that Takushoku had won for many years. They were up against a Wado-ryu team and after four bouts it was a draw, so Omura went up as number five. The man he fought was really fast, but Omura caught him on the chin with what surely should have been an *ippon*. But no point was scored and the contestants continued. Omura stepped in again, same technique. *Ippon*! But no point was given. I couldn't understand what was going on and nor could Omura for he looked at Tsuyama as if to say, 'What else do I have to do?' The combatants faced each other once more and Omura punched his opponent, knocked him out cold and was disqualified. Takushoku had lost.

"Then it was straight back to the Takushoku *dojo*. Everyone was disappointed. Tsuyama said he'd take the squad for freestyle instruction for the next two weeks. I went over to him and said that, as a foreigner, I thought that Takushoku was brilliant, the best I'd ever seen, in the hope that might be some small consolation. There is nothing you can do if you are faced with refereeing like that, but Takushoku felt that they had lost face.

"Another point I remember about those championships was Tadashi Ishikawa, 5th Dan, who gave a display of basics. I thought Ishikawa was superb and he did teach us, as did Yosuke Yamada. The Takushoku team of ten performed *Bassai-dai* as a synchronised *kata*.

"After the championships we toured Japan for three weeks. Firstly, we went to Gifu, where we stayed at the Hotel Oss, which was owned by another Mr. Kato, who studied karate. The local instructor, a JKA 5th Dan, was very good. We were treated as special guests and taken to dinner on a restaurant riverboat. We had fish caught on the river by fisherman not using rod and line or nets, but cormorants. It was an indescribable experience watching these creatures fish by the lanterns at the front of the boats.

"On another occasion we mentioned that it would be nice, because of the heat, to go swimming in the Gifu River, but we didn't have any swimming costumes. This other Mr. Kato, who was a businessman, told us just to strip off and swim, so we did. Now I wouldn't strip off and go for a swim in Aberdeen, but this Mr. Kato lived in Gifu so we did what we were told, thinking that it was perfectly normal behaviour for this part of the world. There we were, three *gaijin* swimming about naked and a little Japanese woman came up in a boat.

"'Lookie, lookie, lookie,' she laughed, and then the police arrived. I thought to myself, 'Oh no! If you blow your nose at the wrong time out here you have to bow a thousand times to say sorry. What are they going to do with three non-Japanese who are showing all!'

"Mr. Kato explained that we were karate men from Great Britain and somehow he got us out of it, but I'm not at all sure he should have got us into it!

"I remember this Mr. Kato, who I got on with really well, said that I had fought really well that day,' and enquired whether I'd like a geisha. Now, I'd been fighting all day, and I didn't want to be 'fighting' all night, so I declined the offer.

"Mr. Kato smiled and said, 'Watt *San*, you are a very good boy!' When I got back to Aberdeen, I have to be honest and say that my mind did stray back, occasionally, to that conversation …

The party, with Kato, outside the Hotel Oss, Gifu (1975)

"There are, as you can imagine, many skyscrapers in Osaka. We were taken to the most prosperous district in the city where the property runs to I don't know how many hundreds of millions of pounds. We were walking along the road in this concrete jungle, passing these enormous buildings towering above us, and I remember the thousands of glass windows glistening in the sun. These buildings

117

The JKA Gifu *dojo*. Watt is standing, seventh from the left (1975)

were filled with banking, insurance and pension businesses. Amongst all these skyscrapers we came, quite unexpectedly, upon a small, though picturesque traditional Japanese house surrounded by trees. It was like something out of a fairytale; it was surreal. We were taken to meet the owner of this house, an old man, with a stick, who, dressed in a *gi* and an old sheepskin jacket, took us to his *dojo,* where he gave us a demonstration with a short staff against a student with a wooden sword. I thought the display, which lasted about fifteen minutes, was wonderful.

"When he finished, he asked the four of us to demonstrate our karate, and we did some *gohon-kumite, ippon-kumite, jiyu-kumite* and *kata*. Then we showered at the *dojo* and were invited back to the old man's house.

"We went back, met his wife and had some tea. Then he took us all out for a meal – beef cooked at the table – helped down with no small amount of beer. It was a first-class restaurant and I said to Kato, 'We can't possibly let this old man pay for all our meals. He only lives in a small house and he hasn't got any money. Let us chip in. Let us pay.' Kato shook his head a little and didn't say anything. Shortly afterwards, this little old man stood up and took out his wallet and paid the bill. I felt really awkward; it was as though we were taking advantage of him and it didn't seem right. It was awful. As we all walked back to the man's house I thanked him for the meal and said how nice it was. When we got back he insisted we had another cup of tea. I felt really sorry for this guy with his little house and nicely manicured garden.

"After we bide our farewells – we were off to Osaka Castle – we were walking down the street and I asked Kato what the man did for a living. I was trying to come terms with my conscience and hoping to clutch at a straw. He stopped, looked up, opened his arms wide and, with a biggest smile you've ever seen said, 'He owns all this!' This old man was one of the wealthiest people in Japan!

"We travelled around Osaka Bay to Kobe. The Rokko Mountains were in the distance. Kobe had been important for the opening up of Japan to foreign trade in the mid nineteenth century. We didn't train in Kobe and I recall seeing famous statues of Buddha.

"I had planned to take my 3rd Dan in Japan, but there was a problem with the flights and the trip was cut short. In one way it was a disappointment, but I felt happy about returning home.

"When I got back to Aberdeen I was so into the Takushoku way of training that I lost most of my students. I ran a special course for SSC clubs from Aberdeen, Stirling, Perth, Keith, Buckie[65] and Elgin, and we raised money to buy eight *makiwara*.[66] The training I was doing was just too hard for them and ninety-five per cent of my students decided to vote with their feet.

"During the 1970s I received a few injuries from *kumite*, especially after I had returned from Japan and was training so hard. I had my arm broken with a kick, received a few broken toes, gave myself a few wobbly knuckles from clashing punches, and I had my fingers kicked back on a number of occasions, but I had some more serious injuries too.

"On one occasion, when engaged in freestyle, I grabbed the sleeve of my opponent's *gi* as I was about to deliver a *gyaku-zuki*. One of my fingers got caught in the folded cuff of my opponent's sleeve as he pulled back and the force snapped my finger, damaging the joint. I went to the hospital to be informed that it could not be fixed, the joint was beyond repair, and it was suggested that they cut the finger off! Well I wasn't going to have any of that. The injury actually made me quite ill and it affected my training as it was really painful every time I touched it. To this day that finger isn't straight.

"I also had trouble with my jaw when I was punched immediately after I'd scored with a good *mae-geri*. 'Let that be another lesson,' I told myself. I could hardly forget the experience though, for every time I ate something it really hurt as I chewed, and I didn't have a pain-free

Watt with his mother at Aberdeen Airport on his return from Japan (1975)

meal for a year.

"I was in a competition at the KUGB Nationals and was up against a very quick black lad. I attacked him with *kizami-zuki* and followed

KARATE

SCOTTISH SHOTOKAN CENTRES

AFFILIATED TO:-
JAPAN KARATE ASSOCIATION
SCOTTISH SHOTOKAN ASSOCIATION

INSTRUCTOR **R. WATT** 2ND DAN J.K.A.

SECRETARY:-
MR. PAUL ALLAN 389 GT. WESTERN ROAD, ABERDEEN 36977

Scottish Shotokan Centres card (*c.* 1975)

this up with an *ura-zuki* with the same hand. A fraction later he stepped back and performed a *kizami-zuki*. I scored first, but he punched me on the eye just as *yame* was called by the referee. This happens sometimes, two things happening simultaneously. The punch gave me concussion and the doctor in attendance wouldn't let me continue. My opponent was disqualified, I couldn't go through to the next round, and I still have a dilated left pupil which stays open.

"My left knee was also a continual cause for concern. I remember being up against a large man, about sixteen stone I guess, and he moved into a powerful forward stance just as I executed an *ashi-barai* on him. My knee cap displaced itself to the side of the leg on impact. It was agony and I thought I'd snapped the leg. Luckily, my good friend Mike Bissett, who is evidently not adverse to torture, pulled my knee straight as I lay on the *dojo* floor. It was badly swollen though and I had to get it checked out at hospital. I was put on anti-inflammatory pills and told to rest for a month, but I was back in the *dojo* two days later. Some might say that I'm my own worst enemy.

"Talking of leg injuries, I was holding a course in Montrose with Hamish Adam [see later] on *kumite* training. The hall was really cold and as I performed a one hundred and eighty degree turn, I heard a loud crack. I actually thought I'd been shot, but the calf muscle had ruptured off the bone. I was off training for several months with that, but attended the *dojo* every day until it healed. To this day, the injury does not look good, but I still function.

"I always go to the *dojo* if I can. I think it's the correct thing to do. It shows commitment. If you can't train, then watch and learn. I tell my students this, but it invariably falls on deaf ears. I had my gall

Watt showing *mawashi-geri* on student, Paul Allan (*c.* 1975)

bladder removed by keyhole surgery on a Tuesday and I was back training on the Saturday with a large bandage wrapped around the middle of my body. At training, one of the black-belts punched me in the abdomen, I screamed and pulled open my *gi* to show him my bandage. He nearly fainted because he was unaware I had recently had an operation. Whilst he was in shock at seeing this, I immediately punched him and laughed. I don't think he quite recovered that day from the shock of my pretended death scream. *Ippon* by deceit, maybe, but it worked!

"Just to show you how many injuries I've suffered over the years, a very good friend of mine, Fritz Wendland [see later], from Germany, said, light-heartedly, to a group of instructors at a course in Bavaria I attended not long ago, as I hobbled in, 'Here comes Ronnie, the old war horse. Look what we did to him in the First World War!' If you practice *kumite* then injuries are to be expected, it comes with the job. But back to my declining student numbers!

"I had to take time out to reflect and I remembered Hamanaka and his students. I had to calm down and realise, once again, that people were choosing to do karate as a hobby after a tiring day at work and probably with family commitments. I had to respect this. I didn't have family commitments and karate was my job, so I had to get my mind around the fact that karate meant different things to different people. In short, I had to temper my teaching and expectations of other people if I wanted to remain a professional karate instructor. I resolved to do this. I know that Enoeda had faced this problem when he went to live in Liverpool.[67] So, I built my clubs up again and decided that I would have expectations for my amateur students based on JKA and SKI criteria and I would have my own personal expectations as a professional. This happens every day in all walks of life, so I thought that this was fair and reasonable and I was happy that I wasn't compromising my karate.

"Today, there is so much political correctness, so much covering one's back, and link to this the notion that everyone has to be a success, not only in general, but in karate too, is a disaster. I think it would be hard for many students to even imagine what karate training can be like. Everything's just become so easy and as such has lost real value. It's like a poster. Nowadays, I plan a poster on my computer, send the design to a printer over the telephone system and collect copies the same day. When I got started as a professional karate instructor, I had to really think about a poster's layout, measure it all up with a ruler to a millimetre, and, importantly, not make a mistake, because it was all hand done. I used to spend hours putting Lettraset on a single poster, checking distance between letters, sticking on individual photographs, and so on. Granted, a lot of time is saved today because of technology, but I feel that there is something lost – less concentration, less commitment, less focus – and we're the poorer for it.

"Not that long after my return from Japan, a matter of months, maybe a year, Omura actually came to my *dojo* with Tsuyama. I gave my black-belts due warning: 'Watch Omura; he's a live wire.'

"I found the years 1973 to 1975 to be difficult times in a political sense; they were a kind of twilight period. I've noted the Kanazawa/Enoeda divide and I had to decide which chief instructor and which association I wanted to align myself to as things appeared

Tsuyama, in kilt, alongside Omura (1976)

to be splitting up and splinters were beginning to fly. I didn't know the ins and outs of it at the time, but I learned later that Kanazawa had formed SKI, which, I believe, was originally intended as an international section of the JKA. In 1977 Kanazawa left the JKA and formed SKI as an independent body. Enoeda remained JKA. Knowing Japanese politics, the whole issue is bound to be horribly complex. But I felt that I got caught up in all this in a small way. Let me give you a couple of examples.

"Kanazawa and Kato were staying at the Dee Motel in Aberdeen and I received a message that Kanazawa wanted to see me. When I got

Tsuyama demonstrates *hidari nagashi-uke* and *migi gedan shuto-uchi* from the *kata Heian Godan* (1976).

there I met someone I knew well, but it isn't appropriate to mention his name here. This other *karateka* went into a room to see Kanazawa and

Kanazawa and Watt relaxing after training (early to mid 1970s)

Kato first and I was asked to wait outside. I thought to myself, 'This is very strange.' After a while this chap came out and I was invited in. I didn't know why I had been summoned and the questioning didn't really give me an answer, though I guessed it was something political. I would, however, like to say that I was just interested in karate and Ford GT40s, but that may not have counted for as much as I might have hoped. The ramifications of that meeting later became apparent.

"I recall going down to a particular town where I had established a club. This town was a good distance from Aberdeen and I had to catch the train. I worked really hard getting this club up and running. I had someone who was the club secretary who I trusted. I was on the train one day and I sat close to another chap who studied karate and who I knew. I asked him what he was doing and he said he was on his way to the same town as me because he had a club there. That came as a surprise to me and I told him that I had a club there as well. It turned out to be the same *dojo*! I went into the club and asked the secretary what was going on, and it turned out that a certain Japanese had been interfering. I'd built this club up from scratch and it had been taken away from me from behind my back. I thought to myself, 'There's nothing honourable here,' and that got me thinking.

"Kanazawa is a great karate man and Enoeda was a great karate man, but I always found there was someone in the middle who'd mess things up. I wasn't at all happy about these interfering third parties. I hadn't aligned myself with anyone really at this time, I had a foot in both camps you might say, because I was just waiting to see how things panned out, and there was a lot of jostling going on. I'd had enough of politics and I decided the KUGB was for me. I was still KUGB, but I hadn't been licensing my students as KUGB members. I telephoned Enoeda and Andy Sherry and told them about the goings-on. I had fifteen clubs under me: Aberdeen, Inverurie, Arbroath, Montrose, Edinburgh, Ellon, Banff, McDuff, Stirling, Coatbridge, Glasgow, Livingstone, Dunblane, Musselbrough, and, Lerwick, in Shetland. I used to go to Shetland one or twice a year for Janice Leask, who ran the club there at Bells Brae School.[68] I was training and teaching seven days a week and I'd sometimes stay overnight.

"I remember one train journey down to Edinburgh, where I used to stay with Heather Houston, who was secretary to the Edinburgh club. There were two oil workers just off the rigs sitting close by and they were both the worse for wear for alcohol. They were sitting opposite one another and a row broke out between them. I naturally looked up to see what the raised voices were all about. As quick as a flash, one of these chaps leapt up and grabbed the hair of the other chap with his left hand and punched him in the head with his right fist. Now this was a serious incident, but when the chap who punched withdrew his left hand, he pulled off the ginger wig the other chap was wearing. The guard came in and separated them and the chap who'd been punched went into the dining car. I had to go to the toilet and passed through the dining area, and this injured chap was sat there with this wig on back to front drinking coffee, trying to sober up. The curly part of the hairpiece instead of being at the back of his head was now stuck over his forehead. When I saw this, I just creased up; I couldn't stop laughing.

"In 1976 then, I became fully part of the KUGB again, in that I licensed my clubs and students through that organisation." A newspaper clipping of May, 1976, noted: 'Mr. Watt has affiliated all his clubs to the KUGB following the recent clarification of the position of the Japan Karate Association instructors in this country. It has now been stated by the JKA that only one organisation per country will be recognised by the JKA ... [what then follows is confused] Mr. Enoeda has agreed to visit Mr. Watt's clubs three times a year and will be conducting a summer course in Aberdeen this September ... [and will be assisted by] two other eminent Japanese instructors.'[69]

Certainly, within a few years, Watt was quoted as saying: 'Aberdeen and the North-east is now one of the best instructional areas [for karate] in the country and the standard here must be one of the highest in Europe.'[70]

III

MASTER NAKAYAMA VISITS ABERDEEN

Watt continued: "The travelling to all the *dojos* was horrendous, but at the time I was young and resilient. I loved cars, as I've said, and I had acquired a second-hand yellow Marcos, which, superficially at least, looked something like a Ferrari but cost a fraction of the price. I recall travelling down to Stirling, thinking about karate, and a lorry past me and I got caught in some kind of uplift. The car almost took off. It was quite frightening actually.

"I remember there was a guy living in Aberdeen who owned a blue Ferrari Daytona. Now, a Daytona is a millionaire's car and it just so happened that I pulled up at a car wash when this Ferrari passed by. The driver looked at my little plastic job and I could see by his face he thought, 'What kind of Ferrari is that!' It was so funny. The chap at the car wash was all over my motor, and suddenly I became somebody different and not the Ronnie in the old second-hand Minis, Escorts and Cortinas. Cars can have that effect, it's strange.

"I started having Enoeda up every three months for courses and gradings and this continued for many years. He'd come up with his assistant, Tomita, who I found to be a very nice person. Tomita was quite small, but strong, and he'd really make us work. I found him a good teacher.

"I used to follow Enoeda around a bit when he was in Scotland. The clubs had a reciprocal arrangement going and I'd trained under Enoeda at the Dempseys' *dojo* in Dundee and Bryceland's *dojo* in Glasgow and they could come up to me. My *dojo* at the time was at the old Teachers' Training College, up by the Sick Children's Hospital, but it's been demolished now.

"I fought in a KUS team against the KUGB team in an England/Scotland match. In our team was Alex Macgregor, Paul and Pat Dempsey, myself, and, I think, Bryceland. Bryceland was my senior and had practised Shukokai before taking up Shotokan; he was very quick with his hands. I remember Terry O'Neill caught Alex with a wonderful *mawashi-geri*, a tremendous kick, but he was disqualified for contact – he actually knocked Alex out – and the Scottish team won. I think I fought Bob Poynton[1], who was an excellent fighter too, strong, and I punched him on the chin, bad control, so he kicked me in the shin and numbed my leg. It was sore and I was hopping about for a week. Enoeda was a referee and he came up to me afterwards and said, 'You punched Bob Poynton on the chin. Why?' I blamed it on nerves. I always found Bob, who is one of my karate heroes, to be very supportive.

"I remember a Scottish Karate Board of Control [SKBC] squad that I was in that Bryceland, as captain, asked me to join. Bryceland had fought for the KUGB team in the European Championships in the late 1960s and had been in the final of the KUGB Nationals [in 1969], but had been beaten by Terry O'Neill. Bryceland, who had been Scotland's captain when they won the All-Britain Championships[2] and an England versus Scotland match[3] in 1972, had been in the British squad to fight at the World Championships in Paris in 1972, and was a terrific fighter.

"I can't remember where this tournament was and who it was against, but I've a recollection that Anton Gesnik, who won an Olympic gold medal in Judo, was there, and so perhaps the Dutch team were competing.

"As I've said, I trained in what might be described as traditional Shotokan and it took me a long time to come to terms with competition. I really struggled with it. Traditional Shotokan and competition don't go hand in hand in my view; they are very different animals. The old style never had competition, it was based on life and death scenarios, and required a different mentality to scoring points. So, whilst I enjoyed competition and competed for about twenty-five years, my heart was always in traditional training. I would argue that traditional *karateka* can practise competition, as long as it's not detrimental to their traditional karate.

"With both traditional and competitive karate you develop lightning-fast reflexes. I remember once, when I was still living in Skene Square, my father brought me, as a treat, my breakfast in bed. He shook me to wake me up and I reacted. I punched him to the floor and my eggs and bacon flew in all directions around my bedroom.

"The next day, when I was asleep, my father came into the room again, this time armed with a broom handle. He whacked me with it and said: 'There's your breakfast you ———!'"

"I recall KUGB seniors like Andy Sherry, Bob Poynton and Terry

Senior KUGB instructor, Andy Sherry, sixth from right, next to Watt, with Aberdeen black-belts (1970s).

Terry O'Neill, sitting, fourth from left, next to Watt, with Aberdeen black-belts.

O'Neill, all from the Liverpool Red Triangle Karate Club. Andy had a tremendously fast *gyaku-zuki*, brilliant punches. Bob was tall and liked to kick. Terry was unstoppable with his kicks – *mawashi-geri, gyaku-mawashi-geri* and *kakato-geris* – really quick and powerful.

Watt's KUGB licence showing grades from 8th kyu to 3rd Dan

"I had Andy Sherry[4, 5] and Bob Poynton[6] up to Aberdeen. I went down to Manchester and Liverpool and stayed with Bob and trained at the Red Triangle. That was tremendous. They were all very kind to me. I've got a lot of respect for those Liverpool lads; I like their karate.

"I had Terry O'Neill up a couple of times too.[7] A photograph by a chap named Ian Mackland of Terry performing a wonderful *kakato-geri* was used a few times in the local press.[5, 8, 9]

"Later, I sparred with another Liverpool great, perhaps the greatest of them all, Frank Brennan.[10] Although I am now with a different organisation, that doesn't diminish the ability of others in my eyes, and I thought some of the Liverpool Red Triangle squad members were superb and they've done a lot to enhance the reputation of British *karateka*.

"I was awarded my 3rd Dan from Enoeda in 1976 [9th September].[11] I received a telegram from Andy, Bob and Frank, congratulating me.[12] I thought that was really nice; they didn't have to do that.

"Aberdeen used to regularly put a team in the KUGB Nationals, but we never got that far. We were only a small *dojo* really, stuck up in the north-east of Scotland and we'd find ourselves competing against the Liverpool Red Triangle, Leeds, Kirkdale, London, and so on. We were there to have a go and we'd sometimes win a few matches before

Watt steps in and scores with a *gyaku-zuki* in the individual *kumite* event at the KUGB Championships (1970s).

Watt in action at the KUGB Championships at Crystal Palace (1970s)

being eliminated. Normally, teams celebrate after winning something, but we never won anything, so one year we thought we'd celebrate the

day before entering. The squad went to a lovely restaurant and no small amount of alcohol was consumed and there was a bet on as to whether Ian Ord could do *Sochin* whilst in his present state. The restaurant owner was delighted we were there because we were the Scottish team. Now, there was a lovely sweet trolley with all sorts of edible delights and one of the team, though it would be unfair to mention his name, who had had more than his far share of booze, got up and performed an *otoshi-shuto* on the biggest cake. Parts of this splendid *gateau* went everywhere and one piece, the largest piece, hit another squad member smack in the face. It was disrespectful, but funny at the same time. We paid up and got out of the restaurant pretty quickly after that.

"Anyway, the next day we had the championships and our team were in a sorry old state, but do you know what, we did better that year than in most others. There's got to be a moral in there somewhere."

Around this time an article by an unknown writer in an unknown magazine entitled, *Scottish Shotokan Centres*, provides a broad synthesis of the information covered to date, noting that, '[The SSC clubs] are all affiliated to the Scottish Region KUGB at Ronnie's insistence and all his members enjoy being KUGB licence holders.' The article notes that Omura and Norimasa Hayakawa[13] had also visited Watt's clubs as had Sherry and Poynton. 'The SSC *dojos* cover an area from Gallashiels in the south to Elgin in the north, a distance of three hundred and fifty miles and encompassing over a dozen main *dojos* with a number of smaller but enthusiastic clubs.'

Watt continued: "When Hayakawa came to my *dojo* I asked him for a private lesson for myself and three other instructors. During the lesson he taught us *Kanku-sho* and I remember that we four students had five senior Japanese in the *dojo* – Enoeda, Tsuyama, Kawasoe, Osaka, and, of course, Hayakawa – and that each *sensei* corrected me differently on the *gedan-barai* in the *kata*! I think this shows that Shotokan 'pure' does not exist and each of us has to find our own path.

"I'd met Osaka in Tokyo of course. I recall, around the time I took my 3rd Dan, that it was his birthday, and Enoeda, Tsuyama, Kawasoe and Osaka came to my house and we got him a cake with candles on it. The Japanese played marjong into the small hours and I made tea for them.

"A funny thing happened that evening. I had a student with me, Malcolm Hogg, a good fighter, and I asked the Japanese about blocking a knife attack. I picked up a banana and attacked Malcolm with it and stabbed him in the throat and the banana broke free of its

Watt and Hayakawa in the Cowdray Hall, Aberdeen

skin and was splattered over Malcolm's neck. The Japanese didn't know it was a banana and they saw this mess like opened skin. I'll never forget the expression on Tsuyama and Osaka's faces – they thought I'd killed the guy."

"I remember when my father died in 1977. It was very cold and he'd been taken ill at work whilst on a building site. The doctor told him to rest in bed for two weeks. It was during this period that I received a phone call from my mother. Whilst at home he'd suffered a heart attack and had been taken to hospital where he was in intensive care. I was twenty-nine, strong, practically minded and 'up for anything', so I thought, 'Okay, we'll fix this problem.' My father survived, returned home and then two weeks latter I received another phone call from my mother to say that he'd suffered another heart attack and a stroke as well. I rushed to the Royal Infirmary to see him. He looked so drawn, his face was contorted and one side of his body was paralysed. I sat there and held his hand. It was terrible, absolutely terrible; words can't describe how I felt. The next day, the twenty-ninth of January, at five minutes to eleven in the morning, he passed away.[14] I registered the death two days later. It was the first time in my life that I'd felt really vulnerable. Karate makes you strong, it builds the body and the spirit, and you can take on adversity, but when you hit something like this, something you can't challenge and overcome, you realise how vulnerable you really are. It took me two years before I could live without his death continually being on my mind and all the sadness it conjured up. I coped with it by denying it happened; it was too painful to admit. If people asked me about his death, I would excuse myself and walk away.

"In 1977 I paid my second visit to Japan when I went with the KUGB British squad to the 2nd IAKF World Championships. I went as the Scottish representative as it were; I didn't compete. I was the Scottish team captain for the KUGB and I would regularly travel south to attend British squad training.

"I organised demonstrations and a KUGB National Squad versus a KUGB Scottish Regional Squad [on the 28th May 1977] competition at the Aberdeen Music Hall, in order to help raise money to finance the trip. Admission was one pound at the door.[15, 16]" Watt was quoted at the time as saying: 'This is a tremendous boost for North[ern] karate. Some of the best fighters in the world will be on view and their visit is sure to be of immense benefit to Scottish karate.'[17]

Watt continued: "Dave Hazard[18] was in the squad and he is a brilliant *karateka*, and so was Mick Dewey.[19] Steve Cattle and his girlfriend, Sandy Hopkins[20], who was the KUGB women's *kata* champion, were also in the squad and so were Terry O'Neill, Bob Poynton, Billy Higgins, Bob Rhodes[21], Mick Wragg, Mick O'Grady and Joe Farley. Enoeda made the decision as to who was going in the team and Andy Sherry was the coach. Kawasoe was coaching too. Only five could be selected for the team. Great Britain went on to take third place. At the championships I saw a number of famous Japanese instructors, including Masaaki Ueki[22], and, I believe, Masatomo Takagi[23], the JKA's General Secretary, who had been an early student of Funakoshi's. I also saw Shoji, and Terry O'Neill asked me to help him bring back some of Shoji's excellent *kata* books.[24] I wanted to see Keigo Abe[25], but he wasn't there. A good friend of mine, George Carruthers, 7th Dan, who was born in Scotland [1953] is chairman of the Japan Shotokan Karate Association (G.B.) and knows Abe. George, who's a practising chiropractic, has invited me to train and meet Abe, but it just hasn't been possible yet, but I hope to do so in the future.

"In one match, Cattle was up against Watanabe, from Brazil, I think. There was a clash and the referee stepped in, and as Cattle turned away Watanable struck him with a *jodan* punch that knocked Cattle down. Enoeda was on the side lines and Watanabe said something to him, the gist being that Cattle was pretending to be

Joe Farley and Watt in the KUGB Scotland vs KUGB (GB) match in Aberdeen (1977).

injured because the punch hadn't been that hard and that Cattle was trying to get him disqualified. I don't think Enoeda would have reacted

Joe Farley and Watt in the KUGB Scotland vs KUGB (GB) match in Aberdeen (1977).

The KUGB (GB) Squad and KUGB Scottish Regional Squad (1977)

The KUGB Team about to board a Japan Airlines plane at Heathrow Airport for the World Championships (1977). On step steps, top to bottom: Keinosuke Enoeda, Andy Sherry, Terry O'Neill, Bob Poynton, Masao Kawasoe, Mick O'Grady, Mick Wragg, Billy Higgins, Ronnie Watt, Bob Rhodes; standing, left to right: Cliff Hepburn, Peter Heal, Joe Farley, unknown, Sandy Hopkins, Steve Cattle.

to that alone, something else must have been said, for he tried to get to Watanabe and had to be restrained by officials. That was exceptional. One always felt that Enoeda was a live wire underneath, but that was

From left to right: Watt, Sherry, Higgins, Kawasoe, Cattle, Hopkins, Enoeda and O'Neill (Tokyo, 1977).

From left to right: Tanaka, Watt, Kawasoe and Yahara at the Budokan (1977)

Sherry, Enoeda, Watt and Higgins at the Takushoku University *dojo* (1977)

the only time I saw him like that. He realised that he'd 'lost it', and thank goodness that he did, for I don't know what would have happened to Watanabe if Enoeda had continued, for no one would have been able to stop him.

"I think it was on that trip that we met Tokyo Rose at the JKA *honbu*. Now that's not the Tokyo Rose from the Second World War of course, who read out propaganda over the radio for the Japanese, rather, this Tokyo Rose was the nickname for a well-built English lass who wore a brown belt. I found her to be quite an odd character to be honest and she asked me, a 3rd Dan, to clean the *dojo* floor! Well, I don't mind cleaning the floor I'm about to train on, that's customary and I do it all the time, and I did on that occasion, but the effrontery of the woman!

"In fact, I can tell you an unfortunate, if not funny story about Tokyo Rose, when she was training, later, in a class in Britain practising the *kata Unsu*. When she performed the 360° jump, she landed on the poor boy behind her who had completed his spin and was on the floor looking forward. The poor chap was flattened and knocked unconscious.

"I also recall when she was taking her Dan grade. Kase was

Famous faces at the JKA Headquarters on the cover of a JKA magazine. Watt collected some of their signatures during his stay. From left to right: Asai, Isamu Baba, Kanazawa, Ishikawa, Nakayama, Osaka, Abe, Iida, Shoji, M. Mabuchi.

speaking to the other Japanese at the table and said something in Japanese to the effect of, 'Well, she's never going to pass.' Not long afterwards, Tokyo Rose went over to the table and spoke to Kase in fluent Japanese. I'll never forget that, or the sight of Kase's lower jaw dropping in amazement. She was quite a girl was Tokyo Rose.

"I remember my second trip to Japan for another reason too. Enoeda visited a Shinto shrine and when he came out he gave me a jar and said to me, 'Whatever you do, don't drop that, it's my life.' I took it that he had received some kind of absolution from a priest, for he told me that it was necessary to purify yourself, let all the bad stuff go, if you wanted to progress. I listened intently. Anyway, I was holding this jar on the bus, intently concentrating on holding the jar and Enoeda suddenly, abruptly, asked me how I was getting on. The shock of his voice made me jump and I fumbled with the jar and dropped it.

"'What have you done!' Enoeda cried. 'You've dropped my spirit!'

"'Oh my God!' I thought to myself. 'Sorry *Sensei*. Sorry,' I said, nervously. He shook his head and looked at me as much as to say, 'Hopeless. What have I done to deserve this?' Then he saw the funny side of it, laughed, and patted me on the back.

"I was captain of the KUGB Scottish Regional Team for many years. I went to Essen, in the Ruhr, Germany, with a view to competing in the European Championships [to be held on the 15th October 1977]. There was a lot of bureaucracy at this time because the powers that be hadn't yet recognised the Scottish Region of the KUGB as an 'official region in the European Union'[26] in its own right, and I wasn't allowed to compete because of this problem.[27]

"Shortly after our arrival in Essen, dressed smartly in our blazers with the KUGB British breast badge, we met Joe Gormley, a well known Union leader who was at a conference and he wished us all the best. We went from a run in the morning with Enoeda and Kawasoe and had some squad training in the park. We visited the competition venue in the evening.

"A surreal thing happened in Essen. There was a meeting, a very important karate meeting and I was asked to attend. It concerned the Japanese, the Arabs and the Israelis. It was deadly serious stuff. There we all were, sitting around this impressive table, trying to sort out this mess, though I was merely a representative, and the Israeli delegate asked if he could get some refreshment. I thought he'd have a glass of water or something. Half-way through this really very important debate, in fact at a crucial point, a waiter knocked on the door and came in carrying a tray with something on it covered in a white cloth.

On reaching the Israeli official, the waiter placed the tray on the table and, in dramatic style, whipped the cloth off, and there, in all its splendour was a most magnificent ice cream, like a huge knickerbocker glory. The official asked for a spoon and when he had one in hand, he started eating. The rest of the delegates sat there in amazement. I still can't believe that happened to this day. The chairman, rather diplomatically I thought, said something to the effect of, 'Now seems a good time to break for tea!'

"I'll tell you a funny incident that occurred in Germany around this time. I was walking past a bridge, leaving a railway station, on my way to my hotel with some fellow *karateka* and a crippled German guy, about sixty, was sitting, propped up against a wall. As we past him he said, with a drunken sneer, 'English swine!'

"I was taken aback, not to say offended and so I answered back, immediately, 'Hey! I'm not English. I'm Scottish!'

"'Okay, okay,' he replied, slurring his words, 'Scottish swine!'

"This was an isolated incident of course and had nothing to do with our German hosts, who treated us really well.

"Another funny incident happened in Essen. I woke up one morning and went to have a wash and shave in my hotel room. There I was facing the mirror, thinking about karate and miles away from what I was doing, when I accidentally shaved off half of one side of my black moustache. If I wanted to keep my moustache, which I did, I had no option than to cut half off the other side too, to match. At the time I had flat, black hair and I'd bought a black leather jacket. With my moustache as it now was, it is true to say that I looked the spitting image of Hitler. The KUGB squad, plus officials, and myself, were on the bus going to the stadium where the competition was to be held and Terry O'Neill, who, bless him, was always looking out for me, said the British squad had brought the bloody Fuehrer with them.

"Many heads turned my way, I can tell you. As I walked into the stadium I felt as though I was about to address one of the Nurembourg Rallies. I expect the Germans thought. 'What sort of simpleton from England comes to Germany trying to impersonate dear old Adolf!'

"Another point I recall about that trip was the squad training, which was taken by Enoeda. I sparred with all members of the national team and I recall coming up against Frank Brennan. Now this chap is a one-off, in a class of his own really, and he caught me with a *mawashi-geri*. Bang! He immediately stopped.

"'Are you okay *Sensei*?' he said.

"I thought to myself, 'Andy Sherry has taught you really well.'

Watt performing a *jodan mawashi-geri* (late 1970s)

"I was mightily impressed with Frank's attitude. He didn't call me *sempai*, he called me *sensei*. He was technically far better than me, yet he respected my years of training, my seniority, and that type of mind only comes from really top *karateka*.

"I took part in quite a few demonstrations and fund-raising events. Mentioning the Aberdeen Music Hall a few moments ago reminds me of a display that a kung-fu *sensei* intended giving that went horribly wrong. I hasten to add this had nothing to do with me whatsoever. I just witnessed it. Roofing tiles lay stacked before the *sensei* and, also, a bucket of water. I didn't understand what he was going to do and so I stayed to watch. He gave it the full ceremony, the build up, and then an assistant came along and poured paraffin over the tiles and over one of his *sensei's* hands. I didn't like the look of it and, as you can imagine, this was the time before Health and Safety. A torch was then lit. This sort of thing is foolhardy in the extreme in my opinion; you can't mess about with fire, let alone with paraffin as well. Anyway, I gathered that the student was going to light the tiles and the *sensei* would bring his hand down on to them, break them, set his hand on fire in the action and immediately extinguish it in the bucket – spectacular maybe, but absolutely crazy. However, the student set light to the *sensei's* hand by mistake, which may, or may not, have had a cloth wrapped around it, I can't remember. There was frantic commotion and the *sensei* drove his hand into the bucket of water, but it was too late and he had to go to hospital with burns, and that was the end of the demonstration.

"Whereas we were not allowed to compete in Essen, Paul Allan and I attended ten hours of EAKF meetings in Belgrade, Yugoslavia, now capital of Serbia, in 1978, after which we were allowed to compete in the championships as Scotland. An Italian delegate gave us the news and we were delighted.

"I felt that the atmosphere at that EAKF congress was not a good. The Cold War was still very much alive and the Iron Curtain certainly divided the congress. I started to realise that karate at this level was very political and was happy to sit back and leave it to my seniors to negotiate, as I was politically naïve, and I'd have been like a lamb being led to slaughter, for all I wanted to do was to train in karate.

"I liked Nishiyama and he was very kind and delighted to see us representing Scotland. I recall that he applauded very loudly when the two of us came into the arena behind the national flag.

"Half-way through the competition, if you can believe it, the coaches and officials were invited up to the reception to meet top government officials. This was really off putting, as you can imagine, for we needed to focus, not be engaged in small talk, but we were obliged to go.

Watt's entry pass to the European Karate Championships in Belgrade (1978)

Watt, centre, with KUGB General Secretary Cliff Hepburn, left, and Paul Allan, pictured at the negotiating table in Belgrade (1978).

"Paul and I entered the *kata* and individual *kumite*. I remember performing *Bassai-dai* and my favourite *kata* at that time, *Kanku-sho*. Terry O'Neill did a superb *Sochin*; I definitely recall that.

"In the *kumite* I beat a Turkish opponent and then drew with a German, Wolf Wichman, who beat me by decision after a two-minute

Watt, left, competing in a KUGB Scotland v Germany match, in Belgrade (1978).

Members of the KUGB England team at the European Championships in Yugoslavia, 1978. From left to right: Sherry, Brennan, O'Neill, Godfrey, Poynton, with Watt.

Enoeda, Kawasoe, Osaka, Tsuyama and Watt at 151 Gray Street, Aberdeen (late 1970s).

extension. Wichman, a German team regular was very nearly twice the size of me. Well, that's an exaggeration of course, but he must have been six foot six inches. I remember kicking a *jodan mae-geri* and he blocked it with a *gedan-barai* with a banged hand! After the championships, I returned to my hotel room and there was a knock on my door. It was Kawasoe and he said, 'Well done; very good fights. See you downstairs for a drink.'

"Allan and I were eliminated after four fights in the round-robin competition, a pooled collection of match losers, but we went for the experience of being up against Europe's best. Our main mission had been to get recognition for Scotland, and we'd got it. In fact, KUGB member George Godfrey, from Liverpool, took the title and the Yugoslavian team took the team *kumite* event.

"I moved out of my home for more than thirty years in 1978 and went to live in a three bedroom masonette at 151, Gray Street, Aberdeen, with my girlfriend of four years and wife to be, Gail [née Ritchie (b. 1/5/1958)]. Because we had extra bedrooms, we were able to invite a good number of *sensei* to stay with us, including Enoeda, Tsuyama, Kawasoe, Osaka, Andy Sherry, Bob Poynton and Frank Brennan. Gail and I lived there a couple of years and we then moved to 43, Sycamore Place, our first detached house. We had absolutely no money left over after we'd bought it and didn't even have a table to eat off. I remember that when Enoeda first stayed with us we all ate breakfast on chairs. Enoeda always enjoyed staying with us and said that he preferred this arrangement to staying in a hotel, because he felt part of a family. He certainly enjoyed punching my *makiwara* in the back garden. We used to watch television and he followed horse racing. I think he liked a bet, well, I know he did. I vividly recall that he was thoroughly engrossed in the war film, *Tora, Tora, Tora,* which was released in 1970 and is about the bombing of Pearl Harbor on the 7th December 1941. What is interesting about this film is that it is viewed from both the American and Japanese positions and employed both an American and two Japanese directors. In the film, the Japanese Air Force bombed the American fleet and *then* declared war. When Enoeda saw this he groaned, audibly.

"After training we'd bring home Chinese take-aways and chat. We tended to go out for special meals after a course had ended. I remember when it was beginning to take a turn for winter and Gail made a real *faux pas* when she said, and Enoeda was standing next to her, 'There's a real nip in the air.' Now 'Nip' is short for Nippon, the Japanese word for Japan, or Nipponese. Enoeda laughed and said, 'Yes, it is cold!' He told me that his good friend, Charlie Naylor, had once used the same expression and explained it to him. However, that was an embarrassing moment for me. We loved having Enoeda stay and he knew that too. I look back on these times with great affection.

"In our home Enoeda was always a real gentleman, but he could be very difficult as well. I remember on one occasion his plane arrived late at the airport and he blamed me! He seemed to have mood swings, but once he was teaching in the *dojo* he'd settle down and always delivered a first-class, inspirational course. When he left Aberdeen, he always said to me words to the effect of: 'Keep up the good work and I'll see you next time.'

"Enoeda hardly ever discussed his past. He never seemed interested in the old masters. I think he was only concerned with the now and, maybe, the future. But he did tell me a few stories about his past and incidents he was involved in.

"I suppose the earliest thing he told me about his life was that he had studied judo at school to 2nd Dan, and that he'd also tried boxing – noting the training was very hard – but found the gloves very cumbersome.

"I remember he said that when he was teaching in the USA in 1967,

Watt and Enoeda (1970s)

he had told an American *karateka* prior to a demonstration to move back and the guy had moved forward instead and Enoeda hurt him seriously. He noted that he had to get back to Britain as quickly as he could as there were all sorts of implications and ramifications if he'd remained.

"On a completely different theme, he said that he once saw someone eating a banana in the JKA *honbu*, thought that this act showed great disrespect, grabbed hold of the culprit and stuck the rest of the banana down his throat before kicking him out.

"Of course we have all heard about the baseball bat incident, where Enoeda, in his youth, and as captain of a baseball team, allegedly smacked a team member around the head with a bat for lying about why he couldn't train. I read about this in an article written by Terry O'Neill in an early *Fighting Arts* magazine.[28] He never mentioned this to me, I suppose there was no reason why he should have, and I didn't ask him, but it sounded like Enoeda all right!

"He also used to tell me about his work in films and I recall that he mentioned the actress Ingrid Pitt, who, I believe, he taught privately. She starred in a couple of Hammer vampire films at the time – *Countess Dracula* [1970], and, *The Vampire Lovers* [1970] – and appeared in *The House That Dripped Blood* [1971]; hardly classics, but everyone to their own. I remember when Pitt and her husband attended the KUGB Championships. But Enoeda liked talking about Sean Connery and the James Bond movie they were in together. The film was, *Diamonds are Forever* [1971], and Enoeda is thrown through screens, kicked in the face and strangled by 007 in the film's opening sequence. Enoeda had appeared in quite a few films in Japan before coming to Britain. He didn't shun the limelight, he wasn't backward in coming forward, and appeared on British television[29] and even in a crisp commercial. I got the distinct impression that he liked the film world, the stars, and the money! He told me he got two thousand pounds for that short clip in *Diamonds are Forever*. He was pushing us very hard once at a KUGB *gasshuku* and I said to him afterwards that I was going to tell James Bond about what he'd done to us. He thought that was really funny.

"Enoeda was a very charismatic man. In my opinion, he was able to get people to do what he wanted because they were drawn to him, though at the same time he encompassed fools gladly. I found that he played a powerful game not only with karate associations and world karate bodies, but also with individuals and their lives. On a good day he was fantastic and lifted the spirits of those around him, but on a bad day he could be very awkward. I found him prone to not being able to deal with people.

"The year 1981 was momentous for me because I managed to get Nakayama to Aberdeen. Nakayama hadn't visited Britain for thirteen years and Enoeda had got him to Britain along with the Japanese team for the KUGB *gasshuku*. Plans had to be made a year in advance and I asked Enoeda if it would be possible for Nakayama to visit Scotland and he was agreeable, so I went about organising it once the dates were given to me.

"The idea was, obviously, to charge students who wished to attend and the money collected would cover the costs. However, it soon became evident that we were talking quite big money when we found out that a party of five would be arriving. We had to find the cost of return flights, top class hotel accommodation, good meals, the hiring of halls, advertising, transport, and so on. We organised some local fund-raising events and I recall we acquired a little sponsorship, so we had some money in the pot and just hoped that the course would be well attended, not only by students from Aberdeen but from further afield as well.

"I went to Aberdeen City Council and told them that the Chief Instructor of the JKA was coming to teach and they agreed to hold a full civic reception for him at Town House, which is the Town Hall.

"I did my very best to organise everything properly, but I did have considerable help from my wife and Paul Allan, our association secretary, and also John Ritchie, the club secretary. I had some notification of Nakayama's visit in the local press.[5, 8]" Watt is quoted so: 'It will be a great honour for our club and a unique experience for the members to have instruction of this calibre.'[5]

Watt continued: "I arranged for a chauffeur in a stretched silver limousine to pick Nakayama's party up at the airport. Some people might say that hiring such a car was over-the-top, but I thought that it would be a bit of fun, make them smile after their trip. However, I also wanted to impress upon Nakayama how seriously we took his visit. Tsuyama, then 7th Dan, national team coach, Osaka, then 5th Dan, and Minoru Kawawada[30], who taught at the Hoitsugan – and still does to the best of my knowledge – and who would later go on to become grand champion at the First Shoto World Cup [1985] and take two JKA All-Japan *kata* titles [1986/87], plus an unknown interpreter made up the group. They flew up from Heathrow in the morning and I took them to the Huntly Hotel, now known as the Copthorne Hotel, in Huntly Street, a four star establishment and one of the best in Aberdeen, on the Friday, just to unwind after the journey.

"The civic reception was held at lunch-time, 12.30 p.m. for 12.45 p.m., and was quite an affair with a nice meal. We had soup as a starter, followed by beef and Yorkshire pudding, and sorbet or ice cream for dessert. A vegetarian alternative was also available. The city did us proud. As I recall, all the Japanese ate heartily. I was sat with Tsuyama to my left and the Lord Provost, Alexander Collie, to my right, and Nakayama sat the other side of the Lord Provost. I chatted quite a bit to Nakayama during the reception. He really liked the Town House and he was shown around and saw the statue of Queen Victoria. There were short speeches too from the Lord Provost and Nakayama. I stood up and recited my carefully prepared welcome piece too. Nakayama was kind enough to present the Lord Provost, that's the English equivalent to Mayor, with an honorary 3rd Dan JKA.[31] I know many *karateka* don't approve of awarding honorary *Dan* grades, and, to be honest, I'm one of them. You have to work hard for years to get a real black belt, and so the honorary *Dan* grade is just a token of friendship, it doesn't mean anything because it hasn't been earned. It was just like when Kanazawa and Enoeda presented Peter Sellers with an honorary black belt when he became President of the KUGB in 1967.

Nakayama at the civic reception at Town House, Aberdeen. From left to right: Paul Allan, interpreter, John Ritchie, Watt, Tsuyama, Nakayama, Kawawada, Osaka, Alex Watt, Mike Bissett (1981).

"After the reception, Nakayama and the other JKA members were taken back to their hotel, via a little sight-seeing, and then we had training at my *dojo* at the College of Education, in Hilton Road. They got changed at the *dojo*. I remember that some of the Japanese were smoking and, just like at Crystal Palace all those years before, they stopped when Nakayama appeared.

"As you might expect, a large number of students turned up to train, about two hundred and fifty, mostly from the Aberdeen area, but also from Edinburgh and Glasgow. I had informed the Aberdeen Tourist Bureau, based at St. Nicholas House, Broad Street, about the course and they offered to help visitors find accommodation, and I put a note to this effect on the course application form. The training was held from 7.00 p.m.–10.00 p.m. at a cost of ten pounds per person. Because this was such an important event, I asked all students to be changed and ready by 6.30 p.m. as I didn't want anyone turning up late, which would have looked slack. I lined everyone up and I introduced Nakayama and the rest of the team, observing the hierarchy, to the class. I introduced Nakayama as the highest graded Shotokan *karateka* in the world; Tsuyama as a lecturer in karate at Takushoku University; and, Osaka as reigning JKA *kata* champion, a JKA *kumite* champion [1976], and former IAKF world *kata* champion

Masatoshi Nakayama (1981)

[1977]. Then we got into *seiza* and it was '*Shihan, nei rei,*' followed by, '*Sensei nei rei.*' We had two classes, beginners/lower *kyu* grades and brown and black-belts."

Nakayama teaching his class of novices and lower kyu grades (1981)

A document of the time, by an unknown writer, records the training:

'Professor Nakayama started the course instructing the novices to 4th kyu and with the help of *Sensei* Kawawada he was stressing the importance of the basics of karate. The master covered all the basic blocking techniques explaining every movement thoroughly, building up a comprehensive picture for the fortunate followers of Shotokan karate.

'At the halfway break in the course, the instructors changed classes and *Sensei* Tsuyama took over the colour belt class and moved on to instruct the students on the *Heian katas*. Through the words of an interpreter, he explained the movements and applications of these important karate libraries, emphasising the importance of these colour belt *katas* as a foundation for the advanced movements of the future.

'Both Professor Nakayama and *Sensei* Tsuyama held the whole of the colour belt class spellbound by their expert instruction and by the occasional display of their world-renowned talents.

'Meanwhile, the black and brown-belts had *Sensei* Osaka demonstrating and explaining the movements of an advanced black-belt *kata* – again the importance of solid basics were stressed. While performing the movements of the *kata* it was easily seen why *Sensei* Osaka is current World *kata* champion [with] each movement flowing with the grace and ease one would expect.

'*Sensei* Tsuyama had earlier been instructing the black and brown-belt class on their stances – he was highlighting the fact that the stances were the true foundation of good karate. A strong stance is obviously required for basic training, *kata* and *kumite*.

'All were impressed with the knowledge that was passed on by the world famous instructors and all the Scottish Shotokan students will benefit from these long-awaited three hours of comprehensive training.'

Watt continued: "After the training, an informal buffet had been arranged at the Huntly Hotel, for 10.30 p.m," where, a report of the time noted, 'the Japanese party were wined, dined, entertained and presented with mementos of their visit to the Granite City. It is sure, by the response of the honorary guests and the students of the SSC, Friday 8th May was a very enjoyable, memorable and informative day.'[32]

Watt continued: "I managed to get Nakayama, Tsuyama, Osaka and Kawawada to sign the invitation card.

"On the Saturday, we had about the same number of students at the same location and Bryceland also came up from Glasgow, which was nice. The training was very basic. I remember Tsuyama taught *shuto-uke/kokutsu-dachi* to *nukite/zenkutsu-dachi* as a way of emphasising stances. He placed a lot of emphasis on the correct use of the hips. He got me out a few times to demonstrate upon and explain what he was doing.

"Nakayama gave his lesson in really good English. Again, it was basics, and he explained how to move and how to drive off from the hips. I recall that we practised the combination *soto-ude-uke/gyaku-zuki, yoko-empi/kiba-dachi*, step across *uraken/gyaku-zuki/gedan-barai* in *zenkutsu-dachi*. Then, another two combinations, *mae-geri/mawashi-geri/uraken/gyaku-zuki/gedan-bari*, and, *mae-geri/kekomi/shuto-uchi/gyaku-zuki/gedan-barai*. Nakayama taught this way, and he had taught Kanazawa and Enoeda who had taught us in the same manner. So, we understood where Nakayama was coming from and what he was trying to show. Nakayama used Osaka to show movements and then he would explain what was going on. The truth of the matter was not so much what we were being taught, but by whom we were being taught.

"I remember we did *Kanku-dai* with Osaka and *Sochin* with Tsuyama."

We are most fortunate that a video record was taken of some of the above events. At the time of writing, there is only one known copy of this video in existence, and as it provides us with a unique opportunity to see Nakayama and his fellow JKA instructors at work in front of a class, and as it is a historically important film, a detailed description of

The buffet at the Huntly Hotel. Sitting, from left to right: Watt, Gail Watt, Nakayama, Tsuyama, Osaka, Kawawada, the interpreter, Allen (1981).

The back of an invitation to a buffet at the Huntly Hotel, Aberdeen, in honour of the visit by Professor Nakayama. From left to right, the signatures read: Nakayama, Tsuyama, Osaka, Kawawada.

its contents will be given here. Although the video is 'home made' and the sound quality variable (which might be expected in a large hall) there is a good sense of actually being in the lesson. The film lasts some one hour and forty-two minutes, and from what is captured,

Nakayama is interesting (if, perhaps, despite his age, technically somewhat disappointing), Tsuyama is an inspiration, Osaka is technically brilliant and Kawawada technically highly accomplished.

For the benefit of less experienced *karateka*, whose technical knowledge might not yet be up to fully comprehending what follows, when the author refers to a particular movement or technique in a particular *kata*, a volume number and a page number are given in brackets, and this refers to the volume and page number in Kanazawa's, two-volume, *Shotokan Karate International Kata*.[33] For example, [I/71] refers to volume I, page 71.

The video starts with a little exercising under Osaka, and then Nakayama emphasises the importance of the elbow, and its correct positioning, in *age-uke, soto-ude-uke, uchi-ude-uke* and *gedan-barai,* to his class of lower *kyu* grades. Nakayama then demonstrates blocks with Kawawada. The class pair-up for *ippon-kumite*, where Student A attacks *jodan oi-zuki* and Student B, his partner, blocks *age-uke* and counters *jodan gyaku-zuki*. Nakayama then demonstrates *soto-ude-uke* in *zenkutsu-dachi* followed by *empi* in *kiba-dachi*. He emphasises the importance of keeping the shoulder down. For a man of sixty-eight, he moves quickly. One gets the impression that Nakayama's *zenkutsu-dachi* shares certain features with *fudo-dachi*, for his back leg does not appear to be as straight as it could be. Our Students A and B pair-up once more and Student A attacks *chudan oi-zuki* and Student B blocks *soto-ude-uke* and counters with a *gyaku-zuki*.

Nakayama proceeds on to *gedan-barai*. One very noticeable feature is that when he moves into the block, he engages his hips into their forty-five degree mode almost from the outset and not either close to the end or at the end. The class then practise the following sequence from *hachiji-dachi*: 1) Step back with the right leg into *zenkutsu-dachi* blocking *gedan-barai* with the left arm, then *gyaku-zuki* with the right fist. Next, advance the right leg forward into the original *hachiji-dachi* position. 2) Step back with the left leg into *zenkutsu-dachi* blocking *gedan-barai* with the right arm, then perform *gyaku-zuki* with the left fist. Next, advance the left leg forward into the original *hachiji-dachi* position. 3) Step back with the right leg forty-five degrees in *zenkutsu-dachi* and block *gedan-barai* with the left arm, then perform a *gyaku-zuki* with the right fist. Next, advance the right leg forward to the original *hachiji-dachi* position. 4) Step back with the left leg forty-five degrees in *zenkutsu-dachi* and block *gedan-barai* with the right arm, then *gyaku-zuki* with the left fist. Students then pair-up for *gedan-barai/gyaku-zuki* practise.

Nakayama demonstrating *age-uke* (1981)

Osaka and Nakayama (1981)

Kihon is resumed and students perform *chudan choku-zuki* in *kiba-dachi*, punching with alternative fists – first one punch, then two consecutive punches, then three consecutive punches. Nakayama makes the point that the reaction fist must be pulled back swiftly as this aids the punching arm.

Throughout his teaching, Nakayama deliberately shows common errors of form and explains why techniques are performed as they are. It is evident that his English is indeed very good. Some forty minutes of film have elapsed at this point.

Then the action shifts to the black and brown-belt class. Tsuyama takes the lesson and Osaka assists. The emphasis here is in stance change and hip movement. The class practise stepping back forty-five degrees from *hachiji-dachi* with the right leg into *kokutsu-dachi* and then shifting to *zenkutsu-dachi* (by moving the front foot to the left), with hands on hips. The exercise is repeated on the left side after returning to *hachiji-dachi* as described above. Then the sequence is practised again, but this time blocking *age-uke* in *kokutsu-dachi* and

Tsuyama leads his class in *kokutsu-dachi* (1981)

Tsuyama leads his class in *gyaku-zuki,* with Osaka in the background (1981). Watt can be seen at the end of the line, by the mirror.

punching *chudan gyaku-zuki* in *zenkutsu-dachi*, first on one side, then on the other. The next sequence follows the same format, except *soto-ude-uke* is performed instead of *age-uke*.

It is evident that Tsuyama generates intensity and is a real motivator. This section last only four minutes, but at the end, when Tsuyama leaves the *dojo*, he is clapped by the class.

The final section involves Nakayama, assisted by Osaka, teaching the brown and black-belt class. The film starts with Osaka performing the *kata Kanku-dai*. One can see why he came to hold the JKA record for successive *kata* wins – he is, quite simply, in JKA terms, in a class of his own.

From the beginning of the first 'active move' (the raising of the hands) of the *kata* to the final 'active move' (*uraken*), fifty-nine seconds have elapsed. Loud applause from the students follows.

The second *kiai* in the *kata* is performed on the *uraken* (many *karateka* perform the *kiai* on the second kick of the jumping *ni-geri* [I/160]).

Nakayama then demonstrates *shuto-uke* to the outside of Osaka's *oi-zuki*.

Osaka demonstrates the first and last 'active' moves from *Kanku-dai* and then Nakayama does too, noting that the parting of the hands at the beginning of the form 'opens' the *kata*, and the move after the *uraken* at the end of the *kata*, 'closes' the form – the arms moving in opposite directions at the end compared to the opening. He notes that this has a 'very important meaning.' Nakayama also performs a *kiai* on the *uraken*.

One notable feature that follows is how Nakayama compares similar techniques in the *katas Kanku-dai* and *Heian Yondan*. Osaka demonstrates the two *kaishu haiwan-uke* at the opening of *Kanku-dai* [I/144-145] and then the first two *kaishu haiwan-uke* at the beginning of *Heian Yondan* [I/70-71], and continues with *Heian Yondan* until completion of the second *empi* [I/73].

There are two features up to this point in *Heian Yondan*, as performed by Osaka, that are worthy of mention, as many Shotokan *karateka* perform the moves differently. Firstly, after the right *chudan morote-uke* (4th move of the *kata* [I/71]), the next move is to come up with the left leg and, rather than bringing the feet together [I/72], Osaka balances in the pre-kicking position with the left foot on the right knee [I/72]. Secondly, after the first *yoko-geri-keage* and *empi*, rather than the right leg coming to the left leg [I/73], Osaka moves his left leg to his right and takes up the pre-kicking position, as noted previously, and then kicks.

Osaka then demonstrates *yoko-geri-keage* on Nakayama and the latter steps slightly further back and Osaka performs a *yoko-geri-kekomi* instead. This is another highlight of the film. Osaka's *kekomis* are breath-taking; there is no other way to describe them.

Nakayama follows this by getting two black-belt students up, asks them to stand side by side, but apart, and form an arch with one hand of each partner touching, and then practising the typical *yoko-geri-keage* and *yoko-geri-kekomi* to under the partner's armpit.

Osaka then demonstrates the next part of the *Heian Yondan* from whence he left off, up to the first *kiai* point [I/75] and Nakayama stresses the importance of keeping low in *kosa-dachi*. From this position, Nakayama then changes to *Kanku-dai* where the *uraken* is employed in identical fashion [I/152] and continues to *morote gedan shuto-uke* [I/155].

Nakayama demonstrates the *ura-zuki hiza gamae* [I/154] and then removes his belt, ties a knot at one end so that it acts like a stick, and swings it upon Osaka who completes the movement and comes to the floor in *morote hiji tate fuse* [I/154], avoiding the belt. Osaka then demonstrates *mawashi-geri* upon Nakayama who sinks low to avoid the kick, and Nakayama shows the importance of the correct head position throughout.

Nakayama demonstrating *shuto-uke* (1981)

Osaka then demonstrates *Kanku-dai* from the position previously stopped to the left *tettsui* in *kiba-dachi* [I/157]. Osaka takes up the *chudan shihon-nukite* which is common to both *Heian Sandan* and *Kanku-dai* [I/60 and I/156, respectively] and shows the turns that follow. Nakayama notes that whilst the countering *tettsui* is evident, for shorter distance, in application, *empi* can be employed.

The class then, by count, perform *Kanku-dai* from *uraken* [I/152] to the end of the *kata,* before performing the whole of *Kanku-dai* to count.

Nakayama explains that the position of the back, left foot in *morote hiji tate fuse* [I/154], should be so that the big toe side of the foot will be along the floor, whereas in *Kanku-sho,* the ball of the left foot should be on the floor [II/198] and that this is to facilitate the next movement.

The class then perform *Kanku-dai* again, to count.

Nakayama demonstrates the difference in weight ratios between *kokutsu-dachi* and *zenkutsu-dachi* and selects a female black-belt who has too much weight on her front leg in *kokutsu-dachi.* Nakayama then demonstrates with this woman by taking up the *oi-zuki* position touching the woman's chin with his fist. The woman is also in *zenkutsu-dachi* and when he instructs her to move to *kokutsu-dachi,* the gap between her face and the punch becomes clearly evident and the value of the stance change is understood. This turns out to be quite an interesting sequence, because the woman, who was called out in front of the class to demonstrate her obvious fault, which Nakayama corrects, is then praised and encouraged by him.

Nakayama then stresses the importance of keeping the same height in *kiba-dachi.*

Returning to *Heian Yondan,* Osaka demonstrates the distance to be covered after the *mae-geri* leading up to the first *kiai* point [I/74-75]. Nakayama makes it quite clear that a length of two stances is required here, and the class practise this move.

The class again practice *Kanku-dai.*

Osaka demonstrates *osae-uke/nukite* [I/147 or I/156] brilliantly. He then demonstrates the *ura-zuki hiza gamae* once more [I/154]. Nakayama selects another black-belt, unties and knots his belt once more, and swings it, catching the student on the back. Nakayama clearly aims a bit lower this time to demonstrate the point that the student must be quick and must keep low entering *morote hiji tate fuse* [I/154].

Osaka then performs *Kanku-dai* once more to Nakayama's count. There are a few interesting technical points here. For example, from the *choku-zuki* [I/144 {position 6}] to the *uchi-ude-uke* [I/144 {position 7}], during the intermediate position [I/144 {position 7a}] Osaka brings his left fist (on the hip) across and close to his body to shoulder height, to act as a reaction. He does this on the following punch/block sequence as well. Secondly, after the second *chudan uchi-ude-uke* [I/145] instead of bringing the right leg back and kicking,

Osaka performing *koshi gamae* from the *kata Kanku-dai* (1981)

Osaka brings the left leg close up to the right leg and then kicks. Thirdly, the reaction arm on the following *shuto-uke* sequence [I/146-147] never reaches full extension. Nakayama explains after the three *shuto-uke/osae-uke/nukite* sequence that the *karateka* should remain at the same height throughout. Fourthly, after the *chudan uchi-ude-uke/chudan gyaku-zuki/chudan zuki* sequence [I/155], Osaka pulls the

168

Nakayama demonstrating the hand movements from the *kata Hangestu* (1981).

right foot all the way back to the left to kick, whereas many other *karateka* bring the left foot in before kicking [I/156].

Osaka's *ni-geri* is expertly delivered and Nakayama comments that the *yame* sequence [I/161-162] should be performed naturally, with 'no power' (to quote Nakayama).

Nakayama then demonstrates the hand position for *shuto-uke* and makes reference to the position of the right hand in the *kaishu kosa-uke* in *Hangetsu* [II/74 {position 10}] and the *tate shuto-uke* in *Heian*

A group shot after Nakayama's Aberdeen course (1981). Sitting, from left to right: unknown, John Main, Kenny Taylor, Watt, Nakayama, Danny Bryceland, Paul Allan, Keith Stewart, Mike Bissett.

Sandan [I/64-65] an demonstrates upon Osaka a right *empi-uke* and *jodan uraken* [I/62-63] from *Heian Sandan* and explains the reason for doing it that way.

Nakayama gives a final, largely inaudible talk before finishing the lesson with a 'Thank you,' and the concluding bowing is interrupted by the need for a large group photo.

Watt continued: "I had total respect for Nakayama: his lineage, his books, what he'd achieved in life. He was an icon in the karate world. I said to my students, 'Look,' pointing to senior Japanese, 'these are 5th Dans and above and they can kill you with a single blow, but they are all bowing to this small man. This is history coming to our *dojo.*' Nakayama's great strength – and we learned this only after his death from the chaos in the Shotokan world that followed – was that he had actually held it all together. I have trouble sometimes with my small group – you know, you never know when the next bombshell is going to fall – but Enoeda held the KUGB together and that, I'm sure, was pretty tricky at times, and I take my hat off to him for doing that, but to keep the JKA intact around the world is mind boggling! It's amazing, and it shows the respect that everyone had for him.

"I'd read so much about this man and now I had him in my living room, sitting on my settee at Sycamore Place, drinking tea and eating

Watt and Nakayama at Sycamore Place (1981)

biscuits. He was smiling and chatting away. He stayed for two hours. I took him up to my study and showed him my karate books and trophies. I don't know how many times I'd opened *Dynamic Karate*, thousands of times I should say, and here was the author signing and dating that old copy in my own house. I've never got over that moment and I'm sure that I never shall.

"I remember that he told me about his skiing accident in the Japanese Alps in the early 1970s [1971] which nearly killed him. He said that he'd been out on the mountains with a group of students from Takushoku when he was caught in an avalanche. He was really lucky to survive and the doctors had told him that it was his level of fitness that had saved him. He was, nevertheless, in hospital for many months. He said that skiing was very good training for both karate stances and the use of the hips and that was why he liked doing it. He recommended it to me as additional karate practise.[34]

"Nakayama also spoke to me about *kokutsu-dachi*. He told me that the stance must not be a low *kiba-dachi* with one leg turned out and the weight shifted back. He also said that the back knee must be in line with the back shoulder and that it is good practice to raise the heel of the front foot slightly off the ground to build strong quadriceps. Then the foot of the front leg could be placed fully on the floor.

"He thanked me for organising the event and commented on the good attitude and technique of my students, all of which, as you can imagine, delighted me. He was such a polite man, well bred, but he

Watt alongside Nakayama at the Aberdeen College of Commerce (1981)

was happy too and that's what I shall always remember about him. To have Nakayama come to my *dojo* to teach myself and my students and then come to my house to have tea, was the highlight, the pinnacle of my karate life. Everything I had worked for in karate – overcoming the

A New Year's Card, in Nakayama's own hand, sent to Watt

A New Year's Card, in Nakayama's own hand, sent to Watt

A New Year's card, in Nakayama's own hand, sent to Watt

problems of my crushed leg, turning out in the pouring rain to train up and down in an empty *dojo*, culminated in that visit. I remember, early on in training, sitting on a drafty old bus and a friend of mine in a Lotus Cortina sped past with a girl I knew sitting beside him. I went to train with a couple of friends in a freezing *dojo* and I thought to myself, 'Why am I doing this?' But Nakayama's visit made it all slot into place. It was better than the trophies, better than sparring with the best in the world, better than all the grades.

"We had Nakayama and his party, essentially, for a weekend course and they flew back to London on the Sunday evening so that they could be at Crystal Palace on the Monday for the commencement of the KUGB *gasshuku*. After Crystal Palace, Fritz Wendland[35] told me that Nakayama went to Germany [and this intent is confirmed from a newspaper clip[5]]."

Watt is quoted in 1986 as saying: 'It cost us nearly four thousand pounds to bring Nakayama and his party to Aberdeen. We would have made a profit of six pounds and sixty-nine pence, but a last minute taxi fare left us with exactly sixty-nine pence!'[36] An account sheet[37] exists that shows incomings and outgoings for the course, and, in fact, the profit may have been twelve pounds and ninety-five pence!

Watt continued: "At the KUGB *gasshuku* that year I attempted my *Yondan* [4th Dan] with Rhodes – a very powerful *karateka* and tremendous at *kumite* – under Kase, Enoeda and Shirai. I passed the *kihon* and *kumite* but the examiners asked us both to come back next time for the *kata*, and they would test only the *kata*. Dan gradings were really tough in those days and I had my grading deferred. I was shattered at the end of that experience and a bit fed up too, but if I wanted the grade then it was up to me to improve my *kata*. That *gasshuku* may have been the time when Shirai asked me to warm up the class, as well as finish the session. I could not believe that he had chosen me out of all the students at Crystal Palace. I felt really honoured and have never forgotten it.

"At the next course, [on the 11th September 1981][38,39], the grading started at 9.00 a.m., but the senior gradings didn't get underway until 5.00 p.m. That was the longest day of my life.

"The '*kata* only' was forgotten and I had to re-take the entire grading, including the freestyle. I was up against top fighters, squad members, attempting 3rd Dan, and I remember this chap whose surname was Fossit. He was a greater sweeper and I watched him demolish his opponent before it was my turn to partner him. He swept me sure enough, but I went with the *ashi-barai* and managed to utilize the uplift at the same time and performed an *empi-uchi* on him just like at the crest of the jump in *Meikyo*. It couldn't have been better if I'd practised it for years.

"Whilst I loved the *kumite*, I dreaded the *kata*, because I knew that one tiny mistake meant failure, and I'd hear the dreaded, 'Please try again next time.' I was asked to perform four *kata*: two *sentei* – which, if memory serves were from *Bassai-dai*, *Kanku-dai*, *Enpi*, *Jion* and *Hangetsu*; one *tokai*, and I performed either *Nijushiho* or *Meikyo*, and one of the examiners choice, which was *Kanku-sho*. I also had to show the *bunkai* to *Bassai-dai*.

"I felt really proud to receive my 4th Dan, as this was a high grade at the time. I had to wait another three years before I held my certificate though! Young people today would not believe what we went through for our grades then. I try and tell them, but they just look at me and say, 'I will be on holiday *Sensei*. Can I grade when I come back?' Times change, but true karate never changes and it makes me feel sad at times to see what is happening in the name of the art. I must be honest and say that, in my opinion, the great Japanese like Kase, Kanazawa, Enoeda, Shirai, Ochi, Asano and Miyazaki, are a dying breed. Well, three of them are dead now. Many of the best of the Japanese came to Europe and America nearly fifty years ago and we benefited from the hard training they gave. Today it's just not the same. I remember a competition I entered with a broken arm, which was in plaster. During the bout I forgot about the arm and punched with it. The pain! I had to have the plaster taken off afterwards and another put on. That wouldn't be allowed now. I feel like a dinosaur sometimes. It reminds me of Turner's wonderful 1839 painting, *The Fighting Téméraire*, an illustrious old wooden sailing ship being pulled to the breakers yard by a much smaller modern metal steamship puffing out black smoke. There is a ghostlike beauty about the old warship as the sun sets behind it, symbolising the end of an era. I know I'm being sentimental, but that 98-gun, Neptune-class ship of the line that was astern of Nelson's *Victory* at the Battle of Trafalgar and played an important role becoming badly damaged, really didn't deserve such a fate. And, dare I say it, karate is going the same way.

"Ninety-nine point nine, nine, nine per cent of students think that they are practising karate when they turn up at the *dojo* twice a week and throw their legs and arms around, but that's not real karate. If what they do keeps them fit and happy then that's fine, but real karate is an art form and that's why Vincent Van Gogh, George Seurat and Amedeo Modigliani are so special, because they gave up everything to pursue it. Their art was a calling and their commitment was total. I mean, you wouldn't get *Irisis, Reclining Nude,* or *The Circus*, respectively, from someone who had a day-time job and painted at the weekend for pleasure, would you? Van Gogh killed himself at thirty-seven, Seurat died of diphtheria aged thirty-two, and Modigliani died of tuberculosis aged thirty-six. The eighteenth/nineteenth century painter Hokusai, who I've mentioned before, lived to eighty-nine, but he existed solely to improve his art, and was called *Gwakiojn*, literally, 'Old Man mad on drawings.' Many great artists are 'close to the edge' as well, like the great Norwegian painter, Edvard Munch; in my opinion his art was never as good after his breakdown. I feel that I come somewhere in between. I train every day and have done so for nearly forty-five years and I try and do my best. I want to get better, but I have had to compromise because I wanted a wife and family and I still want to eat and keep warm in a Scottish winter. I am full of admiration for *real* artists, be they painters, sculptors, musicians or *karateka*, but they are incredibly rare individuals. I believe that if you don't live an art, you don't do it.

"In those days, it was *Taikyoku Shodan*, which we called *Kihon Kata*, for 9th kyu, the *Heian kata*, in order, to 4th kyu, *Tekki Shodan* for 3rd kyu, and, *Bassai-dai* for 2nd and 1st kyu. For 1st Dan, you could choose from *Bassai-dai, Kanku-dai, Enpi, Jion* and *Hangetsu*; for 2nd Dan, *Bassai-sho, Kanku-sho, Jitte, Tekki Nidan* and *Nijushiho*; for 3rd Dan, *Gankaku, Jiin, Sochin, Chinte, Wankan, Rohai [Meikyo], Unsu, Tekki Sandan, Gojushiho-dai* and *Gojushiho-sho*. For all Dan grades, it was necessary to have a thorough knowledge of the *kata* forming the previous Dan set.[40]

"Enoeda had come up to Aberdeen regularly, four times a year, since 1976[41], and then visited with Yoshinobu Ohta[42] on the same basis.[43] Classes were often from more than one hundred to more than two hundred people.[44, 45]"

Watt is reported in 1986 as saying: '[Enoeda] used to come up on the train and it was fish suppers at the end of the night. Now he's chief instructor in Europe for the JKA and flies around the world First-Class.'[46] There is colour video footage lasting some thirty-five minutes of Enoeda, in Aberdeen, teaching the *kata Unsu*, on a course organised by Watt.

Watt continued: "I remember on one occasion when I was in a group being taught by Enoeda, maybe he was demonstrating with me in *kumite*, I can't recall. He kicked me hard with a *mae-geri* and Andy Sherry came up to me in the showers afterwards, when I was nursing

Enoeda counters *kizami-zuki* to Watt's *mae-geri* at the Aberdeen College of Commerce (late 1970s/early 1980s).

my wound, and said that Enoeda liked me. I thought to myself, 'If he likes me and kicks me to this extent, heaven knows what he does to the poor souls he doesn't care for!' Enoeda was a real powerhouse of a man, genuinely dangerous. I paired-up with him on many occasions and I'd charge in. He'd block and then push me back. 'No! Harder!' he'd insist. Then I'd fly in and he'd boot me! There was no winning.

"Enoeda was known at the time as the man with the most powerful punch and I used to promote him as such. He was recorded in the *Guinness Book of Records*, I believe, with his punch being delivered, if I remember correctly, at twenty-two miles per hour with a force of half a ton." Watt is quoted as saying that if Enoeda made 'contact with you [he] would kill you in the first blow. He can control his punch to within one-eighth of an inch of your skin.'[45]

Watt continued: "Enoeda's visits had accompanying gradings of course, and a good number of my students received their Dan grades, 1st to 3rd. I can remember, exactly, the *kihon* requirement for each of the Dan grades. For 1st Dan the sequence was as follows: *kizami-zuki/gyaku-zuki, mae-geri/oi-zuki/gyaku-zuki, yoko-geri-kekomi/uraken/gyaku-zuki, mawashi-geri/uraken/gyaku-zuki, jodan ushiro-*

SCOTTISH SHOTOKAN CENTRES

SPECIAL COURSE

15th - 18th MARCH 1984

Sensei OHTA 4th Dan J.K.A.

Sensei WATT 4th Dan J.K.A.

Sensei ENOEDA
8th Dan J.K.A.

* *

PLUS ! SCOTLAND vs NORWAY INTERNATIONAL TEAM COMPETITION

* *

Thursday 15th March	Sensei OHTA	Novice - 4th Kyu Brown & Black belts	6.30 - 8 pm 8 - 9.30 pm	College of Education Hilton Drive ABERDEEN
Friday 16th March	Sensei ENOEDA & Sensei OHTA DEMONSTRATIONS & INTERNATIONAL TEAM COMPETITION - SCOTLAND vs NORWAY	All Grades	6.30 - 8.30 pm 8.30 pm onwards	Summerhill Community Centre Summerhill Academy Langstracht ABERDEEN
Saturday 17th March	Sensei ENOEDA & Sensei OHTA	All Grades Kyu Grading Dan Grading	11 am - 1 pm 1 pm onwards 2 pm onwards	Summerhill Community Centre ABERDEEN
Sunday 18th March	Sensei ENOEDA & Sensei OHTA	All Grades Kyu Grading only	10 am - 1 pm 1 pm onwards	Westerhailes Education Centre Murrayburn Drive EDINBURGH

* *

Members sitting grading should register no later than 9.30 am on Saturday or Sunday

Typical details for an Enoeda and Ohta course (1984)

geri/chudan gyaku-zuki, mae-geri/yoko-geri/mawashi-geri/ushiro-geri/gyaku-zuki, mae-geri/oi-zuki/gyaku-zuki/ step back *gedan-barai/gyaku-zuki/mawashi-geri/uraken/gyaku-zuki*, and, kicking on the spot with the same leg, *mae-geri/yoko-geri/ushiro-geri.*

"For 2nd Dan: *mae-geri/ni-zuki, chudan mae-geri/jodan mawashi-geri* (same leg) *uraken/gyaku-zuki, jodan mawashi-geri/chudan yoko-geri* (same leg)/*uraken/gyaku-zuki, mae-geri* (step forward)/*yoko-geri* (same leg)/step down then back leg *mawashi-geri/ushiro-geri/uraken/ gyaku-zuki, mae-geri/yoko-geri/mawashi-geri/ushiro-geri/uraken/ gyaku-zuki, mae-geri/yoko-geri/ushiro-geri/mawashi-geri* (kicking on the spot with same leg).

"In fact, there was an alternative 2nd Dan grading *kihon* syllabus that kept the last three movements [of the above] but substituted the first three as follows: *kizami-zuki/gyaku-zuki/oi-zuki*/step back *gedan-barai/mae-geri*/step back *ushiro-geri/uraken/oi-zuki, kizami-zuki/oi-zuki*/step back to *musubi-dachi* and kick with other leg *yoko-geri/ uraken/oi-zuki* (or *gyaku-zuki*), *kizami-zuki/oi-zuki*/step back *gedan-barai/mae-geri*/step back *ushiro-geri*/step down and kick with other leg *ushiro-geri/uraken/gyaku-zuki.*

"For 3rd Dan: *mae-geri/yoko-geri/gyaku-zuki, mae-geri/yoko-geri/uraken/gyaku-zuki, mawashi-geri/yoko-geri/uraken/gyaku-zuki, mawashi-geri/ushiro-geri/gyaku-zuki, mawashi-geri* (front leg)/ *ura-mawashi-geri*/step down back leg *ushiro-geri, kizami-zuki/ gyaku-zuki/mawashi-geri/uraken/gyaku-zuki*/step back *gedan-barai/ gyaku-zuki/mae-geri*/step back *ushiro-geri/uraken/oi-zuki, jodan mawashi-geri/ura-mawashi-geri/jodan ushiro-geri*, with all kicks performed with the same leg.[47]

"I ensured that students wishing to put themselves forward for Dan gradings had to give six months notice of their intent, in writing, and that each intending examinee had a good training record for at least one year beforehand. I did this because I wanted students to focus and to really give of their best, not only for their own sakes, but because when they were standing in front of Enoeda they were a reflection of me too.

"The KUGB was one of the largest, if not the largest karate organisation in Britain with a membership of some twelve thousand at the time.[48] The association was split into five regions, and I was the regional officer for Scotland. The late Geoff Wilding acted for Wales, and, in England, Bob Rhodes acted for the Northern Region [and P. Hardy and R. Waterhouse for the Central and Southern Regions, respectively].

"Being in the KUGB opened up all sorts of opportunities for me in a competitive sense, both home and abroad. When I was the Scottish team captain of the KUGB Scottish Region, I fought in the European

Amateur Karate Federation Championships held in Manchester on the 8th November 1981. I think Cliff Hepburn, a KUGB general secretary, organised that competition.

"The team was selected from four meetings prior to the championship – the Scottish Region KUGB Championship Elimi-nations, held at the Powis Academy, Aberdeen [29th August 1981]; the Scottish Region KUGB Championships and Team Karate Eliminations [20th September 1981]; the Scottish Region KUGB squad training, Aberdeen College of Education [4th October 1981]; and, the KUGB inter-regional competition in Coventry [17th/18th October 1981]. The Scottish squad was made up of myself, as team coach and competitor, Paul Allan as team manager and competitor, George Robb, Alan Simpson, James Kidd, John Main and Linda Main. John Ritchie went as our conference delegate.

"We left Aberdeen by coach early [8.00 a.m.] on the Friday morning via Dundee and arrived in Manchester in the afternoon. We all wore the standard and very smart KUGB uniform, consisting of white shirt, navy blue jacket and tie, grey flannel trousers, or skirt for the female team member, and dark shoes. The jacket sported a Scottish team badge. An official reception was held in the evening along with a buffet.

"On the Saturday, an EAKF meeting was held, the competition draw was conducted and we had squad training. We wore navy blue tracksuit tops and clean white *gis*, and we were required to wear gum shields and boxes. The eliminations were held on the Sunday morning with the finals that evening. We each had an additional two badges, one for the tracksuit top and one for the *gi*. So, each member had three team badges and two of these had to be returned after the event.

"The KUGB English team fought the German team, which had been brought over by Ochi, and Scotland fought Yugoslavia. I went in at number five. I was up against Dusan Dacic, who, although the smallest man in a team of giants, was a tremendous fighter, excep-tionally talented, the best. He was runner-up at the last IAKF World Championships, so you can appreciate the level and experience. Dacic broke my wrist with a *mawashi-geri*, but I took him to an extension and we drew. I consider that, probably, to be the best international fight I ever had. Scotland lost the match by half a point and Yugoslavia went on to take 3rd place with Sweden.

"Apart from fighting Dacic, the other outstanding memory I have of those championships was of Bob Poynton by the side of the *tatami* shouting encouragement."

This is to Certify that

CHP

RONALD WATT

SCOTTISH TEAM CAPTAIN.

Was a contestant in the

EAKF European
Senior Karate
Championships

at Manchester, England
on Sunday 8th November 1981

Organised and presented by
Cliff Hepburn
CHP Sports Promotions

A EAKF certificate showing that Watt was Scottish Team Captain and a contestant.

Terry O'Neill noted that the event attracted contestants from fourteen countries – Austria, Belgium, England, Germany, Greece, Hungary, Ireland, Israel, Italy, Scotland, Sweden, Switzerland, Wales and Yugoslavia. The English team beat the Germans in an exciting final, clinched in the last fight when Cattle won, and the individual title went to Frank Brennan. The *kata* title went to P. Dimitrijevic of Yugoslavia, Brennan was second and Dacic, third.[49]

Watt continued: "The morning after the championships we left Manchester for Aberdeen, a journey of about eight hours."

In 1982 Watt recalled the Scottish team's performance: 'This was a new and relatively inexperienced Scottish team, and for most members was their first taste of European competition ... they acquitted themselves very well.'[50]

Watt continued: "On the afternoon of the 26th January 1982, at the City Registrar's Office, Gail and I got married. In fact, I met Gail when I was sitting in my Marcos on Union Street, Aberdeen, and she came up and opened the door and said, 'Hello!' I told you people see you differently when you drive a flash car! After the service, we went back home for a glass of champagne and sandwiches that my neighbours, Phil and Elizabeth Dudar had kindly arranged. That evening, from 7.00 p.m. until 9.00 p.m., I had a karate class at the Cowdrey Club and after training some of my senior black-belts – John Ritchie, Paul Allan, Ian Ord, Keith Stewart, George Robb, Alan Simpson and Malcolm Hogg – came back home to celebrate.

"So 1982 was a very happy year for me, but it was also a very sad one, for my mother died.[51] When my father passed away it was a dreadful loss for my mother and she pined away really whilst still living at 27, Skene Square. Then, five years later, in 1982, when Roxanne was born, she came alive again. But approaching midnight on the 28th July, my Aunt Kate telephoned me and said that Mum was ill. Then, shortly afterwards, a few minutes after midnight, Aunt Kate phoned me again and said that Mum had died. My mother knew she was about to die because her last words to Kate were, 'I'm going', or words to that effect. I went to the funeral directors a few days later. I felt that I needed to see her one more time. I found it very hard walking into that chapel of rest, alone. She lay in her coffin. She looked so thin, so pale. I touched her cold hand in the hope that I could somehow bring her back to life. I loved her dearly.

"I have never got over the death of my father and my mother. I lost both parents by the age of thirty-five and I think having a family helped me, because I knew that, having had no brothers or sisters, the family line would carry on; that what had been the essence of my parents carried on through my children. With my mother's death came the end of an era though. Mum and Dad never had much in life, but

Gail and Ronnie cut the cake before Ronnie goes karate training at the Cowdray Hall (26th January 1982).

what they had they gave to me. All the happy childhood memories at Skene Square – the Christmases, playing games in the snow and walking to the shops to buy little things – came to an end. But let us not dwell on this subject.

"Because I was spending so much time on the road driving between *dojos*, I decided that I had to drive something a bit more comfortable and so I bought a second-hand Datsun 240Z and, then, a second-hand Daimler V12. I've mentioned that people see you differently if you drive a nice car, but sometimes this can be malevolent. I parked my Datsun and when I returned I found that someone had unscrewed all my wheel nuts!

"That Daimler was a lovely car and I'd drive down to London with five people in it, to attend the KUGB *gasshukus*. At that time petrol was really cheap, so it wasn't a problem. Later, I bought a black replica Porsche Carrerra and then saved up a long time and bought a silver Porsche 911 Turbo. I had to part with them when my children, Roxanne and Reeve [b. 1985] were born as there wasn't any room. Ironically, Reeve worked for a while as a Porsche technician. Both Roxanne and Reeve studied karate with me. Reeve is a 3rd Dan and received 4th place in the individual *kumite* at the 2000 WKC World Junior Championships in Valencia, and Roxanne, who is also a 3rd Dan, received the bronze medal in the team *kata* at the 2001 WKC World Championships, and she is now working as a nurse.

"I treasured that Porsche Turbo; I liked the style and the power – rather as I do karate I suppose. I'd just go into the driveway and admire it, touch it, to make sure it was real. I didn't want to even drive the car in case I damaged it.

"Anyway, I had to have a new starter motor. A starter motor on a Porsche Turbo is very powerful, with about as much clout as a small car's engine – only joking, but you know what I mean. I went to KUGB *gasshuku* in London and I decided to go down by train. I caught a taxi to the station and was sitting in the carriage, looking out of the window, when Gail suddenly appeared. I'd said goodbye to her before leaving home, so I thought one of two things had happened: either she was missing me already, which would have been really nice, or, and this was more likely, a disaster had happened. I regret to say it was the latter. Then a tear came to her eye.

"'What's the matter!' I asked, worriedly.

"'It's your car,' she replied.

"Now the train was about to leave and my mind set was that shortly I would be practising with some of the greatest Shotokan masters in the world. I wanted to think solely about karate, so I took a deep breath, sighed with a sense of resignation and whispered, 'Just fix it.'

"'It's not just the car,' Gail cried, 'it's the house as well.' Then she explained what had happened.

"She was talking to one of the neighbours and she turned the car's ignition on so that she could turn down the windows. Well, she turned the key too much and the car, which was in gear, jumped forward, demolished the garage door and much of the wall at the other end of the garage as well. It had also demolished the front of my lovely Porsche Turbo.

"I'd decided to catch a taxi to the train station specially so the Porsche wouldn't be in a car park, so that it wouldn't even get wet, and here it was now stuck half-way through my garage wall. When I got off the train in London I was still in a state of shock and when Enoeda said hello to me he asked, 'What's the matter? You look very worried.' He was genuinely concerned. I told him the story and he nearly died laughing and proceeded to tell everyone he met.

"We had some good times at those *gasshukus*. I remember a funny incident that occurred after a morning training session. John Ritchie and John Cox, the Two Johns I called them, were real comediennes when they were together. They were brilliant and fed off one another, just like Stan Laurel and Oliver Hardy. The two Johns, some other lads and I, were wandering up to the Sun Sun Chinese restaurant. Suddenly, John Cox, without any warning – though, in actuality, it was in revenge for a tannoy announcement stunt Ritchie had previously pulled – ran up to Ritchie and pulled down his blue over-gi tracksuit trousers and pants to his ankles. Ritchie was standing there showing all that nature had endowed him with and a woman motorist driving passed got the full view and crashed her car into a lamp post. The Two Johns ran up the road as fast as they could with the rest of us in pursuit. Ritchie wasn't too happy about what had happened and he put a head lock on Cox. Cox passed out for about two minutes. After Cox came around, we all carried on to the Sun Sun. I have often wondered what that woman put in her accident insurance report, but I bet it had something to do with having seen the Loch Ness monster!

"Kase, Enoeda and the other Japanese were already eating. We sat down and the Chinese waitress came over to take our order. She asked the first person what he wanted and he said, 'One Coke.' She then went to the second person and he said, 'Two Cokes.' She then moved to the third person and he said, 'Three Cokes,' and so on until the seventh person. She staggered back shortly afterwards with twenty-eight Coca Colas, all opened, when we had meant one Coke each and were just tallying them up for her as we went along. I wish I could have taken a photograph of the expression on the faces of the Japanese."

"I remember when I bit John Cox's ear. We liked pairing up with one another because we could go for it hammer and tongs, get a good work-out, and yet not get any bad or strange injuries. John was one of the best *kumite* men I ever had, good control too, and is still a very good friend. We were paired-up at Crystal Palace on the summer course and when it was time to get a new partner, we changed, and then when it came time to change again we paired up once more. Anyway, I'd heard a story about how a certain Japanese instructor noted for *kumite* and wonderful technique had bitten someone's ear when free-styling, so, for fun, I thought I'd have a go if the opportunity arose. Well, it did, and I jumped up, grabbed John and nipped his ear. I jumped down from his back and pushed him away.

' "That was a good one," he said whilst still in shock. Then he realised what I'd really done. 'You little b———!' he shouted, and then he came after me. I didn't hurt him and he took it in the spirit it was meant. It wasn't as though I'd done a Mike Tyson on him; that would have been a '*hansoku chui.*'

"Kawasoe *Sensei* came over to me afterwards and asked if I'd spar with him. Perhaps it was coincidence, but if not, then I hope he didn't think I was serious about biting John's ear.

"In 1983 I secured a permanent *dojo* in Aberdeen." A typed, undated document, though handwritten 'after 1981', recalls the event under the title, 'New Base for Scottish Shotokan Centre.' It reads:

'After nearly two decades of hard work, the Scottish Shotokan Centres, under the chief instructor, Ronnie Watt, 4th Dan JKA, have found a permanent base in the city. As from April, the club will have a full-time *dojo* (training hall) in the city centre. The *dojo*, which is self-financed, will be completed around April and will be open seven days a week, all day.

'Private lessons, ladies self-defence, businessmen's sessions and lunch-time sessions are planned, as well as the normal karate club. The *dojo* will be fully equipped with exercise aids, plus showers, and the use of a cafeteria and lounge bar. Ronnie Watt commented that for eighteen years in karate, he and the club had made do with sub-standard facilities and he was glad that at last it [the *dojo*] had facilities to match the level of expertise and standards within the club.

'John Ritchie, general secretary of the centre, added that the reason it had become possible to open the centre was the loyalty of the members of staff. 'We don't have a top-heavy management; everybody pulls his weight. We don't have any rooms for individual superstars; that only leads to the work not getting done. Now we have pruned our team through natural selection and wastage, we can run the centre efficiently. Our policy will continue to be loyalty and quality. With the opening of the new centre we will be employing the best in the world to come and teach our members and squad. We will welcome anybody from any style who is interested in training with the best. Our squad is now recognised as one of the top in Europe. We have attained this with little facilities and it is exciting to think that what can be attained with these new headquarters.

'In pursuance of the policy of getting the best, the Scottish Shotokan Centres will be visited in March by Sensei T. Kase, 8th Dan JKA, international Japanese instructor.'

Literature to this course exists to show that Kase taught on Saturday 16th, and, Sunday 17th March 1983. Training times were from 10.00 a.m.–1.00 p.m. with kyu gradings held on both afternoons and Dan gradings on the Sunday only. Training on the 16th was at the Edinburgh Westerhailes Education Centre, Murryburn Drive, and on 17th at the Powis Academy, St. Machar Drive, Aberdeen.

Details of a four-day course by Kase also exist, from the 24th–27th June, though for which year is unclear, though 1983–1986. Training and grading was held as follows: Monday 24th – Burgh Hall, Clifton Road, Aberdeen, 7.00 p.m.–10 p.m. grading for kyu grades; Tuesday 25th – Summerhill Academy, Langstracht, Aberdeen, 7.00 p.m.– 9.30 p.m. training; Wednesday 26th – Westerhailes Education Centre, Edinburgh, 7.00 p.m.–9.30 p.m. training and grading; Thursday 27th – YMCA, Randolf Place, Edinburgh – 7.00 p.m.–10.00 p.m., grading for Edinburgh SSC kyu grades. Additionally, an entry ticket to a course by Kase also exists for the 25th/26th June, but again the year is unknown.

A published report exists on Kase visiting Aberdeen and Edinburgh around this time. It was noted that two hundred and fifty students attended the two-day course. It was recorded that Kase concentrated on *tai-sabaki* and *maai*, and that '*kihon* concentrated on attacking and defending in every direction.'[52] Kase also concentrated on the *kata* *Jion* performed normally and then 'on the other side, all the way through.'[52] As the writer noted: 'Just as our brains adjusted to this development, we then moved on to *Jion* performed backwards … *Sensei* Kase gathered everyone together and explained that the *kata,* as we know it, is just a starting point and that we should perform *kata* on both sides, backwards and in different directions. Then with free-style application for all these ways!'[52]

Watt continued: "At this time we had a good number of women students and Kase enjoyed taking them." In one report, from 1983, it was noted that; 'They [the SSC] occasionally run ladies' self-defence classes. At the end of last year, for example, one hundred and twenty women turned up for the eight-week course. Obviously, in that time

Typical details for a Kase course (1983)

they could learn only very basic self-defence, but they found it extremely worthwhile.'[53]

Watt continued: "Enoeda actually helped me get both Kase and Shirai up to Aberdeen and I recall that he and Ohta attended one of Kase's courses too.[54] Kase spoke about setting-up a Gichin Funakoshi

SHOTOKAN

1983 SPECIAL KARATE SUMMER COURSE

Organised by:

The Japan Karate Association   **European Technical Instruction Centre**
The Karate Union of Great Britain

COURSE DIPLOMA

Name: RONALD WATT   *Club.* ABERDEEN S. S. C

Nationality: SCOTTISH   *Grade:*

The person mentioned attended the Special European Course at Crystal Palace National Recreation Centre

Course No: 1   *Date:* 2. 5 ~ 6. 5. 83

Instructors:

Sensei Kase: ....   *Sensei Tabata:* .... T. Tabata

Sensei Shirai: ....   *Sensei Kawasoe:* ....

Sensei Ochi: ....   *Sensei Ohta:* ....

Chairman (Chief Instructor E.S.K.A. and K.U.G.B.)
Sensei K. Enoeda

Cup competition with both John Ritchie and I and asked us to select a Scottish team to take part in the inaugural contest to be held in Tokyo in September that year[55], though the event didn't happen."

There is some wonderful video footage of Kase performing the *kata Chinte* at Watt's Aberdeen *dojo* around this time. Kase takes

Enoeda, Watt, Kase and Shirai at Crystal Palace (1984/85)

forty-four seconds to perform the *kata* – from the beginning of the movement of the right fist which goes on to form a *tettsui* to the end of the jumps. It is a performance of much depth. The timing is interesting and Kase can move with astonishing speed. His class then performs the *kata*. However, what is particularly interesting about Kase's performance is contained in the twenty-four seconds of video before he begins the form and the twenty-two seconds afterwards. One gets the distinct impression that he is not comfortable about performing the *kata* to onlookers and afterwards, when he walks towards his seated class, he receives a round of applause, looks up, smiles, is obviously pleased, but gesticulates that it was a 'so-so' performance. The two and a half minutes of videotape is a little gem of a real karate master at work and it is hoped that it becomes commercially available. In the author's opinion, based on what he has seen of Kase on film, including Kase performing his favourite *kata*, *Meikyo*, it far exceeds anything else.

Watt continued: "Kase performed his *kata* differently from standard JKA, if I can put it like that. In my experience many Shotokan *karateka* want to become clones of senior Japanese or their instructor, and I understand this, but in so doing they lose what is intrinsically their own. Let us take *Chinte* as an example. Firstly, Kase's timing was different in places. He could be so fast and so crisp in his movements – for example, from the first *kiba-dachi* to the *fudo-dachi* that follows, or from the *age-tate-empi-uchi*, the first *kiai* point, to the *shuto-uke* – that it took your breath away.

"After the *mae-geri* and *kosa-uke*, the leg-hooking movement was followed by a *tettsui-uchi*. This may be a fairly standard application, but Kase could actually do it! Many a time he demonstrated this on me. First he'd hook my kicking leg and I'd go over, and then he'd catch me at the side of the head as I fell, with the *tettsui*. That was real class.

"Then there were the hops at the end. Often, *karateka* bring the left foot to the right foot and hop back at an angle, have a very slight pause, and then finish the form with two other hops, 1 … 2, 3. Kase didn't do this. He hopped, hopped, hopped – 1, 2, 3. His centre of gravity was so low and his balance so good, a fractional pause was not necessary.

"Kase's body wasn't really suited to mainstream JKA practice, he wasn't able to kick high like Kanazawa, Kawasoe and Osaka; he wasn't what many people would call a stylist. So Kase made his own Shotokan with slightly different emphases. When I saw Kase it gave me heart, because, in truth, my body shape isn't ideal for Shotokan either. I'd struggled with this for years, but when I saw Kase I realised that I, too, could make my own Shotokan.

"Kawasoe also came up to Aberdeen a few times. He'd been to KUGB Scottish Region clubs since the mid 1970s[56, 57] and I had been to his wedding. He was a first-class technician, a 6th Dan I recall, and a really well brought up individual. On one occasion he gave me a Tokaido *gi* with his name on. It wasn't a new *gi*, he'd worn it, and that's what I was after. I wanted some of his spirit. Such a notion may seem primitive, but it's true. The Japanese understand this." Evidence has survived to show that Kawasoe went to Aberdeen, singularly, on at least four occasions: 12th/13th November 1983, 11th/12th August 1984, and, the 18th/19th January and 19th/20th May, though the year(s) is/are unknown, for 'special courses.' Training and gradings were held at a number of locations, namely: Powis Academy and Summerhill Community Centre, in Aberdeen; Westerhailes Education Centre, and, Marco's Leisure Centre, Grove Street, Edinburgh; and, Corsewall Community Centre, Corsewell Street, Coatbridge. Often, Watt organised inter-club competitions and arranged discos for members following these courses.

Watt continued: "Kawasoe's trip to Edinburgh in 1984 coincided with Scottish Shotokan Centres' students taking part in the Edinburgh Festival Opening Parade along Princess Street. In an article of the time we learn the following: 'In the parade, the karate contingent, comprised of club members from Edinburgh, Aberdeen, Stirling and Coatbridge, was received with a mixture of enthusiasm and curiosity as they performed basic movements along the route. Some of the

Watt, Kawasoe and Paul Allan at Kawasoe's wedding (23rd June 1980). Watt recalled: 'I did a side-kick after getting out of the car and split my suit trousers beyond repair; I had to wear jeans with my suit jacket' (1980).

higher grades followed behind the main contingent entertaining the crowd with a display of karate techniques.'[58]

Watt continued: "In fact, we'd been part of the Edinburgh Festival Parade the year before and we marched behind a large SSC banner, punching as we went.

Typical details for an SSC Kawasoe course (1984)

"In October 1984, I held a four-way goodwill match between the SSC Aberdeen, SSKA Edinburgh, Kawasoe's Earls Court club, London, and, Kenny Taylor's Tora Kai Karate Club, Glasgow. The matches were held at Champers Nighclub, Aberdeen, and Aberdeen won." Watt noted at the time, 'the result, however, was secondary as the whole weekend was aimed at consolidating links between the

Watt (left) sparring with Kawasoe – Aberdeen (early to mid 1980s)

various clubs.'[59] There was free training that weekend under Kawasoe.

Watt continued: "On one of my Aberdeen courses, a student from Norway came up to me and said that he thought that his instructor in Stavanger, on the west coast, might be interested in me going over to train at his *dojo*. This man's instructor turned out to be none other than Egon Solem, a 5th Dan in Sanku-kai and Nambudo, who was thinking of changing styles[60, 61, 62] and I was, indeed, invited over for a week.[63]

"There was quite a bit of interest in my trip as Stavanger is a sister city of Aberdeen and we both share North Sea oil. Stavanger is known as the Petroleum Capital of Norway and both cities experienced unprecedented growth as a consequence of the oil boom. Grampian Television sent down a reporter and film crew and they came to my *dojo* before I left on my trip. They interviewed me and shot some film footage.[64]

"Solem, who was the senior grade in that area, invited me back a

A moment of relaxation as Watt fishes with Knut Helge Nordbotn, near Bergen.

second time and I went north to Bergen, the birthplace of the composer, Edvard Greig, to the *dojo* of Knut Helge Nordbotn.[65] The Bergen *dojo* was amazing, for it was located in a bunker in the side of a mountain that had been used for storing weapons in during World War II. In fact, the *dojo* was in the cave system. The training was difficult because the air conditioning wasn't very good and the air was really sticky. Water was literally running down the walls.

"All in all, I helped in 'five hundred students changing to the Shotokan style.'[66] The Norwegians were really tall, big men, Vikings, and the training was good, spirited.

"Another *karateka*, Alf Ronny Fagerland, from Karmoy [also known as Karm] Island, had a *dojo* on the island that he established in 1982, and another at Haugesund named the Sentrum Karateklubb[67], which he set up later [1996] and I taught at both. We got from the mainland to Karmoy by the Karmsundbridge and the island quite surprised me because there are some lovely sandy beaches, just like at Aberdeen, and I hadn't expected that in Norway. Fagerland invited me to teach at a three-day course last November [2008] at the Haugesund Karate Festival, Skaaredalhallen. Fagerland is now a 4th Dan and Chief Instructor of the National Karate Federation Norway.

"I also travelled to Sauda, in Rogaland. It was a two or three hour boat trip up Saudafjorden to Sauda and the scenery was spectacular. It

Watt, left, coaches Norwegian team member, Geir Larson, on the beach on the Black Sea, Bulgaria (1983/84).

was because of the waterfalls that there is a large smelting works at Sauda, which I later discovered was Europe's largest, and I found that there was a lack of oxygen in the air that made breathing difficult, or at least that is how it seemed to me. Fagerland is now independent politically, like me.

"I also trained with Geir Arlid Larsen, who is the top man for the JKA in Norway. There's a picture of me sparring with Larsen in Bulgaria, by the Black Sea, when we went there in 1983.[68]

"I went over to Norway for about three years, 1981–1984, and I introduced Enoeda to them. I took him over and a television company came to the Stavanger club and asked him to do a demonstration and he said, 'No! He will!' and pointed at me. Actually, they filmed Enoeda doing some press-ups on his knuckles and I did a display with Nordbotn – swept him, kicked him, and then did interviews.

"I went to Norway with Kawasoe[69] too, who'd been going over there teaching for about ten years, and I remember on one occasion we were training in the *dojo* and there was a festival going on outside. Fair enough, but then a topless maiden walked past the window as part of a procession and that diverted our attention from training for a while!

"It was in Norway that Kawasoe punched me twice, then a third time. I said to him that he must have really meant that last punch. He looked genuinely mystified and replied that it had been the same as the

Egon Solem (left) with Kawasoe and Watt at the Stavanger *dojo* (1984)

previous two. But something was different. Boy, did I feel that technique.[70]

"I think it was on that trip that I gave a speech saying that at one time, in the age of the Vikings, Norway and Scotland had fought each other. I commented on the Norwegian fighting spirit, their heritage, and how it was similar to our own, and that now we had come together

Kawasoe and Watt during a light-hearted moment in Norway

in a martial art to learn Shotokan. The speech seemed to go down well.

"[On the 15th May 1983], we hosted an international competition at the Scottish Shotokan Karate Centres, when I invited Solem over to Aberdeen. A party of twelve arrived and stayed for five days. I had organised a civic reception with the Lord Provost, who was still

Alexander Collie, at Aberdeen's Town House. Solem and his students trained with me around my *dojos* – Edinburgh, Stirling, Coatbridge and Banff. We then had a competition at the Altens Skean Dhu which we won 9-6, against very good competitors.[71]

"A return match was held in Stavanger in October.[73, 73] The five man team I picked was: Ian Ord, Alan Simpson, John Main, Ian Still and David Bremner. Unfortunately, Bremner couldn't go because he was best man at a wedding[74], so a replacement was sought. It was actually a triangular competition with Norway and Denmark. The Norwegians had the Nordic champion in their squad and the all-styles Danish team were the Danish champions of 1982, and SSC beat them both. Ian Still beat the Nordic champion. We were given a civic reception by the Mayor of Stavanger[75] and it was a most enjoyable trip. Frank Gilfeather of Grampian Television covered the trip.

"[On the 12th September] 1985, the SSC hosted another Scotland versus Norway competition at Summerhill Academy and Enoeda and Tsuyama acted as chief judges.[76]

"Then Enoeda and I went over to Bergen, Norway's second largest city, in December [10th-13th] 1986[77], but Enoeda started dealing with the Norwegians directly. At this point my job in Norway was over. I've found this idea of coming in and taking over to be a common feature in karate and I don't like it. Some people apparently don't appreciate what has to be done to get something up and running and they come along and, because of their seniority, bulldoze their way in. Then again, perhaps they do know. You work really hard to get something established and then it's gone. In all, I organised eight major courses in Norway. I'm delighted to say that I am now back working with my friend, Fagerland, and his fantastic NKF Norway.

"My third trip to Japan occurred in August 1984 and was for two weeks duration. Kawasoe organised the trip and Steve Cattle, Kenny Taylor, Lee Smith and a chap called Jim – I don't recall his surname – and I, went. Tokyo was really hot and the humidity draining. We trained at the JKA *honbu*, at 2-11-4, Ebisunishi, Shibuyaku, where we were taught by Osaka and Omura. I saw Omura and Osaka freestyle. That was something special. Omura was a handful and Osaka moved up a few gears to deal with him, something not many people could have done.

"I recall that Cattle and I were practising the *Heian* and *Tekki kata* one day taking it in turns to have the other on our backs. That was really hard training and probably bad for the knees. This was just Steve and I, and when Omura came in he gave us a look as if to say, 'Idiots!'

Watt standing outside the JKA headquarters, Tokyo (1984)

"I remember sparring with Cattle at the JKA *honbu* and Kon was encouraging me from the side of the *dojo*, 'Come on Ronnie; come on!'

"We trained with Asai that time and he took us for *Nijushiho*. He

Watt and Cattle inside the JKA *honbu* (1984)

Akita, Watt and Cattle (1984)

was a brilliant *karateka*, very flexible, and his style, which was unique, reminded me of a large cat, such as a panther. I also remember his very smart Tony Curtis style haircut!

204

"I also met Masahiko Tanaka[78] again, though I didn't have a chance to train with him, but I did see him instructing some JKA seniors. I'd actually met Tanaka in Japan in 1977 and at Crystal Palace too, when I had been given the job of going to his room and collecting him and bringing him down to give a display before the KUGB finals. He signed a poster I had, 'Tanaka Karate-Do.' I'd also met him in Germany, when he was coaching the Swedish team.

"Our party then travelled down to Kyoto by train and practised under Katsuhiro Tsuyama, 8th Dan JKA, that's Katsunori's younger brother, who wore a moustache, before travelling on to Gifu where we trained with Kato, and I must say again that this is not the Sadashige Kato who used to visit my *dojo* and who organised my first trip to Japan. In Gifu we met Tabata, Kon and Tomita. We went sightseeing in the mountains and were roped into Japanese dancing. Kon put on a firework display for us.[79] Later, in 2002 to be precise, I spent a bit of time with Katsuhiro when he visited Ochi in Germany and we all went sight-seeing together.

"Kawasoe took us to train at Nakayama's Hoitsugan *dojo*.[80] I learned that the name 'Hoitsugan' was given to the *dojo* by Nakayama after his time in China. It was, apparently, the name of the first hotel he stayed in when he went there in the 1930s and the name means, 'where people come together with a shared aim.'[81]

"I felt that the old master looked quite frail at the time. He had a small office and he had kept some of the things people had given him on his visits or that he'd bought as souvenirs. These were often little iconic items, like a Dinky Toy London Bus and a model of the Eiffel Tower. That quite surprised me to be truthful, it showed a different side of the man, and I really liked that. He remembered me from his visit to Aberdeen in 1981 and gave members of the party some much appreciated refreshing melon to eat. He wanted to talk to me, but, as a party, we had to keep to a schedule and we'd been invited to go somewhere else and so I was whisked off. That was the last time I saw him before he died. I very much regret hurrying away like that because I'll never know now what he wanted to say to me.

"In [October] 1984, I was asked to write to the Home Office in support of Ohta's work permit. This I was pleased to do and I spent considerable time and thought on it."

Watt's letter has survived, dated the 3rd October 1984, and in it he noted: 'It is essential for my development of the art and consequently that of my pupils that the very best possible instructors are engaged. While the sport has developed greatly in recent years in this country,

Kawasoe and Nakayama in Tokyo (1984)

the simple fact of the matter is that we are still 'novices' in comparison to the Japanese and persons such as Mr. Ohta are vital to the advancement of the sport in the UK at this time.'

In fact, Ohta did leave Great Britain in 1987 to be replaced for a brief period by Yuji Hashiguchi, 4th Dan.

Watt continued: "In 1985, the press got hold of a story about Sean Connery coming up to visit the SSC. They asked me about it[82] and I told them that Enoeda had appeared at the beginning of the Bond film, *Diamonds Are Forever*, and, I believed, both belonged to the same golf club. A mutual friend had apparently mentioned me and the SSC and Connery, who supports things Scottish, apparently had said that he'd be pleased to pay us a visit. However, I'd heard nothing official. Ironically, the piece appeared on April Fool's Day and he never did come, though 'we still hope he can make it privately some time in the not too distant future.'[83] The character of James Bond, brilliantly played by Connery, really did start things rolling on the martial arts front in Scotland, and it would be nice if he could pay us a visit to see how things had developed.

"The 1985 KUGB *gasshuku* [29th April–10th May] was under the direction of Enoeda, Kase, Shirai and Tabata, along with the Japanese instructors resident in Britain.[84] It may have been that year, I can't remember, that Kase gave the black-belts, 3rd Dans and above, if I recall correctly, a very intensive course practising *kumite*. We'd been practising *kata* all week, but on both the normal and other sides, which was Kase's idea. I had prepared all week for this, I knew it was coming, but it is so mentally exhausting under pressure, because you have to think about what the next move is and then perform it on the other side. I recall Frank Brennan saying to me as we went to get changed that he thought that was a hard session. If athletes of that high calibre say that kind of thing, then you know your training close to the limit.

"Tabata had come to assist Enoeda at the KUGB Championships for many years. He was very tall for a Japanese, over six feet[85], but he was surprisingly quick and versatile for a man of his size. I sparred with him once when he paired-up with me as I had no partner. He had a fantastically fast *gyaku-zuki* and his *ashi-barai* was awesome. I really enjoyed his classes. I remember him teaching *Sochin*. He liked the front foot straight in *fudo-dachi* and not slightly turned in. I was very sorry to hear about his strange death.[86] I've always believed that he was a very kind man and this intent did come across in his excellent instruction.

"In 1986, I took 'around sixty pupils'[66] to the KUGB *gasshuku* [28th April–9th May] which was run by Enoeda, Kawasoe and Ohta, with Kase and Shirai flying in. In 1986, Enoeda was 'arranging to come to the club ten times during the year,'[66] but it didn't happen.

"The SSC was still performing demonstrations, and the one I remember from 1986 was the Festival of Martial Arts in Edinburgh that Do-Su, a martial arts' shop, presented. There were displays of kendo, taekwondo, wing chun, muay thai, wu-chia, pencak silat, tai chi, Okinawan weaponry, ju-jitsu, wushu and karate.[87]

"The SSC was going well and it had been decided to split the clubs into sections: North – John Cox; Central – Mike Bissett; West – Heather Houston; and, East – Ray Morgan. All these members were 3rd Dan JKA.[88]

"Around the mid 1980s I was beginning to seriously doubt whether the KUGB was still right for me. I was no longer comfortable about the regional status, when we were a country. Other Scottish *karateka*,

Front row, left to right, Ohta, Enoeda, Tsuyama and Watt, at an Aberdeen KUGB regional course (mid 1980s).

some junior to me, were doing their own thing and not being dictated to. I also wanted to compete with the SKBC, which had been established in 1973, and be involved in that. I understood that I could never compete for the SKBC because, although I was Scottish, I was in, what was effectively seen as an English karate group. I had been toying with the idea of resigning from the KUGB for some time, but what really sealed it was something that happened to me at a *gasshuku* that confirmed that it appeared I was not going to be allowed to grow in the way that I wanted. I don't want to talk about this episode for there are two sides to every story, so let me simply say that, after some twenty years, having experienced something I didn't like, I felt that I could no longer continue in the same manner. However, I'd invested so much emotional energy in the exercise that the whole incident made me ill. I came home from the course and shortly afterwards had a nervous reaction to all the stress. It was psychological and I felt very sad, extremely low, for a long time, more than a year.

"I wanted to join another group, but it was blocked for what I saw as political reasons and Enoeda didn't come up for about six months. Then he returned with Ohta, twice I think, and Enoeda tried to get me back into the KUGB, but I wasn't interested. He told me I wasn't liked and that if I wanted to train with him, because he wouldn't be able to

Watt by his (covered) *makiwara* in Sycamore Place

come to Aberdeen again, that I should go to Edinburgh and train as a guest. I believe that Enoeda was sympathetic to my cause and he helped me get Kase and Shirai up to Aberdeen, as I've said. I remember a long walk the two of us had after training at Jim Wood's club. Enoeda invited me down to London so that we could discuss the problem in-depth. I was still friendly with many of the senior grades in the KUGB, but I felt that my path lay in a different direction. I stopped competing in karate at this time. I was in my late thirties and I'd been in competition for twenty years – the last ten or so of which had been at a high level.

"In Scotland, there were the Dempseys in Dundee, as I've mentioned, and the KUS North; Danny Bryceland, Alex Macgregor and Kenny Taylor were in Glasgow, and the KUS South. Enoeda would visit groups as a JKA instructor because they were JKA, just like the KUGB, at the time, was JKA. Then there were the SKI groups and I didn't want to get involved at all. I was in Aberdeen, miles north, quite literally stuck out on a limb. I was sick of the politics and the worry. I had to go and see a solicitor about my political dilemma. It was a nightmare. All I wanted to do was train and teach, and yet there was all this pressure. There was a lot of correspondence flying about at this time[89] and I decided that I'd had enough, so I made my mind up to do my own thing. I wanted to be independent. I didn't want to be a lackey to anyone nor a clone of the JKA. I simply felt that there was no soul in what I was doing under their direction. Strange things were beginning to happen that made me feel uncomfortable. For example, although this is certainly not the reason why I left the KUGB, I was on a course and I was sparring with Kawasoe. Enoeda shouted over to me above the background noise. Everybody looked up and he asked me to put the lights on. That's fair enough, but why couldn't he have waited until the sparring was over. Better still, why didn't he ask someone standing by the light switch? I felt that it was a belittling act, a deliberate put-down, and I didn't like it because I hadn't done anything to deserve it.

"I remember when I was training at a KUGB *gasshuku* and I had been invited out to dine with Enoeda, Kase and Shirai, at a Japanese restaurant that Enoeda really liked, and that I'd been to before. I got to their hotel in good time, but as I arrived I saw the three of them get into a taxi. Why hadn't they waited until the agreed time? I could have called out but I didn't, because I thought that it would have been rude. So I just stood there and watched the taxi drive away. I felt low and decided to forego the meal and went off to train with Kawasoe instead. The next day, Enoeda asked me what had happened and I explained the sequence and what I had done. He didn't like that at all and I got the distinct impression that I had not been asked out for personal or karate reasons, but for business reasons. I brought a lot of students down to the *gasshukus* with me and I invited the Japanese up to my *dojos* for courses that were well attended. I used to go on nearly all the courses, but I missed one and Enoeda asked me where I had been. I explained that I had been to Japan. He didn't like that either and if looks could have killed! He asked me why I had gone and I told him I went there to train.

"'Just to train?' he asked.

"'*Oss*,' I replied, which was the truth. I didn't realise until afterwards that the poison of politics was afoot.

Too fast for Enoeda! Watt attacks Enoeda with an *oi-zuki* and catches him at the Grampian Television studios (1980s) – and then wished he hadn't!

"I had intended going to the 1987 KUGB *gasshuku* at Crystal Palace that Nakayama was to attend, but he died less than two weeks beforehand.[90] He was going to teach at the course for a week and fly up to Scotland at the weekend and then fly back to London for the

Kawasoe at the Edinburgh *dojo* (28th February 1988)

second week. Jim Wood and I organised the three-hour course, between 5.00 p.m. and 8.00 p.m., which was to include Enoeda, Tsuyama and Tabata, for the 2nd May, at the Wester Hailes Education Centre in Edinburgh. We had a course booklet published and were really looking forward to seeing Nakayama in Scotland once more.[91]

"The last KUGB *gasshuku* I attended was in 1987 [27th April – 8th May], I believe. The Japanese instructors were the same as the previous year, and Tabata was there as well.

"Kawasoe came up to the *dojos* in Aberdeen, Stirling and Edinburgh in November 1987, I think[92], and again at the beginning of 1988. There was talk about a JKA Scotland under Kawasoe being formed, but I'm not sure what happened.[93] I asked one of my senior students, John Ritchie, to go to London to discuss the prospect of us joining a JKA Scotland Number 2, as it were, with Kawasoe. I then arranged for Kawasoe to come up to Aberdeen and had several hundred people attending, but he was unable to and so we missed both the training and the grading. I didn't blame Kawasoe for this in any way; I understand that he was blocked by Enoeda. I spoke to Enoeda on the telephone a couple of times.

"'It is a long time we have been together – no?' Enoeda said, but the atmosphere was very sour. I felt that loyalty is one thing, but to be used is another. It was the end of an era for me. But, you know, even now, more than twenty years down the line, I sometimes have vivid dreams about Enoeda. He is powerful, as always, and he and I are still friends. But I have to be honest and say that I found him to be a political player, and, perhaps, a businessman first, but it cannot be denied that he was a major influence on the British karate movement.

"When I finally decided to leave the KUGB, Paul Allan elected to stay with them. He had a club at Huntly and became their regional secretary. He started running courses[94] with Bob Rhodes and Billy Higgins. Paul lives in Ireland now. We are still friends."

IV

THE KASE AND SHIRAI YEARS

W att continued: "Around this time, 1988–1989, Kase and Shirai split from the JKA and formed the World Karate Shotokan Academy. I liked Kase and Shirai both as *karateka* and as men. Their styles were very much Ying and Yang, and they complemented each other beautifully. Kase was what I have always imagined Yoshitaka Funakoshi's karate to be like, deep *fudo-dachis*, and Shirai was the perfect example of the Shotokan stylist. In my mind I like to see myself move the way Shirai does." Watt noted at the time that he saw these men as 'a constant model to any aspiring *karateka* in both karate technique and mental approach.'[1]"

If numbers are to be believed, the fragmenting that took place in the JKA after the death of Nakayama saw Kase and Shirai's association grow so that there were 'fifty-four countries in WKSA and nine hundred thousand members worldwide.'[2] However, these figures seem, at least to the author, somewhat incredulous.

Watt continued: "I'd been with Enoeda a long time and the split, and what caused it, adversely affected my health again. I was brittle to tell you the truth. But Kase and Shirai understood my position and were very supportive and I shall always thank them for that. Whereas in the past I felt that I was striving to achieve my best and such advancement was being blocked – either that, or my best was never good enough – now I saw a new horizon. I was tired of running into goal posts when you thought you knew where the posts were, because, suddenly, they'd been moved. When you've done everything you can and it is thrown in your face, what do you do? I'll tell you how I felt. It was as if I'd been training as an athlete for twenty years, building up to the Olympic Games, then, having been chosen to represent my county, was told by some bureaucrat that I couldn't compete because of political reasons.

"Prior to this problem, SSC student numbers was good [in 1986 the SSC was 'bulging the five hundred mark'[3]], but I started losing members when these problems occurred. I began to practise karate more by myself during this dark time. Then, slowly, I began to regain my confidence and started to rebuild my clubs up again.

"In 1988, John Cox – whose a 5th Dan now and one of the best fighters I ever had – accompanied me on a flight over to Paris, direct from Aberdeen, to train with Kase and Shirai on a weekend instructors' course. I remember the pictures of Gichin Funakoshi, Yoshitaka Funakoshi and Nakayama, framed in Kase's *dojo*. Kase would often talk about how good Yoshitaka had been and he definitely aligned himself to that type of training. It was his speciality, because he was one of the few *karateka* still alive who had actually trained at the Shotokan *dojo*.[4]"

Kase began his study of karate during World War II at the Shotokan *dojo*, situated in Zoshigaya, Toshima Ward, Tokyo. The Shotokan was the first purpose-built karate *dojo* in Japan, with the inauguration ceremony being held on the 29th July 1939, and it is from this building that the style of karate gets its name. Gichin Funakoshi and his third and youngest son, Yoshitaka, along with his son's wife and child(ren), lived in the adjoining house.

Yoshitaka Funakoshi was born on Okinawa in 1906 and trained under one of his father's principal teachers, Yasutsune Itosu [the other being Yasutsune Azato], on Okinawa. He followed his father to Tokyo and after the premature death of Takeshi Shimoda, from pneumonia, in 1934, he became his father's assistant, instructing at the Shotokan and at various universities. Having suffered tuberculosis from an early age, Yoshitaka died in November 1945, shortly after American bombing destroyed the Shotokan. An extremely dynamic *karateka*, his importance, though often overlooked today, is very considerable.[5]

Kase noted: 'When I started in karate I chose to follow Yoshitaka Funakoshi's way. I have now gone back to teaching this way to advanced students . . . I think now we are looking for original Shotokan from 1944/45. This is when Shotokan reached its maximum. This was training for Budo, for your whole life.'[6]

Watt continued: "There were some good karate people on that course, like Alain Verbeeck from France and Dirk Heene from Belgium. I'd seen Heene before, in Tokyo, at the 1977 World Championships, when he was in the Belgian team. Paris was a great experience and we trained in both the morning and the afternoon.

"Kase invited John and I back to his flat in the rue Jean Jaurès, Vanves, that first evening, for dinner. That was a very special occasion as you can imagine. It was a lovely meal. We started with a salad and then had rice and prawns. It was typical Japanese food and beautifully prepared by Kase's wife, Cheiko. Shirai was there as was his assistant,

Kase, in *fudo-dachi*, prepares to deliver a *shuto-uchi* (1989/90)

Takashi Naito. Naito, who had been a good competitor, being placed in the JKA championships, had appeared in Nakayama's, *Best Karate: Kumite 1*, partnering Mikio Yahara.[7] I think Naito had taught in the Middle-East – Iran, I believe – before going to Italy.

"Kase's apartment wasn't like I had imagined at all. I had this vision of someone who, being world famous and teaching large

From left to right: John Cox, Shirai, Kase, Naito and Watt at Kase's Paris apartment (1989).

numbers of students, would be wealthy, but his flat was quite simple. He was so good at karate that he'd gone beyond money.

"As John and I were strangers in Paris, at the end of the evening Kase asked Shirai and Naito to take us back to our hotel, which they were kind enough to do.

"The second night we were there we went out to see the sights of Paris, and I remember our trips to the Moulin Rouge to see the Can-Can dancing and a visit to Louis XIV's Palace.

"Not that long after Paris, still in 1988, Kase and Shirai invited me to the first WKSA instructors' course held in Hasselt, Belgium. It may have been there, I can't remember, that Kase introduced me, properly, to the *Ten no Kata*. He showed us the sequence once, and then each instructor had to stand in front of the class of instructors and lead the group. It was quite scary actually. I got mine over and done with early on, and Kase said, 'Good.' I think the *Ten no Kata* is excellent training. It speeds everything up and makes the focus sharper. I believe it was Kase who said that Yoshitaka and Motonobu Hironishi devised it, but I'm not sure and maybe that's why Kase was so fond of it. Anyway, I still like to practise the *Ten no Kata* and would recommend it for beginner and advanced grades alike."

According to Hironishi, in the preface of the 1988 edition of Gichin

Funakoshi's, *Karate-Do Nyūmon*, the *Ten no Kata* were 'created and designed under the leadership and guidance of Master Funakoshi.'[8] So, Hironishi makes it pretty clear that Funakoshi did not actually devise the form (which might be more correctly defined as a sequence). Certainly, when Funakoshi wrote in his *Karate-Do Kyohan*, that, *Taikyoku* and the *Ten no Kata* were 'the product of my many years of research into the art of karate,'[9] he makes no direct reference to having devised it. As Kase told Watt, Yoshitaka and Hironishi designed the form under Funakoshi's direction. As we have seen in the References and Notes to the last chapter, Yoshitaka and Miyata are to be seen in the 1941 pamphlet showing the *Ten no Kata*. Whoever was the main player in its design is actually not too important, for the *kata* certainly had Funakoshi's full support, for he wrote that it should be 'assiduously studied.'[10]

In the 1941 version of the *Ten no Kata*, with Miyata, *fudo-dachi* is shown. The 1943 version of *Karate-Do Nyumon* shows *fudo-dachi* being employed, yet in the 1988 version front-stance is referred to. Ernest Harrison in his 1959, *Manual of Karate*, using two earlier Japanese sources, gives *zenkutsu-dachi*. The question is, did *zenkutsu-dachi* replace *fudo-dachi*? Whereas Ohshima appears to employ *fudo-dachi* in the third, 1973 edition of *Karate-Do Kyohan*, the single photograph contained within it (page 34) showing a move from the *Ten no Kata* performed by Egami in the rare second, 1958 edition of the book, is unclear, in that Egami could be in either stance. The question of stance is relevant because Kase favoured *fudo-dachi*.

Watt continued: "The *Ten no Kata* is actually in two parts, *omote* and *ura*; *omote* is practised by oneself and *ura* is practised with an opponent. In *omote* there are twenty movement sets, split half on the left side and half on the right side, each performed from either *hachiji-dachi* or *heiko-dachi* as a preparatory position. There are eight punches moving a step forward, both *oi-zuki* and *gyaku-zuki*, at *chudan* and *jodan* level. The remaining twelve movement sets involve single units stepping backwards, blocking, followed by counter-punches/*nukites*.

"The *ura* element involves putting the last twelve sequences of the *omote* element into operation. The practice is, therefore, like defending in *ippon-kumite* twelve times.

"But what Funakoshi describes in his book is for beginners and Kase took it much further. Kase preferred to perform the *zenkutsu-dachis* as *fudo-dachis*. Actually, I don't think Funakoshi included the *fudo-dachi* in his book, but the 1973 edition, translated by Tsutomu Ohshima, does, and Ohshima uses this stance when blocking and countering too. Although Kase preferred *fudo-dachi*, he sometimes blocked in *fudo-dachi* and countered in *zenkutsu-dachi*.

"Kase would talk about the importance of *tai-sabaki* and *maai* when performing the *Ten non Kata*. Whereas in Funakoshi's basic version students would step only forwards and backwards in the form, Kase would ask his class to step back at forty-five degrees when blocking as well. The counter would always be determined by *maai* and this was partially governed by *tai-sabaki*. We could counter *gyaku-zuki*, or, if the distancing wasn't quite correct because our *tai-sabaki* or *maai* were slightly out, we could slide in, *yori-ashi* style, and counter with the reverse punch. If the distance between the attacker and defender became greater than the *yori-ashi* would allow for, then he would teach *kae-ashi*, which is, basically, where the defender steps forward a half step and punches. If the gap between the two parties was significant, then we could use what Kase termed, *tusugi-ashi*, where, after being blocked, the attacker would withdraw before a counter could be delivered, and the defender would, if the left leg was forward, advance the right foot to the left foot then advance the left foot forward and counter *gyaku-zuki*. If the attacker was much faster retreating, or, the defender was much slower in countering, then Kase would ask the defender to step forward with an *oi-zuki*. Kase was interested in space, timing and distancing, all of which are inter-linked."

Kase and Shirai are advertised in course literature for the 1988 KUGB *gasshuku* (2nd May–13th May). Apart from Enoeda, Kawasoe and Ohta, Tabata, Tanaka and Yahara were also expected. The same eight instructors are to be seen in an advertisement for the 1989 *gasshuku* held between 1st May–12th May. Whether Kase and Shirai attended this course is unknown, but they are not named in the 1989 special September course, which featured Ueki and Tanaka instead. Details on the KUGB's 1990 *gasshuku* (30th April–11th May) show that Kase and Shirai are no longer featured, but Miyazaki, Tanaka and Yahara are present. Likewise, a special KUGB karate course during the first week in September 1990 shows that Tsuyama and Tabata were the visiting instructors.

Watt continued: "I had actually taken the first part of my *Godan* [5th Dan] grading at Crystal Palace under Enoeda, Kase and Shirai in May, 1987. I went back on the next course because I liked training with Kase and Shirai, but I did not grade. Kase and Shirai asked me to do it as I had done so well on the first part. As I've said, circumstances were really very difficult. As I was not one hundred per cent, I said that

I would do it again some time in the not too distant future. However, as I've explained, I left the KUGB in the meantime.

"Shirai and Kase started to come to Aberdeen for me, and it was during one of these that I graded to 5th Dan at the Northfield Academy. Kase signed the grade. The grading was ratified by Danny Bryceland for the SKBC and Barney Whelan. Then, Shirai and Barney Whelan presented me [on the 19th September 1988] with my World Union of Karate Organisation certificate, signed by Jacques Delcourt, Chairman of WUKO, at Powis Academy Assembly Hall. Kase and Shirai were both very disappointed that I had not been able to achieve this at Crystal Palace. The World Shotokan Karate Academy Dan certificates and licences had not been printed at this stage. Kase and Shirai showed me a copy of the new Dan diploma they had designed for their new association and they were soon to have them printed in Japan on special paper. Kase also awarded me the position of kyu and Dan grading examiner in 1991 for WKSA. With the KUGB under Enoeda, I had not been allowed to grade 9th kyu! Kase and Shirai both said they had never heard of so high a grade in Europe not being able to grade a white belt and now I could grade to 2nd Dan.[11] Kase and Shirai allowed me to have an official stamp for my gradings. This decision gave me a great sense of relief, because I was no longer at the mercy and vagaries of other people. I was now in control of what I was doing. I will always thank Kase and Shirai for giving me that.

"Shirai had developed a fantastic Dan grading syllabus, really well thought out, and I practised this with my students assiduously. It wouldn't be fair of me to give details of this syllabus, because it wasn't designed by me.

"The *kata* I chose for 5th Dan was *Meikyo*, because Kase liked it. I thought that if Kase thought that I'd performed it well enough then that was good enough for me. Instead of *zenkutsu-dachi*, he performed *fudo-dachi* and his *kata* had only one *kiai*, on the jump. I also had to write a short report on the form, explaining the *bunkai*. There are a number of variations of this *kata*. For example most *karateka* in my experience perform *gedan-barai/oi-zuki*, then, *gedan-barai/oi-zuki*, on the first and second sets of diagonal movements and then *uchi-ude-uke/oi-zuki*, followed by, *uchi-ude-uke/oi-zuki*, for the third set. This is how Kase performed it when he came to Aberdeen.[12] Kanazawa performs the first set of diagonal moves the same, the second set as *uchi-ude-uke/oi-zuki* and the third set as *age-uke/oi-zuki, age-uke/oi-zuki*.[13]

"I'd been in the KUGB virtually since I'd started karate and despite

Watt's WUKO 5th Dan

Shirai and Barney Whelan of the Scottish Karate Board of Control present Watt with his WUKO 5th Dan (1988).

having a 5th Dan from Kase, I needed to ensure my political position was secure as well. I asked Barney Whelan, who was Chairman of the SKBC, the British Karate Federation, and the Martial arts Commission, to write me a note to say that my qualifications were *bona fide*, and this he was kind enough to do."

A copy of the note exists. Dated the 29th September 1988, written on SKBC headed paper and addressed to 'Whom it May Concern', Whelan wrote:

'I have to advise that all qualifications held by Mr. Ronnie Watt 5th Dan, are recognised by the Scottish Karate Board of Control and through them the British Karate Federation, the Martial Arts Commission and the World Union of Karate Organisations. Anyone requiring further information regarding the standing of Mr. Watt in karate in Britain, should contact B. Whelan, Chairman.'

Watt continued: "When I first had Kase to Aberdeen under these new arrangements, I think a few students who hadn't trained with him before thought to themselves, 'Who is this little guy.' Kase was not tall, about five feet two inches, not supple, and he was pretty rotund, so it was easy to get the wrong impression. I think he sensed this and he asked me to attack him. I charged in and he hit me, with control I might add, but I flew back some fourteen feet into the wall. On another occasion, he hit me under the rib cage, not hard, not deliberately, and I experienced a type of discomfort that I'd never had before. It was weird; it's hard to put into words. Kase could release *kime* at any point on a punch – two inches from his body or two feet, it made no difference. After being hit like that I thought to myself, 'That's it, I've got three months to live. He's given me a delayed death touch!' A few days later a large bruise appeared on my back where the blow had gone through, but I was worried for a while.

"One strange feature about Kase was that sometimes he looked very small and at other times he appeared much larger. I've never been able to work out why that was.

"[From the 7th–10th September 1989], Andy Murdoch of the Scottish Amateur Shotokan Federation and I got both Kase and Shirai over for courses in Wishaw[14, 15] and Aberdeen, in that order, and they spent the last two days with me. Andy's a very good friend of mine and he'd had Enoeda and other Japanese to his *dojo* in the past. In Aberdeen, we trained on the Saturday and Sunday mornings and afternoons at St. Machar Academy. Dan and kyu gradings were also held.[16] We had guests from Norway, France and Belgium over too." As

Shirai demonstrating a clasping block on Watt (18th November 1988)

Shirai demonstrates *tsukami dori mae-geri* from the *kata Kanku-sho* on Watt (18th November 1988).

Shirai demonstrates *morote enshin haito barai* from the *kata Chinte* (18th November 1988).

Shirai in the process of delivering a *yoko-geri kekomi on* Watt (18th November 1988).

Kase and Watt enjoying an evening out at Ferry Hill (4th March 1989)

a report at the time noted: 'On Sunday evening, *Sensei* Shirai and *Sensei* Kase cooked a special Japanese meal in *Sensei* Watt's house.'[1]

Watt continued: "I recall at this time that we went out for dinner and both Shirai and Kase wore kilts as it was St. Andrew's Night.[17] I also organised for pipers, highland dancers and a folk singer to be present, ['and, of course, a first-class meal with haggis as a starter'[15]] and I think that I can truthfully say that a merry time was had by all.

"It was at this time [1989] that Kase graded one of my youngest students to black belt at St. Machar Academy. The young man in question was Christopher Fowler and he was only thirteen at the time.[18] Unfortunately, like many children, he stopped training with me about a year later. Kase and Shirai had no objection to teaching children and there is a nice picture of Kase being punched in the throat by six-year-old Kelly Bissett.[19] Similarly, like me[20, 21], the two Japanese had no problem whatsoever teaching women.

"I've always encouraged youngsters to take up karate, as long as they are serious about wanting to learn and have sufficient attention span. Fowler was a fine example of this, but there were others. Simon Munro was recorded as the youngest black belt holder in Scotland by the press when he achieved 1st Dan at the age of ten. He was awarded his black belt after a grading in Manchester. He was exceptional and was tipped to be a future champion." Watt was quoted at the time as

Shirai in kilt (September 1989)

saying: 'He is dedicated and has extraordinary speed and technique for one so young,'[22] and, 'Simon is brilliant. In fact I would go as far as to say that he is as good as any Japanese student of his age.'[23] Watt continued: "I don't know what happened to Simon. Matthew Grindlay was another real hopeful.[24]

"At the end of the 1980s, Murdoch and I formed the Scottish

Kase, Shirai and Watt in kilts (1989)

Kase and Watt (1989)

Shotokan Karate Centres Association. Andy is a very honest person. I found I could trust him one hundred per cent. He is a family man, and Janet, his wife, and their children all practise karate. Andy is a good friend, who, like me, loves traditional training, and is a hard mentor who takes his karate seriously. He holds the rank of 5th Dan today.

"In 1989, the technical committee of the SSKCA decided to change the kyu belt system to: 9th kyu – red; 8th kyu – yellow; 7th kyu – orange; 6th kyu –green; 5th kyu –green; 4th kyu – purple/blue; 3rd kyu – purple/blue; 2nd kyu – brown; and, 1st kyu – brown. Where the grade changed but the belt colour remained unchanged, a white tab could be worn. The timescale between 2nd kyu and 1st gradings was six months, with one endorsement, and twelve months between 1st kyu and 1st Dan, with three endorsements.

"I now lived in Primrosebank Avenue, Cults, just off the A93 to Balmoral, south-east of Aberdeen. The house was larger than my previous home and so it was no trouble for Kase and Shirai to stay with Gail and I. When Kase was a guest, I always had restless nights, odd dreams, as though my mind was being probed. In the morning I'd knock on his bedroom door to tell him breakfast was ready and the bed wouldn't have been slept in and he'd be sitting in a chair. He say things like, 'You got up at 3.30 a.m. to go to the toilet. You make the noise of an elephant!' He would always say that he had fire in his stomach, by which he meant spirit from all the training. He'd be waiting for you to come in; he was on guard. I do something like that too, for I always sit down with my back to a wall; I'm not comfortable with people walking behind me.

"Kase just lived and breathed karate. If we spoke about something else, somehow we'd always get back to the subject of karate. I remember when he was up for a course and he taught both in the morning and the afternoon. I took him back to his hotel and said I'd pick him up later to go out for a meal. I was exhausted. I went home, bathed, relaxed for a few hours, and then went back to his hotel. When he answered the door, he was wearing his *gi*, sweating profusely, and all the furniture in the room had been moved to the edges. He'd been training by himself!

"I vividly recall training with him in Aberdeen when an astonishing thing happened. I had a real bout of flu and felt truly awful. I should have been tucked up in bed, but as I'd organised the course, arranged everything, it was essential that I went. The sweat was pouring off me and the training was torturous. Anyway, during a series of basic combinations I couldn't get my breath, I was in trouble, and I

Kase blocks Watt's *oi-zuki* (*c.* 1989)

momentarily sunk down on one knee, nearly out of it. I'll never forget what happened next. Kase, as quick as a flash – he didn't have time to think – rushed over to me and took up a *fudo-dachi*, raised a right-handed *shuto* above his head and his left arm out with the hand in *tate-shuto* and glared at the other black-belts. He was guarding me! Shirai, who was at the other end of the *dojo*, looked up. Kase just stood there, positioned as I have described, until I got back up. He was there for me at my moment of need. No one was going to attack me of course, but Kase never thought like that. I've told you that it was real for him. He was like the samurai standing besides a wounded comrade and would go down fighting, protecting him. From that moment on I knew I could rely on Kase and I knew I'd do the same for him. We were brothers in arms and that incident will remain with me for as long as I live. You can't buy that type of thing; it's worth more than material things.

"I later toured Norway with him for a month and took him to Stavanger and Haugseund and I kid you not, after we'd finished my forearms looked like Popeye's from all the *otoshi-ukes* and *soto-ude-ukes* he'd done on me. The trouble was that when he blocked you it was like being hit by solid stone, really. I couldn't feel flesh, or even bone, he didn't seem to be like a normal person, it was just stone. If he blocked *gedan-barai* in *fudo-dachi* you knew what you were in for. He was a dangerous cookie all right. I couldn't even fasten the buttons of my shirt for some time afterwards, that's how sore my arms and hands were. We got on really well, and he invited me back to Japan and said things like: 'You come; we train sixteen hours a day, six days a week. I hit you, you get back up, and then we can do it again! You can have Sunday off.'

"I'll tell you a funny story that happened on that trip to Norway. We were staying at the parents' house of an instructor, Arild Damm, and the parents were away on holiday. I was sleeping in one room and Kase was in another. A woman, a friend of the parents, had drunk too much and, probably looking for the bathroom in the middle of the night, mistakenly found herself in Kase's room. Suddenly, I heard the noise from the room next door of this woman singing Norwegian songs and I went to investigate. Kase slept on a trigger and there he was standing with his dressing gown on looking at this woman. I thought to myself, 'My god! Of all the bedrooms in Norway to fall into to!' Never has someone been so close to death without realising it! Damm came in, apologised, and swiftly took the woman out.

"Kase would drink with part of his hand over the top of a glass so that if anyone knocked it upwards his own hand would strike his teeth

Watt and Kase in Norway (*c.* 1990)

and shattered glass would be embedded in his hand instead of his face. He'd have his chopsticks ready to use as weapons. This wasn't an act. He came from a different generation of *karateka* that had a very pragmatic approach to martial arts.

"Kase was quite rotund, as I've said, and I'm not saying that he didn't like his food and drink, he did – I recall that he really loved a Chinese red wine – but there was a substantial *hara* there as well. No one unnaturally overweight could possibly have moved with the remarkable speed and precision that he did, especially for a man of his age[25], being in his sixties at the time. True, he never kicked high, but he didn't have to. He was from the old school where, at most, you kicked *chudan*, but mostly *gedan*.

"He liked whisky and he'd have a few tots when he came up to Aberdeen, but he never, ever, let it affect his karate teaching or training; he was too serious a *karateka* for that, too professional.

"He had some wonderful stories to tell. I think he belonged to some strange sect – something to do with goats I was told – that he always visited when he went back to Japan. It struck me as a cult and he would talk about old masters who could mesmerize wolves and light fires with their minds, this sort of thing. I remember him saying that his instructor's instructor had been a warrior monk who shunned society and lived in a cave.

"I remember when we were in a sauna in Norway[26] and he was telling me, in good English, stories that, quite literally, made the hairs stand up on the back of my neck, about when he was young and impressionable and worked as a debt collector and bodyguard for the Yakuza. He also told me that Oyama, as a brown-belt, came to practise with him several times as he wanted to train in Shotokan. Kase said that he was very good, but when Kase turned up the heat when they were sparring, Oyama stopped turning up. Kase said that when he was a 3rd Dan, he practised *Tekki Shodan* everyday for four years as this is what Yoshitaka would have wanted.

"Kase related an encounter he had with a large, black American GI sergeant who challenged him to a fight at an USA Air Force base. The GI was a heavyweight boxer and Kase had no hesitation 'picking up the glove.' Kase said that the GI threw a hook and he ducked beneath it and punched his opponent once, to the torso, and floored him. The GI was then taken to hospital. This impressed the onlookers so much that they began training in karate with Kase.

"Kase had been a naval cadet towards the end of the war and I recall a few stories that he told me about this time. He had actually been on the *Yamato*, one of the Imperial Navy's great battleships, with nine eighteen inch guns and a large array of other weapons, including one hundred and sixty-two anti-aircraft guns. She weighed some seventy thousand tons and her sides were made of steel over forty centimetres thick. She was over two hundred and fifty metres in length and took a crew nearing three thousand. She even carried seven aeroplanes; this was a real fortress. Although there were originally planned to be five ships in her super-battleship class, only three were built. Along with her sister ship, *Musashi*, which was destroyed in 1944, she was the largest battleship ever constructed. She was destroyed [31st August 1945] by American bombing after undertaking a suicide mission during the Battle for Okinawa. The smoke from her rose four miles into the air and could be seen over one hundred miles away. Only one-tenth of her crew survived. It's a fantastic story and I understand the Japanese made a film about her recently [2005] entitled, *Otoko-tachi no Yamato*, but I haven't seen it yet. The third ship, the *Shinano*, was converted into an aircraft carrier before being launched. To the best of my knowledge, she was the shortest commissioned battleship of all time. She sailed out of harbour and within a day she was sunk [29th November 1944] by an American submarine, the *Archer-fish*. I love military history, and so, when Kase mentioned the *Yamato*, my mind went back to the model that Kanazawa and I had launched in the bath something like a quarter of a century before. It's amazing to think, now, that when Kanazawa and I did that, only twenty-two or twenty-three years had elapsed since the *Yamato's* sinking, and yet from our bath launching to now, more than forty years have passed. I read recently[27] that one of Kawasoe's uncles, on his mother's side, was killed aboard ship in the Pacific in 1944.

"Kase also spoke of the *kaiten*. Everyone has heard of the *kamikaze* pilots who flew their planes loaded with explosives into enemy ships, well, *kaiten* were the equivalent underwater. The *kaiten* used by the Japanese Imperial Navy towards the end of the war were about fifteen metres in length and carried a fixed three thousand pound warhead. They could be launched from the deck of a ship or submerged submarine. *Kaiten* were, however, not very successful. I don't know whether Kase trained to be a *kaiten* pilot or not, but he seemed to know an awful lot about the subject.

"Another story he told me was interesting because it highlights, in my experience, a facet peculiar to the Japanese. He said that he had been given something to work on by a superior and was working earnestly on it when an officer walked into the room. Kase didn't look up because he didn't want to be seen not to be working otherwise he would have been put on a charge. The officer took out his sword and brought it down towards Kase's head, just stopping short. Kase looked up, the blade of the sword hovering over his forehead.

' "You acknowledge an officer when he walks into a room,' the man said sternly and glared at Kase.

"A few days later, the officer walked into the room once more. Kase said he hadn't seen him enter because he was so engrossed in his task. Suddenly, he caught a glimpse of the man's feet standing besides him. Kase was in an impossible position, for he had to break off from work set by one officer to acknowledge another. If he stopped work that would be an insult to the officer that had set it, but if he didn't acknowledge the officer standing before him, then that would be deemed as being insubordinate. It was a no win scenario. Perhaps the officer was testing Kase's resolve? Kase didn't look up and in a flash the officer brought down his sword, non-blade edge, on Kase's head and cut it.

' "I've told you for the last time,' the officer said. 'If you don't stand up next time I walk into the room I will kill you.'

"Well, the officer did walk in the next day. Kase, once again said

Kase demonstrates *shuto-uchi* upon Shirai (1989/90)

that he was completing his work and didn't look up, and the officer suddenly drew his sword and cut down. Kase recalled that he jumped to one side and the sword cut through the book he had been working on. The officer then walked out. The story shows the impossible position that Kase was put into and serves as an example, no doubt, of the type of bullying that went on in Japan at the time. In truth, I suspect that Kase had called the officer's bluff and forced him into action, but what a dangerous thing to do!

"Kase also told me how men of the Japanese Imperial Navy looked down upon men of the Japanese Imperial Army. Kase said this was because the Navy had originally been trained by the British in the early part of the twentieth century. One day, in 1943 or 1944, he noted that the cadet officers were sent on a special training mission. The officers had to have the respect of their men and be able to show uncompromising leadership. Kase said that the cadets were taken about eighteen miles out to sea in a number of boats, in a strong wind and high waves. Kase asked a friendly officer what they were doing and the officer replied, 'Training.'

'"What sort of training,' Kase enquired.

'"Survival,' the officer replied.

"The purpose of the exercise was to simulate being in the water following a successful enemy attack.

'"What happens if you can't swim,' Kase asked the officer.

'"Then that means that you are not good enough,' came to reply. 'We only want the strongest to survive.'

"The cadets were ordered into the water with the understanding that the boats would return twenty-four hours later. Kase did not say if life jackets or floats were used.

"I was interviewed in Norway[28] and, later, some of the Norwegians [G. Thorsen, A. Damm, Atle Brekke and Tom Bjølgerud are mentioned[29]] came over to Aberdeen to train with Kase and Shirai

"In the *dojo*, Kase was very innovative and I enjoyed his *bunkai*. He had a different slant on things when compared to the JKA and I found it all new, refreshing and fascinating. He didn't mind if, in *kata*, you weren't a wonderful technician, what he wanted was that a student lived the *kata*. That's why he practised the forms back to front and in reverse. He wanted the *kata* to become part of you. I did a lot of training with him on this. The problem is that *katas* are one-sided on many techniques[30], and he sought to balance both mind and body. There is a debate as to whether this kind of training is more beneficial that practising *kata* on one side only. I think it depends on what you're trying to achieve.

"He'd also merge *kata*. For example, when we'd completed the four *shuto-uke* at the end of *Heian Shodan* – the next movement being *Yame* – he would continue on from where the four *shuto-uke* end in *Heian Nidan*.

"Taiji Kase, 9th Dan, was a very unusual man. He was deep, sometimes too deep for me to grasp. He was probably the best I ever trained with and was the closest to my image of the ancient masters. His karate was for real. You get some technically very talented people in karate, but, very occasionally, you get someone who somehow goes beyond that and operates on a different plane and Kase was one of those *karateka*. He got to the stage where he wanted to do his own thing and formed the Shotokan Ryu Kase Ha. It was with great sadness that I learned of his death in 2004.[31] I felt truly awful after I'd heard the news. I wanted to go to his funeral, but work committments prevented me from doing so. I wish I could have gone, I really do, but if I had, then I would have let people, who had booked me a year in advance, down, and that is not the karate way. I've heard it said that after he passed away they found out that he didn't have any money. I believe that he was a martyr to real karate, someone who needed money to live and nothing else and when he became ill he spent what he had on medical bills. I could be wrong, but that's how I want to remember him. He was a very great karate master in my eyes and it was an honour, a real honour to have known him."

After two SSC courses taken by Kase and held on the 11th–12th July1990, in Aberdeen and Stirling, respectively, Kase travelled with Watt to John Waters *dojo* in Liverpool, before continuing to Ireland, where he was a guest of Tim Harte.[32] Watt knew Waters, noting that he'd enjoyed visiting his *dojo*[33], and that Waters had invited him to take a squad of Scottish members to the Shotokan Federation of Great Britain championships, which were held at the Everton Sports Centre. The Scottish squad was: Albert Stables (Aberdeen), John Cox (Banff), Terry Whyte (Peterhead), Stuart Dunn (Edinburgh), David McEwen (Coatbridge) and Alex Laird (Wishaw).[34]

Certainly, Kase's reputation for his *kime* was considerable and many experienced senior grades referred to him in reverential terms. It is on this private seminar in Liverpool, with six students, that we get some more views.

John Cheetham, editor of *Shotokan Karate Magazine*, recalled training with Kase on this course, held on the 13th July 1990. Noting that Kase was a *real* master of karate, Cheetham wrote 'I am absolutely, totally convinced, that Kase *Sensei* could kill any man with one blow to the body. Not the throat or temple which are obvious targets for death strikes, but just simply a punch or, very significantly, a strike to the body. I am not alone in this opinion. Everyone on this very special class witnessed this great man's unbelievable power and samurai spirit at very close range.'[35] John Waters recalled: 'Master Kase's power and *kime* are incredible. As an ex-power-lifter and a solid fourteen stone of muscle, I have felt the power of Master Kase, which is unreal.'[35]

The respected writer on karate, Harry Cook, attended one of Watt's Kase/Shirai courses and recalled: 'The training was split into four two-hour classes with each instructor teaching the seniors and juniors for one hour per session … The first thing that struck me was the sheer enthusiasm they both have for the martial arts, it was obvious to all the people on the course that both of them wanted to transmit as much as possible … it was fascinating to me how he [Kase] could relate various

Shirai, Watt and Kase (*c.* 1989)

aspect of *kata, kihon, kumite, bunkai*, etc, to Yoshitaka Funakoshi and other great names from the past ... Kase *Sensei* mentioned that for fast explosive movements *fudo-dachi* ... is more practical than *zenkutsu-dachi* ...

'The brown and black-belts practised *Bassai-dai, Enpi, Bassai-sho, Jitte* and *Nijushiho*. Teaching centred on trying to perfect details of the various techniques, then applying those techniques with a partner. Kase *Sensei* made the point that if you cannot apply the *kata* as you practise it then either you do not really understand the *kata* or there is something wrong with the way you are performing it. The link between practice and application was strongly made, and this, of course, is the traditional way ... [Shirai], as well as teaching his students the usual Shotokan *kata*, also taught the full-range of Goju-ryu *kata* [recommending *Sanchin* to Shotokan *karateka*, and had taught his Scottish black-belts *Gekisai dai Ichi*] ... [Kase] urged all the students to develop as wide a range as possible of hand techniques – *shuto, haito, kumade, teisho*, etc – instead of relying on 'just a punch' ... [Shirai's] technique is immaculate, and this, combined with an

The SSC exhibition stand at Aberdeen Try a Sport Week (1989)

inquisitive mind, produces skills of the highest order ... Both instructors have developed sets of *kata-kumite* or *yakusoku-kumite*.'[36]

Watt continued: "Kase came up to Aberdeen more times than Shirai. Kase flew direct from Paris, but Shirai had to fly from Milan to Heathrow and then catch another flight. I thought Shirai was another really interesting *karateka*. They were both cultured men, both university graduates, Kase attended Senshu and Shirai, Komazawa. I used to telephone Shirai up at his *dojo* quite early in the morning and arrange things with him. Considering he had spent more than twenty years in Italy, his English was very good indeed. I liked speaking to him directly, without a middleman. The weekend lessons were split up and I'd take one group and either Kase or Shirai would take the other, then we'd swap around. A grading usually followed.

"The SSC took part in numerous activities to encourage people to take up karate, and the Try A Sport Week, run by Aberdeen Sports Council, is a good example. This gave karate very good exposure and the event was held at the Music Hall, Aberdeen. Aberdeen Council have always been very kind to me, supported me, and I am more than happy to support them, which, of course, has a spin off for me, as more students train with me as a consequence – everybody benefits." In an undated letter[37], though probably 1987, we learn that the SSC had some eight hundred and fifty members of whom some two hundred and fifty were juniors (aged five to ten). Watt continued: "We were members of the Aberdeen Sports Council and about forty different sports were represented at these festivals.[38]

"I don't like karate cowboys, especially those who take advantage of parents and children. You get these people sometimes and I will go out of my way to make their life as difficult as I can." An undated letter (but late 1980s/early 1990s) exists, presumably to the editor of a local newspaper, which highlights this very point. The name of the individual so mentioned has been removed. Watt wrote:

'Once again, it is with great regret that I saw your recent article in the *Evening Express* with reference to ———— and his achievements in karate. He starts off by praising his own skills at boxing, then continues to discuss his prowess at karate.

'There are a number of points which I would like to raise for the information of your readers: 1) ———— and his so-called karate style are not recognised by the Scottish Karate Board of Control (which is the government approved body for karate in Scotland); 2) He is not on the Aberdeen Sports Council which is responsible for the development of sport at its highest levels; 3) In the past, due to complaints concerning his standard of instruction, to the Board of Control, irate parents in the Aberdeen area have terminated his classes and sought properly qualified karate instruction; 4) his so-called qualifications have not been awarded by any karate master of any nationally recognised standing; 5) his style of karate has no national recognition and any person training with him would not be eligible to fight with the Scottish team (only Board approved Associations are entitled to participate – in an effort to maintain the highest standards).

'The list could continue for long enough, but it is of grave concern to my Association and other *bona fide* groups that the general public may be duped into allowing their children to take up this excellent sport with unsuitable instruction.'

Watt then refers to the SSKCA, the fact that he brings Kase and Shirai to Scotland, that it is 'recognised instruction,' and so on, and in the last paragraph notes: 'I would earnestly request parents check out all aspects of a club prior to letting their children be taught karate.'

There is much evidence to show that Watt was naturally keen to promote his clubs.[39] For example, Watt and Ritchie were interviewed by Rob McLain and Ken McRobb of Northsound Radio on several occasions and the results broadcasted on Saturday afternoons during the sports programme. Also, Northsound reporter, Gill Fraser, visited Watt's *dojo* to take part and put together a five-minute article for the Sunday morning children's show.[40] One child member got an article published in the local press about children studying karate.[41] The annual SSKCA championships were also sometimes recorded both locally[42] and nationally.[43]

Watt continued: "One thing I will always remember was the contrast between Kase and Shirai when they performed *Bassai-dai*. Kase was solid, like a rock, a living rock, and Shirai, who was very powerful, moved so beautifully, with such good timing. Shirai was graceful in his movements, whereas Kase's was entirely practical; that's the impression I had.

"I've got Shirai performing *Bassai-dai*, *Bassai-sho* and *Jitte* on DVD, when he was up in Aberdeen. I looked at them recently. Shirai learned his *katas* when, I feel, there was more room for person expression. His *katas* seem to have elements of the old style in them, and his *shuto-ukes* are the best example of this, where not so much emphasis is placed on the reaction arm and more attention given to the hips. In *Bassai-dai*, the three *fumikomi* are performed just as *fumikomi* and not remotely with a *mikazuki-geri* feeling.

"When Kase and Shirai were not teaching, I'd take them sightseeing to castles and other places of local interest. I remember going salmon fishing once on the River Dee. We took a hamper, including whisky, and had a go at fishing, but John Ritchie and I didn't know what to do with these very long rods, complicated reels and numerous multi-coloured flies, and Kase and Shirai ended up showing us! They were quite good actually, and I have this image of Shirai standing in the river, casting across stream and working his fly, or lure, back up the current. We told them that the Queen Mother fished the river, but what we didn't know was that whereas we were on a public stretch of water, she had her own beat, with pools, on the Balmoral Estate, where the salmon held up before continuing upstream. It was a dull day, overcast, typical Scottish weather, and we didn't catch anything, but I think they had a nice time and the whisky kept the chill out.

"Steve Cattle came up to train on some of these courses, and, like me really, actually left the KUGB to join Kase and Shirai. Cattle, who was the same height as me, had been a member of the BKF York *dojo*[44] and moved to Liverpool to study, where he set up a *dojo* close to when the KUGB was formed. He'd been in the KUGB team for years and had won the KUGB national *kumite* title twice [1974, 1981] and had been runner-up in both the *kumite* and *kata* many times – he was also a British All-Styles champion – and he held both Kase and Shirai in very high regard. Even though he was a 5th Dan from the KUGB/JKA, he'd wanted a change and followed his heart, not his purse.[2] It was a

Shirai blocks *uchi-uke* to Watt's *oi-zuki* (*c*.1989)

big decision for him to make, he took it[45], and I admired him for it. I've got Cattle on DVD on one such course. He is so committed, so good – he graded to 6th Dan under Kase – so into what he is doing. It's such a shame he was dead within a few years.[46] He was very knowledgeable about karate history and he wrote a number of articles in the martial arts' press to inform and to support, to generate interest in, what Kase and Shirai were trying to do.[4, 47-51]

"These courses were always first-rate. We would practise what I believe Shirai called, *sanbon-genka*, which is like *sanbon-kumite* except that you are in *kamae* and rather than move forwards and backwards (or backwards and forwards) you can arc around. The movements are pre-arranged. Let me give you an example of what I mean.

"Student A and Student B would face each in *kamae*, left legs forward. Visualise Student A at twelve o'clock looking at six o'clock and Student B at six o'clock facing twelve o'clock. Student A would attack Student B with a right *jodan oi-zuki* landing in a right foot forward *zenkutsu-dachi*. Student B would slide in a little with the leading left foot into *zenkutsu-dachi* and block the outside of the attacker's forearm with a left *jodan soto-ude-uke* countering with a right *chudan gyaku-zuki*, which would be blocked downwards with the palm of Student A's left hand. Then, Student A would arc their back (left) leg clockwise ninety degrees and take up the *kamae* guard once more but this time facing nine o'clock. At the same time, Student B would arc their back (right) leg clockwise ninety degrees and take up the *kamae* guard once more but this time facing three o'clock. Then, Student B would attack with a right *jodan mawashi-geri*, stepping down into a right foot forward *zenkutsu-dachi*. Student A would block the kick to the inside of the kicking leg with the right forearm, in *zenkutsu-dachi*, and counter with a left *chudan gyaku-zuki*, which would be blocked by a right *soto-ude-uke* from Student B; then, both students would slide back a little to enter *kamae* once more, Student A with their right leg forward, Student B with their right leg forward. Finally, Student A would kick with a left *chudan mae-geri* stepping forward into *zenkutsu-dachi* and Student B would arc, clockwise, forty-five degrees with their back (left) leg and block with a right *gedan-barai* in *zenkutsu-dachi* and counter with a left *chudan gyaku-zuki* which would be blocked, downwards, by Student A's right palm.

"A variation for black-belts would entail the first two stages being the same as I have described, but instead of Student A attacking with a left *mae-geri*, he/she would bring their left leg up to their right and kick *jodan mawashi-geri* with the right foot. Student B would block with a right *jodan soto-ude-uke* and then counter with a left *chudan gyaku-zuki* which would be blocked, downwards, by Student A's right palm. Student A would end up facing nine o'clock and Student B, at half-past one, both in *kamae*.

"This was the sort of thing that Shirai taught. Firstly, we would practise the movements as *kihon*, taking the role of Student A and then taking the role of Student B. When students paired up, such sequences were performed on both sides and there were three or four different sequences per session. It was good training.

"Here's another sequence we used to practise. Student A and Student B would face each other in *kamae* as before, left legs forward. Student A would attack with a right *chudan mae-geri* and Student B would slide back with his right leg into a *kokutsu-dachi* whilst at the same time performing a *sukui-uke* with the left hand. Student B would then perform a right *chudan gyaku-zuki* in a left foot forward *zenkutsu-dachi* which was blocked by a right *soto-ude-uke* from Student A as he slid back into *kamae*. Student B would then attack with a right *chudan mae-geri* and Student A, standing with their right leg forward, would arc their left leg around anti-clockwise some ninety-degrees sweeping

Shirai demonstrates *shuto-uke* (1989/90)

the kick away with the right palm to the inside of Student B's leg whilst entering *kokutsu-dachi* and then counter with a left *chudan gyaku-zuki* in *zenkutsu-dachi*. Student B would then step back with the

244

Shirai demonstrates *kaiun no te* from the *kata Unsu* (1989/90)

right leg and so face his opponent in *kamae*, with left leg forward. Then, Student A, with right leg forward, would attack by bringing his left foot to the right foot and then advance the right foot and attack *jodan oi-zuki* in *zenkutsu-dachi*. Student B would then slide forward with the left leg into a deep *zenkutsu-dachi* blocking Student A's right attack inside with a left *age-uke* or *haiwan-uke*-type block and counter with a right *chudan gyaku-zuki*. This ended the sequence.

"Shirai would also show, and we would practise, a version of blocking a *mae-geri* with the palm to the outside of the leg, not the inside, as I've described. Shirai's timing was immaculate and he could read an opponent like a book. His *tai-sabaki* was also excellent and I wonder if the *kendo* he told me he'd practised when young helped him with this.

"I have two real Japanese blades. The first is an authentic bone-carved handled *tanto*; the scabbard is also bone carved. A *tanto* is the 'second blade' carried by the samurai and traditionally worn at all times. Because of its short length compared to a *katana* – a *katana* is what most people think of as a samurai sword – its chief function was to stab with, but it could also be a highly effective slashing weapon. I bought it from the Rendezvous Art Gallery about thirty years ago. I don't know the date, but I guess it's from the nineteenth century and that it was made for export. It's much more a decorative piece than a practical weapon. It's a beautiful piece of craftwork though. I had to have some of the metalwork, handle and scabbard repaired, as parts had become lost or damaged. Incidentally, a black-belt student of mine from the 1970s, Pat Wight, who has lived in Australia on and off, is a wonderful craftsman and is very good at polishing Japanese blades. He made me a skein dhu with a fine wooden handle and I gave it to a good friend of mine, Compton Ross, as a present.

"My other sword is a *katana* and was made by a noted sword smith, Kanehisa Ozawa, who died aged thirty in 1945. I bought this sword from a hotel in Kincardine O'Neil, on the River Dee, on the way to Aboyne. Paul Allan had just started karate with me and was working part-time, when a student, delivering bread and he saw the sword hanging in the hotel and told me about it. I went there as quickly as I could and offered the owner fifty pounds, which was quite a lot of money back in the late 1970s. We bargained and I got it for fifty-five pounds. The handle is covered in shark skin, but the blade has a slight finger print on it where someone has touched it and the blade wasn't cleaned afterwards. That just shows you how acidic human beings can be! I showed Kawasoe my swords and he was interested in them. I later read that Kawasoe came from samurai lineage, as did Enoeda, and that his father had to give up the family's ancestral swords shortly after World War II under the American occupation.[52] I think it's likely that quite a few JKA instructors are descendents of samurai.

"I also have a lacquer light-weight samurai helmet that archers wore when on horseback. I bought it at the only auction I've ever been to.

"I had Kase and/or Shirai up to Aberdeen three times a year – I even took Kase to our Shetland *dojo*[53] – and I went to their courses in France and Alicante[54], the latter being at the invitation of the Asociacion Española de Karate Amateur. There was a competition and we won three gold medals.[55]

"[From the 26th-28th October 1990], I organised the Aberdeen Karate Festival '90[56-61], which was held at the Beach Ballroom, Beach Leisure Centre. Kase and Shirai both came up, taught, and acted as judges. Around five hundred students took part and we had people over from Norway [Stavanger], France [Clermant Ferrand], Germany

WSKA Alicante Course (29th September 1990). Steve Cattle is sitting in the front row, fifth from the left; Watt, front row, extreme right, with Naito, fifth right; Kase, sixth right and Shirai, seventh right.

Kase demonstrates *uraken* at the Alicante Course (1990)

Kase demonstrates *haiwan-uke* from the *kata Heian Nidan* upon Watt on the Alicante Course (1990).

John Cox avoids Watt's *mae-geri* whilst Mike Bissett looks on during training on the Alicante Course (1990).

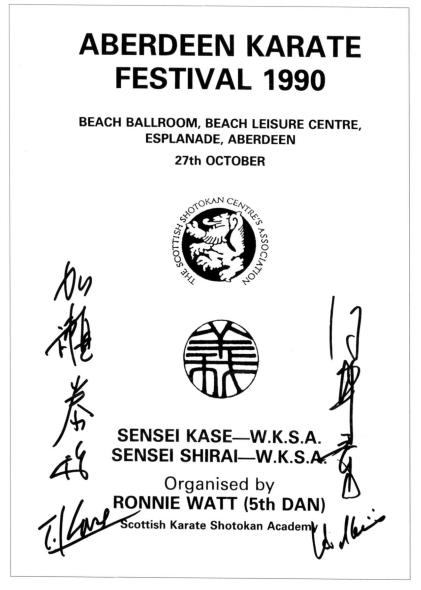

ABERDEEN KARATE FESTIVAL 1990

**BEACH BALLROOM, BEACH LEISURE CENTRE,
ESPLANADE, ABERDEEN**

27th OCTOBER

**SENSEI KASE—W.K.S.A.
SENSEI SHIRAI—W.K.S.A.**
Organised by
RONNIE WATT (5th DAN)
Scottish Karate Shotokan Academy

The cover of the Aberdeen Karate Festival 1990, signed by both Kase and Shirai.

[Regensburg] and Ireland, and up from England and Wales. Kase took the training on the Friday evening and Shirai, who had been teaching at Murdoch's *dojo* in Wishaw, came over on the Saturday morning with some students. We had a grading on the Sunday morning, followed by a six-nation challenge match. It was an exciting competition with Ireland beating France in the final. Scotland were placed third, with Wales.[62, 63]" It was noted at the time that the event was 'watched by well over one thousand spectators.'[52] The meeting, 'which was one of the largest ever staged in the North of Scotland,'[61] showed 'the true spirit of karate and the friendliness of the participating teams was a joy to behold.'[57] Details of the event are to be found in the programme, which includes the names of the competitors of all seven countries.[64]

Watt continued: "That evening, Kase and Shirai along with representatives of the teams, attended the Aberdeen Sports Council's annual dinner.

"I think it was on this occasion that Shirai asked not to stay at my house, saying that he preferred to lodge in a hotel. I felt a bit disappointed to be honest, because Gail and I had, in the past, tried to make it nice for him, but it was his choice and so I said I would organise it. Now Shirai and Kase had joined Nishiyama's International Traditional Karate Federation and Shirai said that it might be a good idea if my Association became a member too. I didn't want to be affiliated and I felt there was pressure being put on me, and I thought to myself, 'Here we go again.' From about 1986 to 1994 I was a member of the SKBC, and I was left on my own, though, individually, I was a member of WKSA. I told Shirai that I was finished with politics and all I wanted to do was engage the world's best and pay them for their services. No more politics, just karate.

"I had been asked to organise the 1991 WKSA *gasshuku* in Aberdeen, in June, but it never happened." Watt recalled at the time: 'It is a great honour to be awarded the WKSA course and we are already making plans to ensure that it will be every bit as good as the Aberdeen Karate Festival '90.'[52]

Watt continued: "At the end of the lesson on the Sunday, Shirai said that he was disappointed by my decision not to affiliate to the ITKF and felt that he should go home immediately and asked me if I could get him a flight straight away. Well, it wasn't possible and so he went back on the Monday morning, as planned. From that point onwards, for one reason or another, I never saw Kase and Shirai again. I did invite both men back to Aberdeen, but they had very busy schedules and weren't able to make it. So, I didn't train with these great men again. My decision also meant that I would no longer see other WKSA friends I'd made either. Throughout this period, for example, there was quite a lot of reciprocal movement going on between myself and the French and members of my *dojo* used to train over there and the French would come to Aberdeen. Alain Verbeeck, a WKSA 5th Dan, was Kase's right-hand man in France and we did a lot of training together. Verbeeck is strong. He took me to a wonderful restaurant on the banks of the River Seine overlooking Notre Dame. Although I actually did see Verbeeck a few more times over the years that followed, all those good times were to remain, essentially, memories.

"I'd had other instructors up to the SSC during this period, and the one that springs readily to mind is Vic Charles, who had been individual world heavyweight karate champion from 1986–1988, and was part of the winning team at the world championships for the same years. He also held British and European titles for individual and team events, so in competitive karate circles he was tops. Before he took his lesson [on 22nd October 1989], Charles was a guest of honour at the Aberdeen Sports Council's annual dinner. He took a three-hour class in the McClymont Halls in Holburn Street – a *dojo* we'd used from about 1984 – and I organised the event in conjunction with Jim Welsh, a Wado-ryu *karateka*.[65]"

There was an SSKCA meeting after the course and in the minutes it was noted that Charles's course had been 'most successful.'

Watt continued: "My old mentor, Enoeda, was still coming up to Aberdeen, but for Alan Simpson and John Main, instead.[66]

"At this time, I was teaching karate seven days a week. On Monday and Thursday evenings at McClymont Hall, Aberdeen; Tuesday evening at the New Inn at Ellon; Wednesday evening at the Community Centre, Cults; and, Friday evening at the village hall in Newmachar. On Saturday morning I taught at McClymont Hall, and on Sunday afternoon at Ellon and Westhill.[67] However, so many people wanted to study karate with the SSC that finding suitable premises was proving to be a problem. I wasn't complaining though, for what a wonderful position to be in! I was actually interviewed in a local paper about it.[68]" In this report Watt is quoted as saying; 'Halls and suitable premises in Aberdeen are very difficult to obtain – not only for karate, but for a wide range of sports … Although property in Aberdeen is very expensive, our executive are on the lookout for any suitable premises to lease – or buy – which has a good open floor space and, preferably, is not too far from the city centre.' It would seem that a good number of halls were being used other than those mentioned above, for SSKA training locations are given as: Monday, Northern College of Education; Tuesday, Ferryhill North Church; and,

McClymont Hall, Holburn Street, Aberdeen. Watt had a *dojo* there from about 1984-1996.

Wednesday, Summerhill Academy.

Watt continued: "We had a new club opening up in 1991 under Ian and Fiona Ellis, based at the Wyness Hall, Inverurie.[69-72] That year was also made the Aberdeen Year of Sport and we participated in the official launch of that event."[73]

But not everything was a bed of roses, as an undated memo, by Watt, to 1st kyu and Dan grades shows, concerning 'the appalling support the Edinburgh senior grades gave both the competition and training sessions just prior to Christmas.' Watt wrote:

'You have been training with SSC for some time now and that I have found it necessary to compile this sheet at all is an indication that discipline, Budo and mental attitude in not all it should be in these grades ... Karate is a martial art, not a sport. Now you have reached 1st kyu, your training and attitudes should be more serious ... The ruling now is that between 1st kyu and *Shodan*, you must have sixty stamps gained from continuous training (if you are off for two months or so your training stamps start at zero again). You must attend all black/brown-belt training sessions (including Stirling and Coatbridge), all pre-grading courses and courses (both in Edinburgh and Aberdeen). During this time, if you are asked to participate, help in any way in either championships, fund raising or courses, then you do so and do not pull out at the last minute or do not turn up. At this stage in your karate, if you are ill or unable to attend courses or ordinary teaching sessions because of work commitments, it is common courtesy and Budo to inform your instructor.

'I understand it is impossible for juniors to comply with these points, but a more serious attitude to training at this stage is definitely required. It will probably mean that juniors will have a year to a year and a half between 1st kyu and *Shodan* in order to bring their standard up to the senior grades, who train up to four times a week.

'Dan grades, even more so, are expected to 'do their bit' for the club and before going on to 2nd Dan will have two hundred and forty stamps, attended all black/brown-belt courses and gradings, helped with teaching and generally be dependable.'

Then, again, in an undated letter, but one or two years either side of the above, Watt laid out precisely what he expected of his Dan grades:

'In recent months it has become increasingly apparent that many black-belts have failed to fully appreciate what is expected of a Dan grade student. To clear up these misconceptions, the following conditions, outlined below, must be closely adhered to, otherwise a Dan grading will no longer be recognised and will be considered by the association to be totally null and void:

'All Dan graded students must 1) hold a current Scottish Karate Board of Control licence; 2) be registered with the Scottish Shotokan Academy; 3) attend a minimum of two training sessions per week*; 4) attend all courses organised by the association*; 5) enter all championships organised by the association and represent the club in all other competitions when asked to do so.*

    * = These conditions will only be waved in exceptional circumstances, that is, when a student is ill or injured, or if a student has unavoidable family or work commitments. The club must be informed in writing of any circumstances which will affect a student's training and participation in club activities. Failure to do so within <u>one month</u> will result in a student's Dan grade becoming NULL and VOID.

    All students are welcome to resume training at any time but must, after a suitable time of re-training, be examined by the black-belt committee. If the student is of a standard below that expected of a black-belt, then the student will be asked to re-sit a full Dan grading.

    Finally, it is the responsibility of all black-belts to promote a high standard of karate and demonstrate, by example, to junior grades, correct discipline at all times before, during and after training sessions.'

The need to secure students who were prepared to train hard was evident elsewhere too. When speaking to a reporter, for example, it was noted that: 'Ronnie adds that, unfortunately, training attitudes are slipping, with students finding it easier to give up rather than committing themselves to some hard work.'[60]

Watt continued: "When students achieve a Dan grade, there is a long wait, years, before the next grading and so, unless they are really focussed, they begin to lose a bit of interest and slowly, but surely, fade away from their training. It's been necessary for me in the past to write to these people and let them know what I expect of them if they wanted to stay practising with me. What I require is dedication, because it's only through regular training that a student can advance and I refuse to lower my standards or those of the Association of whom I'm Chief Instructor. In the SSKCA constitution at that time, under aims and objectives, it stated that 'the object of the association shall be to promote, develop and uphold Shotokan karate on traditional lines. At all times the true ethos of traditional Shotokan karate will be the aim of the association.' My view was that black-belts should support their club and association otherwise the SSKCA aims and objectives weren't being met. I read, recently, that Terry Wingrove, a very early member of the original BKF who actually came up to Aberdeen to teach before my time, said in *Shotokan Dawn*, that 'It's always easier to get easier.' How true that is, and, like Wingrove, it isn't what my karate is about. I'd rather have a few dedicated black-belts in the Association than a ragged collection of fly-by-nights that I'm embarrassed by and can't rely upon.

"In 1991 I got the National Karate Team of the USSR over to Aberdeen in conjunction with the SKBC. I'd been over to Hanover for the European Championships along with other members of the SKBC and it was agreed that the Scots approach the Russian Sports Council with a view to sending a team to Aberdeen.[74] The teams had met the day earlier in the Kelvin Hall, Glasgow, but our event was held at the Music Hall [on the 21st July]. Tommy Morris, Chairman of the SKBC and Hamish Adam, National Coach, came over to take a course prior to the match." Watt was quoted at the time as saying: 'Having Tommy and Hamish join me to take a three-style course in Aberdeen for the first time was most enjoyable and we hope to develop these courses further ... It was good for our club and the city to welcome the Soviets and we look forward to seeing them again.'[75] In a foreword in the event's programme, Morris noted: 'Whilst the Scottish squad is experienced in international competition, being led by John Roddie, European Champion, the Soviet's are comparative newcomers. However, what they lack in experience, is certainly made up for in enthusiasm.'[74]

Watt continued: "In [August] 1991, the SSKCA were invited to instruct at the Boys' Brigade International Camp which was held in Aberdeen. HRH Prince Edward watched our karate class, which we gave in the open air.

"I remember 1992 as the year we met Frank Bruno, who had been invited up to Aberdeen as a special guest for the Telefon Day [19th July], at Duthie Park, an event organised by Aberdeen City Council. I was asked to look after him and generally take him around with my black-belts acting as ushers. What struck me about Bruno when I first saw him, at the reception, was his size and how fit he looked. He just towered over me and beamed good health. He was an absolute delight to be with. We discussed punching and blocking and he said he'd practised a little bit of karate at home and that he liked it. I teased him and asked him whether he'd like to do a bit of light sparring, but he got back at me and said that he didn't want me to hurt him before he could lift the world title form Mike Tyson! We escorted him around the park and kept the overly inquisitive away from him.

"During a break, we went for a run with Frank. I must be honest and say that the squad and I were having trouble keeping up with him. I thought I was fit, but I wasn't a patch on this guy and he inspired me in a way. I thought he was a gentleman in every way. I know karate is different from boxing, but if I could have afforded it I would have

Watt shows Frank Bruno how to deliver a *soto-ude-uke* (1992)

invited Frank up for a course. As it is, I have had to be content with the fact that I was Frank Bruno's minder for a day!

"In [March] 1993, even though I'd left the KUGB, Terry O'Neill came up for a two-day course." A report at the time recalled: 'Terry is a very practical karate man. He has seen situations during his work as a Liverpool doorman in which self-defence/self-preservation is an absolute must. To this end, Terry uses karate in the exact manner for which it was developed ... All the moves demonstrated by Terry were simple, but effective. Throughout the course, Terry stressed that self-defence and competition karate can only be effective if students can harbour their power inwardly and explode into action in an instant. Even when students are listening to Terry, he demands that they are totally alert and totally aware so that when a command to move is

Roxanne, Ronnie and Reeve Watt at their home in Primrose Bank Avenue, Cults, Aberdeen (1992).

given, the students must react immediately.

'From a coaching point of view, Terry has the sense to appreciate that years of karate training takes its toll on the body. Unlike traditional karate instructors who see admission of injury as showing weakness and have often been heard to say 'train harder', Terry recognises that older students training with injuries are wise to avoid over-training [in] techniques which will aggravate [a] condition.

'In conclusion, Terry, a very genial man, impressed the Scottish students with his size, and ability to move with such explosive agility. Nobody in the *dojo* was in any doubt that Terry was anything less than a well-tuned, precision karate man, never to be underestimated.'[76]

The report also gives one student's view of Watt: 'Ronnie exudes fitness and athleticism. As anyone who has ever trained under Ronnie will know, if you can survive a session with Ronnie Watt then you can survive training with anyone. Ronnie has an unmatched talent for teaching a single technique for an entire training session. He can generate such enthusiasm that students fail to realise that they have only worked on a single technique ... Ronnie's approach to karate is

From left to right: Verbeeck, unknown French student and Watt, in France (1993).

an innovation. His ability to isolate, specialise and develop techniques for the individual makes Ronnie's approach to karate unique.'[76]

Watt continued: "I'd had Terry up before, as I've said, but I wasn't the only one in Aberdeen who'd acquired his services. Another chap had Rick Jackson[77] up as well.[78]

"In 1993 [between the 11th-15th June], I took forty SSKCA black-belts over to Alain Verbeeck's *dojo* in France at the Palais des Sports, rue E. Lavezzari, Berck Plage. At the end of the course we had a competition, and although the Scottish men's team lost, the women's team won[79]; there was even a write-up in the French Press.[80]

"In 1993 the SSKCA ran a special European course and international competition at a karate festival between the 3rd and 5th of September, at the St. Machar Academy, and Gracemount Sports Centre, Aberdeen. Hamish Adam, 6th Dan, and Alain Verbeeck and I

Watt, third from right in Gomel, Belarus (1992)

took the training. I had organised teams from Norway [Stavanger], France [Calais and Clermont Ferrand], England and an SSKCA team to compete. I tried to get a team from Gomel, Belarus, in the former USSR, which was twinned with Aberdeen in 1990, to come, under Viktor Drobyshevsky, head of sports development in Gomel, but they had to pull out at the last minute because of difficulties. As an association we were very disappointed ['as it had been hoped to renew the friendships made, when the SSKCA participated in a festival of sport in the former USSR last October'[81]]. The SSKCA had done fund-raising in order to pay for the Belarusian team to come over, but to no avail. When we'd gone over to Gomel, we trained at the Santana Sports Club and I graded students. Quite a few SSKCA instructors went, including, John Ritchie, Ann Robertson, David McDonald, Andrew Thornton, Ian Ellis, Fiona Ellis, Jackie Dorwood of Arbroath, Roddy Morrison of Westhill and Jim Mylchreest of Edinburgh. We'd been invited over by the Mayoress as part of the city's eight hundred and fiftieth celebrations and we accompanied our Lord Provost of the time, Jim Wyness, over.[82] ['Despite the impoverished lifestyle of the people and their relatively basic knowledge of karate, their attitude to training showed why the Soviet Union has been such a major force in the world of Olympic sport'[83]]. It had been the intention that the Belarus team would travel to Aberdeen, via Moscow, by coach, and we were paying their petrol and ferry crossing costs.

"It was only after I got to Gomel, which is sited on the River Sozh, in the south-east of the country near the border with Ukraine, that I realised how close we were to Chernobyl, where only six years before, the world's worst nuclear accident happened, with something like four hundred times the amount of fallout compared to the Hiroshima bomb. I read about it when I got home and Gomel, which is the second largest city in Belarus, must have received a good dosage of caesium-137, iodine-131 and strontium-90. Six years is nothing with these babies and I'm glad we weren't there very long!

"The competition [held on the 4th September] went very well and we had some nice demonstrations.[84]

"Terry O'Neill is a top-class instructor and I invited him back up in [December] 1993. Because he was a friend of Arnold Schwarzenegger, a local paper did a write-up on him." O'Neill is quoted: 'It's always a pleasure coming to Scotland to teach ... I attend courses at all the big centres in England, but the Scots are amongst the most dedicated and enthusiastic you can get.'[85]

Watt continued: "I was promoted to *Rokudan* [6th Dan] in 1994 [20th February]. I was graded by Hamish Adam, Andy Murdoch, in his capacity as secretary of the SKBC, and a panel of senior members from the Scottish Shotokan Karate Association Centres. The grade was ratified by the SKBC and the diploma signed by Adam and Murdoch.[86]

"We also held an Aberdeen Karate Festival in the spring [23rd April] 1994, at the Beach Ballroom.[87] Aberdeen had been crowned Scotland's Most Sporting City the year before and events like this helped it acquire that status. David McDonald organised the festival and Tommy Morris, Hamish Adam and Andy Murdoch were present.[88] We had training at the St. Machar Academy.[89] We were pleased to welcome Alain Verbeeck once more, who came over not only with a good number of black-belts, but with his wife, Joëlla, a WSKA 4th Dan, and their son and daughter too, and they all took part in the festival, as did the two teams he brought. There was an inter-club, 'Scotland versus France' match, and we won on the last bout. The French Consul to Scotland, Mr. Ricard, presented the trophies.[90]

"That was the first year that the SSKCA awarded the Glover Trophy.[91] Thomas Blake Glover was a very interesting man who was born in Fraserburgh in 1838, the son of an English naval officer and his Scottish wife. She actually came from Fordyce in Banffshire. The family moved to Bridge of Don, near Aberdeen, and when Thomas left school he got a job with a trading company. He sailed to Shanghai and then on to Nagasaki in the mid nineteenth century and formed a business that sold arms to rebellious clans. He arranged for the first

Watt's 6th Dan (1994)

metal Japanese warships to be built in Aberdeen's Hall Russell shipyard. He also introduced the first train. He moved in highly influential circles and arranged for Hirobumi Ito, later Japan's first Prime Minister, and others, including two future Foreign Ministers and a Minister of Education, to come to London to receive an education. He sided with the Emperor Meiji during the Boshin War and from then on business relations with the government were assured. Although Glover bankrupted himself in 1870, he continued to manage the Takashima coal mine that he'd once owned. He moved to Tokyo in 1876. He also had a significant part to play in the founding of the Mitsubishi Company, through the building of the first western style shipyard, a pre-fabricated slip dock, in Japan. Additionally, he founded a company that later became the Kirin Brewery. It is said that his wife, Tsuru, was the model for Puccini's opera, Madame Butterfly. Glover had two children, a daughter who died in Korea just before World War II, and a son [apparently not with Tsuru] who committed suicide in 1945, aged seventy-five. Glover was honoured by the Emperor, who

Left to right: Alexander McKay (author of *The Scottish Samurai: Thomas Blake Glover*), Watt, unknown (1994).

presented him with the Order of the Rising Sun. Glover died in 1911, was cremated, and his ashes interred in Nagasaki's Sakamoto International Cemetery. Alexander McKay wrote a book about Glover entitled, *Scottish Samurai: Thomas Blake Glover*, which was translated into Japanese.

"The Lord Provost, James Wyness, presented me with the Glover Trophy for over a quarter of a century's service to karate and the City of Aberdeen. Afterwards, I decided to continue the award under a new name, the Scottish Samurai Award, a national trophy awarded yearly by the National Karate Federation/National Institute of Karate to very special people who we feel have unselfishly contributed to their fellows. This is normally in the field of karate – a number of world champions have been recipients for example – but we also honour individuals who have assisted with the development of karate in other ways, financially or politically. The individual has first to be nominated and seconded, and then our technical committee decide from those put forward. We take the honour very seriously.

"The Aberdeen Sports Council has an annual dinner, which I've already mentioned several times, where they announce the city's sports personality of the year. Towards the end of 1993 [30th October], I was presented with a special [Aberdeen] Sports Council award for service to sport. The presentation was held at the Beechwood Suite,

Watt on the occasion of his being awarded the Scottish Samurai Award. Left to right: James Wyness (Lord Provost), Gail Watt, Ronnie Watt, French Consul General and wife (1994).

Three Scottish Samurai Award winners: Watt (karate), Len Ironside (wrestling) and Berry (judo).

Ronnie Watt with members of the SSKCA team, in France (1995)

Treetops Hotel, Aberdeen.[92]" As was noted near the time: 'This award is specifically for those who have given many years of dedication to their sport … This prestigious award highlights Ronnie's involvement with the Aberdeen Sport Council and the high esteem in which he is held by all sportspersons in the Grampian Region.' Mr. William Berry, MBE, Chairman of the Aberdeen Sports Council, went on to say, 'We fully appreciate the work done by Ronnie, on behalf of the Scottish Karate Board, to maintain the highest possible standards of karate in this area.'[93]

Watt continued: "We had the annual SSKCA championships at the Summerhill Education Centre again that year, and we invariably had more than four hundred people entering the various events." An article in a local newspaper highlighting the coming championships, noted that SKBC members at the time for the Grampian region, were, apart from Watt: Brian Bothwell, 4th Dan (Shotokan); Jim Welsh and Duncan McPherson (Wado-ryu), 4th and 3rd Dan, respectively.[94]

Watt continued: "In 1994 [16th July] the SSKC took part in the Union Street 200 Parade. That was also the year that Andy Murdoch and I formed the National Karate Federation, Scotland.

"I also went over to Verbeeck's *dojo* again in [8th–9th April] 1995[95] with a squad of forty. We had a competition and we did well, winning the men's team *kumite* and Brian Dempster (captain) took the individual title. The women won both the team *kumite* and team *kata* events. Fiona Ellis was the ladies captain. Caroline Johnstone won the individual *kumite*. The cadets did well too." An uncredited report of the time noted: '[Watt had] started preparing his group for this major event at the Scottish Shotokan Karate Centres summer camp in Ibiza in September last year. Extra coaching has also been provided for the group by a series of karate specialists. In December, Sensei David Coulter, the Scottish National Team Coach, put the squad through their paces in a two-day intensive training course. In March, the students received extra help from *Sensei* Aiden Trimble[96] (5th Dan), an ex … [World Champion]. Final preparations for the trip were made on a special weekend course in Arbroath's Saltire Sports Centre, where the squad were instructed on competition karate by Hamish Adam, a very successful competition coach.'[97]

V

THE WKC WORLD CHAMPIONSHIPS: ABERDEEN, 2001

Watt continued: "Between 1995 and 1997 I became independent of all governing bodies. I'd just had enough of the politics, the in-fighting, the continual disappointment. Murdoch and I were going well together with the SSKCA with a good number of *dojos* throughout Scotland.[1]

"Whether the Japanese were there or not, I still insisted that the *Dojo Kun* be said at the end of each lesson.[2] I have always felt that it is important to abide by the precepts of the *dojo*, which, I believe, were devised by Master Funakoshi. The *Dojo Kun* draws attention to the virtues of courage, courtesy, integrity, humility and self-control. To me that is what karate is all about. If a karate technician, no matter how good, does not adhere to these principles, then, to my way of thinking, he or she is no *karateka*.

"In 1995 the SSKCA had our own tartan 'Brave Heart Warrior Tartan', designed by Mike King of Philip King Ltd, who are tailors in Union Street, Aberdeen. The Mel Gibson film, which was highly successful, was, in fact, purely coincidental, but the association certainly helped sales. The tartan was shown to the Minister of Sport with a view to making it available to athletes under the Sports Council[3], but nothing happened. It's amazing how things travel though, for I was featured on the cover of the North American newspaper, *The Scottish Banner* [July 2004], the largest Scottish newspaper outside Scotland, wearing the Brave Heart kilt and they gave me a write-up.[4]

"The Brave Heart tartan is taken from the Royal Stewart, which is a beautiful tartan. The tartan has several variations depending on occasion, such as the Dress Stewart, Hunting Stewart and Black Stewart. Mike King started with the Black Stewart as the model for the Brave Heart, but changed the yellow lines to white with red, purple and green. He created a masterpiece in my opinion. We say it is the first warrior tartan in three hundred years and this reflects our martial

A selection of Watt's *gi* badges

spirit.

"Brave Heart can be in a light wool tartan for the summer, or made from a heavier wool for winter. Heavier wool is used for formal dress and a silk version is available for waistcoats and ladies ball gowns. For my sixtieth birthday, Mike designed a kilt with a black apron, just like the soldiers' kilts worn in World War I. For this kilt, I have a black Bonny Prince Charlie jacket and waistcoat. The kilt is Brave Heart with a military pleat at the back. A military pleat is when all the pleats

are finished with each pleat being folded on the white lines of the tartan to give a wonderful look to it. I also have a red military jacket and waistcoat copied from the officers jackets at Waterloo. On my normal kilt I have a white cockade to show I support the Jacobites!

"Many of the great karate masters who have come up to take courses in Aberdeen have been presented with a tie in the Black Heart tartan. This entitles them to wear our tartan and be members of our clan.

"In [November] 1995 I became one of the first martial arts' professionals in Scotland to be awarded a National Vocational Qualification in assessing karate. The NVQs had just come in at this time. I saw this as an alternative way forward for me, away from the clutches of large, professional organisations. Kase had given me permission to grade, as I've said, and that was good enough for me, personally, but now I could grade pupils and instructors under a nationally recognised framework, officially.[5] I did this NVQ through the OCR – that's the Oxford and Cambridge and Royal Society of Arts Examinations – with an external verifier from the EKGB [English

Karate Governing Body]. I understand that NAKMAS, the National Association of Karate and Martial Art Schools[6], also ran NVQ courses around this time, from England.

"The NVQ was a government initiative, but I had done a similar thing before. Andy Murdoch and I had Dr. Richard Cox of the Martial Arts Commission up for a day's course in 1989." As was noted at the time: 'Nearly thirty senior grades from all over Scotland attended and were put through a most strenuous, though enjoyable day's work. *Kata*, *kumite* and self-defence were instructed at the end of the day, all participants were awarded their MAC Assistant Coach Award.'[7, 8]

Watt continued: "I did a lot of courses in the mid to late 1990s.[9] I became a member of the British Institute of Sports Coaches in 1993 and the National Association of Sports Coaches in 1994.[10] I ran various courses too.[11]

"When the NVQs came in, I undertook the necessary work, reached NVQ Level 4[12], and received RSA Centre Recognition in 1996 and also achieved the RSA Assessor Award in 1998. George Brand, who worked for Aberdeen and Grampian Chamber of Commerce, as well as an external verifier for the OCR, helped me enormously. He took me under his wing and helped me progress through new territory. He attended many of my karate classes and after we became a full NVQ Centre of Excellence, we presented George with life membership of the club. In 1998, I received the Qualifications and Curriculum Authority's certificate for internally verifying the assessment process.[13] Sheila Irvine, Scottish Promotions Manager for the RSA Examinations Board, presented me with my certificate and Councillor George Urquhart also attended the ceremony, which was held at McClymont Hall." Watt is quoted at the time as saying: 'I feel the qualification is the way forward for the sport.'[14] Certainly, it was reported that the SSC had 'the largest amount of qualified candidates in the UK for NVQ Sport and Recreation within the framework of karate.'[15]

Watt continued: "There was no way that someone could come up and say to me, 'Your not qualified,' because I'd done the courses and qualified not only in my own right, but I could assess others as well. I let influential people like the Lord Provost and Aberdeen's Director of Education know what I was doing too.[16] I had over one hundred members registered at NVQ Level 2 by 2002.[17] I actually found the whole NVQ episode hard work, but very fulfilling.

"Andy Murdoch is a full-time NVQ assessor and verifier for the motor trade and along with Peter Leitch, one of his karate instructors,

The Civic Reception at Town House celebrating the City of Aberdeen Karate Festival (1996). Civic dignitaries stand alongside representatives from Scotland, England, Norway and France. The winning Scottish ladies team is seated.

helped me establish our first instructors' course in the NVQ system. Peter guided me to become an assessor in the motor trade as well and registered me with City and Guilds and Scotvec.

"In 1996[18] I was made an Aberdeen Sports Person of the Year." The citation reads: 'Ronald, a 6th Dan, is Chief Instructor of the Scottish Shotokan Karate Centre's Association. This centre has recently received accreditation from the Royal Society of Arts.' The civic reception and dinner were held at the Beach Ballroom on the 7th March.

Watt continued: "We held another Aberdeen Karate Festival in 1996 [20th April], once again at the Beach Ballroom, but this time without SKBC officials. David McDonald organised the event once more and Alain Verbeeck came over with his Clermont-Ferand squad as did the Norwegians [Stavanger] and we had a team come up from England. The Lonach Pipes and Drums opened and closed proceedings. The Lord Provost for Aberdeen, Dr. Margaret Farquar, wrote the foreword to the programme. We finished the day with a civic reception.[19, 20]

"In 1997 I travelled to Japan for a fourth time with the Glover Foundation, a charitable body established the year before, with a team of fourteen. The party included Gail, Anne Malcolm and other Glover Foundation trustees, the writer and poet Alan Spence, film-maker Richard Scott Thomson, council dignitaries, and an interpreter. Our main objective was to attend the annual Glover Commemorative Festival in Nagasaki. Glover is recognised in Japan as being a great man and is an integral part of history and economic syllabi in schools, for he was a major contributor to the westernisation of their country. Our itinerary was organised by the Japanese. We attended a remembrance ceremony and the party received civic hospitality from Mayor Iccho Itoh at Nagasaki City Hall, where we also met the Director of the Department of Commerce, Industry and Tourism, the Chief of the Tourism Section and representatives of the Nagasaki International Tourism and Convention Association. We were also invited to attend a reception given by the President of the Eighteenth Bank and Chairman of the Japan British Society, Mr. Genji Nozaki, and met Professor Brian Burke-Gaffney, who is head of the Faculty of Human Environment at the Institute of Applied Science, in Nagasaki. We met officials of the *Nagasaki Shimbun* [newspaper] and were taken on a tour of the Kirin Beer Factory. We also went to Yokohama, Kyoto and Nagoya.

"At a reception, I was asked to give a short display of karate in my kilt. It was totally unexpected and I thought to myself, 'This is like taking coals to Newcastle.' However, the little impromptu demonstration of *Sochin* went down really well.

"In 1863 Glover built a house overlooking Nagasaki Bay. This house is the oldest western-styled building in Japan. The house and garden are visited by some two million people a year, so, as I say, Glover is well-respected in Japan. In the Glover Gardens I met a man dressed as a samurai who practised karate at university. I asked our guide if he would take a photograph of us – the samurai and the Scotsman dressed in a Brave Heart kilt. I am very proud of that picture because it symbolises the friendship of training through a *Do* – respect through hard training. I find a bond with the clan systems of Japan and Scotland. I know it's archaic, an anachronism, but it's an integral part of both our nations histories and I'm proud to be part of it.

"Glover, of course, wasn't the only British man helping to modernise Japan, and due credit and respect was also paid to W.H. Alt, F. Ringer and Capt. R.N. Walker.

"Overall, the trip was considered a great success. A Japanese film crew from the Nagasaki Broadcasting Company, under the direction of a Masaoki Yamato, filmed our visit in Nagasaki, and I met him again

Watt (in Brave Heart kilt) and samurai exchange *gyaku-zukis* in the Glover Gardens (Nagasaki, 1997).

later when he came to Aberdeen as part of his documentary.[21] I understand a film on Glover, which included our visit to Nagasaki, was shown on Japanese television.

"Prior to departure, through the offices of the Glover Foundation, a proposal was put forward to invite ten Japanese children interested in karate, and their teachers, to Aberdeen to take part in a karate tournament.[22] Although the group would have had to pay the cost of flights, it was proposed that NKF club members would be hosts to our guests, so no expense would be incurred that way. Unfortunately, the proposal was never taken up.

"A funny thing happened on that trip. I was sitting in the gardens dedicated to Glover, admiring the flowers and trees, when I suddenly found myself surrounded by a group of giggling teenage Japanese girls who were certain that I was Sean Connery. They just wouldn't accept that I was not he. I finally got the message through to them when I stood up and they could see that I was a fair bit short of Connery's six feet three inches!

"The following year, I put my name forward for a proposal to visit Nagasaki again as part of a delegation to develop trading links between that city and Aberdeen, but nothing came of that either.

"1997 was a big year for me because I decided to join the World

273

Andy Murdoch, Watt and Dr. Fritz Wendland

Karate Confederation. Andy Murdoch and I approached Dr. Fritz Wendland, President of the WKC, with a view to the SSKCA becoming members. Andy and I then decided that it would be best if we registered independently, so I applied as NKF (Scotland) and he appled as the Scottish Amateur Karate Federation. The WKC had only been formed on the 4th May 1996, in Frankfurt, when nine senior *karateka* from six nations from three continents met. What attracted me to the WKC was that whereas other international karate organisations seemed to be either single style bodies or allowed only one representative body from each country, the WKC allowed more than one group from each country to be members. So, if you had fallen foul of karate politics in your own country and couldn't get access to a world body and its competitions, then now you could. It struck me as a collective body that didn't get involved with individual member politics. They held World Championships every other, odd year, and European Championships every other, even year. An additional benefit was that they also held Children's, Junior and Cadet World Champion-ships. The WKC subsequently has also had two South American Open Championships [2002: Londrina, Brazil; 2003: Buenos Aires, Argen-tina], and two South-East Asian Open Championships [2003: Kathmandu, Nepal; 2005: New Delhi, India].

"The 1st WKC World Championships were held in Arezzo, Italy [with twenty-two federations from three continents being represented]. The championships were held in early late May [24th-25th] 1997, and

Dr. Fritz Wendland presents Watt with his WKC 7th Dan licence (1997)

I think it was before the actual championships that the NKF's application to join the WKC was considered and accepted. We were absolutely delighted, and to this day I have never regretted the move. Needless to say, as the NKF were not members before that time, we did not take part in the event.

"I had good classes for children and held lessons in the afternoons, after school[23] and was taking self-defence classes for both men and women at Robert Gordon University[24] and for Aberdeen City personnel of the Housing, Environment, Consumer Protection and Library Service department.[25]

"In 1997, I was awarded my *Nanadan* [7th Dan] by the World Karate Confederation [on the 10th October]. The diploma shows that Carlo Henke, WKC General Secretary, and Fritz Wendland, WKC President, both signed it.[7] Henke is no longer with the WKC and is with WUKO instead. Nowadays it is customary to wait seven years between 6th and 7th Dan, but I was awarded mine after three years and I'll tell you why. Because of various problems I'd encountered with grading opportunities either not being possible or being blocked, I was behind what the WKC thought I should have been. I'd waited nearly five and a half years between 1st Dan and 2nd Dan for example, when I could have waited only two. Working on the two years between 1st Dan and 2nd Dan, another three years between 2nd Dan and 3rd Dan, another four years between 3rd Dan and 4th Dan, and so on, if I'd graded regularly then I could have been up for 7th Dan in 1996. It was on this basis that I was awarded my 7th Dan. I don't really believe that anyone could have trained harder than I did, so I thought this fair and reasonable. I used the publicity in the local press to make a point about the drug problem, which I have found rife in Aberdeen, and young people's general apathy to sport these days."

A newspaper cutting on this very point is in existence. Watt is quoted as saying just hours after being made a 7th Dan: 'Youngsters today are turning to drugs or would rather sit in front of the TV and watch cartoons than take up a sport ...' Certainly, the reporter, Steve McKenzie, noted that Watt 'claimed a couldn't care-less attitude has decimated class sizes over the last five years,' commenting that some youngsters, after being dropped off by their parents, would just stroll up and down the street rather than attend the karate lesson. When asked whether he might introduce Japanese-style discipline, Watt replied, 'Many people just couldn't handle it here."[26]

Watt continued: "In 1997 I was an Aberdeen's Sports Person of the Year again.

"In June [6th–7th] 1998, I managed the NKF team at the WKC's 1st European Karate Championships staged in an ice hockey stadium in Bratislava, the capital of Slovakia[27], which attracted seventeen European nations.[28] The NKF raised eight thousand pounds so that we could attend.[29] Ladislav Klementis[30], the man who I believe introduced karate to Slovakia, was Chairman of the Organising Committee. Klementis is a very serious exponent of Okinawan karate, an 8th Dan graded on Okinawa, and has since been honoured by the Okinawans for his promoting of Okinawan martial arts throughout the world. We did really well[31] and come home with the bronze medal for the team *kumite* along with Northern Ireland. Germany won that event with Italy second. The team captain was Scott Strachan and members were: Alan Duguid, John Conn and Greg Clancy. We were placed fourth in the men's *kata* event too.[32] We also got a bronze for the female *kumite* team along with the

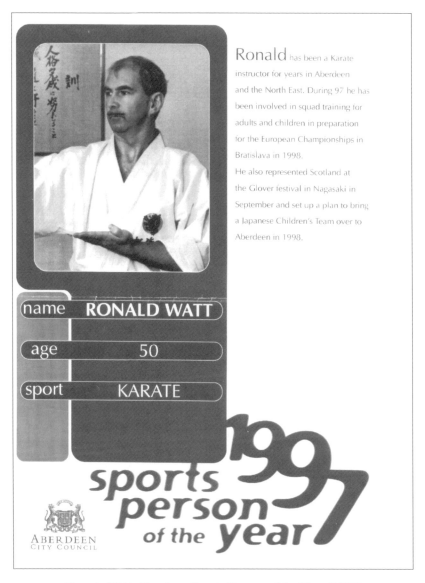

Ronald has been a Karate instructor for years in Aberdeen and the North East. During 97 he has been involved in squad training for adults and children in preparation for the European Championships in Bratislava in 1998.

He also represented Scotland at the Glover festival in Nagasaki in September and set up a plan to bring a Japanese Children's Team over to Aberdeen in 1998.

name	RONALD WATT
age	50
sport	KARATE

sports person of the year 1997

ABERDEEN CITY COUNCIL

Ronnie Watt, Aberdeen Sports Person of the Year (1997)

Czech Republic, with Germany winning and Italy coming second. The ladies team included Fiona Ellis, Ann Robertson and Catriona Hall. At the end of the competition Takeji Ogawa was presented with a WKC 8th Dan. The Lord Provost replied to a letter I had sent her on the trip and she congratulated us on our success in Europe.[33]

Certificate of Sporting
Achievement

presented to

Ronald Watt

in recognition of gaining
National Representative Honours
during

1997

Councillor, Arts & Recreation Committee

"In September 1998, I intended taking a junior squad to Locarno, Switzerland, for the 1st WKC Junior World Championships and World Cup for Children. Locarno is on Lake Maggiore, surrounded by the Alps, and we were all excited about going. Although in Switzerland, the official language is Italian. I wrote to twenty-four companies[34] for

NKF Scotland team at the 1st WKC European Championships, Bratislava (1998).

A WKC diploma recognising Watt's coaching of two bronze medal teams at the 1st WKC European Championships (1998).

sponsorship, but without success, though a good friend of mine, Jim Rogerson of Monyana Engineering Services made a kind donation of five hundred pounds.[35] Our team included Grant Conroy, Andrew Watt, Tracy Maloy and Roxanne Watt.[36] Despite everything being set, we were unable to attend because we couldn't get reasonably priced air tickets. It would have actually cost each member the equivalent of two return fares to the USA to fly to Switzerland and back, which seemed ridiculous. We were all terribly disappointed, as you might imagine.

"In 1998 I was awarded an Aberdeen Sports Person of the Year yet again." The citation on the award reads: 'Ronnie has been coaching karate for thirty-five years. He has coached in Japan and Scotland and has coached his squad to European Championship Level. He has been involved in coach monitoring and has had thirty coaches whom he helped gain their qualifications.'

Watt continued: "I wanted to be able not only to send NKF teams to WKC championships, but also to send judges and referees. [Between the 27th–28th March 1999], I organised a course at the Bank O'Dee Sports Centre and arranged for Bernd Hinschberger, 6th Dan, and Thomas Specht, 4th Dan, to give a course of instruction with judging and refereeing in mind.

"The 2nd WKC World Championships were held in Bochum, Germany, [12th–13th] June 1999, at the Ruhrlandhalle. I was interested in going to Bochum because it was the birthplace of General Alfred Keller, one of the Luftwaffe's most decorated officers. Some three thousand spectators were there and teams from fifty federations from around the world. As part of the opening ceremony, they had Japanese and German drummers, who were tremendous, and the general theme was German/Japanese relations. There were also songs sung by a Japanese women's choir led by Mrs. Ochi and a display of capoeira. The NKF took a men's team made up of Simon Robertson, who was captain, Scott Strachan and Alan Duguid, with Craig Scroggie as the reserve. The women's team included Fiona Ellis as captain, Vivienne Milne, Kim Mylchreest and Roxanne Watt. Ian Ellis, that's Fiona's husband, also came as a referee. It cost approximately six thousand pounds[29] to attend the event and although we didn't win anything, we got through to the last eight in the categories we entered, and had several fourth places, so we just missed out. For us, it was more a case of becoming familiar with such an event and coming up against some much larger federations. All in all, I thought we equipped ourselves very well indeed.

"During the Bochum championships I suggested to Fritz that

A WKC diploma of participation at the 2nd WKC World Championships (1999).

Aberdeen could hold the 3rd World Championships and the WKC committee had a meeting. Then at the end of the Bochum championships, which had been superb, there, in bright lazer lights beamed all around the stadium, it suddenly said, 'World Championships Aberdeen 2001.' That's when it struck me what I had let myself in for. I whispered to myself, 'Oh my God, we've got it!' I knew Russia, the USA and Austria put in bids as well.[37] I experienced a sudden and intense mixture of excitement and fear. I thought it was going to be difficult to organise, but I was wrong, it was very difficult to organise! The official letter from the WKC president came through a couple of days after I'd returned home, noting the NKF were the hosting federation[38] and the press were on to it straight away.[39] The condition set by the WKC was that we present an official body which was going to support the NKF and correspond with the WKC. I took this as meaning I would need civic backing and in September I had a meeting with representatives of the Grampian Enterprise Trust and Aberdeen Council's Economic Development Department. I found the response to be very positive and they asked me to present a business plan three weeks later.[40]

"I also wrote to Anne Begg[41], the Member of Parliament for

Aberdeen South, shortly after returning home and asked her if she could write to the Lord Provost and the Grampian Enterprise Trust to see if she could secure backing for the event, and within a week she had written.[42] Her influence was very important in bringing the championships to Aberdeen.

"On my return from Bochum, I wrote to the Lord Provost too, informing her that I had been successful in bidding for the 3rd WKC World Championships[43], and she wrote back a few days later."

The Lord Provost's wrote that she was 'thrilled' by the news, congratulated Watt on his 'splendid achievement' and noted that he was 'an excellent ambassador for the city.' She concluded: 'It must have been a wonderful sight to see the name of Aberdeen broadcast to fifty-eight nations.'[44]

Watt continued: "In 1999, Aberdeen City Council made me a Sports Personality yet again." The citation reads: 'Ronald has been coaching for thirty-five years in Aberdeen. In 1999 he took a team to Germany to compete at World level. He has convinced the WKC that the World Championships be held in Aberdeen in June 2001.' Watt was also nominated for the Scottish Coach of the Year Awards under the Scottish Sports Council.

Watt continued: "The 2nd WKC European Championships were held at Cluj Napoca, Transylvania, modern-day Romania, [17th–18th June] June 2000. The NKF female teams did very well in both the team *kata* and team *kumite* by taking bronze medals in both, behind Italy and Germany, and, Germany and Italy, respectively. The girls' squad were: Fiona Ellis, Kim Watson, Vivian Milne, Cheryl Rogerson and Alana Tischuk.[45, 46] The men's squad of Scott Strachan, Craig Scroggie, Alan Duguid, Simon Robertson and Reeve Watt, my son, put up a good show. I was actually delighted by our growing improvement against the best in Europe. I felt that we were really getting somewhere.

"The WKC Junior World Championships and World Cup for Children was held at Valencia, Spain, [28th–29th October] 2000. I took a party that included Cheryl Rogerson, Danielle Jamieson, Samantha McCann, Alana Tischuk and Reeve Watt.[47] Alana took a bronze in the individual *shobu-ippon-kumite*[48] and was presented with her medal by HRH Prince Adan Czartoryski Borbon, cousin of King Carlos of Spain. Reeve just missed out and came fourth in the *kumite*. But there was one little boy, Ryan Watt, no relation, that we had intended taking, that I will not forget, and for quite a different reason.

"Ryan was born with a condition – TGA, Transition of the Great

A WKC diploma of participation at the 2nd WKC European Championships (2000).

A WKC diploma of participation at the 2nd WKC World Cup (2000)

Arteries – to do with the heart, which prevented him from receiving enough oxygen. He had three major operations after birth, the first being when he was only one day old, and things did not look good. Ryan is an inspiration to all of us, for he not only survived, but passed his black belt grading as well, aged eight, after three years study.[49-51]

"The question of awarding Dan grades to children is a difficult one. Ryan trained four times a week, hardly ever missed a session. His improvement in health was something wonderful to behold and his technique was really very good indeed. He was exceptional. At the age of sixteen, he would have had to re-sit the grading for adult status and I would not allow anyone under twenty-one to become a 2nd Dan.

"When Ryan took his black-belt things were different. I'm not in any way saying that Ryan didn't deserve his black-belt, he most certainly did, but I've tightened the whole subject up. I found that if a junior achieved a black-belt, then he or she would be inclined to give up, when getting a *Shodan* is just the first real step in karate. Young people just have too many distractions, but I'm after commitment, which I feel is both good for them and good for the NKF. I'm not interested in the buy and throw-away mentality. I currently have two young female black-belts who both train four or five times a week and they are truly excellent, they put many adults to shame, but if they leave for no good reason for two years and then want to come back, then that's fine, but they'll have to start as white-belts again. Also, I have elected for a system of two Dan gradings, whereby a student takes a Dan grading under myself and, if successful, is awarded an NKF diploma, and then, a year later, takes the WKC grading under several world masters who attend our national course. By insisting on measures like this, I have built up a world-class junior and cadet squad.

"I'd actually tried to get the 2000 WKC Junior World Championship for Aberdeen. Indeed, I had been invited by the WKC to do just that, in September, and there seemed to be some preliminary interest, but Spain got the nod.[52] At the closing ceremony of those championships, Mr. Angelo Duato, President of the Federacion Española Unificada de Artes Marciales, who had hosted the event, passed the WKC flag to both Councillor John Reynolds and I, in the presence of Prince Adan and Dr. Wendland. Aberdeen was next …

"In [January] 2001, Bill Berry of the Aberdeen Sports Council and 7th Dan Chairman of Judo Scotland, presented me with an honorary 3rd Dan of the Scottish Judo Federation. Bill has always been supportive of my efforts. He awarded this honour for all my

Watt being presented with his honorary 3rd Dan in Judo from Bill Berry (2001).

work in karate both in Scotland and abroad, and his kind action was most appreciated.

"The Organising Committee for the WKC World Championships in Aberdeen was set up in 2000 with fourteen members. John Reynolds was elected Chairman and took charge of organisation and tourism; I was Vice-Chairman and was in-charge of basic organisation and technical enquiries; Gail was Secretary. Ann Malcolm was Treasurer and David McDonald was Publicity and Promotion, and this included sponsorship and marketing. Then there was Fritz Wendland, Jim Mylchreest, Ken McNeil, Jim Duguid, Fiona and Ian Ellis, Katie Barnett, Alan McCartney and Simon Robertson. A company was set up, the World Karate Championships 2001 Ltd., and we opened an account with the Bank of Scotland.

"Once we'd decided who was going to be responsible for what, the next thing was to identify exactly what needed to be done. We could take absolutely nothing for granted, because we were dealing with large numbers of people from diverse cultures, so everything had to be arranged with extreme care. In a karate sense, it was 'back to basics.'

"Logistics proved to be the greatest problem. The amount of work put in was phenomenal – from designing championship diplomas (and getting the master copy signed before the event by masters around the world who were going to be in attendance) – and organising trophies and medals to sorting out private cars and taxis to pick up officials and contestants from the airport. Broadfield Garage sponsored us with the use of two minibuses.

"We needed two hundred and eight medals [ninety-six for *kata* and one hundred and twelve for *kumite*] and these were actually made in Valencia and supplied through Arthur Booth of the Trophy Centre, Aberdeen. I recall we spent something like two thousand pounds on trophies. The statuettes were about one foot in height and showed a figure performing an *uraken* and *yoko-geri-keage* as in the *kata Heian Yondan*. Peter Carry, one of my black-belts who had to give up training after his father died, is one of Aberdeen's top jewellers and he gave us a large donation to help with the cost of the trophies and medals. His son, David, was in the British Olympic Swimming Team that went to Beijing in 2008. He reached the finals in the freestyle. He is one of the best swimmers Scotland has ever produced and has won two gold medals and one silver medal at the Commonwealth Games. He holds Scottish, British, European and Commonwealth records. He also went to the Athens Olympic Games in 2004. If you want to be good at something, swimming or karate, then, like David Carry, you have to train six hours a day, six days a week. It's about real commitment and it becomes a way of life. I feel confident that he'll be in the 2012 London Olympics, so look out for him!

"Then there were the little things, the easily forgotten items, like whistles, mitts and weighing scales. The lists seemed to go on forever and all the time the costs were rising and the clock was ticking.

"Bill Smith put into fruition my vision for all the artwork and advised me on every aspect in this regard. His assistance and exceptional work were given entirely free.

"We prepared a booklet of recommended pubs and restaurants – American, Chinese/Oriental, French, Indian, Italian, Mexican, fast food, and, seafood – cinemas, nightclubs, taxi services, and so on. We had our own website. We also felt that it was important to get as many children interested as possible." An article at the time recalled Watt saying: 'We will be working extensively with schools in the build up to the championships and would like to get as many children involved as we can.'[53]

Watt continued: "I wanted to give a children's display at the championships and I arranged a series of free classes at the Banks O'Dee Sports Centre with this in mind."[54]

"Then we had to think about the major problem of finance. As soon

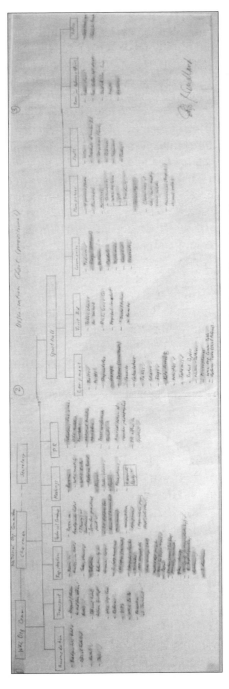

The master plan of the 2001 WKC World Championships

as I had returned from Bochum I'd started making enquiries into obtaining a large hall. The Aberdeen Exhibition Centre, or the Oil Exhibition Centre as it is called, wanted eight thousand pounds per day for the hire of the hall.[55] The eight thousand per day was just for the building and didn't include any extras. Then I was verbally quoted twelve thousand pounds a day for everything, VAT, use of toilets and changing rooms, staff, seating, and so on. That was a real shock, a big worry, and I thought I'd have to cancel the championships there and then. We needed it for four days – two days for the championship and one day either side, known in the trade, I believe, as 'build up' and 'breakdown' days. When all the forecasting and projecting had been done and put into hard numbers, it was estimated that there was a shortfall of twenty-six thousand pounds.[56] No wonder what was left of my hair turned white. It was horrendous. A lovely idea, a glorious vision, was turning into a nightmare. We had general plans, marketing plans, composite plans, and so on. We had to think, and act, on accommodation – we ended up recommending four hotels: the Jarvis Hotel, the Marriott Hotel, the Posthouse Hotel and the Thistle Hotel – transport, registration, technical seminars, meetings, PR, equipment, first aid, ceremonies, manpower, seating, etc., the list went on and on, and each one of these incorporated goodness knows how many more sub-divisions. We had to think about important things like insurance, legal fees and ambulance services in case of an emergency, to smaller but highly impressionable items like flowers, posters, banners and flags. It was a growing monster and whichever way we looked at it this monster was coloured a deep red."

A letter from Diana Morgan, of the Aberdeen Exhibition and Conference Centre, dated the 24th October 2000, to Gail Watt, noted that following a request via Councillor John Reynolds, the Board of Directors of the AECC agreed, given the importance of the championships to the city, to reduce the fee from fifteen thousand pounds to twelve thousand five hundred pounds. This is the only letter of its kind the author has seen.

Watt continued: "There was the possibility of using the facilities at Aberdeen University and I did speak to their people, but I deemed the facilities too small. Luckily, with Gordon McIntosh's help, we were able to apply for a grant from Aberdeen City Council. When they realised I simply couldn't raise that kind of money, they cut the fee by half and we got a grant for another ten [£15,000[57]] thousand pounds, which meant we had to find another eight thousand – though that was just to cover the venue!

Watt alongside his good friend, Compton Ross

"So, at first, despite sterling work by Compton Ross (see below) and a very good package, supported by a letter from Gordon McIntosh, Director of the Economic Development Department at Aberdeen City Council, offering 'the strongest possible support to the organisers'[58] of the championships in their request for sponsorship – six levels of potential participation, ranging from Friend of the Championship, for sponsors willing to put in less than one thousand pounds, to Full Championship Branding for those offering thirty thousand pounds – we had real trouble securing any sponsorship at all.

"It was not looking good and when things had run to the extent that the event could not be cancelled, I seriously thought I'd have to re-mortgage my house. Then a good friend of mine, Compton Ross, of Metrol Technology Ltd., a petro-technological business, came around to see me. Compton, both a former international hockey player and athlete, was already a black-belt in another style of martial arts when he began training with me. Although, initially, he found the change-over quite difficult, he practised hard and achieved his Shotokan *Shodan* in 2000, and, later, in 2004, passed his *Nidan*. He said that he respected individuals who stuck themselves out on a limb and presented me with a cheque. I looked at it quickly as I thanked him, saw a seven and two noughts and thought to myself, 'seven hundred pounds will come in useful.' After he left, I looked at the cheque again and saw three noughts – he'd given me seven thousand pounds! I

Jim and Sandra Rogerson of Monyana Engineering, flank Cheryl Rogerson and Watt (3rd April 2001).

couldn't believe it and telephoned him immediately. I'll never forget that; I was just blown away with his kindness. That was a real strain taken off my shoulders.

"However, we were still a long way short of the money we needed and then, about three months before the championships were due to begin, Jim and Sandra Rogerson from Monyana Engineering, who I've mentioned before and are based in Inverurie, asked Gail and I up one evening to their house. At the end of a very pleasant evening, Jim said that he wanted to give me something for all that I had done for his daughter, Cheryl, an excellent 1st Dan and junior squad member. He handed me a cheque. I thought it read one hundred pounds and thanked him, but I looked again after what had happened last time. I'd put my glasses on and it was just as well that I did, for the sum was ten thousand pounds. What can you say when you have friends like Ross, Jim and Sandra?

"Alistair Greig, an accountant, helped a great deal on the financial front. He assisted us with many a letter to companies for sponsorship, but we found out pretty soon that karate is not top of their agenda. He went to a dinner with some top bankers and Alistair managed to secure some sponsorship from the Royal Bank of Scotland for fifteen hundred pounds. We also got some sponsorship from fish merchants. So, slowly, we started to acquire people who were prepared to help in various ways, small and large, and eventually we had forty-six[59] who assisted to varying degrees, but Monyana Engineering Services and Metrol Technology were our main 'private' sponsers.[60] Scottish Mutual also supported us with six thousand pounds and Price Waterhouse, with one thousand. Scottish Enterprise Grampian gave just over thirteen thousand.

"Also, Aberdeen City Council was later prepared to underwrite the event and this was much appreciated. In this regard, the Lord Provost, Margaret Smith, Councillor John Reynolds, and Councillor Len Ironside are to be particularly thanked. The council also awarded a grant of ten thousand pounds for a co-ordinator for six months.[61] The problem was, we had nearly twice the work, because we had to show the poor girl, whose name was Ella McLean, all the work we had done already to feed this beast I'd brought home from Germany! There was also another woman, Dawn Schultz, the secretary to Gordon McIntosh, who was very good.

"Fritz came over to finalise arrangements in 2000 and to meet the Lord Provost. He gave a wonderful impression and fully backed our efforts. Fritz is tall and has that Germanic air of dignity about him; he is also calm, collected and highly intelligent. Later, there was also a press and photo call at the Altens Thistle Hotel."[62] Dr. Wendland is quoted as saying: 'We are convinced that the Aberdeen Organising Committee will prepare an unforgettable tournament which competitors and officials will speak of in the future,'[63] and, 'All our member federations are eager to come to Scotland. We have realised that the City of Aberdeen is fully supporting this great international event.'[64] In a letter to the Lord Provost, Wendland, thanking her for the reception at Town House, wrote: 'I was very impressed by the efficiency of the councillors and officials of the city. I have visited all the venues and facilities in the city. Everything is suitable to host the 3rd WKC World Championships 2001 in Aberdeen.'[65]

"Fritz stayed at my home. Gail and I have since become particularly good friends with Fritz and his family – his wife, Christine, and their daughters, Elke and Gudrun. In fact, Gudrun and her partner, Joachim Berg, their son, Anton, and daughter, Sophia, came to stay with us recently.

In a 'Message from the World Karate Confederation President,

Watt showing a mock-up of the 2001 WKC World Championship programme to the championship organising committee (21st January 2001).

John Reynolds, Fritz Wendland and Watt at a press conference for the WKC World Championships (2001).

Bill Berry, Prince Adan and Ronnie Watt outside the Aberdeen Exhibition Centre. Note the minibus behind.

Fritz Wendland,' we also learn that Aberdeen City Councillor, John Reynolds, attended both the WKC European Championships in Romania and the Junior World Cup in Spain, and that the WKC 'appreciated his visit and support very much.'

It is also important to record what Wendland thought of Watt and the NKF at this time. Noting, in the above document, that the WKC were 'very happy' to have the WKC Championships in Aberdeen, and that Watt and the NKF were strong members of the WKC, he wrote: 'They have proved from the very beginning of their membership of the WKC [that they are prepared to give] their full support, sportsmanship, loyalty, and good karate spirit to our international body.'

Watt continued: "We presented Dr. Wendland with Brave Heart tartan trews [trousers] and he was happy to accept.

"We had a real boost to our campaign when Prince Adan, honorary president of the WKC, agreed to attend the championships. That gave us a big lift in the press a few months before the event.[66-68] Prince Adan was a 5th Dan in Shito-ryu at the time, having started karate under John McSweeney[69] when at university in Dublin, and had represented his country. Prince Adan is really quite knowledgeable about karate and I would chat to him on the subject.

"Then, in May, we had another big uplift, when Sir Sean Connery agreed to be honorary chairman for the event.[70-72] He wasn't able to attend in person due to filming commitments in the USA, but a trophy, the Sean Connery Trophy, was offered for the most promising youngster, as per his wishes."

In a letter to Watt, Connery is quoted in the press at the time as saying: 'I am happy to support your splendid initiative in bringing world karate to Scotland.'[72] In his undated letter to Watt, though faxed on the 18th May 2001, if this is what is actually being referred to by the press, Connery actually wrote that he was happy to accept the invitation to be Honorary Chairman of the World Karate Championships in Aberdeen, given Watt's, 'splendid initiative in bringing the World Championships to Scotland.'

Watt continued: "The connection with Connery came about when I was speaking to Alex Salmond at the House of Commons and Connery was there, so it was very fortuitous. It just seemed to bring things full circle. I'd started karate, essentially, because of *Goldfinger*, watching Bond and Oddjob at work, and here I was bringing the WKC World Championships to my home city and the man who had played 007 in the movie was supporting the event. It was lovely. They even did a feature on it in the local press[73] and a number of smaller reports. I wrote both to Alex Salmond[74] and to Sir Sean, thanking them."

The letter that Watt wrote to Connery is dated the 22nd May 2001. Watt noted that Connery's acceptance was, 'a tremendous boost for the WKC and all the people here in Aberdeen who have been working tirelessly to bring the World Championships to our city. Your support adds great strength to our efforts to bring karate to the people of Scotland and to demonstrate the qualities which have made karate such an enduring and life enhancing martial art.' [I awarded Connery an honorary [5th] Dan grade from the NKF for his support[4]].

"Like Connery, not everyone we invited could attend, and Mayor Itoh of Nagasaki and Nelson Mandella, are two that I recall.

"We also had a delegation of VIPs from Romania, including a senator from Senate Office, a Republican MP from Upper House, another MP, the Director of the Ministry for Youth and Sport, and the Lord Mayor of Cluj Napoca was also due to attend.

"Stuart Clarkson, a local businessman, gave us five hundred pounds and then agreed to sponsor the tournament brochure for a further two thousand pounds, and you could get tickets from the College Bar and Diner at 9 Alford Place, Holburn Junction, which was one of his businesses.[75, 76] The fact that tickets were on sale was highlighted in the press[77] and we even had a 'Win Tickets' competition, with the question being, 'What is the name for a karate training hall?'[78] The price of tickets was very reasonable: one day –

Stuart Clarkson (left) sponsors the WKC 2001 Aberdeen World Championships (4th May 2001).

adult £6, concession £3; for two days – £10 adult, concession £5.[79] The tickets revealed that doors would open at 8.00 a.m. on the Saturday and the Sunday and preliminaries would follow. The finals would be

The 3rd WKC World Championships programme

at 4.00 p.m. both days. Also, there was a super forty-page programme priced at only £3. We had eight welcomes included: Tatsuaki Iwata [Japanese Counsel General], Sir Sean Connery, Prince Adan,

Aberdeen's Lord Provost [Margaret Smith], Fritz Wendland [WKC President], Carlo Henke [WKC Vice-President], John Reynolds [Chairman of the Organising Committee], and, yours truly as President of the NKF (Scotland).

"We got a two-page write-up in the June 2001 edition of *Traditional Karate*[80], and we also put in a two-page advert in that magazine.

"Unfortunately, not everyone welcomed the WKC World Championships being held in Aberdeen, saying the event lacked official standing.[81] Basically, there were two criticisms.

"Firstly, the amount of money we had been given my Aberdeen City Council to help finance the event caused considerable jealousy, I feel, and no small amount of small-mindedness. Let me read these quotes to you: 'Aberdeen City Council ... warmly welcomed the championships. It agreed to support the event with grants totalling twenty-five thousand pounds and a loan for five thousand, plus underwriting any financial shortfall up to a maximum of ten thousand pounds.'[82] It was quoted that the event would pump one million pounds into the local economy[82, 83], so Aberdeen City Council was being very responsible in my opinion. They were certainly not spending tax payers money recklessly, far from it. For example, when we applied to Scottish Enterprise Grampian with our proposal, I recall that we worked out, based on an estimated figure for competitors, coaches, officials, instructors and supporters who we thought would be attending, the income that would be generated purely on hotel bookings and lunches and dinners bought, would be over two hundred and eighty thousand pounds."[84]

A local newspaper report quoted City Councillor John Reynolds as saying: 'Cities spend thousands of pounds trying to attract events of this scale, but Ronnie has managed to bring the championships here without it costing Aberdeen a penny.'[63] Reynolds then is quoted noting the benefits of the championships with regard to tourism. In another newspaper[85], Reynolds is noted as saying that the event would be a money-spinner for the local economy: 'Scotland is a great tourist spot, and we are hoping that the visitors will stay on an extra few days after the tournament to explore the local area. The early signs are good. We have around two hundred pre-bookings [in January 2001] and most are staying six to eight days'[85], and Anne Begg, the aforementioned MP, replied to Watt noting that 'it is quite a coup for the City, and of course for yourself!'[86]

Certainly, as a headline in Aberdeen's, *The Press and Journal*, suggested, the event would 'bring an international showcase as well as money and prestige to the city.'[64] It was estimated that the event could bring in a great deal of money into Aberdeen[83] and that, 'Attracting the event to the city is expected to be a boon for the tourist industry, as many competitors and their families are likely to stay in the area after the competition.'[64] Similarly, 'It is hoped that the event will bring a one million pound economic boom for the city and put it on the global sporting map.'[87] Even Watt made reference to this point when he said: 'This [the championship] is a huge success for Aberdeen, we have opened the doors for tourism, which has taken a real hit recently,'[88] and, 'We have people coming here from as far afield as Bangladesh, Nepal, Russia and Argentina – it's great for the city.'[90] The Lord Provost, Margaret Smith, wrote: 'We are delighted to be playing host to such a prestigious event and I am confident that our city will prove to be a fitting venue for an event of this scale and significance.'[90] The fact that 'the event is expected to bring a one million pound economic boom to the city at a time when tourism has been hard hit by foot and mouth disease[91]', was seen as an added benefit, and, indeed, in his letter to Watt, Connery noted that the championships would aid tourism in Scotland, 'helping the industry recover from a troubled time.'[92] The figure of one million pounds income for the city appeared in numerous newspaper reports, although it was acknowledged by 'tourism chief', Alan Clark, that karate is not a great spectator sport, but that an event of this size 'raises the region's profile.'[93]

Watt continued: "Secondly, it was felt in certain quarters that the event might scupper karate being included in the Olympic Games. Apparently, the World Karate Federation and the International Olympic Committee had been in talks. Of course the WKC is not the WKF and I suspect that the IOC approves of unification in a sport and these championships were seen as counter-productive, at least by another, more local body. My answer to this point was, and still is, that karate is not suited to the Olympics because it has numerous schools, and if there is some kind of attempt at homogenizing these, then style uniqueness will suffer. Unification may be okay for *kumite* competition, but I don't understand how you could overcome the diversity in *kata* without style dilution taking place.

"My reactions to the objections were shock and sadness; shock by the verbal hostility it generated in certain quarters and sadness that some people should feel as they did. I remember reading an official being reported as alleging that, and I'm going to quote from the report: 'it would be easier for competitors to get awards at the confederation's championships than those of the WKF because the latter were of such a high standard.'[82] The truth of the matter is, of course, that if you were actually at the championships or saw highlights on television, then I'm quite prepared for people to make up their own minds as to the level. I'm not saying the WKC level was better, I wouldn't say that, I'm saying that it was comparable in my opinion." As far as Aberdeen City Council was concerned, a spokesman is quoted at the time as saying: 'We are absolutely certain this is a *bona fide* tournament, bringing a boost to the economy of Aberdeen. The Council is giving it its full support.'[81] No one was saying that the event wasn't *bona fide*.

Watt continued: "It got bad. I heard that there was talk that attempts were going to be made to disrupt the championships. I couldn't believe this was happening. The police were informed and they telephoned me and asked for my opinion as to the risk. I told them that these people could disrupt the event, but I didn't think they'd bomb the Exhibition Centre! I believe that there was a letter suggesting legal action. I asked myself, 'What's all this got to do with the noble art of karate?'

"I thought it was largely sour grapes from administrators. To read that certain people, and I'm going to quote again here, 'agreed actively to oppose the Aberdeen Championships,'[82] was extremely disappointing. But that wasn't all: 'It [a certain body] has also ruled its thirty-two member associations – with a total membership of over fourteen thousand – should not support the event in any way.'[82] I thought to myself, 'Who do these people think they are trying to tell other people what they can do and what they can watch?' If the truth be told, they were probably frightened that members would indeed come along and see for themselves what they were missing.

"Okay, you had to be a member of the WKC to take part in the championships, but the masterclasses that had been arranged and that took place during the two days prior to the championships at the Jesmond Sports Centre, Bridge of Don, were open to everyone – white belt or senior Dan grade, regardless of style or affiliation.

"In fact, a few *karateka* who were not with the WKC did come and watch the championships, and paid too. I said to more than one individual that I was really surprised to see them given the atmosphere. They were very quiet, taken aback I think, because I confronted them directly and they didn't know what to say. Perhaps I should give them credit for at least going against the directive; then again, perhaps they were spies!

A letter exists to show that William Berry, Chairman of the Aberdeen Sports Council, wrote to the Chairman of Sport-Scotland

Watt alongside Bill Berry, MBE, 7th Dan (judo)

fifteen months before the championships, noting that the event had the full backing of the Aberdeen Sports Council and that: 'I would sincerely hope that Sport-Scotland be seen to give this event its full support. I am aware, as your department is, that in the past there have been difficulties with the various karate factions within Scotland. However, on this specific occasion I would respectfully request that matters of the past be laid aside and that Ronnie Watt be given your full support.'[94] This is the only letter of correspondence between the two parties that the author has been privy to. There may, or may not, be others.

Watt continued: "Alistair Greig went up to Sport-Scotland, in Edinburgh, and told me that he waited a long time to see someone. Alistair gave this chappie information about the championships and the official said he'd get back to him. As far as I know he never did get back to him and we had no help from Sport-Scotland whatsoever."

In a letter[95] to the author, Berry, noting that he had known Watt for

Prince Adan, Ronnie Watt, Margaret Smith (Lord Provost), unknown and Dr.
Fritz Wendland at the Town House, Aberdeen (2001).

some forty years as both a friend and fellow martial artist, wrote: 'I
have always admired Ronnie's talent and commitment to his sport,
albeit with little or no support from any sports body within Scotland.'

With Aberdeen City Council behind Watt, one feels that there was
no way that spoilers were going to stop him. Watt was quoted a few
months prior to the championships saying: 'We are absolutely over the
moon that the event is being staged here. It has taken a lot of hard work
and two years of planning, but it is going to pay off.'[87]

Watt continued: "The 2nd Congress of the WKC was due to be held
prior to the championships, and, towards the end of 2000[96], Gail wrote
to the Lord Provost requesting a suitable venue. The congress was held
in the council chamber of the Town and County Hall in the Town
House before the championships [6.30 p.m.–8.00 p.m., 21st June] and
a civic reception had been arranged immediately afterwards
[8.00 p.m.–9.30 p.m.] at no cost to the championships. The honorary
guests at the congress included Prince Adan, Prof. Paul Hoglund, Dr.
Giacomo Bertoletti and George Popper. Dr. Wendland presented the
Lord Provost with the WKC medal for the city of Aberdeen. The
senior referees were staying at the Posthouse Hotel and Prince Adan,
Dr. Wendland and the masters were at the Skein Dhu Hotel, as I recall.
Official meetings, registration and the draw were held at the
Exhibition Centre, I believe, though I did not attend as I was training.

"The two days of seminars were style-based affairs and in the

Karate masters who taught at the seminars before the 2001 WKC World Championships. From left to right: Yukio Kawabata, Yasunari Ishimi, Eugene Codrington, Stan Schmidt, Yoshimasu Kakazu, Hideo Ochi, Kando Shibamori, Takeji Ogawa and Chuzo Kotaka.

mornings and lasted three hours each day. The nine masters from five styles who attended were Hideo Ochi (Shotokan), Stan Schmidt[97] (Shotokan), Kando Shibamori[98] (Wado-ryu), Eugene Codrington[99] (Wado-ryu), Takeji Ogawa[100] (Goju-ryu), Yasunari Ishimi[101] (Shito-ryu), Chuzo Kotaka[102] (Shito-ryu), Yoshimasa Kakazu[103] (Shorin-ryu), and Yukio Kawabata[104] (Shorin-ryu). In the afternoon there were courses in the theory and practice of *kumite* and refereeing *kata*. We also had open classes in the evenings, so *karateka* from one style could get a taster of another.

"I attended the classes under Ochi and Schmidt. The first thing that struck me about Schmidt when I met him at Aberdeen Airport after he'd flown in from Johannesburg, before taking him to his hotel, was how tall he was. When we shook hands, I noticed his large knuckles from the years of *makiwara* training. His reputation preceded him of course, as he'd been the highest graded non-Japanese in the JKA for decades. He was top-notch; we all knew that. I'd seen a large number of photographs of him in action in the various magazines, especially *Fighting Arts*, including the early ones where he was sparring with Enoeda on the cover of the magazine[105], and the one that showed that he'd trained with the best at the JKA headquarters in the 1960s.[106] That was good enough for me! What came across was his friendliness, his eagerness to oblige, and yet he had a spirit of steel and technique to match. I think it's the sign of a real master to have these qualities.

"On the course, he showed some highly innovative self-defence techniques from each of the *Heian kata* and the *sentei kata* with a *bo*, *morote-bo-uke*, *bo-sukami* and *bo-dori*. The *bunkai* was excellent, efficient, and I'd only ever seen evidence of this kind of training before from Ken Wittstock, another South African.

"Stan had been in a nasty car crash years before that affected his hips, resulting, later, in hip replacement. He told me after the master class that he now performed his *kata* to suit his body and particularly favoured *Sochin*. Many people would have given up training after that, but not Schmidt. Kase was like Stan in this, he'd never give in, and would use injury as a learning experience. I recall Kase saying to me that if a leg is badly injured, train on one leg; if one arm is injured, practise with the other. Remember what Kanazawa did with one hand back in 1957 – he won the first All-Japan JKA Championships![107] So I think this is an important point.

"Schmidt gave both myself and my next door neighbour, Pat Tischuk – a local black-belt, whose daughter, Alana, won a bronze medal in the *kumite* at the WKC World Cup for Children and Juniors

Master Ochi performing *keito-uke-nagashi* and *gedan-shuto-osae* whilst in *neko-ashi-dachi* during a demonstration of the *kata Gojushiho-dai* (Aberdeen, 2001).

in Valencia – who drove Stan about, a signed copy of his book, *Meeting Myself: Beyond the Spirit of the Empty-hand*. I really liked Stan and would very much welcome training with him again.

"Ochi's lesson began with the usual stretching and warming up exercises, including *choku-zuki*. On this short session, he concentrated on *tai-sabaki*. The class paired-up and we practised body-evasion to *jodan* and *chudan* punches, and *mae-geri*, *mawashi-geri* and *ushiro-*

geri attacks. After avoiding the attack and blocking, we had to counter immediately. The *kumite* was practised on both the left and right sides.

"The second half of Ochi's lesson was devoted to *Bassai-dai*. He demonstrated the *kata* slowly to the class. I remember in the *choku-zuki/uchi-ude-uke* series, he said that he preferred to use both arms to form the block as he was smaller and getting older and wanted to harness the maximum power that his body could generate for its size. Standing in *shizen-tai*, left arm out and the hand forming a *tate-shuto-uke*, he punched with his right fist, *choku-zuki*, and pulled the left fist back to his left hip, *hikite*. Then, instead of just blocking *uchi-ude-uke* with his right forearm and leaving the left fist on the left hip, he thrust the left arm out again and withdrew the right arm above his left, extended arm, just below the left shoulder and then brought the left fist back to the left hip and formed a right *uchi—ude-uke*. The movement was then repeated on the other side.[108] He instructed the class to do this. However, there was another technical point that he did that he asked us not to copy and I'll tell you what it was.

"In the *shuto-ukes* that follow the above sequence, like many senior Japanese, he did not use a straight reaction arm. The straight reaction arm method is really for lower grades, to make them aware that their shoulders should be square-on until the delivery of the *shuto-uke*, but it is also to highlight the positioning of the hips, which, again, should be in *shomen* until the last moment. This type of training is, therefore, extremely important and you never 'grow out of it.' Senior people cut the basics down and create focus from a shorter distance after many years of *hikite*. Then you can reduce the length of the reaction arm by about fifty per cent. Kase used to do this and you see it in the old films from the 1930s. I thought that Ochi's *shuto-uke* was exceptional, generating a powerful release of energy.

"Towards the end of the lesson, Ochi had everyone punch to a count to ten, in Japanese. Occasionally, someone performed a *kiai* after ten and he gave them a friendly tap on the head and a smile of disapproval, though I don't know why. To finish the class, we had to do one hundred trunk curls, our hands having to pass our knees each time, and that was murder.

"In the afternoons there were seminars for referees and judges, as I've said. The Germans had brought over a team of seven especially to help with these sessions. The seminars were run by Klementis, Bernd Hinschberger of Germany, Joe Mirza[109] of the USA – a genuine motivator and educator – and, Gerold Reifenauer of Austria. Doctor Rony Kluger also gave a lecture on Budo to the coaches. The WKC

Roland Deitrich (Germany), WKC Vice-President

Ilya Gouliev (Russia), WKC Vice-President

Ladislav Klementis (Slovakia), WKC Vice-President

Joe Mirza (USA), WKC Vice-President

Organising Committee was made up of Peter Spanton of England, Dr. Juraj Staffa of Slovakia, and, Roland Dietrich.[110] Dietrich, a tall, calm and refined *karateka*, seems to be one of those rare individuals who is able to overcome any problem. The non English members could speak English, so there was no communication problem.

"One point I find extraordinary is the language skills of the WKC Executive Committee. Marko Nicovic[111] [Serbia and Montenergo] who is now the WKC President, speaks Serbian, English, French, Spanish and German, all fluently. Let's look at the Vice-Presidents too. Dietrich speaks German, English and Spanish; Klementis speaks Slovak, English, Russian and German; Mirza speaks English, Arabic, Farsi and Armenian; and, Ilya Gouliev[112] [Russia] speaks Russian, English and French.[113]

"I found Nicovic to be a very dignified, clever and friendly man, a real 7th Dan. Gouliev is also very friendly and a serious *karateka*.

"The Championships were held at the Aberdeen Exhibition and Conference Centre, Bridge of Don, on the 23rd–24th June 2001, a venue that one reporter of the event called 'a grey utilitarian hangar of stupefying ugliness,'[114] though we preferred to think of it as a 'superb 4000-seater venue.'[115] There were to be four styles represented in competition – Shotokan, Goju-ryu[116], Shito-ryu[117] and Wado-ryu.[118] We also hoped for close on to a thousand competitors and officials and several thousand spectators. In the end, we had some eight hundred competitors from twenty-nine nations [Argentina, Australia, Austria, Bangladesh, Belarus, Brazil, England, France, Germany, Ireland, Israel, Italy, Japan, Nepal, Netherlands, Northern Ireland, Portugal, Republic of Srpske, Romania, Russia, USA, Scotland, Serbia, Slovakia, South Africa, Spain, Sri Lanka, Switzerland, Turkey, Ukraine and Yugoslavia][119] representing five continents, with some three thousand spectators.

"The Championships began at 8.00 a.m. on Saturday, 23rd June with eliminations for the team events, namely, team *kumite* and team *kata*. At 5.00 p.m. we had the opening ceremony, so the opening ceremony was actually held after the team eliminations. This had to be the case because of shortage of time. Proceedings began with a fanfare and a welcome by much respected TV and radio presenter and sports writer, Frank Gilfeather. Gilfeather, who actually originates from Dundee, was a first-class feather-weight boxer in his youth, a Scottish Amateur Boxing Champion, and he gave his services free over the two days. The *Heart of Asia* was the chosen theme tune throughout the event.

"Then there was a march on of teams led by girls, dressed in tartan, from the Albyn School for Girls. In all, sixty girls participated.'[120] This was followed by a march on of officials led by a lone piper. Then came the four introductions/welcomes. Firstly, Fritz introduced the aforementioned karate masters, then Margaret Smith, in her capacity of Lord Provost of Aberdeen, gave a short speech welcoming all to Aberdeen, and then it was my turn to say something. Finally, John Reynolds spoke as Chairman of the Organising Committee. We had three Members of Parliament in attendance in addition to the Consul General of Japan. In fact, Gail and I attended a reception at the consulate in Edinburgh, in January that year, to celebrate the Emperor's Birthday, so I had met Mr. Iwata before."

A copy of Watt's address has survived:

2001 WKC World Championships, from left to right: John Reynolds, Ronnie Watt, Margaret Smith, HRH Prince Adan Czartoryski Borbon, Carlo Henke.

'Dear Friends, distinguished guests,

'In the spirit of Karate-Do, it is my great pleasure, on behalf of the National Karate Federation (NKF) and the Organising Committee, to welcome you to Aberdeen for the 3rd (WKC) World Karate Championships.

'Whether you are competing, officiating, or supporting family and friends, I hope you will have a wonderful time.

'It has been a long and often difficult process to make these championships a reality. But now we are all here, and the action is underway, I know in my heart it has been more than worthwhile. I have dedicated much of my life to Karate-Do and the presence of so many *karateka* from around the world cheers my heart.

'These championships are a great boost for karate in Scotland and the UK as a whole. A world championship is a fantastic opportunity for young people

Some of the teams lining up at the opening ceremony of the WKC World Championships (2001).

and parents to see karate at its very best. Throughout the competition we will witness the tremendous skill, power, strength and discipline that karate demands of its students.

'An event of this scale is a major undertaking and I would like to acknowledge the contribution of the NKF membership and my own students and their families for the tremendous support they have given us over the past two years. The strength of an organisation is drawn from its members and we are fortunate indeed to enjoy such strength. It is my hope that the WKC draws on this strength during these championships and that we grow stronger and stronger as a confederation which embodies the true spirit of Karate-Do.

'My personal thanks go to Fritz Wendland, President WKC and His Royal Highness Prince Adan Czartoryski Borbon; our organising committee, managers and WKC technical staff. Finally, I would like to acknowledge the vision shown by Aberdeen City Council, Scottish Enterprise Grampian and our sponsors who have recognised the prestige of hosting a major world championship here in our city.

'Oss!'

Watt continued: "The Ellon Pipe Band then played and this was followed by Clanranald. We contacted Steve Hern of the Clanranald Trust for Scotland, in Edinburgh, back in 2000, and they put on a fantastic display with their Clan Combat Team. Because of the significance of the championships and the fact that their organisation

Members of Clanranald

had a good number of martial artists in it, they cut their performing costs by two-thirds. They also set up a retail stall with banners and flags that added to the event, as did, without question, the tribal drum and pipe band, Saor Patrol. If I remember correctly, the drums and pipes were playing both during their march into the hall and during the pre-arranged fighting. I think the whole demonstration lasted about twenty to thirty minutes.

"Then we had a display of highland dancing and that was followed by the closing remarks, a short break, and the team finals began at 6.00 p.m. In all, we had forty-two karate federations take part.

"The NKF supplied all the scorers, timekeepers, stewards, announcers and runners. We had thirty-one people on the go, with primary, secondary and tertiary roles. Andy and Alison Anderson sponsored the sport equipment for the officials and the NKF squad. NKF members such as Paddy Jamieson, now secretary to the NKF, Ian Kirk, Christopher Bruce, David 'Jock' Calder, and so on, were invaluable. Then there were all the people in the background, not only NKF members, who were involved in administration, catering, equipment, and others who acted as drivers, translators – and I'd like to mention Nicović's secretary, Rada Stopic, particularly in this regard – and more besides.

"The *kata* competition for the male and female team events was

Sitting, right to left, Hideo Ochi, Stan Schmidt and Norman Robinson during a break in the WKC World Championship opening ceremony.

based on three rounds. In the first round, teams would perform a *shitei kata* and the sixteen teams scoring the highest marks would go through to the second round, where they would perform a *sentei kata*. The eight teams scoring the highest marks would then go through to the final, where they would perform a *tokai kata*. Team scores were not added together and each round was a separate entity in itself."

The list of *kata* in the WKC *Shitei* Section is: Shotokan: *Heian 1-5*, and *Tekki Shodan*; Wado-ryu: *Pinan 1-5*; Goju-ryu: *Gekisai 1* and *2*, *Saifa*; Shito-ryu: *Pinan 1-5*, *Naifanchi Shodan*, *Saifa*. The *Sentei* Section is: Shotokan: *Bassai Dai*, *Kanku Dai*, *Enpi*, *Jion* and *Hangetsu*; Wado-ryu: *Passai*, *Kushanku*, *Jion* and *Niseishi*; Goju-ryu: *Seienchin*, *Shisochin*, *Seisan* and *Seipai*; Shito-ryu: *Bassai Dai*; *Kosokun Dai*, *Jion*, *Tomari no Wanshu* and *Seienchin*. The *Tokui* Section is: Shotokan: *Jitte*, *Tekki Nidan*, *Tekki Sandan*, *Gankaku*, *Bassai Sho*, *Kanku Sho*, *Sochin*, *Nijushiho*, *Chinte*, *Meikyo*, *Unsu*, *Wankan*, *Gojushiho Dai* and *Gojushiho Sho*; Wado-ryu: *Naihanchi*, *Wanshu*, *Chinto*, *Rohai* and *Seisan*; Goju-ryu: *Sanseiru*, *Kururunfa* and *Suparinpai*; Shito-ryu: Matsumura *Bassai*, Tomari *Bassai*, *Bassai Sho*, *Kosokun Sho*, *Jitte*, *Chinte*, *Chinto*, *Wanshu*, *Sochin* (Aragaki Ha), *Unshu*, *Gojushiho*, *Shisochin*, *Nipaipo*, *Niseishi*, *Seipai*, *Seisan*, *Kururunfa*, *Matsukaze* and *Suparimpei*.

Watt continued: "To be honest, I'm not sure why *Ji'in* is missing

Officials, competitors and spectators at the WKC World Championships in Aberdeen, 2001.

from the Shotokan *kata* list. I heard it said that it is because of Ochi. Maybe he doesn't practise it, or maybe it's because there are a number of variations, I don't know. I practise it two ways: the Enoeda way, let's say, and the Kase way. Kase substituted all the *zenkutsu-dachi* with *fudo-dachi*, and, very near the end, after performing a *kosa-uke*, left arm blocking *gedan-barai* and the right arm blocking *uchi-ude-uke*, before you pivot 135° into a *kiba-dachi* and perform another *kosa-uke* so that the right arm forms a *gedan-barai* and the right arm performs an *uchi-ude-uke*, which was Enoeda's way, Kase, and I only ever saw Kase do this, did not perform the second *kosa-uke* in the same way, for he swung round and performed another left-handed *gedan-barai* and a right-handed *uchi-ude-uke*. He didn't just keep them in place, as he pivoted, he brought his left hand to his right collarbone and his right hand swung across.[121]

"Competitors of the four styles represented had their own

312

The Aberdeen Exhibition Centre decked out in matting, showing six contest areas.

competitions, as it is WKC policy to respect the history and development of each style. Only seniors of the style in question could, therefore, judge the event.

"We had six contest areas and two warm-up areas covered in light green *tatami*, which we had hired from the National Exhibition Centre Group, in Birmingham, for some twelve hundred pounds as I recall, though, luckily, we had a sponsor to cover the transporting of all these large mats in a curtain sided articulated lorry, and that cost eleven hundred pounds. I recall the insurance on the mats, worth fifty thousand pounds, whilst in transit and whilst in Aberdeen was about seven hundred pounds. The contest areas were delineated from one another by red *tatami*, with light green *tatami* between the eight metres by eight metres squares as walk areas for officials. We had one hundred and eight red mats and four hundred and fifty-nine green mats, which were twenty-seven inches wide and forty-two inches in length. The mats were of the Geemat variety, judo mats, but noted for

The successful NKF women's *kata* team with their bronze medals. From left to right: Lydia Van De Beers, Roxanne Watt and Fiona Ellis, with Nicol Stephen, Member of the Scottish Parliament.

The winning women's South African Shito-ryu *kata* team in action

reducing mat burns. So, the whole floor was covered. We had them for six days, returning them two days after the event.[122]

"Twenty-two *kata* teams took part. For the Shotokan team *kata* event, the NKF came third in the women's competition, behind Serbia, and the winners, Italy. Our three girls were Fiona Ellis, Lydia Van De

Beers and my daughter, Roxanne. The reserve was Vivienne MacIntyre, now Vivienne Grant. Vivienne had a very capable sister, Angela. We weren't placed in the male event, which was ordered, first to third, Italy, Germany and South Africa, respectively.

"Another point we had to sort out prior to the championships was to ensure that we had all the National Anthems from the participating countries. We only played the anthems for the winners of events.

"Half-way between the *kata* and *kumite* team events, we had a short break from the competition when a lone piper played whilst a children's demonstration was given.

"The teams for *kumite*, of which there were fifty-five, male and female, were made up of three members each, plus one reserve. The *shobu-ippon* event was based on a single point being scored in two minutes, the *shobu-sanbon* event was based on three points, or the most points within three minutes. The *shobu-ippon* was an open weight event, the *shobu-sanbon* was divided into three weight categories: light (male – less than 68 kg; female – less than 55 kg), middle (male – less than 78 kg; female – less than 60 kg) and heavy (male – more than 78 kg; female – more than 60 kg). All the *kumite* events were multi-styled and competitors could enter for the *shobu-ippon* or the *shobu-sandon*, but not both.

"For the men, Serbia won the *shobu-sanbon* event with Yugoslavia coming second; for the women, Yugoslavia took the gold and the USA the silver. For the male *shobu-ippon* competition, Germany won the event and Turkey came second.

"The NKF team were really unlucky in the team *shobu-ippon* competition, because Simon Robertson was badly hurt when an American heavyweight burst his face with an illegal technique after the referee had called '*Yame*.' Simon was a point up when this happened. His opponent just went berserk and was disqualified, but our team could not continue as Simon had to go to the local hospital with severe concussion and bleeding. It was only after this incident that we learned that Simon had one eye, but we didn't know that at the time as he'd never told us. Simon was probably the second best fighter I ever had, after John Cox.

"For the female event, Germany took the title, followed by Italy, and the NKF came third with a very creditable bronze medal, with the same team members as in the *kata*. In the team *kumite*, we gave additional medals to the reserve and the coach.

"We had cracking women's *shobu-ippon* and *kata* teams and they took the bronze medals in these events the following year at the WKC

European Championships held in St. Pölten, Austria [15th–16th June 2002].[123-127] The *kata* team was made up of Angela MacIntyre, Vivienne Grant, Roxanne Watt and Lydia Van De Beers[128], and the *kumite* team: Tina Burgoine, Julia Little and Alexandra McLean.[125] The teams were beaten only by the Ukrainian and German teams. The men did well, too, in the *kumite*. Turkey went on to win gold over Germany.

"In fact, it was that year [2002] that I was made WKC Regional President for Britain and Ireland, which was a great honour[129] and a Shotokan technical director.[125] It was at St. Pölten and at the 2003 WKC World Championships, that I was asked to be a tournament director[124] and that was a tremendous honour too. I also changed the name of my *dojos* from the SSC to the National Karate Institute.

"In the evening of that first championship day, I took all the masters and senior officials to a Chinese restaurant owned by a friend of mine, Sam Ng. I have lunch there about once a fortnight with Bill Berry. We call it our office. Anyway, that evening, there we all were, Fritz, Ochi and his wife, Tomie, Stan Schmidt, Norman Robinson, and so on, and at the end of a truly excellent meal – many people there commented upon the hospitality – Sam said that the meal was on him! I was so taken aback, because I never expected it, and so another good friend had came up trumps.

"The second day, Sunday 24th June, was for individual competitors. We had one hundred and forty-nine individual *kata* entries and two hundred and ninety-six individual *kumite* entries.

"Eliminations began once again at 8.00 a.m. for both *kata* and *kumite* events, and at 5.00 p.m. we had the finals. Between the eliminations and the finals, a *nunchaku* display was given. Once again, the finals were interspersed with a demonstration of karate given by children. In the Shotokan men's *kata* event, Z. Nikolin of Yugoslavia took the title with G. Grolla and F. Comi, both from Italy, coming second and third, respectively. In the Shotokan female *kata* event, B. Gho of Italy came first, then N. Arviji and C. Vitale took silver and bronze for Yugoslavia and Italy, respectively. Because there were three weight divisions for both men and women in the *shobu-sanbon-kumite* in addition to the male and female *shobu-ippon-kumite*, I don't recall who won each event.[130] Although the NKF were not fortunate enough to win medals in these events, I can honestly say that all members gave a good account of themselves and I was really very proud of those who represented us.

"An American female Shito-ryu *karateka*, Elisa Au, won the Sean

Elisa Au, winner of the Sean Connery Award, with Carlo Henke, Chairman of the WKC.

Watt stands alongside the individual men's *shobu-ippon-kumite* winners: 1st – D. Kruegar, 2nd – H. Yildrim, 3rd – T. Schulze and N. Mantock (in tracksuit top, of England). Yildrim was later killed in a motorcycling accident.

Connery Trophy. She took the gold medal in the *kumite* and the bronze medal in the *kata*. We sent Connery a video of the event."[131]

One tongue-in-cheek, if not irreverent, though some might call 'silly' or 'irritating' article, noted that the championships were playing out along familiar lines: 'The Germans are strong and the Americans shout a lot … the Italians naturally reveal themselves to be the most stylish nation here … [and] if the Russians really want to get their hands on some fancy sports gear, they're going to have to defect.'[114]

Watt continued: "Twenty-two federations won medals from nineteen countries. The top three countries, in order, were: Slovakia, Romania and Italy.[132] Scotland came fifteenth equal in the federation list along with Switzerland and Argentina, and fourteenth in the country list with two bronze medals.

"At around 9.00 p.m. we had the closing ceremony where it was announced that the next, 4th WKC World Championships, were to be held in St. Petersburg, Russia, in 2003, as part of that famous city's three hundredth anniversary celebrations. Then one 7th Dan and two 6th Dans were awarded, and this was followed by a farewell party at the Aberdeen Exhibition Centre.

"Grampian TV and presenter Tyrone Smith, who is now with Scottish Television, really supported the Championships with excellent coverage, including filming the arrival and meeting of the masters at the airport, especially Stan Schmidt and Mr. and Mrs. Ochi.

"About one month later [27th–28th July 2001], the championships were shown on Sky Sports 2 at 10.00 p.m. and then the following day on Sky Sports 3 at 9.00 a.m. with Frank Gilfeather and I commentating. Frank, who I've known for years and who has interviewed me for Grampian Television on a number of occasions, really helped me with the voice-over. I found the voice-overs difficult, because they had to match the film clips and so I was restricted in what I could say. We had a full recording studio and the championships tapes ran all day. I sat there with earphones on, facing a microphone with a furry cover over it. What was difficult was trying to explain how a competitor scores points, the two types of *kumite* competition rules, and the differences between the four styles represented, to viewers without any prior knowledge of karate. I also had to keep my Aberdonian Doric accent in check, which I have to do when public speaking. I was shattered after that day in the studio. Both before, during and after the championships, making the programme was just another thing to do in a long line of things that had to be done to make a event like this viable. It was a real baptism of fire, but I grasped the opportunity and did my best. Like Frank, I didn't get paid to do the voice-overs.

"The people who produced the programme and video had twenty-two hours of competition and demonstrations. The film had to be edited for the time slots on Sky TV. I was really quite proud of the end result and I understand that it was shown worldwide. The film captured some of the excitement of the occasion. It featured all four events – team *kata*, individual *kata*, *shobu-sanbon-kumite* and *shobu-ippon-kumite*. We also see the four styles in action.[133] It was only through the donation given by Jim and Sandra Rogerson that it was possible for the programme to be made at all, though it was not possible to bring it out on DVD because of the costs involved.

"The championships were a huge success, even though I say so myself, both in terms of WKC karate and promoting Aberdeen. They cost something in the region of one hundred thousand pounds to stage and brought in about fifteen times that into the local community." Watt had 'dozens of calls from around the world complimenting Aberdeen for putting on such a great show.'[134] He noted that 'it was a great honour for me to bring the world championships to my home town. I

Father and daughter (2001)

would like to thank the people of Aberdeen, the City Council and all our sponsors for their kind support in making the championships such a great success and for extending such a warm welcome to our friends around the world.'[134] Watt wrote to the Lord Provost: 'The Aberdeen world championships were a real highlight for me personally, and for Scottish karate in general. I have received many complements and requests for guidance from federations all over the world on the way we put the championship together. Indeed, the Mayor of St. Petersburg was inspired by the Aberdeen event and is pulling out all the stops for when his city hosts the event in 2003.'[135]

Dr. Wendland wrote on the championships: 'Despite the fact that third parties in Scotland and Britain tried to disturb the preparations of the local organiser, the event proved to be a major success with a very high standard of competitor entering from all over the world ... The team around Ronald Watt, President of the National Karate Federation (NKF) of Scotland, worked very hard and overcame all the difficulties. The championships were a great success ... '[136] Wendland also noted: 'The 3rd WKC World Championships in Aberdeen, Scotland, gave the WKC another decisive push forward. The experiences encountered by the competitors, coaches, referees and the meetings of the presidents, proved to be very fruitful.'[137]

David McDonald of the organising committee commented: 'I'm sure Aberdeen will be fondly remembered by the competitors for its contribution to the 2001 championships.'[138, 139]

In fact, apart from being a showcase for karate competition, it was noted sometime after the event, as predicted, that one and a half million pounds had been forthcoming for the local economy[140], and that it 'provided a major boost for tourism in the north-east.'[141] The Chairman of Aberdeen Sports Council, Bill Berry, later noted that the event 'was a huge success.'[95]

Watt concluded: "*Traditional Karate* magazine gave us six pages of coverage on the championships.[142]

"I took Mrs. Ochi, who is a graduate in English from Tsudajuku University, to the airport on the Sunday evening. Gail and I have met Mrs. Ochi on many occasions and she is a genuinely delightful person. She is very considerate, especially when someone is injured in competition. She is a Shotokan 5th Dan and is WKC Director for Asia. I trained with her in India.

"When I got back from the airport, it just hit me. I was absolutely emotionally and mentally exhausted. That night, to save me driving home and back into Aberdeen the next morning, I shared a hotel room with *Sensei* Ochi. When the alarm went off, I shot out of bed and I think Ochi thought I was going to attack him! Ochi and I have had some good times together, as was the case in Bavaria [2002]. That new day was to be spent taking some of our honoured guests to Balmoral Castle. We took two minibuses and the party included Prince Adan, Fritz, Jurij Staffa and his wife, Andrea, Roland Dietrich and his wife, also named Andrea, and, Thomas Specht and his wife. Just to show

Mrs. Tomie Ochi (Germany)

you how drained I was, I couldn't even recall Balmoral's location and, therefore, which road should be taken to get there!

"On the Tuesday, we went to Stirling, where William Wallace defeated the English in 1297 and then went on to invade England from Newcastle to Carlisle. Of course, the following year Wallace was defeated by Edward I at Falkirk, and that was the end of that – well, at least for seventeen years. But I'll tell you something we saw whilst there and it is an object I shall never forget, and that was an actual sword from the Battle of Bannockburn [1314], where Robert the Bruce defeated Edward II's army and Scotland regained her independence.

"I also took the masters and guests to see Glover's House at 79 Balgownie Road, Bridge of Don. It's fantastic how they have recreated the ambiance of the time, thanks to the City of Aberdeen and Mitzubishi. The Fraserburgh Heritage Centre won a special award for being the best museum in Scotland.

"So, all the planning, the many thousands of man hours, the

Watt and Ochi, dressed in lederhosen (leather trousers), enjoying themselves in Bavaria. As Watt put it, 'I had a beer and Ochi and the Germans had a festival!'

sleepless nights, the seminars, the championships and the visits were over. I breathed an enormous sigh of relief. It had gone smoothly and everyone, I think, went home with happy memories. As I reflected on the event, my mind drifted back those forty odd years following that dreadful industrial injury that so nearly left me with one leg, and to when I was a youth, eagerly learning how to block and punch at the Bugeikwai. Never, not even in my wildest dreams, did I ever imagine that I might one day bring such prestigious championships to Aberdeen. People had said to me, 'Don't try to do it; it's too big; it can't be done,' but with the spirit of karate in my heart and with the help of some very dear friends, it wasn't impossible, because we did it."

REFERENCES & NOTES

CHAPTER I – FROM ODDJOB TO KANAZAWA AND ENOEDA

1. Leslie was born on the 28th August 1914, and died on the 29th January 1977.
2. Marjory was born on the 11th May 1916, and died on the 29th July 1982.
3. The marriage certificate notes that the couple were married at Bon Accord Church, Aberdeen, and Leslie Watt was employed as a plasterer's labourer. Leslie's father, also named Leslie, was a farm labourer and his wife, Annie (née Thomson), was deceased at this stage (they married in 1913). Leslie Watt was living at 3, Windsor Place, Aberdeen at the time of his marriage. Marjory Watt's father was a retired farmer at the time of her marriage, and her mother, previously Stewart, formerly Cowie, was deceased. Marjory was living at 27, Skene Square at the time of her marriage, so Leslie evidently moved in with her.
4. *The Avengers* ran from 1961-1969. The outstanding *Avengers* episode that dealt with karate was entitled, *The Cybernauts*, which was first broadcast on the 16th October 1965. For a description of the karate sequences contained within this episode see *Shotokan Dawn, Vol. I*, pp. 293-294.
5. *The Saint*, based on the character created by Leslie Charteris, was first broadcast in 1962 (concluding in 1969), with Roger Moore taking the lead role. In an episode in the fourth or fifth season (1966-67 and 1968-69, respectively), Kanazawa was featured performing karate.
6. *Danger Man*, starring Patrick McGoohan as John Drake, ran from 1960-61, and, 1964-1967.
7. There is no record in the BKF archive to suggest that Anderson had graded in karate at this time, and, indeed, Bell had largely suspended gradings in the latter half of 1964 and the first half of 1965 awaiting Kanazawa's arrival. It is most unlikely that Allan had graded to yellow belt rank, having joined only two months before Watt began. If they both wore yellow belts, they may have reflected judo grades. However, the attendance and grading records of the 1965 BKF summer school have not survived and it quite possible that Anderson, at least, graded at this time.
8. Anderson signed his BKF membership application form on the 11th April 1964.
9. Allan signed his BKF membership application form on the 29th September 1965.
10. Kanazawa was born on the 3rd May 1931 in Miyako, Iwate Prefecture. He studied judo to 2nd Dan whilst at High School, before changing university from Nihon to Takushoku, so that he could study karate. He began karate training at Takushoku in 1952. He was awarded his 1st Dan in the astonishingly short period of eighteen months and by 1955 he was a 2nd Dan. Upon graduation, he joined the newly instigated JKA's instructors' course in 1956 on the advice of the then Chief Instructor, Masatoshi Nakayama, and successfully pursued the one-year programme. In the first JKA Championships, Kanazawa won the *kumite* title with a broken hand and the following year became the first of only six JKA Grand Champions (to date), by winning both the *kumite* and *kata* events on the

same occasion. As a 4th Dan, in January 1961, he become the JKA representative to Hawaii until 1963, after which he returned to Tokyo. He had been an instructor at the JKA Headquarters, Musashi Industrial University, Mitsubishi Shoji Company and the Arabia Oil Company. Master Kanazawa's story, to the time he came to Britain, is told in the author's book, *Kanazawa, 10th Dan: Recollections of a Living Karate Legend – the early years (1931-1964)* {Shoto Publishing, 2001}). Further details on Kanazawa will be revealed throughout the current book.

11. Bell was born in Ilford in 1921 and an account of his early life and how he established karate in Britain is given in great depth in *Shotokan Dawn, Vols. I & II, The Shotokan Dawn Supplement, Shotokan Dawn Over Ireland, Shotokan Horizon, You Don't Have to Dress to Kill,* and, *The Liverpool Red Triangle Karate Club.* He died on the 27th February 2004 of cancer and his obituary appeared in *The Times* (8th March 2004, p. 28 {page 56 of the compact edition}). He also features in *The Oxford Dictionary of National Biography*, with the entry written by the author.

12. Plee was born in 1923 and is widely regarded as the founder of karate in Europe. He started judo not long after World War II under Mikinosuke Kawaishi and was one of the first Frenchmen to be graded to *Shodan*. He also practised French boxing, where both the hands and feet are employed. After seeing an article in a 1948 edition of *Life* magazine that featured karate, he acquired some Japanese books on the subject and had them translated. In 1953, he met Donn Draeger (1922-1982), a former major in the US Marine Corps who would later become famous for his martial arts books. Draeger introduced Plee to Shotokan karate mainly through a film of Isao Obata (1904-1976) and Masatoshi Nakayama (1913-1987) practising. In 1954, Plee wrote his first book, *Vanquish or Die: Karate-Do.* He was a founder member of the Federation Francaise de Karate et Boxe Libre. Although Bell had been in contact with Plee at least since February 1955 (the date of the first known letter between the two men), it was probably not until 1957 that Bell first trained at his *dojo* at 34, Rue de la Montagne Sainte-Genevieve, Paris 5 (see, *Shotokan Dawn, Vol. I, The Shotokan Dawn Supplement*, and, *Shotokan Horizon*). Bell founded the BKF under the auspices of the Federation Francaise de Karate et Boxe Libre. Plee aligned himself to Minoru Mochizuki's Yoseikan *dojo*, in Japan, which had been the *dojo* of Jean Alcheik and arranged for Minoru's son, Hiroo, to come to Paris in 1956 and stay for two years. In 1957, Plee arranged for another Yoseikan *karateka*, Tetsuji Murakami to stay in France. Both these Japanese had a profound effect on European karate. Plee founded the International Karate Federation in 1958, which listed the following countries as affiliated: Japan, France, Great Britain, Germany, Italy, Switzerland, Canada, Belgium, Portugal, Tunisia, Morocco, USA, Spain, Panama, Uruguay and Argentina. He wrote a good number of books during these early days, including, *ABC of Karate*, and, *Karate by Pictures.*

13. Mochizuki was born in Japan in 1936, the son of the famous *judoka* and *aikidoka*, Minoru Mochizuki (1907-2003). Hiroo spent much of his early life in China, but returned after the war. He was already studying a number of martial arts, including kendo, judo and aikido, before commencing karate in 1952 under Master Hyogo, at his father's Yoseikan *dojo*, in Shizuoka. He enrolled at Tokyo

University to read veterinary medicine in 1954. He then travelled to Paris in 1956 and met Henri Plee. Studying in France for two years, he taught at Plee's *dojo* and it was here that Vernon Bell trained under him. Mochizuki returned to Japan to compete his academic studies, came under the influence of Wado-ryu, and returned to France in 1963. He visited England for the BKF in 1964. He founded, or improved upon, Yoseikan Budo.

14. Murakami was born in Shizuoka in 1927 and started training at the Yoseikan *dojo* at a young age where he trained in a number of martial arts. A carpenter by trade, by the time Plee invited him to Paris, he was a 3rd Dan in Yoseikan karate (his teacher being Masaji Yamaguchi), a 3rd Dan in aikido and a 2nd Dan in kendo. He was also a 1st Dan from the JKA. Murakami arrived in Paris in November 1957 and started teaching for Plee. In August 1958, Bell and three of his students went to train with Murakami in Paris, and in July, 1959, Murakami paid his first of many trips to England for the BKF. Murakami was highly influential at this time, but with the onset of the arrival of JKA instructors in Europe, he lost favour in some quarters. His senior students in Britain were Terry Wingrove and Jimmy Neal. He last taught for the BKF in 1964. He subsequently joined the Shotokai and was graded 5th Dan by Egami. Later moving to Spain, he continued to teach throughout Europe and North Africa. Murakami died of cancer in 1987.

15. Kase was born in Tokyo on the 9th February 1929. He started judo at the Kodokan in 1935 and reached 2nd Dan before beginning karate in 1944. He trained at the Shotokan under both Gichin and Yoshitaka Funakoshi. In 1949, Kase was awarded his 3rd Dan and captained Senshu University's karate club for three years. Brief *curriculum vitae* details provided at the time to Bell by the JKA, show that Kase had instructed at George Higginson's Durban *dojo*, South Africa, for three months in 1964. Kase had also served as a judge at the All Japan Karate Championships from the 1st Championships in 1957, and instructed at Hitotsubashi University. Further details on Kase will be revealed throughout the book.

16. Enoeda was born in Fukuoka on the 4th July 1935 and reached the final of the All-Japan High Schools Judo Championships. He attained 2nd Dan in judo before studying karate at Takushoku University. It was at Takushoku that he acquired the nicknamed 'Tora' (tiger) for his tremendous fighting spirit. By 1956 he was a 3rd Dan and captain of the karate club. In 1959 he undertook the JKA Instructors' Course, and in 1963 took the JKA *kumite* title, defeating Shirai in the finals. Also in 1963, along with Nakayama, Shoji, Iwaizumi and Kisaka, he instructed the military in Indonesia for two months. An instructor to Tokyo Art College, Enoeda came to England as reigning JKA Champion, for there were no JKA championships in 1964 due to the Olympic Games being held in Tokyo. Further details on Enoeda will be revealed throughout the book.

17. Shirai was born in Nagasaki in 1937 and trained in kendo at High School. He attended Komazawa University from 1955-1959 and then undertook the JKA Instructors' Course. He became the JKA Grand Champion in 1962. He was an instructor to Toritsu University and the United States Air Force before coming to Britain. Further details on Shirai will be revealed throughout the book.

18. For more details on the BKF Dundee branch see *Shotokan Dawn, Vol. II*, pp. 86-

87, and, *The Shotokan Dawn Supplement*, pp. 79-85.

19. David Danks was a twenty-year-old journalist when he applied for BKF membership to the Dundee Branch on the 10th October 1964.

20. Layton, C. & Muthucumarana, D. *You Don't Have to Dress to Kill: early female Shotokan karateka of the British Isles (1957-1966)* (Saisho Publications, 2007).

21. Sherry was born in Liverpool in 1943 and joined the BKF in 1961 after studying ju-jitsu. He was the first *karateka* in Britain to take, and pass, a JKA black belt grading, along with Joseph Chialton, in February 1966. He was a competitor of the highest order, taking the first KUGB *kata* title in 1967, and then again for the next three years. He was KUGB grand champion in 1968 and 1970. He won the first British All-Styles Championship in 1966 and became EAKF European *kumite* champion in in 1968. He was a member of the highly successful Liverpool Red Triangle team for many years. He became chairman of the KUGB and was coach to the team that won the World Shotokan Karate Championships in Sunderland in 1990, defeating Japan. Future WSKA championships were also notable. On Enoeda's death, he became chief instructor to the KUGB and, today, holds the rank of 8th Dan. A book on Sherry's life is currently being written by the author.

22. Thompson was born in 1930 and joined the BKF in 1961 after studying judo. He attended Murakami's St. Osyth course that year and shortly thereafter founded the BKF York branch. He was a BKF committee member and was therefore partly responsible for bringing Kanazawa to Britain. He became a founder member of the KUGB, receiving his *Shodan* in 1967. Today, he holds the rank of 3rd Dan and still teaches.

23. A good number of JKA instructors were shown performing *kata*, such as Nakaya, Asai, Sugiura. Shoji and Iwaizumi (*Heian* 1-5, respectively), Sugiura, Shoji and Iwaizumi (*Tekki* 1-3, respectively), Enoeda (*Jitte*), Mori (*Chinte*), Kase (*Jion*), Enoeda (*Bassai-dai*), Iwaizumi (*Bassai-sho*), Ueki (*Gankaku*), Mikami (*Hangestu*), Nakaya (*Kanku-dai*), Mikami (*Kanku-sho*), Shirai (*Sochin*), Asai (*Nijushiho*) and Nakayama (*Unsu*).

24. Details of these individuals, their BKF clubs, correspondence with Bell, and *dojo* members, can be found in *Shotokan Dawn*, and, *The Shotokan Dawn Supplement*.

25. Photographs of these three London *dojos*, both inside and outside, can be found, variously, in *Shotokan Dawn*, and, *The Kanazawa Years: Reminiscences by Michael Randall, 7th Dan, on a golden age in British karate* (Shoto Publ. 1998).

26. Nambu was born in Kobe in 1943. Coming from a family imbued in martial arts, he trained in Shito-ryu under Chijiro Tani from 1961, when studying in Osaka. He was Japanese University Champion in 1963 and was awarded the Medal of Merit. He moved to France in the mid 1960s and taught all over Europe. He founded Sanku-kai and Nambudo.

27. Morris was born in 1938/39 and educated in Glasgow. He trained in judo and was a Royal Marine reserve. In May 1964, he visited Plee's Shotokan *dojo* in Paris, returned to open a karate club, and then returned to Paris where he met Shito-ryu *karateka*, Yoshinao Nambu, who graded him to 1st Dan in September 1965, in Glasgow. Morris set up the Kobe-Osaka Karate Kai and changed to Shukokai. He subsequently travelled to Japan and was graded both 2nd Dan and

3rd Dan in 1967 (uncredited article: *Tommy Morris* {*Karate*, No. 2, 1968}). He became a highly influential figure in Scottish karate.

28.   Layton, C. *Shotokan Dawn, Vol. I: A Selected, Early History of Shotokan Karate in Great Britain (1956-1966)* , pp. 265-275 (Mona Books, 2007).

29.   Details of these individuals, their BKF clubs, correspondence with Bell, and *dojo* members, can be found in *Shotokan Dawn*, and, *The Shotokan Dawn Supplement*.

30.   These displays are recorded in detail in *Shotokan Dawn, Vol. II*, pp. 149-155.

31.   Michael Parkes is an acclaimed painter of animals.

32.   11th March is given in Watt's early KUGB licence, and this probably shows entry date.

33.   Bell's own karate *dojo* was sited at St. Mary's Hall, St. Mary's Lane, Upminster. This was the BKF's first hired karate *dojo* and Bell and his early students started training there just after Christmas, 1957. The building, at least in 1994, was still standing, and must be regarded as one of the most important, if not the most important *dojo* in the history of British karate (see *Shotokan Dawn, Vol. I*, pages 107-111). It was the venue for early training under Murakami and, later, Kanazawa.

CHAPTER II – BECOMING A PROFESSIONAL KARATE INSTRUCTOR

1.   Whether there was a very late (before the split and the formation of the KUGB) BKF club in Glasgow is a mystery. Bell had no recollection of a BKF Glasgow branch despite the presence of an empty file in the BKF archive so marked. Various enquiries came from individuals living in that city and maybe this file once housed those, or had been made-up in preparation of a *dojo*. Certainly, in a list of BKF clubs that appeared on Edward Whitcher's (Whitcher joined the BKF London *dojo* in 1963 and became the first *karateka* to take a *Shodan* grading under Kanazawa in Britain {April 1966}) Certificate of Proficiency (for brown belt junior instructor status) dated the 3rd March 1966, on BKF letter-headed paper and signed by Bell and Kanazawa, whilst Aberdeen and Dundee are mentioned, and, so, strangely, at this late date, is Ayr (Saltcoats), Glasgow is not included on the list that runs down the left-hand side of the page (see *The Shotokan Dawn Supplement*, page 96, for a copy of this certificate). However, Bell noted in correspondence that, in April 1966, the Glasgow branch's representative was a C. Bauldry. If Bauldry was a BKF member, nothing has survived. In his letter to Bell dated the 16th May 1966, Anderson mentioned that there was a branch in the process of being formed in Glasgow, and that 'we are trying to finalise the formation of a branch in Fraserburgh.' There is no evidence whatsoever of a BKF Fraserburgh club. Anderson intended calling a meeting of representatives of the Aberdeen, Glasgow and Fraserburgh *dojos* in mid June 1966. One supposes that these *dojos*, if they were indeed founded around mid 1966, because of the political/organisational uncertainly following the BKF meeting already alluded to, never registered with the BKF.

2.   Sumi was born on the 23rd June 1936 in Shiritori. He gained his 1st Dan in 1957 after training under Eiji Takaura and joined the JKA in 1962. Today, an 8th Dan, he resides in Tokyo, but heads the Karate Union of Australia and continues to

travel, teaching karate.

3. John Allan stated on his BKF application in answer to the question, 'State how you became interested in karate …': 'Whilst in Japan with Royal Navy.'

4. Kanazawa recalled, when living and teaching in Hawaii (1961-1963): 'I bought a nice red car with a white line down the side, a Ford Saloon, with a special GT engine,' and, later, 'When I got back to Japan I had no money because of the car. I hadn't bought the Ford, I'd acquired it on hire purchase, but it had taken all my money.' (Layton, C. *Kanazawa, 10th Dan: Recollections of a Living Karate Legend – the Early Years (1931-1964)* (Shoto Publ., 2001), p.156 and p. 160, respectively.

5. Michael Randall recalled this event: 'Kanazawa was heavy handed with Sumi during a freestyle demonstration. He hit him hard across the face, very hard in fact, with the palm of his hand – slapped him, if you like. You could clearly hear the sound of the slap in the audience. It was really quite embarrassing. I took it as a deliberate 'put you in your place' act' (Layton, C. *The Kanazawa Years: Reminiscences by Michel Randall, 7th Dan, on a golden age in British karate* (Shoto Publ., 1998), p. 136.

6. Nakayama was born in Yamaguchi Prefecture in 1913, the son of a surgeon who held the rank of colonel in the Japanese Imperial Army. He spent a substantial part of his schooling in Taiwan, where his father was stationed, before entering Takushoku University in 1932, studying Chinese. He took up Shotokan under Funakoshi and his son, Yoshitaka, and in 1937 went to China. Returning to Japan in 1946, in 1949 he was a founder member of the JKA. He taught karate to American military personnel and became Professor of Physical Education at Takushoku. He set up the JKA Instructors' Course in 1956 under the Ministry of Education, and was instrumental in organising the All-Japan JKA Championships which commenced in 1957. His main contribution to karate was his sending JKA instructors abroad, and thus he affected the lives of millions of people. His book, *Dynamic Karate*, first published in 1966, became *the* reference work on Shotokan the world over, and this was followed by his *Best Karate* series, though he wrote a good number of other books as well. Nakayama death in 1987 caused political disruption in the Shotokan world.

7. Naylor, C. & Goodbody, J. *Report on the KUGB '68 Summer Course* (*Karate*, No. 2, 1968).

8. Miyazaki was born in Saga City on the 17th June 1938. He entered Takushoku in 1956, where he became a member of a highly successful university team that included Kisaka, Ochi and Asano. He resided in Belgium from 1967 as representative of the JKA. He died on the 31st May 1993, of stomach cancer. A photograph of Miyazaki is to be found in Nakayama's, *Dynamic Karate*, p. 259. See also, photographs in: Layton, C. *The Kanazawa Years: Reminiscences by Michael Randall, 7th Dan, on a golden age in British karate* (Shoto Publishing, 1998), p. 126.

9. Shiro Asano was born in Shinjuku, Tokyo, on the 29th October 1939. He is reported to have graded to 1st Dan at the age of sixteen before enrolling at Takushoku University, where he had a highly successful competition career. He qualified as a JKA instructor in April 1963. He taught in Germany for two months before coming to Britain in 1968, where he was first, briefly, based in

Liverpool before moving to Nottingham. He is now Chief Instructor, briefly, SKI (GB) and the SKI European Federation. He currently holds the rank of 9th Dan (awarded in 2001).

10. Akio Nagai was born in Yamaguchi in 1942. He trained firstly in Shito-ryu before changing styles to Shotokan when he attended Takushoku University. He moved to Germany in 1965. Today, an 8th Dan, he heads SKI Germany.

11. Koichi Sugimura was born on the 24th March 1940. He read law at Keio University and today, as a 7th Dan, is JKA Chief Instructor to Switzerland.

12. Sadashige Kato was born on the 22nd July 1943 in Kochi. He attended Takushoku University. He taught karate in Germany in 1966 before coming to Great Britain. Today, he is 8th Dan of the International JKA.

13. The fact that Iwai was in attendance is confirmed in Naylor, C. *Liverpool Dominate '68 KUGB Championships* (*Karate*, No. 1, July 1968).

14. Naylor, C. & Goodbody, J. *Report on the KUGB '68 Summer Course* (*Karate*, No. 2, 1968). It is noted that Miyazaki beat the record for drinking a yard (three pints) of ale. He apparently managed this in an astonishing twenty-one seconds, as timed by Nakayama.

15. O'Neill was born in Liverpool in 1948 and joined the BKF in 1963. Receiving his *Shodan* in 1968, he became one of the great competitors of British karate. He took eleven individual KUGB titles between 1969 and 1978 (*kumite*: 1969, 1973, 1975, 1977; *kata*: 1971-1975, 1977, 1978) being grand champion three times. He was a Liverpool Red Triangle team member for many years and an international competitor for nearly twenty years. He won the gold medal in the South African Games in 1969, was captain of the British All-Styles that beat the Japanese at the World Championships in Paris, in 1972, and was part of the All-Styles squad that beat the Japanese at the World Karate Championships in Long Beach California, in 1975, and took the title. He was placed joint third in the 1974 World Championships held in Japan. His competition career came to an abrupt end following a knee injury in a bout against Italy in 1983. He was editor and publisher of *Fighting Arts* magazine (later to become *Fighting Arts International*, and, *Terry O'Neill's Fighting Arts International*), that ran for ninety-three editions from 1972-1997. At the time of writing, he holds the rank of 7th Dan. He took up acting and has appeared in numerous films and television dramas.

16. Naylor, C. *Liverpool Dominate '68 KUGB Championships* (*Karate*, No. 1, July 1968).

17. The KUGB grading syllabus for kyu grades was published in 1969 in three issues of *Karate* magazine, as follows: 9th kyu-6th kyu (No. 7, pp. 12-14); 5th kyu-3rd kyu (No. 8, pp. 16-17); 2nd kyu-1st kyu (No. 9, pp. 6-7).

18. Kisaka was born in 1938 and, after attending Takushoku University graduated from the JKA Instructors' Programme in 1961. Photographs of Kisaka are to be found in Nakayama's, *Dynamic Karate*, pp. 21-22.

19. Ochi was born in 1940. He entered Takushoku University and, after graduating, embarked upon the JKA Instructors' Course, graduating in 1963. He became JKA grand champion in 1966 and followed this up taking the *kumite* title in 1967 and the *kata* title in 1969. He returned to competition in 1976 and took the *kata* title once more. At the time of writing, he is Chief Instructor to JKA Europe and

the German Karate Federation, and holds the rank of 8th Dan. Photographs of Ochi are to be found in Nakayama's, *Dynamic Karate* – for example, p. 69; see also, *Fighting Arts International*, No. 40, p. 63.

20. Yoshimasa Takahashi, a graduate of Komazawa University and a Buddhist priest, died in a motorcycle accident in 1975. He won the JKA *kata* championships three times (1970/72/73) and was a member of the Japanese team at the world championships in 1972. For a list of JKA winners, *kata* and *kumite*, from 1957-1989, see Layton et al, *A Shotokan Karate Book of Facts, Vol. I*, (Shoto Publ, 1997), pp. 38-39.

21. Anderson, J. *Aberdeen University Karate Club* (*Karate*, No. 3, 1968).

22. Uncredited. *Aberdeen University Karate Club* (*Karate*, No. 8, 1969, p. 13).

23. Martin, D. 1969 University Championships (*Karate*, No. 8, 1969, pp. 9-11).

24. Martin, D. *1970 Universities Championships* (*Karate*, No. 13, 1970, pp. 6-7).

25. Uncredited piece in unknown newspaper, entitled, *YOU can be a black-belt: Shotokan club extends welcome to all youngsters.*

26. Instructors at the KUGB *gasshuku* that year were: Enoeda, Shirai, Miyazaki, Asano, Kobayashi, Takahashi, Nagai, Sugimura, Sumi and Kato (*Karate*, No. 7, p. 4). Training was from the 4th-8th May, and, 11th-15th May.

27. Doran, A. *Letter* (*Karate*, No. 11, 1969, p. 6).

28. Hironishi was born on the 1st January 1913, and died in December 1999. He was reputedly Funakoshi's favourite student. After graduating from Waseda University, he joined the army and saw service in China. He taught at the Shotokan *dojo* as a 4th Dan during the Pacific War. He was a founder of Shotokai and was an instructor to Mitsusuke Harada, whose reflections of him are to be found (including photographs of Hironishi) in the author's two books*: Karate Master: The Life and Times of Mitsusuke Harada* (Ronin Publ. 1997), and, *Reminiscences by Master Mitsusuke Harada* (KDS Publ., 1999).

29. Egami was born on the 7th December 1912, in Fukuoka Prefecture, and died on the 8th January 1981. He was a highly regarded *karateka* who graduated from Waseda in the mid 1930s. He was a founder of Shotokai, and, later, President and Chief Instructor of Japan Karate-Do Shotokai. A lecturer at Waseda and instructor to a number of other universities, including Chuo, Gakushuin and Toho, he was later plagued by ill health. He became mentor to Mitsusuke Harada, who was his private student for eighteen months, and whose reflections on Egami are to be found (including photographs) in the author's two books*: Karate Master: The Life and Times of Mitsusuke Harada* (Ronin Publ. 1997), and, *Reminiscences by Master Mitsusuke Harada* (KDS Publ., 1999). Egami wrote the book, *The Way of Karate: Beyond Technique*, later published as, *The Heart of Karate-Do* (Kodansha, 1975).

30. Layton, C. *Karate Master: The Life and Times of Mitsusuke Harada* (Budo Publ., 1997), and, *Reminiscences by Master Mitsusuke Harada* (KDS Publ., 1999).

31. Layton, C. *Karate Master: The Life and Times of Mitsusuke Harada* (Budo Publ., 1997), p.142. It is noted that Ken Waight accompanied Harada 'about once a fortnight, assisting on courses in Scotland ...' Waight trained with Harada from 1964-1970.

32. Whether there was a very late (before the split and the formation of the KUGB)

BKF club in Edinburgh is a mystery. Bell had no recollection of a BKF Edinburgh branch despite the presence of an empty file in the BKF archive so marked. Apparently, a Kenneth Budge was planning to start a BKF Edinburgh branch in 1965, and so perhaps Bell opened a file in anticipation. There are no membership forms in existence for Edinburgh, so it is likely that the venture, at least in BKF terms to mid 1966, never got off the ground. Certainly, in the aforementioned list of BKF clubs in March 1966 (Note 1), Edinburgh is not mentioned. In a letter of the 22nd July 1965, Budge wrote to Bell in response to a letter from Bell of the 22nd June. Budge was 'extremely disappointed that your [Bell's] previous promises have not been fulfilled,' and requested why his 'outfit and licence' had not materialised. In a reply of the 12th August, Bell apologised, but noted that both *gi* and licence had been sent two months previously. Bell was prepared to send replacements of both, hoping, 'we can be assured of your continued support and loyalty, and as a potential Area Officer you are invited to a special meeting.' A new licence exists for Budge.

Whilst what became of Budge is a mystery, he wasn't the first Scot from Edinburgh to show interest in BKF karate. A certain J. Doyle, from Rosyth, living just across the Forth Bridge, was curious enough to send for details as early as July, 1957. Also, a certain M. Robertson from Edinburgh wrote to Bell on the 25th October 1963 (*BKF Register of Enquiries* entry 372), and literature was sent three days later. Doyle and Robertson appear not to have joined the BKF, or, if they did, no evidence has survived.

33. Harris, W. *For the Chop: Ronnie Hits Out at the Karate Cowboys* (*Evening Express*, 10th February 1986, page unknown).

34. For example: Reid, M. *Majorca – Here We Come: Frearsome foursome ready to give Romeos the chop* (unknown newspaper of unknown date, though 1970s); Uncredited and untitled report in unknown and undated newspaper (though 1970s); Uncredited report in unknown and undated newspaper (though 1970s), entitled, *Knees Up Mrs. Watt*; Uncredited report in unknown and undated newspaper (though 1970s), entitled, *Women Learn the Martial Arts*; Uncredited report in unknown and undated newspaper (though 1970s), entitled, *First Lesson in Self-defence for City Women*; published photograph of Watt instructing a large class of women at the Cowdrey Club, Fonthill Road, in 1978 (*Evening Express*, 16th September 2008); various adverts.

35. Taken from a document from 1970. Minor corrections have been made.

36. Taken from a document from 1973.

37. A ticket survives for the showing of *Sanjuro*.

38. A photograph of Kanazawa using such a *makiwara* and a description by its joint manufacturer, Michael Randall, is to be found in the author's, *Kanazawa Years: Reminiscences by Michael Randall, 7th Dan, on a Golden Age in British Karate* (Shoto Publ., 1998, pp. 145-147), so: 'I went into the manufacturing of *makiwara* with Chris Adamou. Kanazawa *Sensei* helped us on that and another venture, and on one occasion loaned us the money to get started – about two hundred pounds I believe, which was a lot of money in those days. Chris and I were happy-go-lucky lads, carefree, disorganized, living from day to day, and Kanazawa said that we would have to structure ourselves if we were going into business. He had a degree in economics, so we listened. 'Oh! Mr. Randly. You

will have to write a schedule for the whole day and tick off as you complete each task.' That was good advice, and it worked for us. We made and sold the *makiwara* through a company we set up called Hiraku Importing, which had an oak leaf logo, upon which was a rising sun badge. It looked really nice, and on each *makiwara* there was a gold sticker which read: 'This Hiraku product has been tested and is recommended by Hirokazu Kanazawa,' and then followed Kanazawa's signature. With each *makiwara* came a four-page pamphlet, 'The Reasons and Needs for Using a MK1-69 *Makiwara*,' which I think we wrote and Kanazawa put his name to. The *makiwara* was set on to a large wooden base and supported by a triangular metal frame. The frame was just over ninety degrees, because the ash blade would bend with use, and this obtuse angle prevented this from happening. In fact, we made two blades. The first was thicker and had a soft striking pad, and was intended for the beginner, as it was considered ideal for learning to feel one's own muscle tension. The thin blade with the hard rubber striking pad, was for the more advanced student, and was designed for training in speed and *kime*. For kicking techniques, the thicker *makiwara* was recommended, irrespective of level of expertise, but the thinner blade could be used for snap-kicks.'

39. The centre spread in issue 12 of *Karate* magazine (1970) shows the advert for the *makiwara* and five photographs of Kanazawa using it with *gyaku-zuki*, *empi*, *mawashi-geri*, *yoko-geri-kekomi* and *ushiro-geri*. It was priced at £14.

40. In 1972, Kon was reported being both a 6th Dan in judo and a 6th Dan in karate in *Fighting Arts International,* Vol. 1, No. 2, p. 24, where a photograph shows him refereeing the KUGB *kumite* final. For a photograph of Kon and other Japanese instructors at the 1977 KUGB summer school, see the author's, *Masao Kawasoe, 8th Dan: Recollections of a Shotokan Karate Master – the Early Years (1945-1975)* (Mona Book, 2008, p. 137).

41. An advert for this course is to be found in *Fighting Arts* (Vol. 1, No. 1, p. 29).

42. Tabata was a regular contestant in the JKA Championships and although he never won a title, he was placed third in the *kumite* event in 1971, and was part of the winning Japanese team at the IAKF World Championships in 1976. He graduated from the JKA Instructors' Course in 1966 and went to Taichung, Taiwan, under Asai. A photograph of Tabata is to be found in Nakayama's, *Dynamic Karate*, p. 69. Also, in the 1971 JKA Championships, *Fighting Arts*, Vol. 1, No. 1, p. 5, and, variously, in later *Fighting Arts* editions.

43. An advert for this course is to be found in *Fighting Arts* (Vol. 1, No. 4, inside cover).

44. Hideo Tomita came to Britain in 1972 to act as an assistant to Enoeda and stayed ten years, to return to Japan to enter the family's porcelain business. He was a highly regarded instructor and well liked by British students.

45. Yushio Shimohara was an interesting man and a fine artist of note. He was born in Kobe, though the year is unknown. He attended the highly prestigious National University of Fine Arts and Music and studied Shotokan whilst there, and captained his university. He resided in Belgium where he continued to paint and train until his death in 2005.

46. The statements about Kato and training courses under him are confirmed from adverts, write-ups in local newspaper clippings and Kato's business card.

47. Watt's JKA 2nd Dan certificate shows the registration date of 23rd August 1974 and is signed by Nakayama and Kanazawa.

48. Gilfeather, F. *Not-so-gentle art proves a big hit with the girls* (*Evening Express*, 17th March 1973, p. 5).

49. Higgins was born in Bootle in 1945. He began his karate training with Wado-ryu in 1965 and quickly established himself in the BKCC squad. He joined the KUGB in 1970 and there followed a distinguished competition career including being placed second in the 1972 WUKO World Championships in Paris and again in Long Beach, California, in 1975, when, as captain of the British All-Styles team, they took the World Championship title. He was in the KUGB squad for many years that won the European championships five times. He became coach and manager of the English Karate Board team. At the time of writing, he holds the rank of 7th Dan.

50. Watt's BKCC certificate shows that his 1st Dan was registered on the 1st October 1972.

51. Uncredited piece in unknown newspaper entitled, *Karate Expert Goes East*.

52. Miyata (1916-1975) was one of the greats of the JKA, who held the same rank as JKA Chief Instructor, Nakayama. After graduating from Takushoku University, Miyata trained at the Shotokan *dojo* and is to be seen in a 1941 pamphlet with Yoshitaka Funakoshi performing *Ten no Kata* (See, Cook, H. *Shotokan Karate: A Precise History* {2001} p. 111, for pictures of Miyata at this time). For photographs of Miyata refereeing in the JKA championships, see, *Kanazawa, 10th Dan*, pp. 166-167. A photograph of Miyata, blocking Nakayama, is to be found in Nakayama's, *Dynamic Karate*, p. 202. A photograph of Miyata performing in a 1971 JKA demonstration is to be found in *Shotokan Karate Magazine*, No. 44, p. 11. Little is known of Miyata in the West. Kanazawa referred to Miyata in, *Kanazawa, 10th Dan* (pp. 59-60): 'Minoru Miyata would very occasionally come and teach us. He was based on Kyushu. He was two years junior to Nakayama at Takushoku, but they held the same grade. Miyata was really strong. His favourite stance was *fudo-dachi*, which he learned from Yoshitaka [Gichin Funakoshi's third son] at the Shotokan *dojo*. All the students noticed that Miyata and Nakayama had different form, but we never said anything. It was only later that I learned that their backgrounds were different, but it was at this time that I began to formulate in my mind that Shotokan 'pure' does not exist.'

   Kawasoe received his 1st Dan from Miyata and recalled in the author's *Masao Kawasoe, 8th Dan* (pp. 40-42): 'Miyata was based in Fukuoka prefecture, where he ran a food shop. I visited that establishment, about twenty-five miles away, with Tsuyama. One of Miyata's top students, eight years my senior, is [Ryusuke] Sakai. Sakai is alive and training and a member of the JKA. Of course [Yoshiharu] Osaka, also from Fukuoka, was Miyata's student. That was one reason why Osaka and I became such good friends. Miyata was an interesting man. He was not tall, looked perfectly normal, and, indeed, appeared to be a soft person, but his eyes, which were hard to read behind his glasses, revealed a depth and a very strong spirit if ever they caught you. I saw him perform a display, much later, 1970s, at the Budokan, where he demonstrated simple, but highly effective *ippon-kumite*. He liked *fudo-dachi* and he blocked in that stance then countered with a punch. He was from the old school, and I believe that he had very strong *kime*. I remember Nakayama telling me that if I wanted to study punching, then Miyata was the man to observe. There was something different about his style; it was very relaxed. I think it likely that Yoshitaka Funakoshi had a major impact on his form and way of thinking ... Miyata died in 1975 or 1976, aged fifty-nine or sixty. I think it was cancer.'

53. Nishiyama was born in Tokyo in 1928, the son of a lawyer. He began karate training in 1943 and joined the karate club at Takushoku University in 1946, where he trained under both Funakoshi and Nakayama. Graduating in 1951, in 1953 he was part of a contingent of seven *judoka* and three *karateka* (the other two being Isao Obata and Toshio Kamata), to tour United States Air Force bases both in Japan (with Funakoshi and Nakayama) and the USA and Cuba for four months. Instrumental in establishing the JKA as a body under the Ministry of Education, he was appointed Chief of the Instruction Committee, teaching many of today's great masters. In 1960, *Karate: the Art of 'Empty-Hand' Fighting* was published, and became one of the most famous Shotokan karate books ever written. In 1961, he moved to California and formed the American Amateur Karate Federation. He headed the International Traditional Karate Federation until his death, from lung cancer, on the 7th November 2008.

54. Okazaki was born in Nogata, Fukuoka Prefecture, Kyushu, in 1931. He began karate training in 1947/48 and entered Takushoku in 1949. He was an early and influential instructor for the JKA, justly famous for his kicking ability, especially *yoko-geri-kekomi* (which is on film). He became the first JKA instructor to reside in the USA (1961) and lives in Philadelphia, Pennsylvania, heading the International Shotokan Karate Federation, which he formed in 1977. He holds the rank of 9th Dan. Photographs of Okazaki performing *yoko-geri-kekomi and yoko-tobi-geri* upon Nishiyama can be seen in Nakayama's, *Dynamic Karate*, pages 89 and 166, respectively. Okazaki also appears frequently throughout Nishiyama's, *Karate: The Art of 'Empty-hand' Fighting,* including performing *yoko-tobi-geri* on the book's famous cover.

55. Shoji was born in 1931, in Yamagata Prefecture. He graduated from Takushoku University in 1954 after being vice-captain of the karate club. He was a *karateka* of the first-order, winning the first All Japan JKA individual *kata* title in 1957, with *Unsu*, and again in 1960. Master Nakayama wrote in Shoji's book on *Unsu* that, 'It was Mr. Hiroshi Shoji who fascinated the spectators fully by his excellent performance, full of power and beauty,' and Master Nishiyama, in the same volume, described Shoji's performance of this complex form as 'flawless.' At the end of 1963, along with Nakayama, Enoeda, Iwaizumi and Kisaka, he travelled to Indonesia to teach, by invitation of President Achmad Sukarno, who had attended that year's JKA championships. Shoji was an instructor at the JKA headquarters (a photograph of Shoji at the JKA Instructors' Class in 1970 can be seen in *Fighting Arts*, Vol: 1, No. 5, p. 17). Kawasoe recalled: 'In my second year, Shoji was in-charge of the Instructors' Programme. He was a very quiet man, modest, serious, introverted, and yet sociable – an interesting combination. He liked company, he wanted to be with people, have a drink, but he did not say much. His technique was very sharp, both punching and kicking – he had a full appreciation of *hara* and hips. He was always caring

towards the students. He was truly excellent at *kata*, of which his favourite was *Unsu*. He featured in a complete book devoted to it. I was told that he was unsurpassed in this *kata*, but I never had the chance to see him perform it. He was a top-level *karateka*' (*Masao Kawasoe, 8th Dan* {Mona Books, 2008, pp. 97-98}). Kanazawa, recalled that Shoji was 'a very quiet, modest, and serious man' (*Kanazawa, 10th Dan* {Shoto Publ., 2001, p. 75}). Shoji died in 2003.

56. Asai was born on the 7th June 1935, on Shikoku, and attended Takusoku University before enrolling on the JKA Instructors' Course. He won the JKA All-Japan *kumite* title in 1961 and the *kata* title in 1963. He replaced Kanazawa as JKA instructor to Hawaii in 1963, staying five years before moving to Taipai, Taiwan. Asai died of leukaemia on the 15th August 2007, aged seventy-one.

57. Tsuyama was born in Saga City, Kyushu, Japan, in 1937. As captain of the famous Takushoku Karate Club, his astonishing ability, especially in *mawashi-geri*, allowed him to reach the first JKA *kumite* finals whilst still at university, in 1957, where he lost to Kanazawa. Tsuyama joined Takushoku University's physical education department in 1968, first as a lecturer, and, later as professor of physical education. He remained in that academic role until 2002. Between 1988 and 1992, he acted as head coach to the Japan Karate Federation (founded in 1964) of which the JKA was a member, before becoming manager in 1993; a position he held until 2000. From 2002-2007, he was a JKF committee member, and then an advisor. In 2007, he became *Shihan* of Takushoku University Karate Club.

58. Kawasoe was born in Korea in 1945. He began Shotokan under Tsuyama in Saga City, Kyushu, in 1960, after witnessing the 1957 All-Japan JKA *kumite* finals on a news clip in the local cinema. He was awarded his *Shodan* from Miyata in 1963 and received a full karate scholarship to Takushoku University. On completion of his degree in 1968, he undertook the JKA Instructors' Course and then taught in Taiwan and Madagascar, before settling in Britain in 1974. For a detailed account of the first thirty years of his life, see the author's, C. *Masao Kawasoe, 8th Dan: Recollections of a Shotokan Karate Master (the Early Years (1945-1975)* (Mona Books, 2008).

59. Osaka was born in Nagasaki, Kyushu, Japan, in 1948, and started Shotokan in 1963, training under Miyata. He attended Takushoku Karate Club from 1966-1970 and, upon graduating, joined the JKA Instructors' Course. His ability was evident early on and he won the JKA student individual *kata* title in 1969. He won the JKA *kata* title from 1978-1983, thus, including his *kumite* title, he took seven JKA individual titles in total. Only Ueki equalled this record (again with six *kata* and one *kumite* title). Osaka accompanied Nakayama to many countries. Today, Osaka is an 8th Dan and a senior within the JKA.

60. Omura was born on the 1st May 1953, in Shizuoka Prefecture. After attending Takushoku University, where he had a highly successful competition career, winning the Kanto Area University Championships in 1975 and taking 2nd place at the All Japan University Championships in 1977, at the IAKF World Championship that year he took the *kumite* title. He graduated from the JKA Instructors' Class in 1978. In 1979 he took the All Japan JKA individual *kumite* title (taking 2nd place in 1980). He took the IAKF World title again in 1980. Today, as a 7th Dan, he is JKA Chief Instructor to Thailand.

61. For an account of Omura's success at the 1979 JKA Championships, see: Robertson, J. *The JKA National Championships* (*Fighting Arts International*, Vol. 4, No. 1, pp. 12-13).
62. Harris, W. *For the Chop: Ronnie Hits Out at the Karate Cowboys* (*Evening Express*, 10th February 1986, page unknown).
63. Hamanaka was a student at Takushoku from 1961-1965, and was captain in his last year. Kawasoe's recalled: 'Hamanaka was a small man, but very strong in mind and body. He excelled at combinations, *gyakyu-zuki/mawashi-geri*, that type of thing. I remember that he was very understanding and kind towards *kohai*' (Layton, C. *Masao Kawasoe, 8th Dan: Recollections of a Shotokan Karate Master – the early years {1945-1975}*, p. 73).
64. Uncredited piece in unknown newspaper, entitled, *Flights Chop Ronnie ... But His Trip to Tokio Wasn't Wasted.*
65. There is a fragment of an unknown and undated newspaper entitled, *Kárate Enthusiasts Form Shotokan Club at Buckie.*
66. Uncredited and undated report in local newspaper entitled, *Aberdeen Host to Karate Teams.*
67. Layton, C. *The Liverpool Red Triangle Karate Club, Origin and Early Years (1959-1961) & the Formation of the KUGB* (KUGB, 2008), pp. 119-120.
68. Uncredited report in unknown newspaper of unknown date (*c.* 1980), entitled, *First Display by Local Karate Club.*
69. Uncredited piece in unknown newspaper entitled, *Shotokan and the KUGB.*
70. Guthrie, A. *Aberdeen the Karate Capital of Europe* (unknown paper and undated, though after 1975).

CHAPTER III – MASTER NAKAYAMA VISITS ABERDEEN

1. Poynton was born in Liverpool in 1949 and began training at the Liverpool Red Triangle club in 1965. He became a competitor of note and was in the KUGB Liverpool Red Triangle and British KUGB and All-Styles teams from 1968-1985. He won the KUGB *kumite* title in 1976 and the Shoto cup three times, on two occasions of which he was grand champion. Today, he is National Administration and Finance Officer to the KUGB and, at the time of writing, holds the rank of 7th Dan.
2. Martin, D. *'All Britain' Report* (*Fighting Arts*, Vol. 1., No. 1, p. 16), for an account of the match.
3. Martin, D. *Karate Home International; England v. Scotland* (*Fighting Arts*, Vol. 1, No. 1, pp. 22-23), for a report.
4. Uncredited and undated (though 1976/77) newspaper report.
5. Uncredited report in unknown newspaper of unknown date (though 1980/81), entitled, *Top Karate Man for Aberdeen.*
6. Uncredited report in unknown newspaper of unknown date entitled, *Karate Coaching.*
7. Uncredited and untitled report in unknown newspaper of unknown date (though 1980/81).
8. Uncredited report in unknown newspaper of unknown date (though 1980), entitled, *Top Karate Men in Action.*

9. Ian Mackland photograph and caption in *The People's Journal* (7th February 1981, p. 15).

10. Brennan was born in Liverpool in 1960 and started training at the Liverpool Red Triangle in 1973. His competition career was truly astonishing, the greatest of any British shotokan *karateka*, winning twenty-four individual KUGB titles (*kata*, 1979-1992; *kumite*, 1979-1980, 1982-1986, 1988, 1991-1992 {Grand Champion ten times}), and was a member of the Liverpool Red Triangle and national squads for nearly two decades from 1975. He became Grand Champion of Europe four times, and captained the team that won the 1990 World Championships in Sunderland. At the time of writing, he holds the rank of 7th Dan.

11. Watt's JKA 3rd Dan certificate shows the registration date of 9th September 1976 and is signed by Nakayama and Enoeda.

12. The greetings telegram is dated 13th September 1976.

13. Hayakawa was a graduate of Taisho University and a Buddhist priest. He graduated from the JKA Instructors' Course in 1971. He was killed in a car accident in 1983. Kawasoe recalled: 'He was a really good friend of mine, very close, and one year my junior. To this day I miss him. He was a tremendous fighter – his specialities being *kizami-zuki* and *gyaku-zuki* – and he was in the Japanese team that won the world championships in Paris, in 1972' (*Masao Kawasoe, 8th Dan* (Mona Books, 2008, p. 99). Hayakawa was a regular contestant in the JKA All-Japan Championships. He never won a JKA title in Japan, but gained second place in the *kumite* event in 1976, losing to Osaka. However, he did win the individual *kumite* in the First Asian-Pacific Karate Championships. Photographs of Hayakawa are to be found in *Fighting Arts*, Vol. 1, No. 5, pp. 15 & 17; and, Vol. I, No. 6, p. 19; *Fighting Arts International*, No. 37, p. 28.

14. Leslie Watt's cause of death, as given on the death certificate, was due to cerebrovascular haemorrhage and myocardial infarction.

15. Advert for event provides specifics.

16. Uncredited report in unknown newspaper of unknown date (though 1977).

17. Bremner, G. *Karate Union Squad to Visit Aberdeen* (unknown newspaper report of unknown date {though 1977}).

18. Hazard was born in London 1952 and began Shotokan at the famous KUGB Blackfriars *dojo*, London, in 1969. He graded to *Shodan* in 1972, under Enoeda, and embarked upon an impressive competition career which included being a finalist in the individual *kata* at the IAKF World Championships in the USA (1975), bronze medallist in the individual *kata* at the 1976 European Shotokan Karate Association Championships, and took the KUGB *kata* title that year (and runner-up in the *kumite).* He received a team *kumite* bronze in the IAKF World Championships, in Japan, in 1977. He graded to *Sandan* under Nakayama in 1977 after training at the JKA for one year. He became Technical Director to the Shotokan of England Karate Union, and, today, holds the rank of 7th Dan and is Chief Instructor to the Academy of Shotokan Karate, which he formed in 2003. He is co-author of *Fundamental Karate*, with Aidan Trimble, with whom he features in the *Applied Karate* DVDs.

19. Dewey was born in 1946, beginning Shotokan in Portsmouth in 1967. He graded

to *Shodan* in 1977 under Enoeda and was in the KUGB squad from 1975 (when he gained second place in the individual *kumite* at the KUGB Championships) to 1980. He also became a member of the BKCC squad from 1975-1978. He trained at the JKA headquarters after taking part in the IAKF World Championships in 1977, and, as a *Sandan*, he was part of the British team that took gold medal at the European Championships, in Brussels, in 1979. He became Chief Instructor to the Shotokan of England Karate Union in 1982, and was appointed a member of the EKGB Technical Committee in 1994. At the time of writing, he holds the rank of 7th Dan.

20. In 1977, Hopkins had won the KUGB *kata* title five times in a row and would win another five in a row, making her the undisputed champion for an astonishing ten years (1973-1982).

21. Rhodes was born in Leeds in 1946 and began karate training in (*circa*) 1966, before joining Ron Wade's club in Leeds. He established himself in the KUGB and British All-Styles teams, and was a member of the team that took the 1975 World Championships title. At the time of writing, he holds the rank of 7th Dan.

22. Ueki was a graduate of Agia University before graduating from the JKA Instructors' Course in 1961. He went on to take seven individual JKA titles (*kata*: 1965, 1967, 1968, 1971, 1974, 1975; *kumite*: 1968; he was, thus, grand champion in 1968), a record equalled only by Osaka. Photographs of Ueki are to be found in Nakayama's, *Dynamic Karate* – for example, pages 21-22.

23. Takagi was born in 1912/13 and had attended classes under Funakoshi at the Meisei Juku, Suidobata, Tokyo, in the 1920s, before becoming a founder member of the karate club at Takushoku University. Takagi, a journalist by profession, spent the war in China, returning to Hiroshima. He was a highly significant figure in the establishment of the JKA, including finding the JKA's first *honbu* at 13, 1-Chome Yotsuya, Shinjuku-ku, Tokyo. He described himself as 'the gatekeeper of the JKA' (*Thinking at the Gate {Karate-Do*, Vol. 1, No. 2, pp. 17-18, 1965}) being the first person people encountered (given the position of his office) when entering the JKA building. Kanazawa recalled: 'Takagi was a very nice man, honest and kind. He looked after everyone, especially, later, the foreign students, who liked him. It was Takagi who acquired the JKA *dojo*, and things may have been very different if Nakayama hadn't approached him for help' (*Kanazawa, 10th Dan; Recollections of a Living Karate Legend – the Early Years (1931-1964)*, p. 96). Two photographs of Takagi may be seen in the said Kanazawa book, pages 97 and 98.

24. The books, produced in the mid 1970s by Fukushoda Publishing, are entitled: *Shotokan Karate Kata Series*. There were five books in all featuring the *katas Unsu, Gojushiho-Dai, Gojushiho-Sho, Nijushiho, Chinte, Sochin* and *Wankan*.

25. Abe was born in 1938, in Iyoshi, Ehime Prefecture, on Shikoku. An engineering student of Nihon University, he followed the JKA Instructors' Course after graduating. A stalwart of the JKA for many years, he was a member of the 1972 World Championship team. In 1999 he formed the Japan Shotokan Karate Association. At the time of writing, he holds the rank of 8th Dan. A photograph of Abe can be seen in *Fighting Arts*, Vol. 1, No. 6, p. 19. See also, *Fighting Arts International*, No. 34, p. 4; No. 37, pp. 28. He appeared in the Bond film, *You Only Live Twice* (1967).

26. Guthrie, A. *Ronnie and Paul Chop Down Karate Barrier* (*Evening Express*, 14th October 1978).
27. Guthrie, A. *Red Tape May Chop Karate Experts' Hopes* (*Evening Express* - undated {though 1978} newspaper article).
28. O'Neill, T. *The Tiger of Shotokan Karate* (*Fighting Arts*, Vol. 3, No. 1, pp. 6-12). The current author once asked Enoeda about the alleged incident at the end of an interview session. Enoeda did not wish to discuss the subject.
29. Enoeda performed a demonstration on *Open Door* (27th October, 1974; 2nd November 1974).
30. Kawawada was born (*c*. 1953) in Iburaki Prefecture and studied karate at High School before attending Takushoku University. After graduating, he taught at the Hoitsugan *dojo* before completing the JKA Instructors' Course in 1978. After Nakayama's death, he became chief instructor of the Hoitsugan.
31. Uncredited photograph and caption in unknown newspaper of unknown date (though 1981).
32. Taken from uncredited and undated documents.
33. *Kanazawa's Shotokan Karate International Kata, Vol. I* (SKI, 1981).
34. Similar information is to be found in Randall G. Hassell's, *Conversations with the Master: Masatoshi Nakayama* (Focus publ., 1983, p. 13).
35. Fritz Wendland was born on the 10th April 1942, in Germany. He studied at the universities of Hamburg and Göttingen, before becoming a teacher in French and history. He started karate in 1963 under Jurgen (this is how his first name is popularly written, actually, 'Juergen') Seydel (1917-2008), the founder of karate in Germany (and student of Murakami), under whom all kyu grades were awarded, and was graded to *Shodan* in April 1965, under the visiting JKA party of Kase, Kanazawa, Enoeda and Shirai. In 1966, he spent three months training at the JKA headquarters in Tokyo. He interspersed teaching with travelling in Asia and Australia. From 1976-2003, he was professor at the National Border Police College. He continued his studies in political science and history at the university of Hanover, gaining both M.A. (1996) and D. Phil (2003) degrees. His involvement with karate politics is impressive. From 1975-1988, he was President of the Deutscher Karate Bund, and President of the unified national karate federation until 1995. He was President of the European Amateur Karate Federation (1976-1977) and Director of the International Amateur Karate Federation 1976-1985. From 1988-1994, he was Vice-President of World Union of Karate Organisations (since 1992, World Karate Federation) and the European Karate Union. From 1976-1994, he was involved in negotiations concerning the unification of the two world bodies, WUKO (WKF) and IAKF (ITKF), and with International Olympic Committee officials with a view to trying to secure a place for karate in the Olympic Program. From its formation in 1996, he was President of the World Karate Federation, and he continued in that role until 2005, before passing responsibility over to Marko Nicovic.
36. Harris, W. *For the Chop: Ronnie Hits Out at the Karate Cowboys* (*Evening Express*, 10th February 1986, page unknown).
37. The income for the course is reported as follows: 221 people at £10 per head = £2210; grant from council = £250; sponsorship = £300. Total income £2760. Outgoings: presents for instructors = £162.95; hotel fees for instructors = £150;

instructors fees = £1000; reception meals for guests = £182; air tickets for instructors = £392; hire of hall = £50; petrol and meals to London = £120; advertising = £60; repay sponsorship = £300; air tickets for travel to British Championships = £178; Accommodation in London for one night = £32; petrol and meals for return from London = £120. Total expenditure = £2747.05. Balance = £12.95. The sum quoted here is twelve hundred and fifty-three pounds less than the sum mentioned in the newspaper article.

38. Uncredited report in unknown newspaper of unknown date (though 1981) entitled, *Europe Top Karate Expert Coaches City Man.*

39. Watt's JKA 4th Dan certificate shows the registration date of 11th September 1981 and is signed by Nakayama and Enoeda.

40. This *kata* order is confirmed in a memo sent to Watt by Enoeda.

41. Watt, R. *Scottish Shotokan Centres* (booklet), (1986), p. 7.

42. Yoshinobu Ohta was born in Chiba in 1959. After attending Takushoku University and undertaking the JKA Instructors' Course, he came to Britain to act as Enoeda's assistant in 1982 and remained in that position until Enoeda's death in 2003. Today, he is Chief Instructor to JKA England and holds the rank of 7th Dan.

43. There is considerable documentary evidence to support this statement. For example, in 1982: 26th-28th March, Kase and Enoeda to Aberdeen and Stirling; 4th-6th June, Enoeda to Edinburgh; 3rd-5th September, Enoeda and Shirai to Stirling or Edinburgh; 3rd-5th December, Enoeda to Aberdeen and Edinburgh. In 1983, details survive of Enoeda courses, 3rd-5th June, 23-25th September, and with Kase or Ohta (different documents), 16th-18th December. In 1984, details survive of Enoeda and Ohta courses: 23rd-25th March, at Coatbridge, Edinburgh and Aberdeen (though this is likely to have changed to the 15th-18th March and Coatbridge not included); 15th-17th June, at Stirling, Edinburgh and Aberdeen; 14th-16th September, Aberdeen and Edinburgh; 14th-16th December, Edinburgh and Aberdeen. A good number of separate sheets, showing times of the month, but no year, are also n existence to show Enoeda/Ohta/Tsuyama visits.

44. Uncredited article in unknown Aberdeen newspaper (though 1980), entitled, *They're Chop of the Class.*

45. Uncredited article from fragment of unknown Edinburgh newspaper.

46. Harris, W. *For the Chop: Ronnie Hits Out at the Karate Cowboys* (*Evening Express*, 10th February 1986, page unknown).

47. Watt, R. *Scottish Shotokan Centres* (booklet), (1986), pp. 33-36, confirms these *kihon* sequences.

48. This figure comes from a KUGB advert of the time.

49. O'Neill, T. *Another Victory for England at the 1981 EAKF European Karate Championships* (*Fighting Arts*, Vol. 4, No. 6, pp. 28-31).

50. Watt, R. Unknown magazine from 1982, p. 10.

51. Marjory Watt's cause of death, as given on the death certificate, was due to myocardial infarction and ischaemic heart disease.

52. Uncredited. *Kase in Scotland: Top Karate Master Holds Special Training Course (Fighting Arts International*, No. 33, pp. 23-25).

53. Munro, M. *It's Punch, Block and Kick on a Hot Afternoon* (*The People's Journal*, 25th June 1983, p. 9).

54. Uncredited article from unknown newspaper fragment, though stamp dated 30th March 1985.

55. Uncredited article from unknown newspaper, entitled, *Move to Start Worldwide Karate Contest*, stamp dated 13th July 1985.

56. Allan, P. *Mr. Kawasoe in Scotland* (unknown piece, but probably internal KUGB Scottish Region news circular {1978}).

57. Uncredited piece in unknown newspaper entitled, *Japanese Karate Expert to Visit Aberdeen.*

58. Hunter, S. *Spotlight on Shotokan: SSC in Festival Parade (Fighters*, December 1984, pp. 15-16).

59. Uncredited. *Shotokan Comes Together in Aberdeen (Combat*, 1984, p. 67).

60. Uncredited article in an unknown magazine entitled, *Ronnie Watt.*

61. Uncredited report from unknown and undated newspaper, entitled, *Karate Expert Calls In.*

62. Houston, B. *Watt a Scot! Ronnie Watt, 4th Dan, Pillar of Scottish Shotokan* (unknown and undated magazine article {*c.* 1983}, pp. 52-53).

63. Uncredited article on page 6 of an unknown Norwegian newspaper entitled, *Kraftkaren Watt*, and dated 14th September 1984.

64. The footage lasts for nearly two and a half minutes and Watt speaks for nearly two of them. Karate footage shows Watt and his students training in *kata* and *kumite* and there are also some callisthenics.

65. Also written as 'Nordbotten.'

66. Watt, R. *Scottish Shotokan Centres* (booklet), (1986), p. 9.

67. Uncredited (maybe Torgeir Hellesen) report in unknown Norwegian magazine/newspaper entitled, *Slar et Slag for VM* (though this may be only part of the title).

68. Uncredited piece entitled, *Karate Success (Aberdeen Advertiser*, 17th February 1984, page unknown).

69. Gray, G. Uncredited photograph and caption (*The People's Journal*, 21st April 1984, p. 22).

70. Kawasoe noted: 'Sometimes odd things, unexpected things, happen during training, using body dynamics and we remember them, but we cannot repeat the effect. Something happens, but there is no control .... I recall a demonstration when I hit Kenny Taylor very lightly, *chudan*, by accident. It was nothing, just a touch. But a few days later he had a large bruise appear on his back, but there was nothing where I had struck him. So, as I say, these things happen. (Layton, C. *Masao Kawasoe, 8th Dan: Recollections of a Shotokan Master – the Early Years (1945-1975)* (Mona books, 2008), pp. 141-142.

71. Bremner, D. *International Karate Match in Scotland (Fighting Arts*, Vol. 5, No. 3, p. 55).

72. Uncredited, unknown newspaper cutting, entitled, *Top Karate Events.*

73. On a SSC list of dates, the 21st-24th November is recorded.

74. Uncredited report from unknown and undated newspaper, entitled, *Dan Dave's First Choice.*

75. Uncredited report from unknown and undated newspaper, entitled, *Shotokan Team Show 'Em in Norway.*

76. A ticket to the event confirms details.

77. An A3 size poster exists showing course details.
78. Tanaka was born in Tokyo in 1941. He is one of the great karate competitors, winning the JKA All-Japan individual *kumite* title twice (1974, 1975) and was IAKF World Individual *Kumite* Champion in 1975 (Los Angeles) and 1977 (Tokyo). In 1980, in Bremen, he was part of the Japanese team that took the IAKF World Team *kumite* title. A photograph of Tanaka in 1973 can be seen in *Fighting Arts*, Vol. 1, No. 6, p. 19. See also, *Fighting Arts International*, No. 37, pp. 28.
79. See Hunter, S. *British JKA Visit Japan* (*Fighting Arts*, Vol. 5, No. 5, pp. 22-23), and, *Pilgrimage to Japan* (*Combat*, No. —, pp. 14-15).
80. Kawasoe, who lived in an apartment above the *dojo* for a short while, provides a description of the Hoitsugan *dojo* situated in the Ebisu district, a quiet part of Shibuya Ward, Tokyo, so: 'Nakayama lived above the *dojo* .... The Hoitsugan *dojo* was built were Nakayama's previous, Japanese style house had been sited. It was knocked down to make the *dojo*, which was located in the basement, with some six apartments above it. Nakayama didn't own it; there was some agreement with the owner ... The *dojo*, being in the basement, had no windows. One proceeded down a flight of stairs and through a small entrance. As one entered the rectangular *dojo*, which wasn't that large, on one's immediate left there was a sauna and showers, and to the right, an office. The floor was cedar wood and sprung. As one progressed into the *dojo* proper, on the left, about half way down, there was a shrine, and, on the right-hand side of the *dojo*, a changing room. A mirror was mounted on the wall opposite the shrine. At the end of the *dojo*, a sandbag hung in the left-hand corner, I believe, and *makiwara* were to be found in the right-hand corner' (Layton, C. *Masao Kawasoe, 8th Dan: Recollections of a Shotokan Master – the Early Years (1945-1975)* (Mona books, 2008), p. 117.
81. In *Shotokan Karate Magazine* (No. 54, p.18), in an article entitled, *Minoru Kawawada, 7th Dan JKA*, by K. Wight, we have 'Hoitsugan' translated as, 'the place where people with the same goal practice and study together.'
82. Harris, W. *Karate Club Gets a Kick* (unknown newspaper, 1st April 1985).
83. Private communication with author (3rd June 2008).
84. An advert for this course is to be found in *Fighting Arts* (Vol. 5, No. 5, p. 48).
85. Tabata stood six feet one inch.
86. Tabata died in 2003, a few days before Enoeda, under mysterious circumstances. Kawasoe recalled: 'He was shown on camera leaving his hotel, alone, on the morning of the day he died, and was found dead in the sea. It is a mystery; no one knows for sure what happened. I asked a good friend of his what had occurred and he said that he'd tried to investigate. He couldn't get to the bottom of it and said that there were many rumours ... I found Tabata to be a gentle man, genuinely caring, who would go out of his way to help if there was a problem' (*Masao Kawasoe, 8th Dan: Recollections of a Shotokan Karate Master: the Early Years (1945-1975)* (Mona Books, 2008, pp. 99-100).
87. Specific details taken from the 1986 programme.
88. This information is confirmed from an advert of the time.
89. The author has read much of this.
90. The course had been arranged for 27th April – 1st May, and, 4th May – 8th May,

1987. Nakayama died on 15th April aged seventy-three, reputedly of a stroke.
91. A copy of the course brochure confirms these details.
92. Uncredited report entitled, *Shotokan in Scotland* (*Fighting Arts International*, No. 47, p. 45).
93. See the author's, *Masao Kawasoe, 8th Dan: Recollections of a Shotokan Karate Master – the Early Years (1945-1975)* (Mona Books, 2008), p. 138. Kawasoe left the KUGB in 1990.
94. Weekend courses (8th & 9th October 1988 and 21st & 22nd October 1989) organised by Allan are to be found advertised in *Fighting Arts International*, No. 54, p. 57, and, No. 58, p. 65, respectively). Both courses were located in Cumbernauld.

CHAPTER IV – THE KASE AND SHIRAI YEARS

1. Uncredited. *Kase and Shirai in Scotland* (*Traditional Karate*, November 1989, pp. 52-53).
2. Cheetham, J. *Steve Cattle, 5th Dan: Back to the Roots* (*Shotokan Karate Magazine*, No. 23. pp. 4-8). This in-depth interview explains the reasoning behind Cattle leaving the KUGB/JKA.
3. Watt, R. Scottish Shotokan Centres (booklet), (1986), p. 9.
4. Cattle, S. *A Meeting with Kase Sensei* (*Traditional Karate*, Vol. 2, No. 6, 1988, pp. 4-12).
5. For a detailed description of the Shotokan and for Harada's recollections of Yoshitaka, see: Layton, C. *Karate Master: The Life and Times of Mitsusuke Harada* (Bushido Publ., 1997, and, *Reminiscences by Master Mitsusuke Harada* (KDS, 1999).
6. Tilley, D. *Sensei Taiji Kase, 8th Dan: Part II* (*Shotokan Karate Magazine*, No. 26, pp. 24-25).
7. Yahara was born in Ehime Prefecture in 1947. After attending Kokushinkan University he joined the JKA Instructors' Course. For more than a decade he was a famed fighter the world over and was part of the JKA team that won the World Championships in 1972. He had a unique and unpredictable style that made him a fearsome opponent. Amongst his titles, he was the JKA All-Japan *Kata* Champion in 1984. He formed the Karatenomichi World Federation in 2000, and, at the time of writing, holds the rank of 8th Dan. For photographs of Yahara see *Fighting Arts International*, No. 37, pp. 20-28.
8. Funakoshi, G. *Karate-Do Nyumon* (Kodansha 1988), p. 7.
9. Funakoshi, G. *Karate-Do Kyohan* (Kodansha, 1973), p. 35.
10. Funakoshi, G. *Karate-Do Kyohan* (Kodansha, 1973), p. 9.
11. The fact that Watt had recently been promoted to 2nd Dan examiner is noted in an advert of 1989 (*Evening Express Community Guide*, p. 19).
12. On *YouTube*, Kase can be seen performing *Meikyo* with the first two sets as being *gedan-barai/oi-zuki* and the third set *uchi-ude-uke/oi-zuki*, as does the early 1930s film of Funakoshi performing *Meikyo*.
13. For reference, see Kanazawa's, *Shotokan Karate International: Vol. I, Meikyo*, moves 3-6, 11-14, and 19-22.
14. Uncredited and untitled piece (*Fighting Arts International*, No. 61, pp. 26-29).

15. Uncredited. *Scottish Amateur Shotokan Federation* (*Traditional Karate*, January 1990, p. 94).
16. Course details reveal that training on the Friday evening was between 7.00 p.m. – 9.30 p.m. The training in Aberdeen was from 11.00 a.m. – 1.00 p.m. and from 2.00 p.m. – 4.00 p.m. on both the Saturday and Sunday. A Dan grading was held after training on the Saturday and the kyu grading after training on the Sunday.
17. This is confirmed in: McDonald, D. *Busy Year End for the SSKCA* (*Martial Arts Illustrated*, No. —, p.61).
18. (Aberdeen) *Sunday Post*, 10th September 1989.
19. Uncredited. *Shotokan Karate Masters Hit Aberdeen* (*Press and Journal*, 11th September 1989, p. 12).
20. Uncredited. *A Perfect Way to Beat the Bullies: Karate (Ann Robertson)* (unknown newspaper, but dated 8th June 1994, p.7).
21. Uncredited piece in unknown and undated newspaper entitled, *Women Armed by Self-defence*.
22. Uncredited and undated (though between 1978-1980) report in the *Evening Express*, entitled, *Simon, 10, Chops His Way to Success*.
23. Melvin, A. *Karate Gives Them a Kick* (unknown and undated newspaper clipping, but between 1978-1980).
24. Uncredited and undated report entitled, *Matt Gets his Kicks Out of Heading for a Record*.
25. See Layton, C. *Speed of Technique and Age in Shotokan Karateka* (*Perceptual and Motor Skills*, 1993, Vol. 76, pp. 1001-1002).
26. *Gashuko Avis*: Details of a Norwegian course with Kase and Watt, in Norwegian.
27. Layton, C. *Masao Kawasoe, 8th Dan: Recollections of a Shotokan Karate Master – the Early Years (1945-1975)* (Mona Books, 2008), p. 20.
28. Uncredited. *Intervju med Ronnie Watt.*
29. Uncredited piece in unknown Norwegian article (though 1990) entitled, *Sommerlier 1990.*
30. See Layton, C. *Sidedness in Shotokan Karate Kata* (*Perceptual and Motor Skills*, 1993, Vol. 76, p. 242).
31. Kase suffered a major heart attack in 1999 and despite resuming training and giving a come-back course the following year, he never fully recovered. On the 24th November 2004, he was fatally struck down by another heart attack at his home in Paris. He was seventy-five years old. He was cremated on the 30th November 2004, at Père Lachaise, Paris. He was survived by his wife and daughters.
32. McDonald, D. *Scottish Shotokan Karate Centres Association* (*Shotokan Karate Magazine*, No. —, p. 33).
33. Cheetham, J. *Ronnie Watt, 5th Dan: Liverpool Course* (*Shotokan Karate Magazine*, No. 23, p. 34).
34. Uncredited: *Scotland and England Do Battle in Shotokan* (*Traditional Karate*, April 1990, p. 87).
35. Cheetham, J. & Water, J. *Taiji Kase 8th Dan: Story and Interview* (*Shotokan Karate Magazine*, No. —, pp. 4-7).
36. Cook, H. *Shotokan Karate: The Kase & Shirai Way* (*Fighting Arts International*, No. 61, pp. 26-29).

37. Main, L. Letter to M. Stainforth of the *Press and Journal*. Main was a 3rd Dan and secretary to the Scottish Karate Centres Association, Aberdeen.

38. This information is confirmed in a letter from the Aberdeen Sports Council, to Watt, dated the 1st February 1989.

39. There are a good number of differing adverts for the SSC and the SSKCA.

40. Undated SSC handout.

41. Fuller, J. *How to be a Karate Kid* (unknown newspaper article, but dated 9th October 1993).

42. Uncredited. *National Wins for City Club* (Unknown local newspaper cutting, but hand dated 24th November 1993).

43. Uncredited. *SSCA Hold 'Successful Karate Championships* (*Traditional Karate*, May 1994, pp. 89-90).

44. Stephen John Cattle signed his BKF application form on the 2nd October 1963 (*Shotokan Dawn: Vol. II*, p. 100). He was also highly skilled in judo, a 2nd Dan, and represented Britain at the World Student Games in Tokyo, in 1967.

45. Terry O'Neill noted in his write-up of the 1990 KUGB Championships that 'a notable exception this year was Cattle who has now officially left the KUGB to join a new association' (*Fighting Arts International*, No. 66, p. 44).

46. Cattle died as a consequence of an epileptic fit aboard a train from London to Liverpool on the 21st February 1995, after attending a karate course in Europe. He was forty-seven years of age at the time of death and held the rank of 6th Dan.

47. Cattle, S. *The Tangled Web: A Short History of the Japan Karate Association, Part II: The Golden Age – 1922-1946, 'The Fearful Symmetry'* (*Traditional Karate*, May, 1989, pp. 54-61).

48. Cattle, S. *The Tangled Web: A Short History of the Japan Karate Association, Part I: What the Afternoon Knows, the Morning Never Expected* (*Traditional Karate*, April, 1989, pp. 54-59).

49. Cattle, S. *A Short History of the Japan Karate Association, Part III: The Golden Age – 1946-55, 'The Law of Tooth and Claw'* (*Traditional Karate*, June, 1989, pp. 54-58).

50. Cattle, S. *History of the JKA, Part IV* (*Traditional Karate*, July, 1989, pp. 56-59).

51. Cattle, S. *A History of the JKA, 1966, 'The Turning of the Tide'* (*Traditional Karate*, September, 1989, pp. 30-34).

52. Layton, C. *Masao Kawasoe, 8th Dan: Recollections of a Shotokan Karate Master – the Early Years (1945-1975)* (Mona Books, 2008), p. 24.

53. Uncredited in unknown and undated newspaper: *Japanese Instructor Shows How to Get a Kick Out of Karate*.

54. Watt's course certificate shows the course was held on the 30th September 1990 and is signed by Kase.

55. Internal SSC memo confirms this.

56. Uncredited. *The Scottish Shotokan Centres Association's Aberdeen Karate Festival '90* (*Fighters*, January 1991, pp. 74-75).

57. Uncredited piece in unknown newspaper (though from 1990) entitled, *Karate Proves a Big Hit*.

58. Uncredited piece in unknown newspaper (though from 1990) entitled, *Karate Festival is a Real Knockout*.

59. Uncredited piece in unknown newspaper (though from 1990) entitled, *Karate a Big Hit.*

60. Uncredited. *Karate Masters to Kick Off Major City Festival* (*Aberdeen Herald & Post*, 27th October 1990, p. 4).

61. McDonald, D. *Aberdeen Karate Festival '90* (*Shotokan Karate Magazine*, No. 26, p. 34).

62. McDonald, D. *Scottish Shotokan Karate Centres Association* (*Shotokan Karate Magazine*, No. —, p. 33).

63. An advert for this course, entitled, *Don't Mess with These Men! Top Karate for the North-East*, in an unknown magazine, confirms the facts.

64. The welcome to the event in the programme is given by the Lord Provost of Aberdeen, Mr. R. Robertson.

65. Two uncredited pieces. The first, in an unknown newspaper, hand dated 14th October 1989: *Karate Great Visits City*; the second, in the *Press and Journal*, dated 24th October 1989, entitled, *Champ Kicks in with a Few Tips.*

66. Confirmed in an advert in the *Aberdeen Herald & Post*, 19th January 1991, p. 6.

67. An advert from the time, showing Kase, confirms the locations.

68. Uncredited. *Success Brings Home Big Problem for Shotokan Karate Club* (*Aberdeen Herald & Post*, 19th January 1991, page 2).

69. Uncredited. *New Karate Club for Inverurie* (*Inverurie Advertiser*, 4th January 1991).

70. Uncredited. *New Club Set to Get Going* (*Inverurie Herald*, 4th January 1991).

71. Uncredited. *High-Kicking Karate Hits Town* (*Inverurie Herald*, 18th January 1991).

72. Uncredited. *Karate Instruction Now Available in Inverurie* (*Inverurie Advertiser*, 18th January 1991).

73. A certificate from the City of Aberdeen confirms this.

74. Details are confirmed in the programme to the event. The Scottish squad, as detailed in the programme were: S. Cunningham, M. Ingram, A. Sinclair, M. Gillan, A. Elliott, A. Thomson, R. Mallinson and J. Roddie.

75. McDonald, D. *Scotland vs Russia: Scotland Outclass the Russians* (*Traditional Karate*, October 1991, pp. 92-93).

76. Uncredited. *Report on the Ronnie Watt and Terry O'Neill Course 27th-28th March 1993.*

77. Jackson was born in 1951. He began Shotokan in Coventry in 1966 and was a member of the KUGB. He went to Japan to train at the JKA headquarters in 1973 and practised under many leading JKA instructors. He wrote a series of articles in 1985/86 in *Fighting Arts International* magazine on his exploits (*Karate Training ... The Japanese Way* – {Part 1, FAI, No. 33, pp. 12-17}, {Part 2, FAI, No. 34, pp. 2-9}, {Part 3, FAI, No. 35, pp. 2-8}). At the time of writing, he holds the rank of 8th Dan.

78. In a report entitled, *Special Shotokan Karate Course in Aberdeen*, by an unknown author, we learn that O'Neill and Jackson had taught for Bothwell during a weekend course (*Fighting Arts International*, No. 45, p. 29) in 1987/88.

79. Uncredited. *Scotland Versus France* (*Traditional Karate*, November 1993, p.75).

80. Uncredited. *Des Ecossais à Berck-sur-Mer: Entre Kilt et Kimono, un échange interclubs musclé ...*(*La Voix Du Jeudi*, 17th June 1993).

81. McDonald, D. Undated press release.
82. Uncredited piece in undated newspaper. *Ronnie Rattles into Russia* (*The Suburb Review*, p. 6).
83. McKenzie, W. *NE Aim to Help Russians* (unknown newspaper, but dated 19th May 1993, p. 9).
84. Course details/adverts/programme, etc, survive to confirm facts.
85. McKenzie, W. *Total Recall: Arnie? Oh He's Just a Mate!* (*Midweek Green*, 22nd December 1993, pp. 6-7).
86. The SSKCA and SKB certificate shows the date 27th February 1994, as the date of registration. In fact, Watt had also been presented with a 6th Dan certificate dated 20th February 1994.
87. Robertson, R. *Le Crunch Match for Scots* (unknown report in unknown paper of unknown date {but 1994}).
88. Details are confirmed by programme to event.
89. Uncredited piece from undated newspaper, entitled, *International Flavour for Karate Festival.*
90. Uncredited and untitled piece in unknown newspaper, but hand dated, 24th April 1994.
91. Aberdeen Karate Festival 1994 programme.
92. A letter to Watt dated the 13th October 1993, by Bill Berry, Chairman of the Aberdeen Sports Council, confirms this information.
93. Uncredited. *SSCA Hold 'Successful Karate Championships* (*Traditional Karate*, May 1994, pp. 89-90).
94. Uncredited piece from undated newspaper, entitled, *Aberdeen is Venue for Karate Championships.*
95. A leaflet showing course details confirm this.
96. Trimble was born in Nottingham in 1960 and trained primarily with Asano, taking his *Shodan* in 1977. He began a remarkable competition career when he was part of the British team that took the SKI European Championships in Dusseldorf in 1978. Numerous British and European titles in both *kumite* and *kata* followed, with the SKI world individual *kumite title* in 1983, in Tokyo, being his crowning glory. He left SKI in 1986 to form the Federation of Shotokan Karate and, at the time of writing, holds the rank of 7th Dan. He has authored a good number of books, including those with Dave Hazard and Vince Morris. He has also made the *Applied Karate* DVDs with Hazard.
97. Uncredited piece, probably for SSC internal readership, entitled, *Scottish Shotokan Karate Students Win in France (1995).*

CHAPTER V – THE WKC WORLD CHAMPIONSHIPS: ABERDEEN, 2001

1. A SSC leaflet provided contact numbers for: Aberdeen, Aboyne/Tarland, Arbroath, Banff and Buchan, Carnoustie, Dunblane, Edinburgh, Ellon, Glasgow, Inverurie, Laurencekirk, Livingstone, Montrose, Musselburgh, Perth, Shetland, Stirling, Tayside, Westhill.
2. The *Dojo Kun* is, in Japanese: *Hitotsu! Jinkaku kansei ni tsutomuru koto! Hitotsu! Makoto no michi o mamoru koto! Hitotsu! Doryoku no seishin o yashinau koto! Hitotsu! Reigi o omonzuru koto! Hitotsu! Kekki no yu o*

imashimuru koto!

3.   Uncredited. *The New Tartan Special* (*Evening Express*, 27th October 1995, p. 8).

4.   Millar, J. *Japanese Tartan: one of the newest tartans to be registered in Scotland is the Samurai* (*Scottish Banner*, Vol. 28, No. 1, July 2004, p. 15).

5.   Uncredited piece (photo and caption) in an unknown newspaper, but hand dated 1st November 1995.

6.   NAKMAS advert (*Traditional Karate*, December 1996, p. 98).

7.   Uncredited. *The Scottish Shotokan Karate Centres and the Scottish Amateur Shotokan Federation Student Course and Coach Award* (*Martial Arts Illustrated*, August 1989, p. 56).

8.   In fact, Watt's MAC certificates reveal that he received his Assistant Coach award and his Coach award for a seemingly indefinite period starting the 14th November 1987 and 13th December 1987, respectively.

9.   A number of lists and certificates exist of courses Watt attended during the 1980s and 1990s. Some courses appear to have been taken more than once and some dates differ. The list includes: Structure of the Body, Developing Endurance, Strength and Flexibility, Coaching Children, Prevention and Treatment of Injuries, Planning Your Programme, Coach in Action, The Body in Action, SKB Referee Course, SKB Practical Referee Course, Safety and Injury, Improving Technique, Understanding and Improving Skills, Developing Flexibility, Mind Over Matter, Developing Strength and Speed, Planning and Practice, Working with Children, Working with People with a Disability, First Aid Certificate (Immediate Care), Mental Training, and, First Aid certificate.

10. Certificates confirm this.

11. For example: Karate/Bodybuilding course (19-20 September 1992) with champion bodybuilders, Colin Buchan and Graham Russell.

12. Uncredited piece in unknown newspaper of unknown date entitled, *Karate Coaching Director Qualifies.*

13. Certificate confirms this.

14. Uncredited. *Watt and Award for Ronnie* (*Evening Express*, undated, p. 28).

15. Uncredited. *Karate NVQ Success* (*RSA News*, p. 5).

16. Four letters, two from the Director of Education of Aberdeen, John Stodter, and two from the Lord Provost, Dr. Margaret Farquhar, during 1997-1998, confirm this.

17. Uncredited piece in unknown newspaper of unknown date (though 2002) entitled, *Karate Kudos.*

18. Uncredited. *The City of Aberdeen Sports Awards: Cream of the Crop* (*Evening Express*, 24th February 1996).

19. Aberdeen Karate Festival 1996 programme.

20. A ticket to the event shows that the Aberdeen Karate Festival was held between 12.30 p.m. – 3.30 p.m. and the Civic Reception was at 4.30 p.m. [in the Northern Lights Suite, Beach Ballroom {separate sheet}].

21. Letter from Watt to Mr. Yamato dated 30th December 1998.

22. Uncredited piece in unknown newspaper of unknown date (though 1998) entitled, *Watt a Prospect.*

23. For example: uncredited piece entitled, *Karate at Kippie* (*Kippie*, 1999, p. 9).

24. For example: uncredited piece in unknown magazine entitled, *Self-Defence*

Classes at RGU (1999).

25. Uncredited. *Self-Defence Strategies* (*City Lights*, No. 3, Spring 1998).
26. McKenzie, S. *Karate's Fight Against Drugs* (unknown newspaper dated 20th November 1997).
27. Certificate confirms this.
28. Uncredited. NKF Scottish Squad at WKC European Championships 1998 (*World Karate Confederation Newsletter*, No. 1, 1999, p. 2).
29. Letter from Watt to Carlsberg Tetley, dated 14th March 1999.
30. Klementis was born in 1948, starting karate in 1965. He attended the Economic University in Bratislva and worked as a manager. He co-founded Slovak Karate and was Slovak *kumite* and *kata* champion on several occasions, and coached many European and World Champions.
31. Uncredited. *Karate* (*Aberdeen Press and Journal*, 11th June 1998).
32. Uncredited. *Scots Win Europe Bronze* (*Aberdeen Herald and Post*, 1st July 1998). The women's *kata* team also qualified for the last eight and team members included Fiona Ellis, Ann Robertson and Catriona Hall.
33. Letter from M. Farquhar to Watt dated 24th July 1998.
34. Letter from Watt to Bernd Hinchberger dated 14th September 1999.
35. Letter from Watt to J. Rogerson dated 15th July 1998.
36. Letter from Watt to a Mr. Conroy, dated 28th August 1998.
37. Letter from Watt to Baroness Mary Goudie, of the Scottish Enterprise Forum, dated 27th June 2000, mentions these three countries.
38. A letter to Watt from Dr. Wendland dated the 16th June 1999, confirms this.
39. Uncredited piece in unknown newspaper of unknown date entitled, *Karate Kicks in for Aberdeen Bid.*
40. Letter from Watt to Wendland dated 4th September 1999.
41. Letter from Watt to Begg dated the 2nd July 1999.
42. Letter from Begg to Watt dated the 8th July 1999. Letter from Begg to Angela Park of GET dated 8th July 1999.
43. Letter from Watt to Margaret Smith dated 14th June 1999.
44. Letter from Margaret Smith to Watt dated 17th June 1999.
45. Uncredited piece in unknown publication of unknown date entitled, *European Karate.*
46. Uncredited piece in unknown publication entitled, *City Fighters Bound for Romania* (hand dated June 2000, p. 33).
47. Moir, A. *Karate Kids Aim for Euro Glory* (unknown publication hand-dated 17th March 2000).
48. Uncredited. *Alana Fights for a Bronze* (*The Piper*, 24th November 2000, p. 34).
49. Uncredited piece in unknown newspaper entitled, *Black Belt Ryan Strikes a Blow for Courage* (2000).
50. Uncredited piece in unknown newspaper entitled, *Fighting Fit: Black-belt Defeats Illness* (2000).
51. Horne, M. *Battling Ryan's Black Belt Joy* (unknown newspaper, 26th June 2000).
52. Letters from Watt to Mr. B. Woodcock, Director of Arts and Recreation, Aberdeen City Council (23rd April 1999); the Lord Provost (24th May 1999); and, Michael Seed of Aberdeen City Council (24th May 1999).
53. Smith, P. *North-east Karate Coup* (unknown and undated newspaper).

54. Uncredited. *Ronnie Wants Karate Kids* (unknown newspaper dated 3rd February 2001).
55. Letter from Watt to Dr. Wendland dated 12th July 1999.
56. This figure is supported in a forecast statement.
57. In Steele's article of the 5th June 2001, it notes that Aberdeen City Council gave grants totalling £25,000, a loan of £5,000 and would underwrite the event to a maximum of £10,000.
58. McIntosh, G. Open letter of support to potential sponsors dated 10th November 2000.
59. A list of sponsors at the back of the WKC 3rd World Championship programme reveal the following names: AVC Media, Mike Bisset Plastics Ltd., Jewel in the Crown, Friends Provident, Norwich Union, Scottish Mutual, GrantPrint Ltd., Monyana Engineering Services, Metrol-Technology Ltd., Aberdeen City Council, Scottish Enterprise Grampian, Bank of Scotland, Park Row Associates, National Karate Federation, Wood Group, Omega Data Services, C. P. Cables, Oilphase Sampling Services, Thistle Hotel, Marriott Hotel, Poste House Hotel, University of Aberdeen, First Bus, XFM Printers, Expro, Aberdeen Leisure, Thomas Blake Glover Foundation, Cohen and Co., Trophies International, Scottish Choice Itineraries, Joseph Robertson – Fish Processors, Cabbies (Mairs Taxis), Kamikaze (Scotland), Clanranald, Compaq, Albyn School for Girls, Ranger Oil, Murgitroyd and Co., ASDA, Town and Country Motors, Broadfold Garage, Heath Lambert, Managemenet Ltd., Price Waterhouse Coopers, P. B. Development Co. Ltd., Sam's Hau Zhong Xim. Also, the name of Agip and an Arts and Rec. Trophy grant appear in a composite plan.
60. *World Karate Confederation Newsletter* (No. 1, 2001, p. 4).
61. Uncredited and undated report in unknown newspaper entitled, *Karate Event Could Bring £1m Boost.*
62. The date of the visit is uncertain and may have been more than once. A document shows he was due to visit for the period 19th-21st February 2000, to met officials from the Aberdeen City Economic Development Department, the Director of Education and the Lord Provost. There is also press notification/invitation for the 19th May 2001.
63. Uncredited. *World Championship for City* (*Bon Accord*, May 2001, p. 2).
64. Gillard, J. *Martial Arts Masters* (*The Press and Journal*, 29th January 2001).
65. Wendland, F. Letter to the Lord Provost, Margaret Smith, dated 26th February 2000.
66. Uncredited report in unknown newspaper of unknown date (though 2001) entitled, *Prince to Attend Karate Event.*
67. Uncredited. *Karate Prince Backs City Event* (*Evening Express*, 12th April 2001).
68. Uncredited. *Prince to Attend Karate Event* (*Aberdeen & District Independent*, undated, p. 60).
69. John McSweeney was born in New York, the son of a lawyer, whilst his mother was a teacher. He began training in boxing, and whilst serving with the US Army in Japan, practised judo, achieving brown belt rank. Returning to the United States, he practised karate with Edmund Parker, in Los Angeles, who awarded him a black belt in September 1962. In December that year, McSweeney took up residence in Dublin, before leaving for New York to open a kenpo *dojo* in 1965.

Whilst in Ireland, there was considerable unpleasant rivalry between Vernon Bell and McSweeney over legitimacy (see the author's, *Shotokan Dawn Over Ireland: A Selected, Early History of Shotokan Karate in Eire {1960-1964}*). The founder of the American Kenpo Karate Association, and author of a book, *Street Karate*, McSweeney died of a heart attack on the 26th February 2002, in Fort Myers, Florida, at the aged of seventy-four.

70. Uncredited report in unknown newspaper of unknown date (though June 2001) entitled, *Sean's Chop and Change Campaigning*.

71. Bath, R. *Connery Acts to Kick-Start Karate Masterclass* (*Sunday Herald*, 24th June 2001, p. 19).

72. Uncredited report in unknown newspaper dated 16th May 2001, entitled, *Connery Gives his Backing*. In another Uncredited report entitled, *North-East Host Karate World Championships* (*The Advertiser*, 25th May 2001), the quote attributed to Connery is slightly different again: 'I am happy to accept, given your splendid initiative in bringing the World Championships to Scotland.'

73. Campsie, I. *James Bond Changed Ronnie's Life For Ever* (*The Sunday Post*, 3rd June 2001, p. 41).

74. Letter from Watt to Salmond dated the 22nd May 2001.

75. Uncredited report in unknown newspaper of unknown date (though 2001) entitled, *Tickets for Sale as Karate Experts Head for Aberdeen*.

76. McDonald, D. *World Karate Championships Tickets on Sale: Press Release – Immediate Use*. This release actually stated the wrong dates, giving the Championship dates as 23rd-24th July!

77. Uncredited and untitled report in the *Herald and Post*, 9th May 2001.

78. Advert in the *Aberdeen Independent* confirms these facts.

79. These prices are confirmed in adverts in local press (2001).

80. Uncredited. *World Karate Championships 2001* (*Traditional Karate*, June 2001, p. 24-25).

81. Steele, D. *Row Casts Cloud Over Karate Championships* (*The Press and Journal*, 5th June 2001, p. 3).

82. Steele, D. *Rivals Decry World Karate Contest in Aberdeen* (unknown paper of unknown date {though 2001).

83. Uncredited. *Flying Start to World Karate Championships* (unknown paper dated 25th June 2001).

84. This is confirmed in a proposal document. The estimated figure was actually £283,900.

85. McKay, D. *Kick-Start for Karate* (*Aberdeen & District Independent*, 25th January 2001, p. 77).

86. Begg. A. Letter to Watt dated the 7th April 2000.

87. Nicol, G. *Karate to Kick-Start City Economic Boom* (unknown newspaper of unknown date {though 2001}).

88. McKay, D. Title unknown (*Aberdeen & District Independent*, June 2001, p. 72).

89. McKay, D. *Get Along, Chop Chop* (*Aberdeen Independent*, undated {but 21st June 2002}).

90. Smith, M. Notice dated 5th May 2000.

91. Uncredited report in unknown newspaper entitled, *Countdown On As City Prepares For Karate Showcase* (10th May 2001).

92. An uncredited report in unknown newspaper dated 16th May 2001, entitled, *Connery Gives his Backing,* attributes the words to Connery as being: 'the tourism industry recovery from a troubled time.' In another uncredited article entitled, *North-East Host Karate World Championships* (*The Advertiser*, 25th May 2001), the quote attributed to Connery is: 'It will be a great boost to the sport and also to tourism.'

93. Uncredited piece in unknown newspaper of unknown date (though 2001), entitled, *Karate Sparks Spending Spree.*

94. Berry, W. Letter to the Chairman of Sports-Scotland dated 17th March 2000.

95. Letter from William Berry to the author dated 8th August 2008.

96. A letter from Mrs. Gail Watt to the Lord Provost dated the 2nd November 2000, confirms the date.

97. Stan Schmidt was born on the 6th October 1936, in Kokstad, Transkei. Originally studying judo, he began karate in 1963, training at the JKA headquarters (whilst on honeymoon). He studied to Masters' degree level in Communications at the University of South Africa. He was the first non Japanese to be awarded a 7th Dan by the JKA. A founder member of the International Karate Society and founder of the College of the Open Hand, he has written a number of books, including, *Spirit of the Empty Hand*, and, *Meeting Myself: Beyond Spirit of the Empty Hand.*

98. Kando Shibamori was born on the 16th December 1945, in Ibaragi, Japan. He began karate in 1962 under Sakai Kazuo, in Yokohama, and gained his 1st Dan two years later. He moved to Linz, Austria, in 1973, and has been national coach for Wado-ryu to both Austria and Hungary. He teaches widely throughout Europe, including Romania, Italy, Germany and France.

99. Eugene Codrington was born on the 29th October 1953 in Jamaica. He began Wado-ryu under Toru Takamizawa and graded to 1st Dan in 1973. He was British, European and World champion – in 1975, as part of the British team that beat the Japanese in Long Beach, USA. He also took a silver medal in the 1977 World Championships in the individual *kumite*. In 1996, he was elected Chief Technical Advisor of Wado-ryu, for the WKC.

100. Takeji Ogawa was born in 1942 in Chiba, Japan, and trained under Yoshihiro Urakawa and Hiromisu Kikuchi. Ogawa moved to Austria in 1970 and today teaches widely throughout Europe.

101. Yasunari Ishimi was born on the 30th October 1943 in Hyogo, Japan. He began karate in 1956 and attended Kobe Gaidai University where he graduated as a Master of Philosophy. In 1967 he went to Spain and became the national coach and today is the Chief instructor of the European Shito-Kai Association.

102. Chuzo Kotaka was born of the 11th November 1941 in Osaka. He began Shito-ryu in 1949 under Genryu Kimura and was a competitor of note, winning an All Japan Championships in 1962. He taught karate in the USA in 1963 and today is based in Hawaii, though he has taught widely. He is President of the International Karate Federation Shito-ryu Karate School, Kotaka-ha Shito-ryu, and in 2001 held the rank of 9th Dan

103. Kakazu is an Okinawan and Chief Instructor of the Shorin-ryu Kyudokan *dojo*.

104. Kawabata is an Okinawan with an impressive competition record in both *kumite* and *kata*.

105. The *Fighting Arts* Watt refers to is Vol. 2, No. 4.

106. The *Fighting Arts* Watt refers to is Vol. 1, No. 5, p. 17.

107. For a photograph of Kanazawa fighting Tsuyama in the 1957 JKA *kumite* finals, where Kanazawa's heavily bandaged hand is clearly evident, see the author's, *Kanazawa, 10th Dan*, page, 116, or, *Masao Kawasoe, 8th Dan*, page 33.

108. See Kanazawa's, *Shotokan Karate International Kata* [I/121-123] for these moves but without the inclusion of Ochi's reaction arm, which would be apparent during movements 11A and 13A.

109. Mirza was born in 1952 and began training in karate in 1967 and today holds the rank of 8th Dan in Shito-ryu. He is President of an engineering company.

110. Dietrich was born in 1959 and began Shotokan karate in 1976. He competed nationally and internationally for many years. He works as an engineer and holds the rank of 4th Dan (under Ochi).

111. Nicovic was born in 1946 and read law at the University of Belgrade. It was during this time he began karate (1966) becoming an international competitor. He trained at the International Police Academy at the FBI in the United States and became Chief of Police for Belgrade before the civil war. Today, he works as a lawyer.

112. Gouliev was born in 1955 and began Shotokan at the age of fifteen, in Rio de Janeiro, Brazil (where his father was First Secretray of the Soviet Embassy), under Yoshitaka Tanaka. He graduated in international law from Moscow State University of Foreign Affairs and continued his studies in international relations and diplomacy at the Higher Diplomatic Academy. Today, he works as a lawyer. In 1995, he founded the Union of Shotokan Karate-Do Organisations of Russia, and holds the rank of 6th Dan.

113. This information is confirmed in the *WKC Newsletter*, No. 2, 2005, p. 2.

114. Smith, A. *No Fancy Dans in the Chop Window of Karate* (*Scotsman*, 25th June 2001).

115. As noted on an advert of event.

116. Goju-ryu (hard and soft school) was founded by Chojun Miyagi (1888-1953) after extended training under Kanryo Higaonna (1853-1917) of Naha-te. It is reported that Miyagi, who would become a man of independent means, first began training with Higaonna in 1902, though Miyagi trained with Ryuko Aragaki beforehand. After Higaonna's death, Miyagi travelled to China staying a short while. When Crown Prince Hirohito visited Okinawa in 1921, Miyagi performed *kata* and did so again, in 1925, for Prince Chichibunomiya. Miyagi taught karate at the Okinawan Police Academy and then travelled to Tokyo, taking up teaching posts at Kansai and Ritsumeikan universities, amongst others. The name 'Goju-ryu' was formally registered with the Japanese Martial Arts Association in 1933. In 1934, Miyagi travelled to Hawaii to teach and stayed eleven months. During the war years he stopped instructing, but in 1946 he took up the post of Director of the Civil Association of Physical Education on Okinawa and resumed teaching at his home, where many of the subsequent great masters of Goju-ryu trained, such as Seiko Kina, An'ichi Miyagi, Eichi Miyazato, Eiko Miyazato, Seikichi Toguchi, and Meitoki Yagi. Funakoshi only recognised the karate of Naha-te and Shuri-te (he does not seem to mention the karate of Tomari-te). He appears to have disliked home-grown Japanese karate

(as distinct from Okinawan) seeing them as being aberrations and/or unworthy amalgams.

117. Shito-ryu was founded by Kenwa Mabuni (1888-1952) a student of both Yasutsune Itosu (*c.* 1832-1915 – of whom a single photograph has recently been discovered) of Shuri-te and Kanryo Higaonna of Naha-te. Shito-ryu *kata* include those practised by both Itosu and Higaonna. Funakoshi was a student of Itosu and many Shotokan *kata* have their origins in Shuri-te. It has been reported that Funakoshi sent Nakayama to Mabuni to learn the *Gojushiho* and *Nijushiho kata*. The *kata Hangetsu* is said to come from Naha-te. Mabuni, on leaving Okinawa, settled in Osaka, so as not to interfere with Funakoshi's attempts to establish karate in Tokyo. There are photographs of Funakoshi and Mabuni, together, covering many years.

118. Wado-ryu (Way of peace school) was founded by Hironori Ohtuska (1892-1982), a quiet, educated man and son of a physician. Ohtsuka trained under Funakoshi from 1923-1932 before combining his knowledge of early Shotokan with Shindo Yoshin Ryu Jujitsu, to form Wado-ryu in 1939. There are a number of stories about the relationship between Funakoshi and Ohtsuka, some say their parting company was amicable, others not so. However, it is likely that whilst Funakoshi liked Ohtsuka as a man, he did not approve of his actions, for he wrote in his *Karate-Do Nyumon*: 'There are also a great many people who try to blend a little knowledge of jujitsu with a tiny bit of karate study. The result is strange and unworthy of being called either' (p. 28). Whether Funakoshi was thinking of Ohtsuka when writing is unknown. However, Ohtsuka had studied jujitsu some twenty-five years when he came to leave Funakoshi, so this can hardly be called a 'little knowledge,' but Funakoshi may have considered some nine years of karate a 'tiny bit of karate study.' Nevertheless, Wado-ryu spread worldwide and Ohtuska, who taught karate at a number of universities, including Meiji, Todai, Chuo, Rikkyo, Nichidai and Hitotsubashi, was decorated by the Emperor of Japan for his services to the martial arts. The Wado-ryu *kata* remain largely unchanged and reflect 1920s training.

119. The list shows thirty-one countries and various written accounts refer to differing numbers of nations participating. Ronnie Watt's CV notes thirty-two countries attended. A list of other WKC member countries found in a file of the championships, though it may not be a list from that time, includes Bosnia and Herzegovnia, Chinese Taipei, Czech Republic, Hungary, Kazakhstan, Macedonia, Tajikaistan, Uzbekistan, USA and Wales. Other than the NKF, other Scottish karate organisations listed as WKC members are the Central Scotland Karate Association and Zanshin-Kai Karate Association Scotland.

120. A letter from the headmistress of Albyn School for Girls, Miss Jennifer Leslie, to Mrs. Gail Watt, confirms this.

121. For reference, Kanazawa, on pages 242-243, in Volume 1 of his *Shotokan Karate International Kata* shows these moves. Unfortunately, to confuse matters, Kanazawa performs the first *kosa uke* (move 30) with the arms in the reverse position of what is described in Watt's description. The JKA and SKI (Kanazawa) versions differ. However, moves 31a and 31 show the arm positions and manner Kase got into *kiba-dachi* as described by Watt. According to Watt, Enoeda used to perform move 32 slowly, whilst Kanazawa performs it quickly.

122. Two letters from the NEC confirm the hire of the mats to be £1180.85 excluding VAT, and the collection and return dates. A letter from the haulage firm confirms the price of transporting, excluding VAT. It was estimated that the lifting of between 18-20 pallets of matting would be required.
123. Uncredited. *Moving on Up* (*Traditional Karate*, September 2002, p. 7).
124. Uncredited. *Ladies Shine* (unknown newspaper, 18th July 2002).
125. Uncredited. *Karate Trio Win Bronze Medal* (unknown newspaper, 31st August 2002).
126. Uncredited. *Karate News* (*Aberdeen Sports Council Newsletter*, November 2002, p. 3).
127. Uncredited. *Success for Women* (unknown newspaper dated 5th July 2002).
128. Uncredited piece in unknown newspaper entitled, *Karate Girls Hit Bronze* (2002).
129. Uncredited. *National Karate Federation Scores Bronze in Europe* (*World Karate Confederation Newsletter*, No. 2, 2002, p. 3).
130. The full *kumite* results were, from first to joint third: Men, *Sanbon* – 68k: P. Broda (Slovakia), A. Santos (Brazil), R. Mujanovic (Yugoslavia), V. Ossipov (Russia); 78k: B. Jelicic (Serbia), D. Flati (Italy), R. Hanga (Romania), E. Kabashi (Switzerland); 78+: M. Mackovich (Slovakia), M. Hacko (Slovakia), D. Blagojevic (Serbia), M. Lazic (Slovakia); *Ippon*: D. Krueger (Germany). H. Yildrim (Germany), T. Schulze (Germany), N. Mantock (England). Women, *Sanbon* – 55k: E. Silva (Brazil), M. Grbic (Yugoslavia), A. Sanchez (Spain), K. Banicova (Slovakia); 60k: T. Petrovic (Yugoslavia), D. Drndarevic (Yugoslavia), M. Regules (Argentina), V. Gazzamiga (Italy); +60k: E. Au (USA), S. Dragoni (Italy), T. Galajdzic (Serbia), L. Krunic (Serbia); *Ippon*: A. Ciocoiu (Romania), B. Gho (Italy), T. Richards (USA), A. Myzhyrytska (Ukraine). Results taken from the *World Karate Confederation Newsletter* (No. 2, 2001).
131. Watt wrote to Connery on the 23rd August 2001 and received a reply from Connery's personal representative, James Brown, dated 24th October 2001.
132. WKC 2001 WORLD CHAMPIONSHIPS MEDAL TABLE (see table on page 358).
133. The DVD the author saw was in four parts: team *kata*, lasting some nine minutes; individual *kata*, lasting some eleven minutes; team *shobu-sanbon* and *shobu-ippon*, lasting some eleven minutes; and, individual *kumite* events lasing some twelve minutes. Competitors, male and female, from a good number of nations were included. The Shotokan *kata* shown, in whole or in part were, for the male team event: *Nijushiho* (Germany) and *Unsu* (Italy); female, *Sochin* (Scotland) and *Unsu* (Italy). For the individual event, male: *Unsu* (Italy and Yugoslavia); female, *Gojushiho-dai* and *Unsu* (Italy).
134. Uncredited. *Sky's the Limit for Ronnie* (*Evening Express*, 27th July 2001).
135. Watt, R. Undated letter to the Lord Provost, Margaret Smith.
136. Wendland, F. *From the President* (*World Karate Confederation Newsletter*, No. 2, 2001, p. 1).
137. Wendland, F. *From the President* (*World Karate Confederation Newsletter*, No. 1, 2002, p. 1).
138. Uncredited piece in an unknown newspaper of unknown date (though June 2001), entitled, *World Karate Championship is a Hit*.

139. Third, P. *Championships Prove a Success* (unknown newspaper of unknown date {though June 2001}).
140. Uncredited. *Scotland the Brave* (*Traditional Karate*, August 2003, p. 7).
141. Uncredited. *Chop Chop* (*Aberdeen & District Independent*, 3rd January 2002, p. ix).
142. Uncredited. *The 3rd WKC World Championships: Aberdeen Exhibition Centre* (*Traditional Karate*, February 2002, pp. 40-45).

WKC 2001 WORLD CHAMPIONSHIPS MEDAL TABLE

GOLD	SILVER	BRONZE	FEDERATION	COUNTRY
5	2	4	SFKBU	Slovakia
5	1	1	FRK/WKC	Romania
3	6	5	FESIK	Italy
3	4	1	YKU	Yugoslavia
3	2	1	DJKB	Germany
2	1	4	KSRS	Republic of Serbia
2	1	2	AAU	USA
2	1	1	ASK	South Africa
2	1	0	CBKI	Brazil
1	1	1	SSK	Spain
0	2	0	FEWR	Spain
0	2	0	WKC	Austria
0	1	0	ETKA	Turkey
0	0	3	FKSR	Russia
0	0	2	NKF	Scotland
0	0	2	SWKO	Switzerland
0	0	2	UAK	Argentina
0	0	1	FEKO	England
0	0	1	FEUAM	Spain
0	0	1	HKK	England
0	0	1	UKC	Northern Ireland
0	0	1	UKF	Ukraine

APPENDIX I

THE ORIGIN AND FORMATION OF THE BKF
ABERDEEN CLUB

It is believed that the first karate club in Scotland, at least BKF Shotokan, met in disused stables on the south-west coast between Saltcoats and Stevenson, North Ayrshire, under Edward Ainsworth. What is known about this *dojo* is recorded in the author's short, yet to be published work, *Scotland's First Karate Club?* Ainsworth, who was interviewed for the book, began his karate training when he attended the third BKF *gasshuku* held at St. Osyth, near Clacton, Essex, from the 5th–12th August 1961. The Saltcoats club's last BKF member joined in 1963, and whilst further karate practice continued until the later 1960s, it gave away to Ainsworth's first love, judo.

There is evidence that pockets of *judoka* were experimenting with karate using the books of H.D. Plee, E. J. Harrison, and, Nishiyama and Brown for guidance in the late 1950s and early 1960s. However, as it may be deemed virtually impossible, if not impossible, to learn karate from books, especially at this time, and whilst these pockets no doubt practised with good intentions, they were almost certainly without proper tuition, whereas Ainsworth had trained and graded under both Vernon Bell and Tetsuji Murakami. For that reason the author considers him to be the founder of Shotokan, if not karate, in Scotland.

It is highly likely that Ainsworth was aware of the beginnings of the BKF Aberdeen branch, despite it being some one hundred and fifty miles away as the crow flies, though there is no mention of it in his correspondence with Bell. Ainsworth certainly knew of the existence of the later BKF Dundee branch, some sixty miles from Aberdeen, for in 1964 he noted that he had offered to teach at the newly founded *dojo*, but that the offer had been declined. In fact, whilst the BKF Dundee *dojo* did get established under William McGuire, subsequent to his applying to Bell for details on the 19th February 1964 and literature duly being sent off on the 25th of that month (BKF *Register of Enquiries,* entry 415), the Aberdeen *dojo* had paid up members the previous year. So, let us take a closer look at the founding of Scotland's second Shotokan karate *dojo* under the BKF. Details of the period where this appendix concludes, and when Watt joined the BKF, are to be found in the main text of this book. Some of the following information has been taken from *Shotokan Dawn, Vols. I & II*, and, *The Shotokan Dawn Supplement*, and enlarged upon.

Entry 320 of the BKF *Register of Enquiries* records that a certain Stewart Duncan applied for details of the BKF on 17th April 1963 and literature was sent back to him, either by Vernon Bell or his father, Leonard, on the 22nd

Stewart Duncan

April. On the 2nd May, the BKF *Register of Enquiries* also records that Bell sent a personal letter to Duncan. Duncan, a married, twenty-seven year old clerk, signed his BKF application form that same day.

Duncan had been in the army for three years reaching the rank of lance corporal and was demobilised in 1956. He declared his interests as hill-climbing, reading, basketball and judo, the latter of which he practised at the Aberdeen Judo Club, in Riverside Drive. In the *Register of Enquiries*, he is noted as having graded to 2nd kyu. He became interested in karate after reading an article on Nishiyama. His single referee, the Rev. R. Flockhart, wrote: 'I have no hesitation in recommending Mr. Duncan as a person of good character. He is reliable and trustworthy and is well endowed with common sense an initiative, and is likely to prove a keen and enthusiastic member of the karate federation.'

In a letter of the 5th July 1963, in reply to a lost letter from Bell of the 2nd July, Duncan accepted the post of BKF Area Officer and set about starting the Aberdeen *dojo*, for, as he noted, 'I'm glad to say that things are progressing well as regards interest in the BKF and the use of suitable premises as a *dojo*.'

Duncan's first student was a friend, Eric Scott, a single, thirty-one year old power loom tuner, who signed his BKF application form on the 18th July 1963. He had seen National Service in the infantry and had also held the rank of lance corporal. He declared interests in climbing, folk singing, football,

Eric Scott

hockey, table tennis and judo, and was a 1st kyu (Scott letter to Bell {26th July 1963}) of the Aberdeen Judo Club. He cited Duncan as his source of introduction to karate. A Mr. J. Callan Anderson acted as a referee for Scott, writing: 'He is a person of sound character and sober habits. He combines admirably the ability to organise with that of getting alongside people and helping them realise their own potential. Mr. Scott has been a judo instructor over the past session [at the '62 Club, in Summer Street, Aberdeen] and will be appointed to this post for the session 1963/64. His own enthusiasm for the art has introduced others to judo and he has built up a strong section here which he has done much to make judo more easily understood by the community. In addition, Mr. Scott is greatly respected as a member of staff. I have no hesitation in commending him and I have great faith in his ability as a person, an instructor and a group worker.'

In a letter to Bell dated the 8th July 1963, Scott wrote: 'I would like to meet you when I am in London next week and (if accepted) to become a member of the BKF in time for the course at Middlesbrough. Because we want to start off with authentic karate instruction, we (Stewart Duncan and I) are prepared to make a five hundred mile round trip for this one day course.

'I hope that I may take the liberty of telephoning you next week and perhaps arrange a visit to your *dojo*. [In another letter to Bell of the 26th July 1963, we learn that Bell's telephone number was Hornchurch 42580].

Vernon Bell, the founder of the British karate movement (1957)

'I am interested only in real karate under proper, qualified teachers – unlike our friend whose card I have enclosed and whose performance, to say the least, was disgusting.'

Who this 'friend' was is unknown for sure and what prompted the word 'disgusting' can only be left to the imagination.

In Duncan's letter to Bell dated the 21st July 1963, we learn that 'Scott was down in London for a week and tried to get through to you [Bell] on the phone several times. He was disappointed of course, but it was just one of those things. Anyway, rest assured that we are both eagerly looking forward to our weekend in Middlesbrough and an introduction to true Karate-Do.'

Duncan wrote to Bell on the 25th July 1963: 'Regarding other would be members, I have several other people interested ... The Aberdeen Judo Club Committee, to whom I have applied for use of the *dojo* on a temporary basis, meets this week to discuss – and approve!

'1) Regarding *makiwara*, am I right in assuming that I shall be shown how to construct [one] at Middlesbrough, as the Judo Club are interested in knowing whether any structural alterations will be necessary.

'2) I sent for J. Milom's of Manchester, price list. They have for sale karate outfits priced at £2-2-0. Are these the genuine article?

'3) Have I your permission to have club letterheads printed and if so, are they to be on similar lines as say North-East Yorkshire and South Durham Branch?'

The said course under Murakami was held at the BKF Middlesbrough *dojo* run by Fred Kidd[1] and Walter Seaton[2] on the 4th August 1963.

But Duncan and Scott (if, indeed, he did attend) may have had a third member with them, and that was Kenneth Melville, a single, twenty-one year old motor engineer, who signed his BKF application form on the 30th July 1963. Melville's name appears in the BKF *Register of Enquiries* (entries 347 & 354) for July 1963. Melville declared his interests to be tennis, badminton and P.T. He was also captain in the Boys' Brigade and a member of the Aberdeen Judo Club. Like Scott, Melville cited Duncan as having introduced him to karate. One of Melville's referees, a Mr. W. Broomfield, noted that Melville was 'a young man of exceptional character and above average intellectual ability . . .' and the Rev. J. Tyrrell wrote: 'I can testify that he is a man of the highest character, and, indeed, of the highest Christian character . . . he has shown notable qualities of leadership, having a deep understanding of people and always a pleasant and approachable manner. He is of the strictest honesty and personal integrity.'

On the 8th August 1963 Duncan wrote to Bell: 'Firstly, I would like to thank you for your hospitality at Middlesbrough last Sunday. Secondly, to say how impressed I was with both Mr. Murakami and the training I received. It's a pity time was so short all around. Have you any leaflets relating to the sequence of training, Mr. Bell? If so, they would prove invaluable. As requested, I have enclosed a copy of a provisional letterhead for your approval before submitting to the printer.' As a postscript, Duncan wrote: 'I'd be obliged if you could send me some application forms,' and, as an afterthought, 'Have you any objections to James Baxter (see shortly), our would be black-belt, applying for membership?' On the top of this letter Bell wrote: 'Re[plied] 13/8/[1963], Yes to Baxter to join BKF.'

Whether Scott or Melville attended Murakami's course is unknown. Duncan makes no reference to them directly in his letter and makes no use of plural pronouns, so, maybe, that is suggestive. Bell was a stickler for procedure, especially when it came to attendance at Murakami's courses, and it is unlikely that he would have allowed a non-BKF member to train. As late as October 1963, Melville was awaiting confirmation of membership, for on the 15th of that month he wrote to Bell: 'I wonder if there has been any word from the [BKF] Committee of its decision. I have no wish to cause any inconvenience in any way, but as I am attending an introductory class to the art in Aberdeen under Mr. Duncan, I am naturally keen to have this information as soon as possible.' What is certain is that Duncan trained, however briefly, with Murakami, and he is, to the best of the author's knowledge, the only karate student for certain, from Aberdeen, indeed Scotland, bar Ainsworth, ever to do so under the BKF.

Bell received another letter from Duncan on the 6th September 1963. Duncan wrote: 'Have just arrived back from my holidays and am keen to get started. I am glad to say things are taking shape now and I would be much obliged if you would send me at least six sets of application forms as soon as

Tetsuji Murakami

possible.' This is the last letter from Duncan in the BKF archive and how and why he chose to leave the BKF is unknown.

Correspondence between Bell and the Aberdeen *dojo* is lost between September 1963 and the 14th May 1964. During this period a most important event occurred. Bell had been corresponding with the Japan Karate Association and in a letter dated the 22nd October 1963, Masatomo Takagi, Secretary of the JKA, wrote to Bell: 'We, of course, would welcome you and

364

your Federation to join our Association directly, as a national organisation for Britain, to conduct all business from now onward on all karate matters ...'[3] In the same letter, Bell was notified that he was to be awarded *Shodan* of the JKA. Bell replied for the BKF on the 16th November 1963 accepting both offers. The JKA affiliation diploma and Bell's *dan* diploma were dated the 5th February 1964. The fact that the BKF joined the JKA is important to further developments of Shotokan in Scotland.

In May 1964, the JKA's magazine publication, *Karate-Do*, appeared in English. The first edition had a green cover with an etching of a stork-like bird upon white. The publisher was Masatomo Takagi; the editor of the magazine was Kazuo Nagai, and the associate editor Mineo Higuchi. The magazine, which was intended to be quarterly, cost $5 a year. Under the heading of, '*Overseas Affairs,*' and a sub-heading of, '*The British Karate Association Affiliate,*' it was stated that: 'JKA authorized the British Karate Federation as an official representative of JKA for the territories of Wales, Scotland, North Ireland, Channel and Icelus [presumably meaning the Channel Isles]. Mr. V.C.F. Bell, Chairman of the association, was granted *Sho-dan.*' Amazingly, England was not mentioned as under the BKF/JKA auspices and clearly this was an oversight, though in an accompanying translation of the affiliation certificate, signed by Masutani, President of the JKA, reads: 'I, the undersigned, certify that the British Karate Federation has been recognised as an exclusive representative of the Japan Karate Association for the territories of England, Wales, Scotland, Northern Ireland, Channel and Icelus [*sic*], in accordance with the rules and regulations set forth by the Japan Karate Association, and has been registered as such in the official book. The British Karate Federation is requested to devote itself for the development of the true art of karate in co-operation with its principal.'

Melville wrote to Bell on the 15th May 1964 resigning from the BKF due, apparently, to work commitments. This letter is of considerable interest because we learn about the aforementioned Baxter, Duncan, and a young man who was later to play a most important role in the Aberdeen *dojo*, John Leeds Anderson.

On Baxter, feelings were running high. Melville wrote: 'Take my word for it, up here he is no friend and least of all to us. To quote ... Stewart Duncan, 'Baxter has done as much for karate as smallpox has done for the human race.' I had the sickening experience along with J. Anderson and S. Duncan, of an introduction to karate at an Aberdeen club, by Baxter, who at that time didn't know his left from his right. S. Duncan challenged Baxter to a contest after the demonstration. If you excuse my language – bloody nearly killed him – why not I shall never know. He (Baxter) was lucky to get off with a severely stubbed toe caused by an *oi-zuki* by S. Duncan against a *mae-geri* by Baxter. Of course, the whole demonstration was a farce. We hadn't heard of him again until you ... [word not clear] and we are now taking steps (indiscreetly) to find out what he's up to. Personally, I can't see what good another challenge to a contest would do, by any of the present club members.

Perhaps your 1st kyu would speak to him when he comes up, if we can arrange this. Mind you, if I have to, I will personally challenge him, inexperienced as I am.'

The 1st kyu in question was Terry Wingrove, a London based *karateka* who joined the BKF in July 1959, and who, along with his *dojo* colleague, James Neal, was the highest graded student in the BKF. Wingrove had captained the BKF team at the first European Karate Championships in Paris, on the 14th December 1963. Wingrove recalled, 'Yes, I taught in Aberdeen once and froze ... if I'm correct, it was February.'[4]

On Duncan, Melville noted: 'We also now suspect S. Duncan of teaching karate to *judoka* of 6th and 5th kyu ... [word unclear] at another club in Aberdeen and along with his crony, D. Haig, a 4th kyu, whose application to the BKF, should it arise, I would most strongly contest since his intentions are definitely not for the good of the BKF. I repeat, most strongly contest. My accusation which ... [words unclear] but we are also keeping an eye on him. We intend to refuse him admission to the class, but J. Anderson awaits your reply here.'

On John Anderson, Melville wrote: 'John Anderson ... is the man I would recommend as LDO [presumably, Local District Officer {i.e. Area Officer}].'

John Leeds Anderson was a seventeen-year-old schoolboy from Aberdeen Grammar School when he signed his application form to join the BKF on the 11th April 1964. He declared his interests as being Japanese philosophy, judo, kendo, angling and keeping tropical fish. He was a member of both the Aberdeen Bugeikwai (Judo Club) and the '62 Club, and had been introduced to karate by Duncan.

Anderson's letter (same date) that accompanied his application noted: 'Over two years ago I took up judo as a sport and a means of self-defence. During my training I became interested in the philosophical side of the art and began to read many books on Zen. I then developed a keen interested in kendo (which I practise at the Aberdeen Bugeikwai) and aikido (which I have been unable to practise ... because of their philosophical attachments). At this time I dismissed the thought of practising karate because it seemed more like a crude form of fighting than anything else. However, since then I have been informed of some of the methods of karate training and their results and have read H.D. Plee's book on the subject. Both these factors have convinced me that karate is deeper than I thought as first and after awakening to my mistake I lost no time in trying to take up the study of the art.'

The single reference to have survived supporting Anderson's BKF application for membership comes from J. Skinner, Rector of Aberdeen Grammar School, who wrote that Anderson: 'is to the best of my knowledge and belief of sound and dependable character.'

At the time of Melville's last letter, the following individuals were additional members of the Aberdeen *dojo*; they are presented in the order each signed their BKF application form and ages and occupations are also given: Ian Massie, 18, factory worker (23.3.64); George Wood, 16, schoolboy

Terry Wingrove in action with Tetsuji Murakami (1961/62)

(12.4.64); Graham Leitch, 17, student (26.4.64); Donald Ross, 15 schoolboy (26.4.64); Charles MacPherson, 15, schoolboy (—.5.64). Leitch attended the same school as Anderson.

Unfortunately, all the letters between Anderson and Bell between May 1964 and until the 21st November 1965 have not survived. However, we know that correspondence was taking place, and that the Aberdeen *dojo* appreciated Bell's hard work. Bell, of course, was full-time secretary to the BKF and this sometimes put him in an embarrassing position where he felt it necessary to justify his position. In response to a letter by Ken Roebuck of the BKF Rotherham branch, dated the 3rd October 1965, where his committee had discussed Bell's 'new salary, rent, etc.,' Bell responded on the 5th October noting (and the present author includes this because it has relevance to Anderson as a BKF Area Officer): 'I do fully realise the amount of work that all the Area Officers put in as unpaid officials in organising their branches, but I would also point out that they also have their full-time paid

The '62 Club, Aberdeen, was a haunt for a good number of early BKF members.

jobs as security which they had prior to taking up karate. In my case, the matter is a little different, in that as full-time secretary of the Federation, which has been brought about more by increasing demands and expansion as a national body than anything else, then I rely on drawing my weekly salary from the Federation in order to earn my living, so that I may devote all my time, every day, nearly seven days a week, to the routine affairs of the Federation. For this, I need and require the continued goodwill and close support of the Area Officers ... the Nottinghamshire, Portsmouth, Aberdeen and Blackpool branches have now given support to me, as well as your own branch, in the proposals put in my [lost] letter, and I thank you for your support in this matter, which has given me great personal concern for the welfare of my living and family.'

In the intervening period when correspondence between Bell and Anderson is lost, a good number of students, for whom details have survived, joined the BKF Aberdeen *dojo*. For the remainder of 1964 and presented in order of signing (though they were all signed in November) they were: Kenneth Stopani, 17, schoolboy (15.11.64); James Brown, 38, civil servant (22.11.64); Robert Noble, 19, student (22.11.64); Charles MacDonald, age unknown, office boy (29.11.64); D. Taylor, 22, student (29.11.64). For all of 1965: Thomas Sprott, 17, storeman (16.3.65); Derek Butler, 19, draughtsman (29.8.65); Norman Dickinson, 28, telegraph officer (30.8.65); John Franklin, 18, apprentice (15.9.65); Angus MacDonald, 18, apprentice (18.9.65); John Mitchell, 18, clerk (19.9.65); John Allan, 29, scaffolder (22.9.65); Angus Watt, 30, male nurse (15.10.65); John Macphie, 17, schoolboy (16.10.65); Henry Morrice, 17, electrician (19.11.65); Alexander Williamson, 29, veterinary surgeon (27.11.65); John Clark, 32, barman (18.12.65); Conrad Fraser, 21, mason (19.12.65); Ronald Robertson, 20, joiner (21.12.65). As we have seen, Ronnie Watt began training at this time, but registered as a BKF member in March 1966.

REFERENCES & NOTES

1. Fred Kidd applied to join the BKF on the 13th June 1960. For a photograph of Kidd see page 55 of, *The Shotokan Dawn Supplement* (Mona Books, 2007), or, page 29 of, *You Don't Have to Dress to Kill: Early Female Shotokan Karateka of the British Isles (1957-1966)* (Saisho Publ., 2007).
2. Walter Seaton applied to join the BKF on the 6th February 1962. For a photograph of Seaton see page 55 of, *The Shotokan Dawn Supplement* (Mona Books, 2007), or, page 29 of, *You Don't Have to Dress to Kill: Early Female Shotokan Karateka of the British Isles (1957-1966)* (Saisho Publ., 2007).
3. A letter Takagi sent to Bell on the 19th December 1963, stated, once again, that the BKF become the official 'authorized executive representative in Great Britain of the Japan Karate Association.'
4. Private correspondence with author (5th March 2008).

APPENDIX II

BKF ABERDEEN BRANCH MEMBERS FOR WHOM PHOTOGRAPHS HAVE SURVIVED

John Mitchell

Henry Morrice

Robert Noble

George Rennie

Ronald Robertson

Donald Ross

Archibald Sim

William Smith

Thomas Sprott

Kenneth Stopani

David Taylor

Angus Watt

Alexander Williamson   George Wood

APPENDIX III

AUTOGRAPHS OF JKA INSTRUCTORS COLLECTED BY WATT

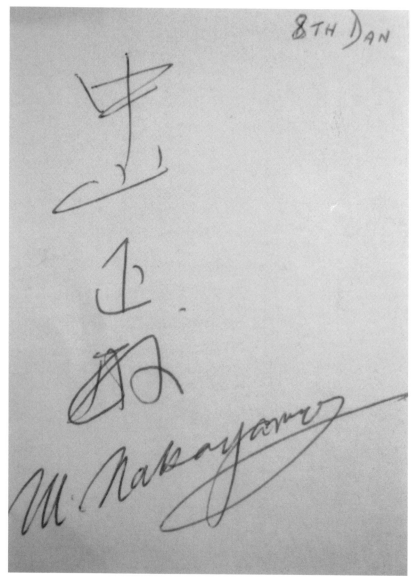

Masatoshi Nakayama

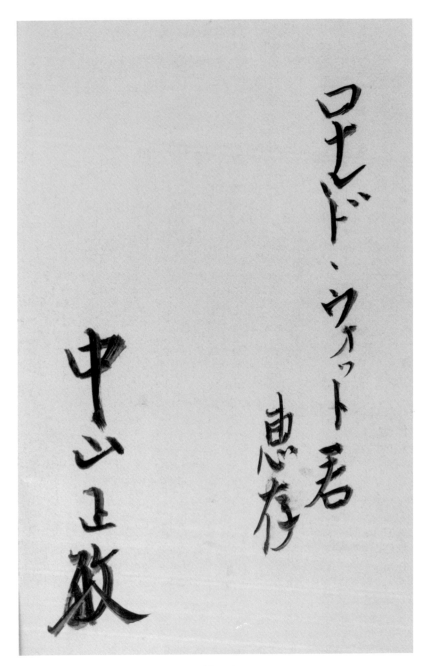

Masatoshi Nakayama

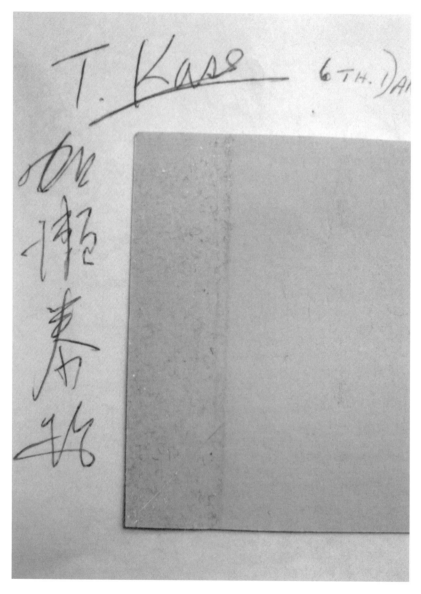

Taiji Kase

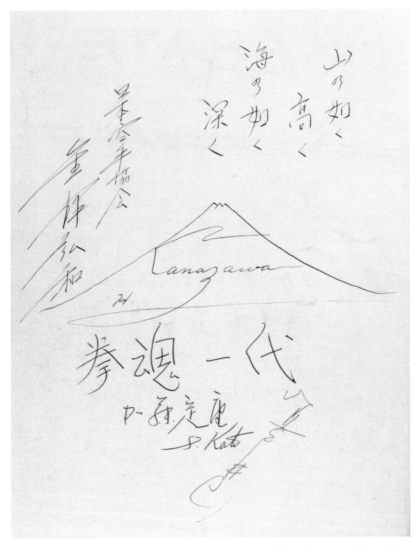

From top to bottom: Hirokazu Kanazawa's Mount Fuji signature, Sadashige Kato, Hiroshi Shirai.

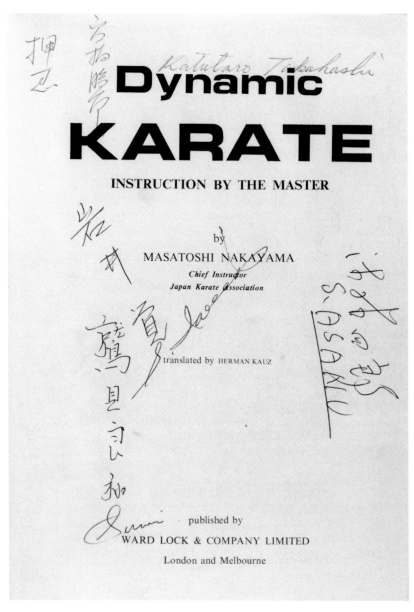

Dynamic
KARATE
INSTRUCTION BY THE MASTER

by
MASATOSHI NAKAYAMA
Chief Instructor
Japan Karate Association

translated by HERMAN KAUZ

published by
WARD LOCK & COMPANY LIMITED
London and Melbourne

From top to bottom: Katsutaro Takahashi, Keinosuke Enoeda, Shiro Asano, Yoshikazu Sumi.

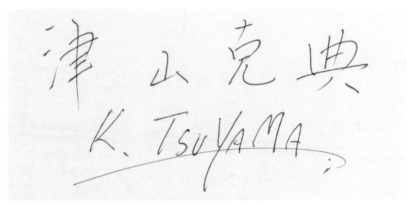

Katsunori Tsuyama

Masao Kawasoe

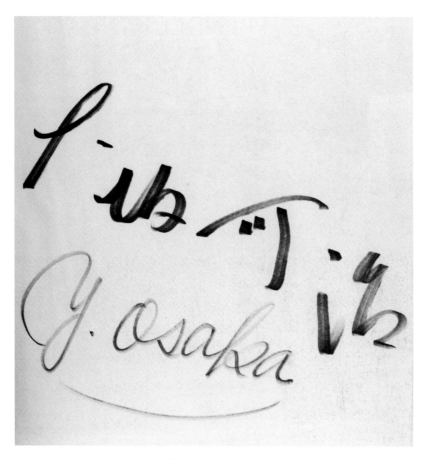

Yoshiharu Osaka

APPENDIX IV

RONNIE WATT, 8th DAN

Watt being presented with his WKC 8th Dan diploma by Dr. Fritz Wendland, in Bratislava (3rd June 2006).

Watt's WKC 8th Dan diploma

GLOSSARY
(including terms found in References & Notes)

Age-uke – rising block

Age-tate-empi-uchi – rising vertical elbow strike

Aikidoka – student of aikido

Ashi-barai – foot sweep

Bassai-dai – to storm a castle {major} (a Shotokan and Shito-ryu *kata*)

Bassai-sho – to storm a castle {minor} (a Shotokan and Shito-ryu *kata*)

Bo – staff

Bo-dori – staff-taking

Bo-sukami – staff-grasping

Bunkai – application of *kata* techniques and movements

Chinte – strange hand (a Shotokan *kata*) also 'calming and soothing' is a Shito-ryu translation

Chinto – (an earlier name for *Gankaku*) a *kata* practised by Shito-ryu and Wado-ryu

Choku-zuki – straight punch

Chudan – middle level

Dan – black belt rank

Deshi – student

Do – Way

Dojo – place of the Way (training hall); often used to describe a club

Dojo Kun – Precepts of the *dojo*

Empi – elbow

Empi-uchi – elbow strike

Empi-uke – elbow block

Enpi – flying swallow (a Shotokan *kata*)

Fudo-dachi – rooted stance

Fumikomi – stamping kick

Fuse – turn down (hand)

Gaijin – foreigner

Gankaku – crane on a rock (a Shotokan *kata*)

Gasshuku – training camp

Gedan – lower level

Gedan-barai – lower level downward block

Gedan-gamae – lower level guard (actually *gedan-barai*)

Gekisai – attack and destroy (a Goju-ryu *kata* {*Gekisai dai ichi* – attack and destroy major 1})

Geta – wooden or iron clogs

Gi – karate suit

Godan – 5th Dan

Gohon-kumite – five-step sparring

Gojushiho-dai – fifty-four steps {major} (a *Shotokan kata*)

Gojushiho-sho – fifty-four steps {minor} (a *Shotokan kata*)

Go-kyu – 5th *kyu*

Gyaku-mawashi-geri – reverse roundhouse kick
Gyaku-zuki – reverse punch
Hachiji-dachi – open leg stance
Hachi-kyu – 8th *kyu* (the first grading undertaken at the time)
Haito – ridge hand
Haito-barai – ridge-hand sweep (block)
Haiwan-uke – back arm block
Hajime – begin
Hakama – a Japanese pleated skirt
Hangetsu – half-moon (a Shotokan *kata*)
Hanmi – (hips) half-facing (45°)
Hansoku-chui – warning (given in *kumite* competition)
Hara – abdomen
Heian – peaceful mind (a set of five Shotokan *kata*, ranked: *Shodan, Nidan, Sandan, Yondan, Godan*)
Heiko-dachi – parallel stance
Heisoku-dachi – informal attention stance
Hiji – elbow
Hikite – return fist
Hiza gamae – knee guard
Honbu – headquarters
Ippon – one point
Ippon-kumite – one-step sparring
Ji'in – temple grounds (a Shotokan *kata*)
Jion – temple sounds/a Buddhist saint (a Shotokan, Wado-ryu and Shito-ryu *kata*)
Jitte – ten hands (a Shotokan and Shito-ryu *kata*)
Jiyu-ippon-kumite – semi-free one-step sparring
Jiyu-kumite – freestyle sparring
Jodan – upper level
Judoka – student of judo
Kae-ashi – whole step forward
Kaishu – open hand
Kaiten – (literally, 'turning of the heavens' effectively a piloted suicide torpedo)
Kakato-geri – axe kick
Kamae – guard
Kamikazi – suicide pilot (literally 'divine wind')
Kanku-dai – to view the sky {major} (a Shotokan and Shito-ryu *kata*)
Kanku-sho – to view the sky {minor} (a Shotokan *kata*)
Karateka – student of karate
Kata – form (set movements in a set sequence)
Kata-kumite – *oya kumite* sparring application of *kata*
Keage – snap (kick)
Kekomi – thrust (kick)
Kendo – Way of the sword
Kiai – a special kind of yell that helps channel the *ki* (vital energy) in the body
Kiba-dachi – straddle-leg stance
Kihon – basic

Kihon-ippon-kumite – basic one-step sparring

Kihon Kata – see *Taikyoku*

Kime – focus

Kizami-zuki – jab

Kohai – junior

Kokutsu-dachi – back stance

Kosa-dachi – cross over stance

Kosa-uke – cross over block

Kosokun-dai – (a Shito-ryu *kata* {see *Kanku-Dai*})

Kosokun-sho – (a Shito-ryu *kata* {see *Kanku-sho*})

Kumade – bear hand

Kumite – sparring (of which there are various types)

Kururunfa – end and fight (a Goju-ryu and Shito-ryu *kata*)

Kushanku – a name (Kung Hsiang Chun, in Chinese {an alternative name for *Kanku*})

Kyu – non black belt rank

Maai – distancing

Mae-geri – front kick

Makiwara – striking pad on a tapered post

Matsukaze – pine tree wind (a Shito-ryu *kata*)

Matsumura Bassai – Matsumura's version of *Bassai*

Mawashi-geri – roundhouse-kick

Meikyo – bright mirror (a Shotokan *kata*)

Mikazuki-geri – crescent kick

Morote – augment

Morote-bo-uke – augmented staff block

Morote-uke – augmented block

Musubi-dachi – informal attention stance

Naifanchi Shodan – (literally) inner step advance (a Shito-ryu *kata*)

Naihanchi – (an earlier name for *Tekki*)

Nanadan – 7th Dan

Nei rei – we bow

Nidan – 2nd Dan

Ni-geri – double kick

Nijushiho – twenty-four steps (a Shotokan *kata*)

Nipaipo – Twenty-eight (a Shito-ryu *kata*)

Niseishi – twenty-four steps (an earlier name for *Nijushiho*, and a Shito-ryu and Wado-ryu *kata*)

Ni-zuki – two punches

Nukite – spear hand

Nunchaku – rice flail

Oi-zuki – lunge punch

Omote – front (by oneself, in relation to the practice of *Ten no Kata*)

Osae-uke – pressing block

Otoshi-nakadaka-ken – dropping middle finger knuckle fist

Otoshi-shuto-uchi – dropping knife-hand strike

Otoshi-uke – dropping block

Passai – to penetrate a fortress (an earlier name for *Bassai*)
Pinan – peaceful (*kata* practised by Shito-ryu and Wado-ryu). *Pinan* is an earlier name for *Heian*
Rei – bow
Ren-geri – alternate kicking
Ren-zuki – alternate punching
Rikishi – strong man (sumo wrestler)
Rohai – white heron (an alternative name for *Meikyo*)
Rokudan – 6th Dan
Roku-kyu – 6th *kyu*
Saifa – destroy and smash (a Goju-ryu and Shito-ryu *kata*)
Saki – rice wine
San – mister (polite addressing to an individual)
Sanbon-genka – a version of *sanbon-kumite*
Sanbon-kumite – three-step sparring
Sanbon-zuki – three consecutive punches
Sanchin – three battles (a Goju-ryu *kata*)
Sandan – 3rd Dan
Sanseiru – thirty-six (a Goju-ryu *kata*)
Seienchin – control and pull fight (a Goju-ryu and Shito-ryu *kata*)
Seiken – fore-fist
Seipai – eighteen (a Goju-ryu and Shito-ryu *kata*)
Seisan – thirteen (a Goju-ryu, Shito-ryu and Wado-ryu *kata*)
Seiza – formal seating position
Sempai – senior
Sensei – teacher
Sentei kata – middle range *kata*
Shichi-kyu – 7th *kyu*
Shihan – master (instructor to instructors)
Shihon-nukite – four finger spearhand
Shisochin – four direction fight/teaching bravery and calmness (a Goju-ryu and Shito-ryu *kata*)
Shitei kata – preliminary *kata*
Shizen-tai – natural position (in Shotokan *Bassai-dai* this takes the form of *heiko-dachi* {parallel stance} or *hachiji-dachi* {open-leg stance})
Shobu-ippon-kumite – one point contest
Shobu-sanbon-kumite – three point contest
Shodan – 1st Dan (lowest level of Dan rank)
Shomen – (hips) square-on (180°)
Shuto – knife-hand
Shuto-uchi – knife-hand strike
Shuto-uke – knife-hand block
Sochin – to suppress (a Shotokan *kata*); the Shito-ryu version is Aragaki Ha
Soto-ude-uke – outside (to inside) forearm block
Sukui-uke – scooping block
Suparinpei – one hundred and eight (a Goju-ryu and Shito-ryu *kata*)
Taikyoku – first cause (a Shotokan *kata*)

Taikyoku Shodan – the first (of three) *Taikyoku kata*
Tai-sabaki – body evasion
Tameshiwari – trial by wood (board breaking)
Tatami – straw mat
Tate – vertical
Tate-ken gyaku-zuki – vertical fist reverse punch
Tate-shuto-uke – vertical knife-hand block
Tate-uke – vertical block
Teisho – palm heel
Tekki – horse riding (a set of three Shotokan *kata*, ranked: *Shodan, Nidan, Sandan*)
Ten no kata – the *kata* of the universe
Tettsui – hammer fist
Tokai – favourite (chosen) form
Tomari Bassai – Tomari version of *Bassai*
Tomari no Wanshu – Tomari version of the *kata Wanshu* (a Shito-ryu *kata)*
Tusugi-ashi – slide step (back leg to front then front leg forward)
Uchi-ude-uke – inside (to outside) forearm block
Unshu – Cloud hand (a Shito-ryu *kata* {see *Unsu*})
Unsu – to part the clouds (a Shotokan *kata*)
Ura – rear (with a partner, in relation to the practice of *Ten no Kata*)
Uraken – back-fist
Ura-mawashi-geri – close (actually *gyaku*) roundhouse kick
Ura-zuki – close punch
Ushiro-geri – back kick
Wankan – king's crown (a Shotokan *kata*)
Wanshu – (an earlier name for *Enpi* {named after Wang Shu, a Chinese envoy, and practised by Shito-ryu and Wado- ryu})
Wazari – half-point
Yakusoku-kumite – a form of *sanbon-genka* (maybe another name for such)
Yame – stop
Yoi – get ready
Yoko-empi – side elbow
Yoko-geri – side kick
Yoko-geri-keage – side snap kick
Yoko-geri-kekomi – side thrust kick
Yoko-tobi-geri – jumping side [thrust] kick
Yondan – 4th Dan
Yori-ashi – slide step (back leg half-way to front leg then front leg forward)
Zenkutsu-dachi – front stance
Zori – straw sandals (flip flops)

INDEX OF SURNAMES

ABOUT THE AUTHOR

Clive Layton was born in Hertfordshire in 1952, the son of an architect. He began his martial arts training with judo in 1960 under Terry Wingrove, and started Shotokan karate in 1973 under Michael Randall and the Adamou brothers, Nick and Chris, gaining his black belt from Hirokazu Kanazawa in 1977. Originally studying environmental design, he later read for M.A and Ph.D degrees from the University of London, and is a Chartered Psychologist, Chartered Scientist and teacher. Doctor Layton has appeared on both BBC television and radio in connection with his academic work. A prolific writer, with over one hundred publications, including twenty-four books on karate and numerous learned research notes, he has emerged not only as, almost certainly, the most productive (with well over one million published words), but, arguably, the finest writer on Shotokan in the world. He has co-authored with famed Okinawan Goju-ryu master, Morio Higaonna; former British manager/coach to the world champion All-Styles karate team, Kyokushinkai master, Steve Arneil; the founder of British karate, Vernon Bell; Michael Randall; and, fellow historian, Harry Cook, amongst others. Doctor Layton's biographies, *Kanazawa, 10th Dan*; *Masao Kawasoe, 8th Dan*; *Karate Master: The Life and Times of Mitsusuke Harada*, and, *Reminiscences by Master Mitsusuke Harada*, along with, *Funakoshi on Okinawa*, a portrait of life on Okinawa in the 19th century, have been published to much acclaim, as has his two volume work, *Shotokan Dawn*, and its Supplement, which, along with *Shotokan Dawn Over Ireland*, *Shotokan Horizon*, *You Don't Have to Dress to Kill*, and, *The Liverpool Red Triangle Karate Club*, chart the first ten years of Shotokan karate in the British Isles in astonishing detail. He has been the recipient of the Historian of the Year award (2004) and Writer of the Year award (2008) of the International Ryukyu Karate Research Society (of which he is also a Technical Advisor), and a holder of the Scottish Samurai Award of the National Karate Institute (Scotland). He was a correspondent for *Fighting Arts* magazine from 1984-1997 and has also acted for twenty years as a consultant reader to the journals, *Perceptual and Motor Skills*, and, *Psychological Reports*, on experimentation into the martial arts. Any spare time is taken up researching new books, pursuing his love of archaeology, genealogy and world cinema, and enjoying the peace of rural life, by the sea, with his wife, daughter and labrador. A highly innovative and deep-thinking *karateka*, he currently holds the rank of 7th Dan.